PALENQUE

PALENQUE

PALENQUE

Recent Investigations at the Classic Maya Center

Edited by
Damien B. Marken

ALTAMIRA
PRESS

A Division of Rowman & Littlefield Publishers, Inc.
Lanham • New York • Toronto • Plymouth, UK

AltaMira Press
A division of Rowman & Littlefield Publishers, Inc.
A wholly owned subsidiary of
The Rowman & Littlefield Publishing Group, Inc.
4501 Forbes Boulevard, Suite 200, Lanham, MD 20706
www.altamirapress.com

Estover Road, Plymouth PL6 7PY, United Kingdom

Copyright © 2007 by ALTAMIRA PRESS

British Library Cataloguing in Publication Information Available

Library of Congress Cataloging-in-Publication Data

Palenque : recent investigations at the classic Maya center / edited by Damien B. Marken.
   p. cm.
   Includes bibliographical references and index.
   ISBN-13: 978-0-7591-0874-5 (cloth : alk. paper)
   ISBN-10: 0-7591-0874-9 (cloth : alk. paper)
   ISBN-13: 978-0-7591-0875-2 (pbk. : alk. paper)
   ISBN-10: 0-7591-0875-7 (pbk. : alk. paper)
   1. Maya architecture—Mexico—Palenque (Chiapas) 2. Maya pottery—Mexico—Palenque (Chiapas) 3. Excavations (Archaeology)—Mexico—Palenque (Chiapas) 4. Palenque Site (Mexico) 5. Palenque (Chiapas, Mexico)—Antiquities. I. Marken, Damien B., 1977–

   F1435.1.P2P256 2006
   972'.7501—dc22

                          2005028881

Printed in the United States of America

™ The paper used in this publication meets the minimum requirements of American National Standard for Information Sciences—Permanence of Paper for Printed Library Materials, ANSI/NISO Z39.48-1992.

Contents

Figures and Tables

Figures

Tables

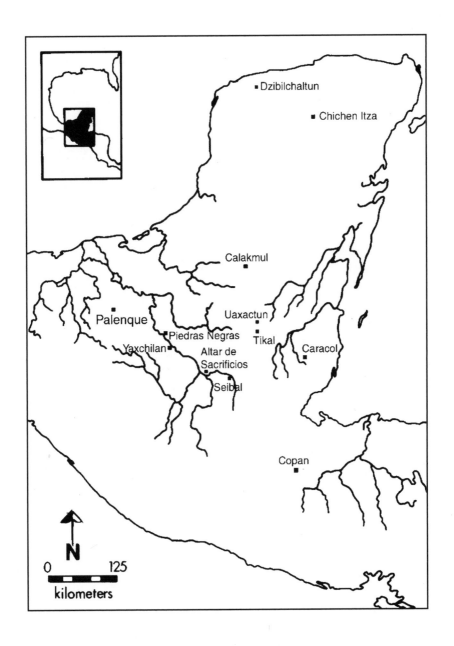

Map of the Maya Area

Foreword

Merle Greene Robertson

Forty years at Palenque—since 1964 when I first started working there—has been a long time full of wonderful and exciting memories. The town itself is much the same, of course larger—more shoe stores, more restaurants (there was only one back then), many more hotels (only one then, the Le Croix), many more grocery stores (then there was only that of my good friend Socorro Cordoba de Martínez), and many things now that were not there back then at all, such as sidewalks, streetlights, camera stores, and ice cream parlors. But Palenque still has its abundance of extraordinarily wonderful people, and many of my good friends from those days are still there.

There is Chencho (Aucensio Cruz Guzman), without whom none of the work I have accomplished at Palenque, from doing the "rubbings" to the photography, could have been done. This was especially true in measuring and drawing roofcomb details: he would be on a ladder, bracing me while I was on the roofcomb. I always knew he wasn't going to let me fall. He and his wife Deleri were an indispensable part of our household at Na Chan-Bahlum and are still my dearest friends.

Alfonso Morales Cleveland, who as a young boy spent most of his time at our house, Na Chan-Bahlum, with my husband Bob and me, read everything in sight in English and helped me in unbelievable ways, like fixing anything electric, rebuilding our jeep, no matter what the problem, serving as my photographic assistant in recording the entire corpus of sculpture, and measuring every inch of the buildings, from their basements to their roofcombs.

Where did all of this lead for Alfonso? To university, of course in archaeology. First it was a scholarship to Tulane, then to the University of Texas where he is now finishing his doctoral dissertation. Of course in the meantime he gained several years of valuable field experience at Copan, Honduras, and Caracol, Belize. Alfonso has been the Principal Investigator in charge of the Pre-Columbian Art Research Institute's joint Proyecto Grupo de los Cruces (PGC) with the Instituto Nacional de Antropología e Historia (INAH) and later CHAAAC. It is to his credit that the "state of the art" excavation and restoration of Temple XIX at Palenque has become a model to be followed in restoring an archaeological ruin.

We have always had a wonderful crew on the Palenque projects. On the Sculpture Project and the Florida State Museum Project there was Paul Saffo, now a director of the Institute for the Future, Palo Alto, and Miguel Molina, son of Arq. Augusto Molina and Marta (Foncerada de Molina), my very dear friends in Mexico City. Augusto, at that time on the INAH Consejo, came to Palenque, and the site director introduced Augusto to a new official just as "the father of Miguel." Augusto loved to tell that story.

John Bowles was the youngest of the group on the first Stucco Project, so he bore the brunt of all the pranks. In this first group were Linda Schele, Malcolm Cleary, Peter Mokler, and Mark Turner, who was my "second hand" in sculpting the piers for the Florida State Museum.

From the start, we had a great work crew for the PGC. I remember the fun we had with all the excitement going on, and everyone so happy and congenial. When we first started the PGC, in Stevens Plaza doing ground-penetrating-radar (GPR), our personnel consisted of Donald Marken, father of Damien and then-president of the GeoOntological Development Society; William Hanna, Claude (Pete) Patrone, and Roger Helmandollar, geophysicists using the GPR instruments loaned to us by Stanford University; Lee Langan, a computer and geophysical consultant; and archaeologists Maureen Carpenter, Christopher Powell, Chato Morales, Julie Acuff, Christin Cash, Richard Bidstrop (topographer), Julie Miller, Arnoldo González Cruz, Alfonso Morales, and myself as director.

Maureen Carpenter, with a degree in archaeology from University of California at Berkeley and a diploma from the University of Athens in Greek Archaeology, has had major responsibilities at numerous archaeological sites, including sites in Belize, Greece, Ecuador, and the states of California and Nevada, and has been in charge of the excavation of Temple XX from the beginning. I remember clearly the day the tomb in Temple XX was discovered. I can still see Maureen, in a yellow hard-hat, down in the 3-m deep pit with Alfonso Morales and Christopher Powell supervising the workmen. A workman pulled out a loose stone and lo and behold, a tiny 10-cm hole was behind it. By putting our heads sideways against the stone, and holding a tiny flashlight into the hole, we could see an amazing crypt below. A digital camera was inserted through the hole and hooked up to a computer Julie Miller had brought out to the site. Everyone crowded around the computer to see the wondrous things in the tomb of Temple XX-sub showing up on the computer—red mural-painted figures on three walls, a floor covered with jade beads, and eleven intact vessels. By this time all of the workers at Palenque had heard of the "find" and came rushing up to watch the computer. It was quite a day.

Of the early crew, there was Christopher Powell, who has nearly finished his Ph.D. dissertation and is still working at Palenque. Yvonne Haralson, a great laboratory person, is also still with us. Kirk Straight, who has been in charge of the Temple XIX excavations (along with Christopher), has written about that structure in this book. Rudy Larios, the best there is in architectural restoration, has been invaluable.

Robert Rands, the great ceramist, taught me ceramic illustration the hard way. In 1964 when I was illustrating thousands of ceramic sherds for Bob, I was also doing the "rubbings" of Palenque. I would work all day, and he would stay up all night going over my drawings. If a line was 1/4 mm off, it was wrong. I learned fast. What a teacher he was. Later, when I did ceramic illustrations of Dzibilchaltun for Bill (E. Wyllys IV) Andrews in Merida, Bill said to me, "well Merle, with your training and illustrating of thousands of ceramic pieces for Rands, I don't need to go over your drawings." Kirk must feel the same way after working for Rands for three years. Bob is still working with us on the PGC and has included two chapters in this book. When Bob Rands, Ed Sisson, and I were working at Palenque, our very good friend Mario Leon was site director. He and his new bride Amalia Huerta supplied us with lots of goodies that we lacked, as Amalia was having a great time testing out her cooking. They are both still at Palenque, and everyone of our crew knows the best restaurant in town, Amalia's "Maya Cañada."

David Stuart, the PARI epigrapher for the PGC from the beginning, I have known and watched grow since he was twelve years old and gave a paper at the Third Mesa Redonda de Palenque, "Some Thoughts on Certain Occurrences of the 565 Glyph Element at Palenque." I remember his dad, George, sitting in the front row chewing his fingers as David started his talk. He need not have worried, because David was as nonchalant and relaxed as if he had been giving talks for years. David has always seemed like one of my sons. He and his mother Gene spent one summer with us at Na Chan-Bahlum, she writing, in the tropical heat of Palenque, a story about polar bears and the Arctic for National Geographic, while David spent all of his time in our library trying to decipher glyphs. Linda Schele who was also living with us, and working with me, kept yelling at David, "you just go and figure it out."

My colleague Peter Mathews has written the introduction to this book. I could write another book just about Peter's and my adventures together, and I am sure he could do the same. He has been one of my very favorite friends since way back when we had the First Mesa Redonda, and Peter came, taking Dave Kelley's place. This was the famous year when the names of the Palenque rulers were figured out by Peter, Linda, and Floyd Lounsbury. Some of my remembrances include the terrible El Cayo highjacking of Peter and his crew, and us trying to rescue them, the time spent with him in Australia a couple of years ago, and his working with me at Chichen Itza, as well as Palenque. Then there was the time when it looked like the Temple Olvidado was going to topple over. Peter and I, with our good helpers Lee Jones, Chencho, and Charlotte Alteri, measured every inch of that temple; it's a wonder it didn't fall down on us, considering some of the places we had to get measurements.

But I'm not forgetting the great times we had during the summer he lived with Bob and me at Na Chan-Bahlum. Every morning, and I mean "every," before breakfast they played a game of cards in which they had a book where they kept score every day. Now this game of chance was one that was almost impossible to win, and a month had gone by and neither of them had won even once. They had kept after me to come and play also, but my response was always, "not that stupid game." Finally they egged me on to play "just once" and then they would leave me alone. Okay, I played once, and WON. They were ready to kill me. "Well that could never happen again," they said, and dared me to play once more. Okay, once more. I WON. I had to disappear. They wouldn't even speak to me. Purely accident, of course, but they didn't think it was a bit funny.

Others who have been doing great work with us on the PGC during the last few years include Patricia Aguirre from Mexico City, Adrienne Tremblay from Tulane, the artist Mark Van Stone, and Marcia Valle. Those who have contributed chapters in this book are Damien Marken, whom I have known since he was four years old, and who at six was explaining the iconography of Pakal's sarcophagus lid, a poster of which was laid out on our kitchen table at Na Chan-Bahlum, to college professors attending one of the Mesas Redondas de Palenque. Ed Barnhart and Kirk French of the Palenque Mapping Project, and Joshua Balcells, now working on Temple XX, have also contributed chapters.

This book is about Palenque, so of course, besides all the work on Palenque projects—and it was enjoyable work—there were a lot of fun things going on all the time. Everyone going to their archaeological "digs" in Chiapas, Belize, or Yucatan always stopped off in Palenque on their way to, or returning from, the field. Our list of friends coming to spend a day or two with us reads like a "Who's Who" of Maya archaeology.

Over the years our crew working at Palenque got to know an incredible group of friends—Dra. Beatriz de la Fuente, the first art historian to ever work at Palenque; Will Andrews from MARI, Tulane; George Andrews, the architect from Eugene, Oregon; Tony Aveni, the astronomer, and Claude Baudez from Paris, who was working at Tonina part of the time I was working at Palenque. Alfred Bush brought his crew from Princeton and helped with early mapping. Mike Coe, now Professor Emeritus at Yale, who has become a fisherman and Khmer-Angkor Wat enthusiast, whose newest book *Angkor* has just come out, came many times to Palenque. Arlen Chase, my student at the Stevenson School, and his wife Diane, with their three kids, my "adopted grandkids," still stop every time they are on their way to and from the famous site, Caracol, in Belize. Then there was John Carlson, astronomer, Paul Gendrop from Mexico City, Norman Hammond from Boston University, Dave Kelley from Calgary, and Gillett Griffin from Princeton, who helped immensely with our photography project, especially "holding lights at midnight" while we photographed the piers of the Palace.

Katherine Josserand and Nick Hopkins played a big role in almost everything we did at Palenque. Then there were Lee Parsons, George Stuart, who was there so many times I can't remember, and Eric Taladoire from the Sorbonne, Paris, who spent a good deal of time with us every time he was going to work at Tonina. Jeff Wilkerson came from his institute near Gutierrez Zamora and was so many times such an incredible help to me that I will never be able to thank him enough. Gordon Wasson, the author of *Soma: Divine Mushroom of Immortality*, and *Maria Sabina and her Mazatec Mushroom Velada*, who spent two days with us going over my research on Usumacinta mushrooms, was a most interesting character and a pleasure to meet for our staff.

Then there was the summer of 1975 when Mary Miller and Virginia Miller, both Fulbright Scholars, stayed at our place with Bob and me. We became very good friends, both of them returning often to Palenque, especially Mary Miller, now the Vincent Scully Professor of History of Art at Yale. She, along with Kathleen Berrin, curator at the Fine Art Museums of San Francisco, is now deeply involved in the opening of the exhibit "Courtly Art of the Ancient Maya" at the National Gallery, Washington, D.C., and the Palace of the Legion of Honor in San Francisco.

And of course, everyone knows Don Moises Morales (Moi), Señor Palenque himself, and the greatest "storyteller" in all Palenque.

Those working at Palenque the last five or six years have been able to know some brilliant scholars—David Stuart, Simon Martin, Marc Zender, Nikolai Grube, Stanley Guenter, and Joel Skidmore, all working on deciphering hieroglyphs, and who have been spending a good deal of time at Palenque.

It was Charlotte Alteri, a biologist living next door, who stayed with me during the eruption of the volcano El Chichon when just about everyone else, including the mayor, left town during this dreadful time.

Then for excitement, and there was always something going on at the same time we were working, Otis Imboden came with his National Geographic air balloon and set it up in the Inscriptions Plaza early one morning. What a thrill for everyone, especially me, as I got up in it and sailed all around Palenque.

Some of the most important events that took place at Palenque were the Mesas Redondas de Palenque, which PARI sponsored for twenty years, and are now being continued by INAH. The First Mesa Redonda in 1973 started with 36 people, but at PARI's last Mesa Redonda in 1993 there were 435 participants from most of the major universities in the United States and from 13 countries. Palenque had become the seat of one of the major Mesoamerican conferences in the world.

My very dear friend Linda Schele spent a good deal of time from 1971 until her untimely passing in 1998 with me at Palenque, and shared in so many of the serious and fun things that were always going on. We will always remember Linda. A *ceiba* tree has been planted at the ruins in her remembrance.

Besides all the work, we did have fun. A typical Thanksgiving would be

Katherine Josserand and I planning dinner for about fifty people, everyone we knew in Palenque and all our crew besides. What kind of dressing to have, hers or mine, was the big question.We settled by having both. Cranberries, well no one in Palenque knew what they were, let alone had any. After the first few years we brought cranberries from the States.

If any of our crew stayed for Christmas, instead of going home, they were in for a treat also. Christmas at Palenque started with a huge feast given by Carlos Morales upstairs in the La Cañada restaurant where young and old ate turkey, ham, pork roast, pies galore, and all kinds of goodies, and danced until the wee hours of the morning. Then everyone went home and stayed there until noon on Christmas Day. Bob and I decided to change that, so the next year we invited everyone to Na Chan-Bahlum for eleven o'clock brunch, expecting them to come at "Mexican" time, about one o'clock. They came at ten. We had loads of food, and when it was gone, people went home and brought more, along with their guitars. Thus, Christmas Day lasted until well into the evening, eating, drinking, singing, and dancing at Na Chan-Bahlum. No one wanted to go home, and upon leaving, reminded us that they expected to be invited the next year.

So this is Palenque, thought by many of us to be the most beautiful ancient Maya site anywhere, a Maya ruin that is in a delightful setting for archaeologists to work, a great crossroads meeting place for archaeologists and people from around the world, and a town that still boasts of so many wonderful people, and feels like "home" to so many of us.

Damien Marken has done a remarkable job in bringing together, in these fourteen papers, the latest information on the ongoing research and accomplishments at this world-renowned archaeological site, Palenque. I have mentioned the significant contributions by Robert Rands, Rudy Larios, David Stuart, Ed Barnhart, Arnoldo González Cruz, Joshua Balcells, Kirk French, and Kirk Straight, but it is the brilliant conclusion by Damien Marken and Kirk Straight that brings everything together with up-to-date, thought-provoking information.

Merle Greene Robertson
Chrm. of the Board, PARI
Director, Proyecto Grupo de las Cruces, Palenque
San Francisco, CA
March 1, 2004

Preface

Damien B. Marken

This volume represents the final product of a conversation I had in a café one sunny June afternoon in Paris' Latin Quarter. Sitting with me on that terrace in 2002 was David Freidel, who eventually became my graduate advisor following my studies in France. The previous spring, David had been the discussant, and I a participant, at a 67th Annual Meeting of the Society for American Archaeology (SAA) symposium in Denver, entitled "Palenque Transformed," organized by Kirk French and Ed Barnhart. While having a beer in Paris, David suggested that I put together a collection of articles on Palenque for publication in an edited volume, adding to the Denver symposium set of papers articles by those archaeologists who were working at Palenque but unable to attend that year's SAA Meeting. Earlier versions of Chapters 4, 6, 8, and 12 were presented in 2002 at the Denver symposium; other chapters and revisions were requested and received by the various contributors throughout the following three years. The reader is forewarned that this volume is not specifically aimed at newcomers to Palenque's archaeology and history. The authors' contributions are highly detailed; the goal of the volume was to publish as much new archaeological information as possible on Palenque. However, this is a strength of the volume: the chapters present new data from five different archaeological projects, both Mexican and foreign, conducted in and around Palenque during the past ten years.

My involvement in Palenque archaeology began when I first went to work for Merle Greene Robertson and Alfonso Morales Cleveland as a member of the Proyecto Grupo de las Cruces (PGC), at Palenque in 1997. Although I had previously visited Palenque in my adolescent years several times, I had never worked in the Maya area. At the time, the PGC was working on the west and north sides of the Temple of the Cross pyramid substructure. The following summer, Kirk

Straight and I began excavation of Temple XIX at Palenque; excavation and restoration of Temple XIX would take the next two years. The Temple XX-subtomb was also discovered during that period of work sponsored by the Pre-Columbian Art Research Institute (PARI), Mexico's Instituto Nacional de Antropología e Historia (INAH), and funded by the GeoOntological Development Society. In the summer of 2000, the Center for the History of Ancient American Art and Culture (CHAAAC) of the University of Texas, Austin, assumed responsibility for PGC funding as we continued work on Temple XX. Each PGC field season held new challenges and insights and I feel extremely lucky to have been a part of such enjoyable and memorable investigations.

Prior to, and concurrent with, the PGC, the Proyecto Arqueológico Palenque, and its various sub-projects, directed by Arnoldo Gonález Cruz, conducted one of the most extensive large-scale excavation programs ever at Palenque. Building on the invaluable work of Miguel Ángel Fernández, Alberto Ruz Lhuillier, and Jorge Acosta, during the past decade or so, INAH archaeologists have significantly increased the available excavation data for Palenque. The investigations of both González Cruz, and that of Rodrigo Liendo Stuardo from the Universiadad Nacional Autónoma de México, illustrate the advances in our knowledge of Palenque that have been gained by the near-continuous archaeological work carried out by Mexican archaeologists in and around the site core.

Acknowledgments

First and foremost, I would like to thank all the contributors to this volume. Without their hard work and punctual submissions, this volume would have been impossible. Over the years we have all shared in lengthy discussions regarding Palenque's ancient history, archaeology, and Classic period population, which have certainly benefited my understanding of the site, as I am sure those conversations have benefited each of us.

Many of the following chapters are based upon work carried out as part of either the PGC or the Palenque Mapping Project (PMP, directed by Edwin Barnhart). A multitude of thanks are due to Merle Greene Robertson, director of the PGC, and Alfonso Morales, the project's principlal investigator. I have known Merle for much of my life, and she has been an inspirational role model and friend. Over the years, Alfonso has always looked out for me, exceeding what is expected from a project director. I would also like to thank all current and former members of the PGC and PMP, in particular Constantino Armedariz, Joshua Balcells, Ed Barnhart, Maureen Carpenter, Cristin Cash, Elizabeth Corin, Anabell Coronado, Alfonso Cruz, Jim Eckhartd, Kirk French, Yvonne Harelson, Heather Hurst, Lucas Johnson, Alonso Mendez, Julie Miller, Christopher Powell, Robert Rands, Rogilio Rivera, Stephen Siemer, George St. Clair, Kirk Straight, and Andrienne Temblay. Our Tzeltal and Chol workmen deserve tremendous praise. George St. Clair, also was kind enough to translate Chapters 9 and 13 from Spanish to English.

I would like to thank the funding agencies that made our work possible, namely CHAAAC, the Foundation for the Advancement of Mesoamerican Studies Inc., the GeoOntological Development Society, and PARI. I would also like to thank PARI for allowing AltaMira Press to publish Figures 4.2a, 4.3a, 4.6b, 6.3, 12.3, 12.5, 12.8, 12.9, and 14.2. I also cannot forget to thank Joel Skidmore of PARI for personally ending the "loss" of my field clothes when he bought a washer and dryer for the project house.

Archaeological work at Palenque would be impossible without the support of the Instituto Nacional de Antopología e Historia of Mexico. Their commitment to the development of the archaeological site and to further uncovering the site's ancient history has always been instrumental to the better understanding of Classic Palenque. Special thanks go to the amiable and helpful site director of Palenque [while I was working there], Juan Antonio Ferrer, Arnoldo González Cruz, the site archaeologist, and Roberto López Bravo, the director of the site museum.

The comments and suggestions of several scholars who read earlier drafts of contributions to the volume significantly improved the content and presentation of this volume. In particular, Robert Sharer's extremely thorough comments on the entire volume were immensely helpful. Michael Coe and David Freidel's early reviews of the volume were crucial to its overall development. Further comments by Ronald Bishop, Marcello Canuto, Keith Eppich, Héctor Escobedo, Stanley Guenter, Roberto López Bravo, Eric Taladoire, and David Webster broadened the scope of specific chapters. While communication and collaboration between the volume contributors were an important part of developing this book, Bob Rands and David Stuart's unsurpassed knowledge of Palenque's ceramics and epigraphy, respectively, served as an invaluable resource. Since we met while working on Temple XIX at Palenque, Kirk Straight has been a good friend and helped me immensely in various phases of the editing process. The interpretations in the following chapters do not necessarily reflect the views of the reviewers. Any errors or omissions are the fault of the individual contributors and myself.

I would like to thank Mitch Allen and his colleagues at AltaMira Press for all their help in organizing this volume. Mitch's enthusiasm to publish a book on Palenque certainly pushed everyone's ability to meet deadlines. Lee Langan deserves special praise for getting the manuscript into camera-ready form. Lastly, I would like to thank my family, especially my mother, my late father, and my brothers and sisters. Thank you for your love and support throughout my life.

Damien Marken
San Francisco, CA
August, 2004

Part I

INTRODUCTION

Chapter 1

Palenque Archaeology: An Introduction

Peter Mathews

It is now a little more than two hundred years since Palenque first gained world-wide attention. Nestled in the lush forested foothills that overlook the coastal plains at the southern edge of the Gulf of Mexico, Palenque is one of the great archaeological sites of the world. It is characterized by some of the most beautiful architecture built by the ancient Maya, as well as for its elegant carved stone monuments and graceful modelled stucco.

History of Archaeological Investigation at Palenque

Two hundred years ago, Palenque lay in an almost forgotten corner of one of Spains numerous colonies, the Kingdom of Guatemala, and official notice of the ancient "Stone Houses" was initially addressed to the king of Spain, Charles III, in the 1780s. But gradually word spread more widely about the ruins, sparking a number of travellers to visit the site. The most famous of these travellers were John Lloyd Stephens and his artist companion Frederick Catherwood, who visited in 1840 and whose riveting travel books and beautiful, accurate illustrations brought instant fame to the Maya ruins in general and Palenque in particular.

By this time Palenque was no longer part of the Spanish Empire, but rather a remote little town in an independent Mexico. Visitors following in the footsteps of Stephens and Catherwood included the Frenchman Désiré Charnay, who took the first photographs of Palenque in 1857. Charnay also made papier mâché moulds of the Palenque sculptures, and in 1882 he taught the technique to a young English explorer, Alfred Maudslay at the ruins of Yaxchilan. In 1891, Maudslay explored Palenque and documented the ruins with such precision with his photographs, plaster casts, maps, and drawings, that his publication was to remain the standard reference work on Palenque for most of the twentieth century.

During the 1920s, the Mexican government began a period of almost continual research at Palenque, through the agency that ultimately became the Instituto Nacional de Antropología e Historia (the National Institute of Anthropology and History; INAH for short). The maintenance of the site, and the posting there of guards, was instituted many decades ago, and there have been numerous seasons of archaeological excavations at Palenque, steadily liberating its temples and other buildings from the green tide of the tropical forest.

The most famous of the Mexican archaeologists to work at Palenque was Alberto Ruz Lhuillier, who directed excavations from 1949 through 1958. In 1952, Ruz made the most dramatic archaeological discovery at Palenque, and one of the greatest achaeological finds ever encountered in the New World. For four years he had been digging through the solid rubble that was packed into an interior stairway in the pyramid beneath the Temple of the Inscriptions. Finally Ruz reached the end of the stairway blocked by a huge triangular slab of limestone. On June 15, 1952 he turned the stone aside, and he and his colleagues gazed upon an intact tomb, with modelled stucco figures on the walls mutely gazing upon a beautifully carved stone sarcophagus with a single human skeleton inside.

In the 1950s, the tomb's inhabitant was not referred to as a king. At that time, the Maya hieroglyphic writing system was largely undeciphered. The chronological part of the inscriptions—the dates—had been deciphered over fifty years before, but little further headway had been made. This led scholars during the first half of the twentieth century to talk about "calendar priests" and the "worship of time." Gradually the arguments evolved into claims that the inscriptions dealt only with calendrical affairs, and that in fact it would have been sacrilegious to have recorded such things as history, or the names of individuals in the beautiful, sacred hieroglyphic texts. Further, places like Palenque were not ancient cities; rather they were inhabited only by a few priests and their retainers. The great mass of the population lived in scattered hamlets dotted throughout the forest, and only came to the "vacant ceremonial center" to witness key calendrical events. The inhabitant of the tomb below the Temple of the Inscriptions, then, must have been an important priest.

We now know that the tomb is that of Palenque's greatest king, K'inich Janab Pakal I, who lived from A.D. 603-683. The great advances made in the decipherment of Maya writing enable us now to piece together a fairly complete account of his life and times, and the inscriptions do indeed bring to life a rich pageant of Maya kings and queens, the world they lived in, and their remarkable deeds. Archaeological research has identified hundreds of residential buildings around the site center, and it is now clear that Palenque and the other great Classic Maya sites (like Tikal in Guatemala, Caracol in Belize, and Copan in Honduras) functioned as the capital cities of their respective kingdoms.

The site of Palenque holds a special place in the field of Maya studies for several reasons. As one of the first Maya sites brought to the attention of the "Western" public, Palenque has fascinated archaeologists and afficianados for over a century. Over a long period of research, Palenque was one of the best-documented Classic Maya sites due to the detailed published reports of scholars such as Teobert Maler and Maudslay.

In the winter of 1973, a small group of Maya scholars met at the house of Bob and Merle Greene Robertson in Palenque to discuss the art, architecture, and hieroglyphs of Palenque. Those in attendance at what would be named the First Palenque Mesa Redonda, included such eminent scholars as E. Wyllys Andrews V, Elizabeth Benson, Michael Coe, Beatriz de la Fuente, Paul Gendrop, Gillette Griffin, Floyd Lounsbury, George Kubler, Arthur Miller, Robert Rands, Donald Robertson, and George Stuart. At that meeting Linda Schele and I presented the dynastic sequence for Palenque, the first such list put together for a Classic Maya site. There the Mesa Redonda attendees first gave the name "Pakal" to the individual now known as K'inich Janab Pakal I. Today, K'inich Janab Pakal I is perhaps the most famous of all the ancient Maya. He is one of the few individuals whose skeleton we can match with near certainty to his Classic Maya name. That conference and the subsequent Palenque Mesa Redondas, or Round Tables, represent a significant development in Classic Maya studies in general, and of Palenque in particular.

Over the past thirty years, the advances in archaeological and epgraphic research into the Classic Maya have revolutionized our understanding of this remarkable civilisation, and Palenque has been at the forefront of these advances, especially due to the decipherment of its beautiful and relatively complete hieroglyphic inscriptions.

Palenque's History

The history of Palenque can be pieced together from a variety of sources. First, of course, is the material gained through archaeological excavations at the site. The archaeological foundation for a chronology of the site is its ceramic assemblage, long and painstakingly worked out by Robert Rands. The ceramic history of Palenque has been divided into several different phases. To this chronological skeleton can be correlated such things as individual buildings and the changing architectural styles at Palenque. Also, of course, there is the hieroglyphic history of Palenque.

I shall not launch into an extensive glyphic history here, because it is detailed in several other sources, most notably the recent book by Simon Martin and Nikolai Grube (2000: 154-175). But briefly, the official royal line of Palenque began in A.D. 431, with the "founding" of Palenque (perhaps its official beginning as a kingdom) by a king called K'uk' Bahlam I.

Before this time, we have only fairly sketchy remains in the form of scattered ceramic remains at Palenque. Preclassic (c. 1000 B.C. - A.D. 250) sherds are particularly sparse, and usually are found mixed in with later deposits. The same is true of the Early Classic Picota ceramic phase, which dates to approximately A.D. 250-400. Picota remains have been mostly found in the western part of Palenque (near the stream after which the phase was named), but have also been found in the fill below the Temple of the Count in the central precinct of Palenque. It would appear that settlement at Palenque in these early times was fairly small and dispersed, although it is fair to say that many parts of the site have barely been touched archaeologically, so future excavations may alter this picture.

To return to the official dynastic records: during the century and a half after the brief reign of K'uk' Bahlam I, there was a series of successor rulers, and it seems that the kingdom of Palenque was beginning to attract attention as a regional power. Late in the sixth century, however, Palenque suffered a series of devastating military defeats at the hands of several older kingdoms to the east and northeast. A young king who officially came to the throne of Palenque in the middle of this time of troubles, in A.D. 615, ended up being the kingdom's salvation.

This young king, K'inich Janab Pakal I, lived until A.D. 683 (when he died he was buried in the tomb below the Temple of the Inscriptions). He stabilized the kingdom and commissioned a series of buildings in the section of the city visited by tourists today. This zone quickly became the central precinct of the city, and reign by reign buildings were added by K'inich Janab Pakal I's sons and successors. The kingdom remained vibrant throughout the seventh and eighth centuries, but by A.D. 800 the city was in decline. The latest hieroglyphic date we have from the site is A.D. 799, when we are told that another king named Janab Pakal (his full name is Wak Kimi Janab Pakal III) acceded to the throne. But Palenque by this time was not so grandiose: the accession event was recorded on a small blackware vessel found in one of the residential sectors of the city, rather than being inscribed on a limestone tablet in the inner sanctum of some great temple. Probably by the early ninth century, the forest had largely reclaimed the great city.

Combined, the various lines of evidence give a very detailed and precise history of Palenque. In Table 1.1, I list the ceramic phases (although see Rands, Chapter 2 for a more detailed discussion), kings, and major buildings of Palenque, along with their Christian dates.

Introduction to This Volume

This book contains chapters that derive largely from the most recent research at Palenque, largely conducted in two recent series of excavations. One of these was undertaken by Mexico's INAH, under the direction of Arnoldo González Cruz. The other excavation program is the Proyecto Grupo de las Cruces, conducted with permits from INAH under the direction of Merle Greene Robertson and Alfonso Morales Cleveland. The latter project, as its name implies, has concentrated its research on the Cross Group buildings and the pocket of temples to its immediate south, especially Temples XIX and XX. Both projects have added immeasurably

**Table 1.1: Correlation between Ceramic Phases, Rulers, and
Major Buildings of Palenque**

Ceramic Phase	Dates B.C./A.D.	Ruler	Buildings/Temples
Huiple	Post-A.D. 820		
Balunte	c. A.D. 750-820	Janab Pakal III Kan Bahlam III? K'uk' Bahlam II	
Murcielagos	c. A.D. 700-750	Janab' Pakal II Ahkal Mo' Nahb III K'an Joy Chitam II	XVIII, XIX, XXI Palace House A-D, Tower?
Otolum	c. A.D. 620-700	Kan Bahlam II Janab Pakal I	XVII, XIV, Cross Group Inscription, Palace Houses D,A,C,E, Count, Olvidado
Cascada	c. A.D. 500-620	Muwaan Mat Aj Ne' Ohl Mat Lady Yohl Ik'nal Kan Bahlam I Ahkal Mo' Nahb II K'an Joy Chitam I Ahkal Mo' Nahb I	
Motiepa	c. A.D. 400-500	Butz'aj Sak Chiik "Casper" K'uk' Bahlam I	
Picota	c. A.D. 250-400		

to our knowledge of the ancient city, and I hope after reading the chapters in this excellent volume that you will agree that these are very exciting times for Palenque archaeology. The chapters cover a wide range of topics, from architecture to hieroglyph texts, from broad issues of chronology to settlement to theoretical and methodological issues concerning architectural excavations. Most of the contributions are written by young scholars who represent the next generation of Mayanist scholars; some chapters discuss the results of dissertation research; and all of them engage the reader in the excitement of current research activity at this wonderful Classic Maya center. In the brief introduction to individual chapters that follow, I shall not necessarily follow the order of presentation within the book.

To my mind, the obvious starting point for discussion is the chapter by Edwin Barnhart (Chapter 6), for it is an example of how much our knowledge of Palenque has increased over the past few decades. His chapter also follows directly from the exhaustive mapping of the site that Barnhart completed a few years ago and which formed the basis of his doctoral dissertation (Barnhart 2001). As a result of Barnhart's seasons of surveying at Palenque, he knows more about the layout and extent of the site than anyone alive. In 1784, Josef Antonio Calderón documented some 215 buildings at Palenque. Subsequent explorers were not able to raise that total much for almost 150 years, since all the early visitors to Palenque confined their research to the central precinct of the site, focusing on the Palace, the Temple of the Inscriptions, and the Cross Group. Maudslay's 1890-1891 map, for example, is a superb site plan (and has been used until very recently as a major source), but it only covers the central 600 m by 350 m area of the site.

In 1922 and 1923, a young Dane, Frans Blom, was commissioned by the Mexican government to undertake an archaeological assessment of Palenque, and he was the first person to investigate the site away from the central precinct. Blom's map (Blom & La Farge 1926-1927, I, f.p. 180) gives the first true indication of the extent of the ancient capital. He shows that the site extended along the ridge for well over a kilometer, and that it was crossed by several small streams flowing down the slope to the north. In fact Blom overlaid the limits of Maudslay's map on his own: it is evident that he expanded the known limits of the site about fivefold.

The trouble is that Blom's draftsmanship was not the best. Some of his maps look more like a bowl of spaghetti thrown against a wall than natural contour lines overlain by rectangular structures. Blom had shown how large the site was, but it still remained to accurately plot the ancient city of Palenque.

Although INAH archaeologists such as Ruz made precise plans of Palenque, they also concentrated their archaeological work, and their mapping, on the central precinct of the site. In the 1970s Linda Schele began to compile a compass-and-tape map of the site. Linda's map formed the basis for the Palenque map published by Merle Greene Robertson (1983: map 3); it included over three-hundred buildings.

This brings us to Edwin Barnhart's precise and detailed mapping of the Palenque site core—all the more remarkable when one considers the difficult terrain and thick vegetation. Barnhart and his team (working as part of the Proyecto Grupo de las Cruces) mapped almost fifteen hundred structures over the "core" area of the site.

In his chapter, Barnhart turns to the issue of urbanism. This subject has been (and still is) a prickly one in Maya studies. As was noted earlier, not long ago scholars believed there were no cities in Classic Maya civilization, that major sites like Palenque, Tikal, and Copan were "vacant ceremonial centers." This view was held because few non-ceremonial buildings had been excavated; in other words, for a long time it was poorly understood where the general population lived. Now it is clear that the larger Maya sites had permanent populations numbering in the thousands. Barnhart estimates Palenque's peak population was as high as 6,000, and that the city had one of the highest population densities of any Maya site. But population density is not of course the only criterion involved in the issue of urbanism, and there is still some debate as to whether "urban" is an appropriate way to describe Classic Maya centers. Barnhart discusses the issue of Maya urbanism and, supported by the wealth of his survey data, makes a strong argument for urbanism at Palenque.

Just as we now know much more about the layout and population of the ancient city of Palenque from the work of Barnhart, we are also learning much more about Palenque's sustaining area (Chapter 5). This knowledge comes from recent work by Rodrigo Liendo Stuardo, who since 1997 has been conducting survey and excavation in a zone stretching just beyond the northern edge of the city.

Liendo and his team have surveyed over 400 sites in an area of just over 400 km². What he has found is a rural settlement pattern that developed relatively late in Palenque's history, with the earlier settlements being situated closest to the best soils. At the beginning of the Palenque royal dynasty (c. A.D. 430), it seems that most of the population increase—including the rural workers—was contained within the city limits. Presumably the population was still small enough that farmers could walk to their fields from the growing city, and "rural" settlements in the zone north of Palenque were very few. By the seventh century, however, Palenque's population was increasing rapidly, and agricultural land was becoming a priority. At this time there is evidence of intensive agriculture and even *sacbes*, or ancient Maya roads, linking outlying sites to the Palenque core. Nevertheless, Palenque's rural settlement was always quite low compared with that of other Maya sites. It was only in the Balunte period that the rural population increased substantially, and even then it was relatively small. One of the issues that Liendo explores is the correlation of political organization with these changing rural settlement patterns north of Palenque. There is still plenty of work to do. It is likely that Palenque's traditional hinterlands were in the valleys and limestone ridges to the south of Palenque, a region barely touched by archaeologists.

One of the archaeologists whose name will always be associated with Palenque is Robert Rands. Rands first worked in Palenque in 1951, as the project ceramicist working with Ruz. He has been analyzing the ceramics of Palenque and sites in the area ever since and is responsible for most of what we know about Palenque's ceramic history (he worked out the ceramic sequence of Palenque shown in Fig. 2.1) and external ceramic relationships (e.g., Rands 1974, 1987, Chapter 2).

In this volume, Rands concentrates on the Preclassic (c. 1000 B.C.-A.D. 250) ceramics from sites to the north and east of Palenque (Chapter 3). Rands has been studying the ceramics from this region, like those of Palenque, for many years. With his colleagues Ronald Bishop and Garmon Harbottle, he pioneered the sourcing of clay deposits (and the ceramics produced from them) by the technique known as neutron activation analysis. In Chapter 3, Rands discusses the Preclassic ceramic assemblages from Palenque and four other sites. (In general, Palenque's ceramics can be characterized as conservative and regional: Classic Palenque ceramics do not share many of the characteristics of Maya pottery to the east.)

The Preclassic ceramics of the four sites to the north and east of Palenque also show varying affinities. Earlier on, they indicate possible relationships with Olmec sites to the west. Later Palenque texts talk of a "king" who was born in 993 B.C. and came to the throne in 967 B.C., deep in Olmec times, perhaps a recollection of these Olmec ties. Indeed, late Olmec, or "epi-Olmec" monuments and smaller objects have been found throughout the region of eastern Tabasco north of Palenque. Other ceramic influences and relationships come from far and wide: the Pacific piedmont of Chiapas and Guatemala, the upper Usumacinta and Pasión river drainages, as well as the Peten Maya "heartland" to the east.

What is clear is that anything definable as a Palenque ceramic "sphere" does not occur in the plains north of Palenque until much later than the Preclassic period (and even then it is never strong). Remember that Palenque's traditional base is likely to have been not the northern coastal plains, but rather the limestone ridges and valleys to the south of the site. In any case, Palenque did not influence regional ceramics until much later, during the Classic period (A.D. 250-900).

Kirk French's chapter concerns water management at Palenque (Chapter 7). Tourists to Palenque notice the famous "Palace Aqueduct," running along the eastern side of the Palace. Even though about half of its corbelled roof has collapsed, this aqueduct is a most impressive piece of engineering, being roofed and reaching a height of four meters for much of its length of 120 meters. It serves to channel water safely through the main ceremonial precinct at the site, and to prevent its flooding during the heavy rainy season. What most tourists do not know, however, is that this is not the only aqueduct at the site: there is another roofed aqueduct about one kilometer to the west of the Palace. This and other features were mapped by French as part of Barnhart's Palenque Mapping Project. French points out that in fact nine streams flow through the site of Palenque, and there are also several dozen springs. All the watercourses have been modified in various ways to channel and direct water safely down the hillside without flooding and undermining the numerous buildings of the city. The importance of water at Palenque is indicated by the fact that the ancient name of the city was *Lakam Ha'*, which can be translated as "Big Water" or "Wide Water."

Damien Marken's chapter is an important contribution to the study of Palenque's architecture (Chapter 4). Marken provides a detailed analysis of the various criteria that can be applied to a seriation of Palenque's major architecture, from floor plans and vault shape to wall construction and the type of mortar. When correlated with associated ceramics and hieroglyphic texts, the seriation is quite sophisticated and precise. Marken's chapter serves as an excellent introduction to several other chapters in this book, which focus on individual architectural types and buildings.

The chapter by Damien Marken and Arnoldo González Cruz concerns residential compounds at Palenque that belonged to the city's non-royal elite (Chapter 8). Several of these groups have now been intensively excavated by González Cruz and others. Marken and González Cruz's chapter discusses three such groups, and well illustrates the wide variety in form and function of individual structures within the groups.

One of the things apparent at Palenque is that a large number of these elite residential groups exists in the city, even though only a few have been excavated. It is unclear whether this indicates a higher-than-average elite population at the site relative to "commoners." Certainly however, the non-royal elites were a powerful force at Palenque. They are mentioned (and portrayed) in hieroglyphic texts from the time of K'inich Janab Pakal I on, and in later Palenque times seem to have been quite powerful, to judge from the portraits of them in courtly scenes and rituals. One of them even commissioned his own carved monument—the Tablet of the Slaves—upon the occasion of his 60th birthday! Many would have been heads of important lineages within the kingdom, and some, we know, had noble offices.

Many different types of buildings exist in ancient Maya cities such as Palenque. One of the most interesting is the sweatbath, which was an important feature of Mesoamerican life in general, and is still used in traditional Maya communities today, rather like the sweat-lodges of many contemporary North American First Nation communities. The purpose of the sweatbath is ritual as well as practical: they were used particularly before, during and after childbirth, and for other "symbolic" birth rituals ("rites of passage"). They were even associated with the birth of the gods.

Mark Child (Chapter 12) has investigated the sweatbaths at the site of Piedras Negras, some 90 kilometers to the east of Palenque. On current count, Piedras Negras is the Classic Maya site with the most sweatbaths, with eight, while Palenque comes in second with two. Palenque, however, also has a number of symbolic sweatbaths: the beautiful sanctuaries of such temples as the Sun, Cross, and Foliated Cross, where we are told that the birth of Palenque's patron gods took place. Even the hieroglyph for sweatbaths has been identified (Houston 1996: 136; Stuart 1987: 38).

In his chapter, Child guides us through the architectural, hieroglyphic, and ritual aspects of Maya sweatbaths and demonstrates how the Cross Group sanctuaries were built to commemorate king K'inich Kan Bahlam II's rite of passage at age nine, when he passed from childhood to adulthood and the status of heir apparent of Palenque. In the process, Child predicts the nearby presence of a real sweatbath: the unexcavated Structure XIXaa, which is located adjacent to the spring where the Otolum stream begins its course through the central precinct of the site.

Kirk Straight's chapter considers the architecture of Temple XIX, one the buildings recently excavated by the Proyecto de las Cruces (Chapter 10). Temple XIX is of great interest not only for the beautiful stone and stucco sculpture found inside its collapsed remains, but also for its surprising architectural form. Although the proportions and size of Temple XIX fit within the standard range for Palenque temples and palace buildings, it is a much more open building inside, with seven piers running along its long central axis instead of the more solid central wall of other structures. An obvious question here is whether this signifies a different function for Temple XIX from that of other Palenque temples (Straight thinks it does, and I agree with him). Straight also discusses the construction techniques used in Temple XIX, and compares them with those used in other Palenque temples.

In the same precinct of Palenque as Temple XIX and the Cross Group is Temple XX, which is currently being excavated by members of the Proyecto de las Cruces. The chapter by Joshua Balcells González summarizes the current knowledge concerning this large structure (Chapter 9). From the summit of Temple XX one can look north toward the Cross Group and the Palace, and in Palenque's heyday the temple must have been one of the most imposing in the central zone of the city. Today, Temple XX is in a rather sorry state, for unlike most other temples at Palenque it has suffered greatly from collapse. Built on top of a small natural hillock, and in parts just a thin veneer of construction was built on top, resulting in a very unstable pyramid, which was apparently remodelled several times. The temple on top is badly destroyed, and perhaps the most noteworthy feature of Temple XX is a vaulted tomb with beautiful painted walls. The murals are quite early in style (the tomb is situated within the substructure of Temple XX), probably dating to the sixth-century A.D. If so, the tomb may be that of one of Palenque's early kings, one of K'inich Janab Pakal I's forebears. Another early king is buried below nearby Temple XVIIIa, and it appears that this precinct of Palenque was an important one from very early times, even though most of its construction is later.

The Guatemalan archaeologist Rudy Larios is one of the finest architectural excavators in the business. He has worked at a number of major Maya sites, from Copan to Uaxactun, and in all of them made major discoveries and important contributions in techniques of excavation and strategies for dealing with complex, multi-phased architecture. His contribution to this volume is a rather pensive one, investigating the fundamental issue of the purpose of archaeological restoration (Chapter 13). Should architectural excavation and restoration be made in order to glean the most information from the remains, going as far as one can from the evidence but no further, or should it follow national objectives and demands such as touristic development of the site? In a country as beautiful and as touristed as Mexico, this debate is always present, and the archaeologist often has difficult choices to make, especially when dealing with badly damaged buildings.

A book on Palenque would not be complete without at least one chapter about its beautiful art and hieroglyphic texts. The recent excavations at Palenque have shown that exciting sculptural finds can be made in quite unlikely locations. The discovery of the beautiful carved tablets in Temple XIX are a prime example of this, and recently another tablet was found in Temple XXI. The inscriptions of Temples XIX and XXI are the subjects of David Stuart's chapter, and through his work we enter the magical world of Maya mythology (Chapter 11).

The tablets of Temples XIX and XXI were commissioned by the Palenque king K'inich Ahkal Mo' Nahb III, who ruled Palenque from A.D. 721-c. 740. Temple XIX was dedicated in A.D. 734, and the throne of Temple XXI two years later. The tablets of the two temples are noteworthy for showing several nobles of the Palenque court in association with the king. But their inscriptions are even more significant: they talk about kings, gods, and great cosmological events. As Stuart cogently argues, they record some of the most explicit details of how Maya kings identified themselves with gods and viewed themselves as divine beings who reenacted great mythological events of the past. Louis XIV of France might have said, "L'état, c'est moi," K'inich Ahkal Mo' Nahb III is more likely to have said, "I am the world," or even "I am the cosmos." On one of the tablets from Temple XIX, K'inich Ahkal Mo' Nahb III represents himself as one of the patron gods of Palenque (referred to simply as "GI") on the date of his accession. Part of the reason for this is that K'inich Ahkal Mo' Nahb III calculated his accession date to repeat significant calendrical cycles of the accession of GI himself. In other words, the king's accession was a cosmological repetition of the god's, and K'inich Ahkal Mo' Nahb III was identifying himself with supernatural forces. The tablet of Temple XXI also talks of Palenque's patron gods, but the scene's central figure is the great K'inich Janab Pakal I. K'inich Ahkal Mo' Nahb III was his grandson and probably recorded this scene in part to show his legitimacy within the royal line.

Summary

I hope that you will agree with me that this book contains many exciting chapters that well reflect the dynamic research that is currently being conducted at Palenque. This work could not have been done without the generous support of Mexico's INAH, and the Proyecto Arqueológico Palenque, directed by Arnoldo González Cruz, nor the Proyecto Grupo de las Cruces, directed by Merle Greene Robertson and Alfonso Morales. The members of both projects deserve great credit for bringing so much new information to light and making it available to the public. While the term "conjunctive approach" is rather hackneyed these days, the chapters in this volume show the truly interdisciplinary nature of research at

Palenque. The scholars who have contributed to this volume are following in a long tradition of research on the wonderful city of Palenque, and the work they are doing continues to expand our understanding of the kingdom of K'inich Janab Pakal I and his successors.

References

Barnhart, Edwin L.
    2001   *The Palenque Mapping Project: Settlement and Urbanism at an Ancient Maya City*. Unpublished Ph.D. dissertation. University of Texas, Austin.

Blom, Frans, and Oliver La Farge
    1926-27 *Tribes and Temples*. 2 volumes. Tulane University, New Orleans, LA.

Greene Robertson, Merle
    1983   *The Sculpture of Palenque. Vol. I: The Temple of the Inscriptions*. Princeton University Press, Princeton, NJ.

Houston, Stephen D.
    1996   Symbolic sweatbaths of the Maya: Architectural Meaning in the Cross Group at Palenque, Mexico. *Latin American Antiquity* 7(2):132-151.

Martin, Simon and Nikolai Grube
    2000   *Chronicle of the Maya Kings and Queens*. Thames & Hudson, London, U.K.

Rands, Robert L.
    1974   The Ceramic Sequence at Palenque, Chiapas. In *Mesoamerican Archaeology: New Approaches*, edited by Norman Hammond, pp. 51-75. Duckworth, London, U.K.

    1987   Ceramic patterns and traditions in the Palenque area. In *Maya Ceramics: Papers of the 1985 Maya Ceramic Conference*, edited by Prudence M. Rice and Robert J. Sharer, pp. 203-238. BAR International Series, 345(i). Oxford, U.K.

Stuart, David
    1987   *Ten Phonetic Syllables*. Research Reports on Ancient Maya Writing 14. Center for Maya Research, Washington, D.C.

Part II

CHRONOLOGY

Chapter 2

Chronological Chart and Overview of Ceramic Developments at Palenque

Robert L. Rands

Traditional chronological charts position ceramic complexes horizontally, lines being drawn to separate one complex from another. A little-used alternative (e.g., Rands 1973: Fig. 6) is to employ slanted instead of horizontal lines. Followed here, the latter procedure has at least two major advantages. (1) There is no misleading implication that the complexes are firmly dated; rather, a range of possible dates is indicated. (2) A visual suggestion is made that complexes overlap instead of having the clear-cut separation that would be indicated by a series of parallel horizontal divisions. To deal with such transitions, Rands and Bishop (2003) have employed the concept of dominant and secondary phases, although this terminology is not used here.

Emphasis is accorded the Classic period chronology. See Chapter 3 for an overview of the Preclassic at Palenque, which present observations directed toward the Preclassic-Classic transition. Brief consideration is also given to the Terminal Classic-Postclassic.

Preclassic-Picota

The Piocta Complex could be characterized, as originally described (Rands 1974), as a strange variant of the Early Classic. It is equally tempting to consider it, in part, as representing the Preclassic-Early Classic transition at Palenque (Rands, Chapter 3). Thus, a portion of the line separating the Preclassic and Picota is broken. The steeper slant shown for the beginning of Picota, in contrast to the only somewhat arbitrary symmetry in the slant of the lines separating the later phases, indicates the poor control of absolute dating in the lower part of the chart.

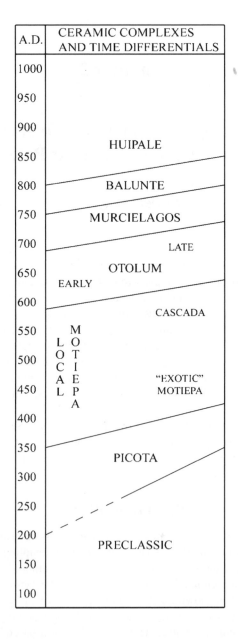

Figure 2.1: Ceramic complexes at Palenque, Chiapas

Early Classic

Ceramic chronology in the chart is presented in a highly unorthodox manner, and a brief review of the ordering of phases at Palenque is necessary. Originally the Early Classic was divided into two complexes, Picota and Motiepa, and a "Middle Classic" Cascada complex was later added (Rands 1974, 1987). Faceting of the subsequent Otolum complex was a factor in reducing the scope of Cascada. Of greater significance, accumulating evidence showed the strength of Peten-like influences early in Motiepa. Yet these influences were seemingly of relatively short duration, apparently being contemporaneous with only a small segment of an ongoing tradition, termed Local Motiepa, which was in large part derived from Picota. Although some incorporation of Peten styles occurred, the subsequent trajectory was toward marked regionalism. In an attempt to reconcile these developments, status as a full complex is not indicated for Cascada although the name is retained as a sometimes useful subcomplex. The Peten-like materials are termed "Exotic Motiepa," rather than being designated a "trade subcomplex" in the terminology of Willey, Culbert, and Adams (1967: 304). It is unknown if widespread trade actually occurred. An alternative scenario might postulate outsiders, including potters trained in a non-Palenque technostylistic tradition, residing in a foreign barrio at the site. In any event, throughout the post-Picota Early Classic, Local Motiepa tends to be dominant. This presentation carves out somewhat arbitrary subdivisions but, if it is substantially correct, a period of recurring instability is implied.

Picota. Deep dishes, with massive solid slab feet, are distinctive, the slab feet being unlike those of Teotihuacan. Vertical groove-incision is common on dish exteriors, a general treatment having less frequent although sometimes highly visible occurrence in subsequent complexes. Much of the pottery is sandy-textured, although the early presence of a fine orange-brown paste warrants attention. Both pastes continue, with some fluctuation in frequency, throughout the Classic sequence. Certain aspects of Palenque's Classic ceramic tradition seem to have been established in Picota, perhaps with roots extending back into the Preclassic.

Local Motiepa. When a determination can be made that pottery is slipped, monochrome red is characteristic. Dishes are deep, recalling those of Picota but with substantial differences. Interior-beveled rims, sometimes associated with concave wall interiors, appear in a variety of forms. Jar pastes, as opposed to the usual sandy texture for other forms, are commonly carbonate or a quartz sand-carbonate mixture. Later trends include the presence of orange slip, perhaps reflecting influences, on a simplified scale, derived from "Exotic" Motiepa.

"Exotic" Motiepa. In sharp contrast to other Classic ceramics at Palenque, slips are glossy, hard, well preserved, and serve as a basis for classification in the type-variety system. Pastes are fine-grained carbonate, again contrasting with other Palenque pottery. In view of the paste, the contrast is not simply an artifact of sampling ceramics having unusually good post-depositional preservation. Best

represented in current sampling are Aguila Orange, Pita Incised, Lucha Incised, and Paradero Fluted.

Cascada. Contemporaneous with the latter part of Local Motiepa, Cascada ceramics can perhaps most simply be characterized as a revival of fine pastes, sparsely represented since the Picota complex. Fine Blacks represent the beginning of a tradition that was to be partially truncated early in the Late Classic only to emerge, with renewed vigor, later in that period.

Late Classic

Otolum. Probably the most extensive use of polychrome occurs at Palenque, although poor surface preservation requires that such an assertion be qualified. Slight traces of primer with a fleck or two of orange on a sherd does not constitute a basis for quantifying polychromes, although a few clear examples are known. Dichromes, especially red-on-orange, are often a distinct possibility, or perhaps the sherd is monochrome orange. Although extensively used, the orange slip is poor, being especially subject to weathering. When observable, polychromes are geometric, like other orange slipped ceramics being largely restricted to tripod plates. Noteworthy for these plates is an exceptionally wide everted rim, this constituting the major single criterion for distinguishing Otolum. Patterning exists in rim eversion. Early Facet plates are uptilted, eversion in the Late Facet being relatively horizontal. Black surfaces are very rare, leading to the suggestion that Fine Black, beginning to emerge in Cascada as one of Palenque's most powerful traditions, was in competiton with the Otolum polychromes as desired service pottery and temporarily lost out.

Murcielagos. As always weathering is a complicating factor, but monochrome reds, blacks, and to a lesser degree creams seem largely to replace the orange-based pottery of Otolum. Fine pastes increase markedly, especially for the blacks, which include members of Chablekal (Fine Gray) and the Yalcox (Fine Black) ceramic groups. The major Otolum marker, the widely everted rim, declines to the point of extinction, although more modest rim eversion is common on plates. Plastic decoration is far more frequent and elaborated than in Otolum, occurring on ritually oriented forms such as incensarios, occasionally on dishes and basins, and more commonly on necks and sublabial ridges of jars. Red paint, often linear, also occurs on necks of the otherwise unslipped jars. Semicylindrical vases maintain Otolum shapes but are more commonly incised, fluted, impressed, or stamped. Serving bowls increase in frequency and are often decorated, especially with surface alteration. Design treatments often incorporate those found on Telchac composite, a member of the Chablekal group, and an unanswered question is that of imitation from outside sources versus development within a localized, Palenque-based tradition. The Chablekal group appears in substantial quantities midway through Murcielagos, extending into the following Balunte complex. Although overlapping in time, the less-consistently decorated Yalcox group is known somewhat earlier than Chablekal ceramics, later incorporating decorative treatments such as those found on Telchac composite.

Balunte. Service pottery is largely unslipped although usually well polished. Abrupt changes occur in jars, now coarsely textured and undecorated. Tripod plates with hollow feet, known in Murcielagos, increase greatly in size during Balunte. Large basins have continuity in general shape with those of Murcielagos, although impressed decoration differs in treatment and placement; the presence of widely everted rims and distinct pastes underscores differences from the Murcielagos basins. Vases assume true cylindrical form, become larger and are often stucco painted. Stucco painting extends to serving bowls, which otherwise have relatively minor differences from those of Murcielagos.

Terminal Classic-Postclassic

Huipale. Post-collapse, the occupation may have been intermittent (the so-called squatters, known at many late Southern Lowland Maya sites.) Accordingly, this is not a firmly based complex and may prove to be divisible with sufficient archaeological investigation. There is no claim to total abandonment of Palenque at the end of Balunte; this also remains to be tested. Fine Orange, although rare, is a major diagnostic, representing the Altar, Balancan, Silho, and Matillas ceramic groups. According to traditional chronology this indicates a long duration, until the Middle Postclassic, although if a "total overlap" interpretation is followed the Fine Orange differences are spatial rather than temporal (Andrews & Sabloff 1986; Ball 1979a, 1979b; Lincoln 1986; Rice & Forsyth 2004; Willey 1986).

Comments

The preceding overview focuses on major trends, not transitions or minor occurrences. For example, the everted rim basins characteristic of Balunte are in part coeval with the lightly bolstered, thumb-impressed Murcielagos basins, and both forms are securely placed in a middle Murcielagos context. Frequencies peak differently, however, and it is in Balunte that eversion becomes wider and more elaborated.

Palenque's geographic and natural settings are relevant to its ceramic development and to archaeological interpretations of that development. From a Maya-oriented perspective, the site's location in the far west has the potential for isolation, and regionalism seems to be reflected in much of its Classic period pottery. Palenque lies on a partially natural plateau that has been enhanced through time by extensive secondary deposition, borrowing, and redeposition. Stratigraphy is therefore complex, being supplemented by seriation. A search is made for agreement in the two approaches, resulting in degrees of chronological control that, for different subsets, vary from excellent to poor.

Changes in slip are accorded importance in the present overview, although these do not constitute the primary criterion for chronological ordering; the poor surface preservation of most of the pottery justifies this reiteration. In developing a ceramic sequence, modifications in shape provide substantially greater information, additional insights resulting from the technologically informed investigation of paste. Classification needs to be flexible enough to use whatever kind of information is relevant and available.

Notwithstanding the quest for chronological refinements, minimally leading to recognition of ceramic complexes and their subdivisions as exemplified in Figure 2.1, this approach is insufficient. Also important are drifts or trends cutting across ceramic complexes. Three examples are given: (1) Decreasing height: diameter ratio, the popularity of plates increasing at the expense of dishes. This trend is observed across the entire Classic sequence. (2) Long-sustained traditions undergoing marked variation in popularity. This is exemplified by fine paste ceramics: orange-browns, blacks, creams, and finally the better known grays and oranges. In this presumably untempered pottery, the general development, although with numerous exceptions, may roughly be described as from silty to very fine. An interplay exists between the potters' techniques and available natural resources, the latter apparently changing as the site and its immediate area of intensive interaction expanded into new microzones. (3) Another tendency, believed to have archaeological utility in spite of differential sampling and untested inferences, is indicative of increased redundancy within a given form: over time a greater number of shapes, each standardized, is made and used to meet the same basic function. The latter trend seems to have some applicability in earlier times but is most pronounced as Murcielagos is contrasted with the preceding Classic complexes. Factors responsible for this are unknown but might include an increase in the number of localized yet semi-independent workshops (Rands & Bishop 2003).

These differing trajectories downplay total reliance on subdividing a sequence into complexes if our aim is to combine chronological, cultural and socioeconomic understandings. A long-range view is necessary, examining the permutations undergone by a tradition or set of traditions.

References

Andrews, E. Wyllys, V and Jeremy A. Sabloff
  1986   Classic to Postclassic: A Summary Discussion. In *Late Lowland Maya Civilization: Classic to Postclassic*, edited by Jeremy A. Sabloff and E. Wyllys Andrews V, pp. 433-456. School of American Research Press and University of New Mexico Press, Albuquerque.

Ball, Joseph W.
  1979a   Ceramics, Culture History, and the Puuc Tradition: Some Alternative Possibilities. In *The Puuc: New Perspectives*, edited by Lawrence Mills, pp. 18-35. Central College, Pella, IA.

1979b   The 1977 Central College Symposium on Puuc Archaeology: A Summary
         Review. In *The Puuc: New Perspectives*, edited by Lawrence Mills, pp. 46-
         51. Central College, Pella, IA.

Lincoln, Charles
1986   The Chronology of Chichen Itza: A Review of the Literature. In *Late Lowland
         Maya Civilization: Classic to Postclassic*, edited by Jeremy A. Sabloff and
         E. Wyllys Andrews V, pp. 141-196. School of American Research Press and
         University of New Mexico Press, Albuquerque.

Rands, Robert L.
1973   The Classic Collapse in the Southern Maya Lowlands: Chronology. In *The
         Classic Maya Collapse*, edited by T. Patrick Culbert, pp. 43-62. University of
         New Mexico Press, Albuquerque.

1974   The Ceramic Sequence at Palenque, Chiapas. In *Mesoamerican Archaeology:
         New Approaches*, edited by Norman Hammond, pp. 51-76. University of
         Texas Press, Austin.

1987   Ceramic Patterns and Traditions in the Palenque Area. In *Maya Ceramics.
         Papers from the 1985 Maya Ceramic Conference*, edited by Prudence M.
         Rice and Robert J. Sharer, pp. 203-238. BAR International Series 345(i).
         Hadrian Books Ltd., Oxford, U.K.

Rands, Robert L. and Ronald L. Bishop
2003   The Dish-Plate Tradition at Palenque: Continuity and Change. In *Patterns &
         Process: A Festschrift in Honor of Dr. Edward V. Sayre*, edited by Lambertus
         van Zelst, pp. 109-132. Smithsonian Center for Materials Research &
         Education, Suitland, MD.

Rice, Prudence M. and Donald Forsyth
2004   Terminal Classic-Period Ceramics. In *Terminal Classic in the Maya Lowlands*,
         edited by Arthur A. Demarest, Prudence M. Rice, & Don S. Rice, pp. 28-59.
         University Press of Colorado, Boulder.

Willey, Gordon R.
1986   The Postclassic of the Maya Lowlands: A Preliminary Overview. In *Late
         Lowland Maya Civilization: Classic to Postclassic*, edited by Jeremy A.
         Sabloff and E. Wyllys Andrews V, pp. 17-52. School of American Research
         Press and University of New Mexico Press, Albuquerque.

Willey, Gordon R., T. Patrick Culbert, and Richard E. W. Adams
1967   Maya Lowland Ceramics: A Report from the 1965 Guatemala City Conference.
         American Antiquity 32(3):289-315.

Chapter 3

Palenque and Selected Survey Sites in Chiapas and Tabasco: The Preclassic

Robert L. Rands

A small subset of Preclassic pottery is considered here, based on fieldwork carried out between the 1950s and 1970s. Archaeological work was focused on the center of Palenque, but included the recovery of Preclassic remains at various survey sites in Chiapas and Tabasco, Mexico. Because of the initial problem orientation (Rands 1967), which gave priority to understanding the ceramic sequence at Palenque, and because very small quantities of Preclassic were recovered at the site, ongoing research has emphasized developments during the Classic period. A partial exception has been the Preclassic sequence at Trinidad. Clearly, it is past time that the Preclassic be considered in greater detail, although a more comprehensive treatment of interaction between Palenque and outlying sites, from the Preclassic to Terminal Classic, is still in preparation. Data and interpretations presented here are, therefore, incomplete and somewhat speculative.

The Preclassic is considered from four sites in addition to Palenque. To the north lying on or near the Usumacinta River, are Trinidad and Zapatillo (the latter also referred to as Nueva Esperanza). To the south and east are Chinikiha and Paso Nuevo. Distances from Palenque are generally in the 40 to 45 km range, although Paso Nuevo is closer, approximately 10 km away (Fig. 3.1). Preclassic data are more detailed than at Palenque, and ceramics from these sites are treated first. This order also permits a more efficient comparison between Palenque and the survey sites.

Before turning to Preclassic pottery from the survey, the status of ceramic work at Palenque, in the perspective of site archaeology, merits brief attention. Leveling of the somewhat natural plateau to form plazas has led to varying amounts of earthen and rubble fill, sometimes rich in pottery, but at other times virtually sterile. Rarely, small Preclassic sherds have been recovered from fill the

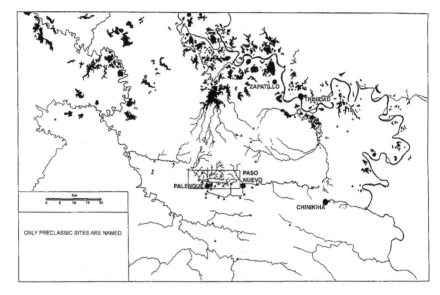

Figure 3.1: Palenque region, Chiapas, Mexico

most frequent pottery of which is of a much later date. Still more rarely, Preclassic and Early Classic ceramics are found in association, providing the possibilities of transitional development or of fortuitous mixing. Moving away from the site center, where architectural construction is greatest, it has required less extensive penetration to recover Preclassic sherds, but the lack of meaningful context for subdividing the Preclassic remains. At the present time, a sound Preclassic sequence is lacking for Palenque, and all the comparative insights to be gained from better contexts at other sites is necessary.

Trinidad, Tabasco

As noted, the Preclassic at Trinidad has been reported on in greatest detail. Early to late, it is sequenced as the Chiuaan, Xot, and Chacibcan ceramic complexes, with a provisionally named Bacha floating somewhere between or overlapping Chiuaan and Xot (Rands 1969, 1987). All fall within the broadly defined Middle Preclassic period. Except for Chacibcan, the Preclassic ceramics are mostly from mound fill, underlying Classic pottery, at a depth of approximately three to six meters. In this churned fill situation, cross-ties from outside the survey provide the major basis for chronological partition. Seriation also indicates developmental trends but tends to be specific to a given form class rather than integrating a number of these classes into sharply defined complexes.

Chiuaan. Chronologically, Chiuaan is early in the Middle Preclassic. In personal communications from a number of years ago, Jeremy Sabloff saw Chiuaan ceramics as a Xe equivalent at Seibal, and Michael Coe considered some of the same sherds as close to Nacaste at San Lorenzo. These observations illustrate, for what has traditionally become known as the "Northwestern Zone" of the southern Maya Lowlands (see Culbert 1973: Fig. 1), that cultural correspondences at the beginning of the Middle Preclassic extended within the Maya area to the southeast and to the Olmec in the west.

For the most part, Figure 3.2 shows thick and thin tecomates and restricted bowls approaching tecomates. White slipped, (a-c) may be earlier than most of the other sherds. For example, (c) corresponds closely to La Mina White convex-base miniatures identified as "paint dishes" from the San Lorenzo phase (Coe & Diehl 1980: Fig. 149a-d); the thick, perforated white-slipped tecomate (a) may equate with Camalote White of the succeeding Nacaste phase, perforation of tecomates extending farther back in time. Horizontally ovoid, (d) is subglobular with an essentially flat base.

Much of the material in Figure 3.2 can be placed early in the Middle Preclassic. Connecting arcs in (e) and the strong occurrence of black, including white-rimmed black (i) are common at this time (Green & Lowe 1967: 67). Fluting (f) is well represented in tecomates and near-tecomates at Trinidad.

In general, Figure 3.3 illustrates slightly flared dishes or bowls of simple silhouette. Black is important, including white-rim black (a, b). Otherwise, slipped surfaces are rare ([e] is non-waxy orange). The double-line break is present ([d] and potentially so [c]), and a field of incised diagonal lines also occurs (e); both are important in the Middle Preclassic (e.g.,, the Nacaste phase at San Lorenzo, Coe & Diehl 1980: Fig. 164). Incising includes motifs of great time range, including the sine curve ([h]; compare Lowe 1989: Fig. 4.9) and, in (a), a fragmentary design having probable relationship to that shown, e.g.,, by Susanna Ekholm (1969: Figs. 35i, 45h, 48h, 57g) at Izapa. Although unreliable for cross-dating, these motifs are not at home in the Maya Lowlands, suggesting Greater Isthmian prototypes. A temporal position early in the Middle Preclassic again seems to fit. As sampled, the absence of features such as carving and red-banded or rocker-stamped tecomates precludes a substantial Early Preclassic occupation.

Angled or composite silhouette bowls are also present in Chiuaan ceramics (Fig. 3.4a-e). Non-waxy red (exterior) and black (interior) are common, the single-line break (e), impressed half-circles (c), and a horizontal groove-incised field (b) also occurring. Sharply thinned toward the rim, (d) recalls various Early Preclassic sherds, although these are mostly flat-based simple silhouettes. Angled sherds of this shape occur, however, in the Duende phase at Izapa (Ekholm 1969: Fig. 62o, 63m).

Bacha. As noted, this attempt at temporal discrimination is provisional, lacking stratigraphic substantiation. Nevertheless, the flared bowl with rim molding and interior-beveled rim (Fig. 3.4f-i) is highly distinctive. In this shape class, the incised arc of (f) is an early Middle Preclassic treatment (pointing toward

Chiuaan) and the cloudy resist in (i), although differing in the absence of slipped surfaces, suggests Xot (later in the Middle Preclassic).

Jars (Fig. 3.5). The mixed fill again poses problems for a temporal separation. A complete, unslipped jar from a Chacibcan level (d) does, however, provide an anchor for seriation at the close of the sampled Preclassic occupation. Standing apart in treatment and abundance are high-necked jars with thickened interior-faceted rims, unobliterrated coiling marks, and red daub exteriors (a, e). Due to similarities in surface treatment to Palma Daub, I was first inclined to place these on a Mamom level—i.e., a temporal equivalent of Xot. To do so, however, introduces complexity into what otherwise would be a smooth development (b-c-d).

Xot. Xot ceramics are well represented in the mound fill and elsewhere at Trinidad, but show less variation than Chiuaan, the latter perhaps covering a wider span of time that is potentially subject to subdivision. Rounded shallow dishes, often with a very low height:diameter ratio, are a major characteristic of Xot (Fig. 3.6a, c). These are usually red slipped (non-waxy), occasionally with one or two incised horizontal lines below the rim. Cloudy, blotchy resist occurs (c), generally on a well-smoothed but unslipped interior and a red-slipped exterior. Volcanic-bearing pastes continue, although a greater admixture of quartz sand is sometimes noted.

Chacibcan. Set apart stratigraphically from the earlier ceramics, Chacibcan is not well represented. Changes, however, are marked, including a lustrous orange, waxy slip; comparatively thick dishes with flared, everted rims (Fig. 3.6b) and carbonate temper (striking due to the inaccessibility of limestone in the alluvial floodplain environment of Trinidad). Perhaps the small amount of volcanic ash-tempered pottery bearing a waxy red slip (not illustrated) also is to be placed in Chacibcan. Cloudy resist, now slipped on both the interior and exterior (d), conforms to Tierra Mojada as described for Seibal in Escoba Mamom (Sabloff 1975). The thickened everted-rim dish has close shape analogs in the Malecon Complex at Edzna (Forsyth 1983: Figs. 3z, 6y). In the ceramics, Mayanization appears to have been underway at Trinidad during Chacibcan times, but was cut short, a near-hiatus, as sampled, occurring from the Middle Preclassic until well into the Classic.

Zapatillo (Nueva Esperanza), Chiapas

Excavations were limited, most of the pottery being collected from a newly opened road, portions of three mounds having been bulldozed for fill. The possibility of multicomponent mixing is obvious. The name, Nueva Esperanza, has a wide application, and the chance of confusion with other sites in the general region is likewise apparent.

On a modal level, heavy rim bolstering in Figure 3.7a recalls Greater Isthmian, including materials of Early and Middle Preclassic date, and Xe. Blacks, some of which are white rimmed (Fig. 3.7m), are well represented, but form and slip characteristics differ from Trinidad. Also shown in Figure 3.7, folded rims (f, l) and circle-impression (j, k) are common, the latter sharing attributes of shape with white-slipped ceramics (h, j, k, m), the punctate fields being reminiscent of Middle Preclassic at Mirador (Agrinier 2000: Fig. 62). The jar form (i) occurs at Trinidad (Fig. 3.5c) and widely throughout the survey region, often with volcanic ash or pumice temper. More elaborate, the shape of the black jar in (e) is almost duplicated in Figure 3.8c, also from Zapatillo. Figure 3.7d strongly resembles a cache vessel from Chiapa de Corzo, dated as Jiquipilas (Mason 1960: Fig. 9b) and stylistically similar materials from, for example, Tres Zapotes (Weiant 1943: Fig. 22). In general, connections of the Figure 3.7 ceramics seem to be primarily to the west, rather than with the Maya Lowlands.

Lowland Maya affiliations are stronger in the waxy, red-slipped pottery of Figure 3.8, some examples relating to the Late Preclassic. Thus, (d) can be equated with Laguna Verde Incised and the medial-flange sherd in (e) with Sierra Red. The red jar (c), referred to above (Fig. 3.7e), has localized characteristics, including shape and precisely executed fluting.

Fairly late in the Middle Preclassic—at least as seen from a Southeastern Mesoamerican perspective—sherds in Figure 3.9 extend the ceramic repertoire at Zapatillo. Cloudy resist, flared-wall dishes (a-c) and elaborations of everted rims, including groove-incising and rim tabs (a, b, d, e) are common. Slips are waxy, (a) corresponds to the double-slipped Tierra Mojada Group, as described for Escoba Mamom at Seibal (Sabloff 1975) and to Chiapa III materials; the double-line break, generally ascribable to Xe rather than Mamom in the Maya Lowlands, is present (cf. Adams 1971: Figs. 1gg, hh, 7i). Variations of the cloudy resist technique occur: (b) is a smudged orange resist with blobs and trickles, and (c) has a mainly red surface with orange showing through. In a strong pattern as observed for Zapatillo, orange is largely restricted to cloudy resist, most of the waxy slips being red (for the widespread occurrence of cloudy resist see Lowe 1977: 223-224; Demarest & Sharer 1982; Demarest 1986; Andrews 1986: 33; Brady et al. 1998: 20, Fig. 2).

The presence of specular hematite red slip, which sparkles when turned to the light, is of special interest (Fig. 3.10a-g). Monochrone red and red-on-cream occurs. The Preclassic associations of specular red are mostly early—a broad Ocos horizon, concentrated on the Pacific Coast of Chiapas and Guatemala, with extensions as far as Oaxaca and the Tehuacan Valley. Closer to Zapatillo, specular red occurs not only in the Mal Paso region, but at La Venta and Tres Zapotes. At La Venta it is recorded only in passing by Drucker (1952: 96) but is considered at greater length on reexamination by E. Wyllys Andrews (Andrews 1990: 34, 43, Fig. 11g, h). According to Andrews, the La Venta-Tres Zapotes specular reds differ in slip and rim forms from Early Preclassic examples at Ocos, being "more appropriate" for the Middle Preclassic. In passing, the Late Classic occurrence of specular red-on-cream at La Blanca, Guatemala, should be noted (Love 2002: 145).

Absence of "gadrooned" lips and general simplification of rims set the Zapatillo specular reds apart from the Ocos horizon (contrast Figure 3.10a-g with, for example, Coe 1961: Fig. 19; Ekholm 1969: Fig. 25; Ceja Tenorio 1985: Fig. 39q-aaa). Although fragmentary, (a) and (d) are possible cuspidors. Incising and groove-incising, mostly horizontal, characterize the rather small sample. Almost all sherds have a hard, dark over-all red exterior slip, the interior combining red below the rim with white or light buff. This pattern is present on non-specular red (h). Somewhat divergent, the specular red is weaker in (g), the incurved wall has a lightly bolstered rim, and vertical rather than horizontal groove-incising is present.

In summary, as sampled, Zapatillo includes sparse ceramics dating back to a Chiuaan-like horizon with linkages outside the Maya Lowlands, undergoes apparent intensification and "Mayanization" later in the Middle Preclassic, and continues into the Late Preclassic. To suggest ceramic complex names for these developments would be unwarranted at the present time, however, in view of sample size and lack of stratigraphic control.

Chinikiha, Chiapas

Small quantities of Preclassic ceramics were obtained from several mixed deposits, notably caves. Correspondences are close to the high-neck daub jars of Trinidad, although at Chinikiha red completely covers the sherd exterior (Figure 3.11a, b). Aside from Tierra Blanca, an Usumacinta site just upstream from Trinidad, Chinikiha is the only other site in the survey region where this daubed, volcanic-glass bearing type is known.

Other Preclassic jars from Chinikiha are shown in Figure 3.11c-e. Widely distributed in the survey region, the shape class in (c) occurs, with only slight variation, at Trinidad (Fig. 3.5c), Zapatillo (Fig. 3.7i), Paso Nuevo (Fig. 3.15f, j), and Palenque (Fig. 3.18c). Volcanic ash temper is characteristic. Fluted rim moldings (Fig. 3.11d) are also known on jars from Palenque (Fig. 3.18d), the form being relatively less common there, however, than at Chinikiha; coarse carbonate temper is usual. With folded rim and slightly grooved lip, the Chinikiha jar in Figure 3.11e is closely paralleled at Zapatillo (Fig. 3.7l) and (not illustrated) at Palenque; again carbonate temper is characteristic. Chinikiha, therefore, is important for its intraregional ceramic cross-ties. Figure 3.12 expands comparative material from the site on an interregional basis.

In discussing affiliations between Komchen and La Venta, Andrews (1986: 34-39, 43, Figs. 11b, i, k, 12d-m) illustrates sharply everted and downturned dish rims; dates may be on the order of B.C. 600/500 to 400/300. Perhaps slightly less strongly, Chinikiha dishes also fit into his illustrated range (Fig. 3.12a, b), and a generally similar form occurs at Palenque (Fig. 3.16f). At least occasional ceramics from the Palenque survey seem to reflect the inferred contacts, perhaps rendering unnecessary the direct seagoing route between the Olmec area and Yucatan posited by Andrews (1986: 41-42).

The possibility of Olmec-Chinikiha affiliations is strengthened, on at least a modal (shape) level (Fig. 3.12c, d). Nuances of rim and wall curvature correspond closely to types of the San Lorenzo phase, as known both at the type site (Coe & Diehl 1980: Fig. 154) and at Mirador (Agrinier 1984: Fig. 36w). Red-on-white is also shared in this form class (d) and for the early Olmec horizon we may approach a typological, rather than simply modal, level of comparative analysis.

Paso Nuevo, Chiapas

Paso Nuevo is geographically much closer to Palenque than the other survey sites considered here. Most Preclassic ceramics known from Paso Nuevo were recovered from a low platform, slightly less than a meter in height. A stone retaining wall, at one end of the platform, contained five stacked dishes (Fig. 3.13a-e). This cache should provide a minimal date for the platform and its redeposited, multicomponent sherds. The cached Sierra vessels are similar: interior and exterior waxy red slip; flat base; flared walls with outturned rims; and rim moldings that are sometimes groove-incised. Generally similar ceramics occur in the mound fill (Fig. 3.13g, h).

Earlier ceramics are abundant in the fill (Fig. 3.14). The exterior thickened band in (a) slants downward, the tecomate otherwise resembling, for example, ceramics of the Duende phase at Izapa (Ekholm 1969: Fig. 66w) and Tok at Chalchuapa (Sharer 1978: Fig. 6a3, g5). Sharply incurved, (c) also has Tok-Colas correspondences at Chalchuapa (Sharer 1978: Figs. 6a2, g5, 7f 10, 11), and (d) is Xe-like. White slips (a, e-g), sometimes with a fugitive, mottled black interior, also contrast with the Paso Nuevo cache vessels and with the thickened, everted, or bolstered forms shown elsewhere in Figure 3.14 (see Lowe 1978: 360-362 for a discussion of Middle Preclassic white wares). In (n) the rim is interior faceted, a closely similar red sherd being illustrated for Palenque (Fig. 3.16i). Figure 3.14m closely resembles shapes from Zapatillo and Chinikiha (Figs. 3.7l, 3.11e). Incised semicircles have analogs at Trinidad (cf. Figs. 3.4c, 3.14h); for concentric squiggles (Fig. 3.14k) compare the Cantera phase at Chalcatzingo (Cyphers Guillen 1987: Fig. 13.26). Similarities are widespread on a modal level, ranging from the Early to Middle Preclassic.

Jars from Paso Nuevo are shown in Figure 3.15. Red or white monochromes and dichromes occur, along with a monochrome black (b-f, j); necks of (a-c) are of a moderate height. In spite of such differences, the cited examples contrast with thick, coarsely finished high-neck jars flaring toward exterior-faceted rims (g-i). Exterior beveled rims (a-c, g-i) occur in other form classes at Paso Nuevo (Fig. 3.14f, m) and are characteristic of the site, perhaps replicating their prominence at Chalchuapa in the Tok, Colas, and Kal phases (Sharer 1978: Table 3B7, Figs. 6a, 7d-f, 8a); also compare jars at Tres Zapotes (Drucker 1943: Fig. 19). The tapering, long-neck jar (Fig. 3.15a) approaches a La Venta bottle form (cf. Drucker 1943: 118, Fig. 39d) and Middle to Late Preclassic Mal Paso materials (Lee 1974: Fig.

43b); see also earlier ceramics in Coe and Diehl (1980), Sisson (1976), and comments by Lowe (1978). White or red-on-white jars are common at Paso Nuevo (Fig. 3.15b, c, e, f); conversely, (h) is a rare example of striation and (j) is bituminous. The strap handle (b) is very rare in the Palenque survey and, generally, in the west (see Lowe 1978: 347). Compared to Chiuaan at Trinidad and some of the Zapatillo ceramics, black is rare at Paso Nuevo and, when present, tends to be distinctive, sometimes recalling the fugitive mottled black-and-whites seen in Figures 3.14e and 3.14f.

At Paso Nuevo, as in other survey sites considered here, modal similarities suggest relationships outside the Maya Lowlands on early Middle Preclassic and even Early Preclassic levels, followed by ceramics more characteristic of the late Middle to Late Preclassic. The appearance of waxy-surfaced pottery, primarily red but often lacking some of the more distinctive features of Sierra Red, appears pivotal, transcending even the Early and Middle Preclassic distinctions. This said, the apparent absence of a number of Early Preclassic diagnostics constitutes an argument against a pervasive occupation at that time.

Palenque

Most Preclassic pottery known at Palenque has been subject to marked redeposition and breakage. The lack of extensive penetration of sealed deposits has contributed to the failure to define ceramic complexes for the period. However, time depth is present.

This is seen especially in Figure 3.16. Tecomates, although highly fragmentary, occur in thick and thin forms (a, b). Simple in silhouette, (d) is Xe-like. Waxy slips, when present, are almost exclusively red (e-k). The labial-flange sherd (k) helps to identify the poorly represented Chicanel horizon. Characterized by a field of parallel cursive, preslipped incised lines, (j), although monochrome red, otherwise closely resembles Correlo incised-dichrome (Smith 1955: Fig. 84k). In other treatments, comparisons are close to Paso Nuevo (Figs. 3.14n, 3.16i) and extend to Chinikiha (Figs. 3.12a, b, 3.16f). Vertically groove-incised, (h) may anticipate an Early Classic (Picota phase) treatment at Palenque.

Preclassic examples of wide-everted rim dishes, usually slightly upturned, are given in Figure 3.17. The thick-walled, shallow to heavily grooved rim (a) is probably the earliest; other rims are waxy red, groove-incised, plain, or (in the thin-walled versions of [d, e]) rectilinear-incised. Years ago I pointed out that at Palenque the Preclassic tradition of everted rims carried over into the Classic, undergoing changes in intensity and type of elaboration (Rands 1961). The reemergence of this shape is best seen on Otolum (Tepeu 1 equivalent) polychromes.

Preclassic Palenque jars are illustrated in Figure 3.18. Most are apparently unslipped—many surfaces are gone—but (a, b) are waxy red and may well be earlier than (d-g). The flared rim with vertical neck and horizontal upper wall (b) corresponds closely in shape to Lowe's "Initial Olmec" (1989: Fig. 4.3–the San

Lorenzo phase of Coe & Diehl 1980: Fig. 149g). Intraregional correspondences are also illustrated: (c) is widespread (see comparisons given for Chinikiha); (d) has a more limited range but likewise is present at Chinikiha (Fig. 3.11d); outside Palenque, (e-g) is best known at Paso Nuevo.

Methodology and Closing Comments

The extended discussion given to Preclassic jars merits attention. This shape class, especially if unslipped, usually plays a limited role in type-variety analyses of Maya ceramics. The Palenque focus of the investigation is a partial reason for this emphasis. Due to the extensive loss of surface finish, chronological partition at the site is heavily weighted toward unslipped pottery or toward sherds on which slip characteristics cannot be determined. This has carried over into shape-oriented comparisons outside Palenque.

Beyond this, shape carries a significance that is often overlooked. On a broad level, form classes are related to use or function as opposed to the construction of chronologies (cf. Dunnell 1978). Use imposes constraints, and this should be borne in mind if shape is to be employed as a chronological indicator. Nuances of form must be sought on levels that are reasonably attributed to style, and this requires attention to detail and accurate illustration. Ideally, a constellation of attributes—linking shape, surface finish, color combinations, decoration, and technological features with archaeological context—should be used in chronological partitioning, but, rarely if ever met, this ideal certainly is not achieved here. Instead, modes—too often in isolation rather than showing covariation—have been noted in a conceptual framework organized along broad shape classes.

Modes may well have persisted over substantial periods of time, reappearing as archaisms—traditions of formal, stylistic, and technological mannerisms, presumably reinforced by ideology—that constitute a "pool" of which potters were more or less cognizant and from which, depending in large part on what was fashionable, they drew. As repeatedly noted for Palenque and its environs, the occurrence of ceramic features having their greatest occurrence in the Early Preclassic but apparently in contexts more characteristic of the initial Middle Preclassic perhaps relates to this proposed cultural dynamic. The general phenomenon has been attributed by Demarest (1989: 319) to a "common material culture substratum" of the Greater Isthmian region, local variants appearing over a protracted span of time. In any case, many of the observed features seem more at home on the fringes of the Maya area or outside it than within the Maya Lowlands. Palenque is a partial exception.

The Preclassic-Classic Transition at Palenque

Developments leading from the Preclassic to Classic periods are considered briefly for Palenque. In general, a contrast can be made between the Preclassic, in which a relatively small sampling shows basic Maya affinities, and most of the Classic, when Palenque ceramics diverged markedly from Maya norms. The weak development at Palenque of such important Classic Maya traits as polychrome, figural painting, painted glyph bands, basal flanges, and ringstand bases, as well as the absence of many specific types, is indicative of a kind of cultural isolation, or drifting away, from patterns more strongly diagnostic of the lowland Maya. Instead, Palenque emphasized the plastic treatment of surfaces: modeling, incising, impressing, punctation—attributes known throughout the Maya area but with a lowered relative frequency. The strength of these observations is mitigated by the high degree of surface weathering of Palenque pottery; for most of the Classic sequence we cannot justify the contrast. Also informative is the substitution of incising for painting in those rare occasions where a glyph band occurs. Considering the unusual importance given the human figure devoid of regalia in sculpture and stucco at Palenque, the rarity of the human form on pottery is also notable. Although numerous ceramic figurines and some incensarios present outstanding treatments of humans, again the plastic manipulation of the surface, not painting, is a Palenque hallmark.

Consideration of Preclassic to Classic developments focuses on the Picota phase, apparently shortly after the time of Christ and prior to the strongest influence of Classic Maya ceramics on Palenque, early in the Motiepa complex. Neither Picota nor early Motiepa are well anchored in time, although the Peten-like ceramics, intrusive in Motiepa, could date to the general range of the foundation of the Palenque dynasty in A.D. 431 (Martin & Grube 2000: 156; Mathews, Chapter 1). Although Picota influences waned, there was a continuation of the localized tradition. Time differentials are somewhat arbitrary but it is useful to refer not only to Local Motiepa, but to the apparently shorter-lived intrusion as "Exotic" Motiepa, later trends within the broad Motiepa framework being for renewed ceramic organization (Fig. 2.1).

Within this developmental framework, which might well have a bearing on aspects of culture additional to ceramics, comparisons are made between subsets of the Preclassic and Picota pottery. First, however, one of the most important criteria for differentiating the two complexes, although almost axiomatic, should be noted: the presence of a waxy slip, Sierra Red, in much of the Preclassic pottery, and its absence from Picota. Shape change in unslipped jars is another major criterion (cf. Fig. 3.18d-g; Rands 1974: Fig. 4a-c). The focus of continuity is on the widely to moderately everted rim dish with massive solid slab feet. Preclassic incised decoration seems largely restricted to the interior of the everted rim (Fig. 3.17d-e; Rands & Bishop 2003: Figs. 5 & 7) whereas, in Picota, vertical groove-incising of the wall exterior is characteristic (Rands 1974: Fig. 3d, f; Rands & Bishop 2003: Fig. 7).

The everted rim dish, with roots reaching deep into the Preclassic, is a long-lived tradition at Palenque. In the Classic, the size of the everted rim decreases from Picota to Local Motiepa, the feature being unknown in the "exotic," Peten-influenced aspect of the phase. Wide rim eversion, often greater than that of the Preclassic, is reasserted as a major diagnostic of Otolum oranges—polychromes, dichromes, and/or monochromes—only to become smaller in Murcielagos. Although the tradition was always strong, a sense of waxing and waning is pervasive in size of the everted rim, and to some extent in frequency. Conceptually, this appears akin to the term "archaisms" which I employed in closing comments about Early Preclassic features found in Middle Preclassic contexts.

Acknowledgments

The present paper builds on previous work: a presentation at the Conference in honor of Gareth W. Lowe (November 2000) and a report submitted to the Foundation for the Advancement of Mesoamerican Studies, Inc. (2002). Fieldwork was supported by the National Science Foundation (grant GS 1455X). The sustained interest of John E. Clark is appreciated, along with suggestions by Robert J. Sharer, and insights, made available from time to time, by Richard E. W. Adams, Michael D. Coe, T. Patrick Culbert, Gareth W. Lowe, Jeremy A. Sabloff, and Gordon R. Willey.

Key to Illustrations

Scale: All ceramics illustrated at approximately one-seventh of natural size.

Radius: Width is normally given, dashed lines indicating a close approximation and dotted lines indicating a lower but still reasonable degree of probability. Although also indicating orientation, dotted lines without a vertical marker signal that the radius cannot be approximated.

Decoration: Interior decoration is shown in juxtaposition to the radius, exterior decoration being placed to the right.

Color bars: Used extensively. Solid framing lines indicate reasonable certainty for slip color. Dashed framing lines have multiple functions, sometimes raising the possibility that additional slip or paint may have been present; in other cases the indicated color is somewhat questionable. Stippling in color bars indicates unslipped areas on a daubed surface.

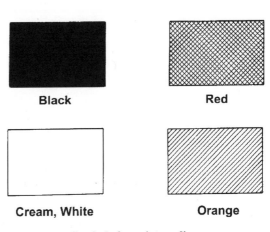

Black

Red

Cream, White

Orange

Symbols for paint or slip

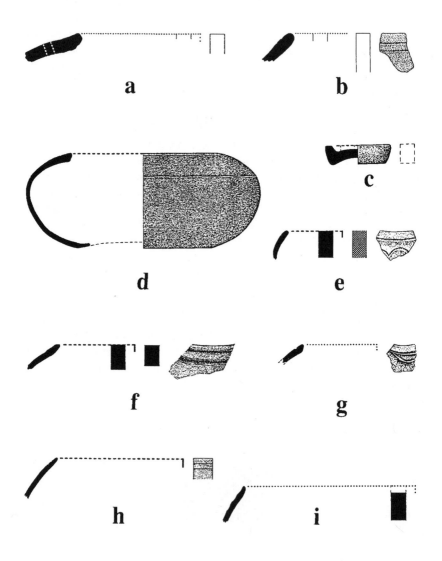

Figure 3.2: Trinidad, Chiuaan phase

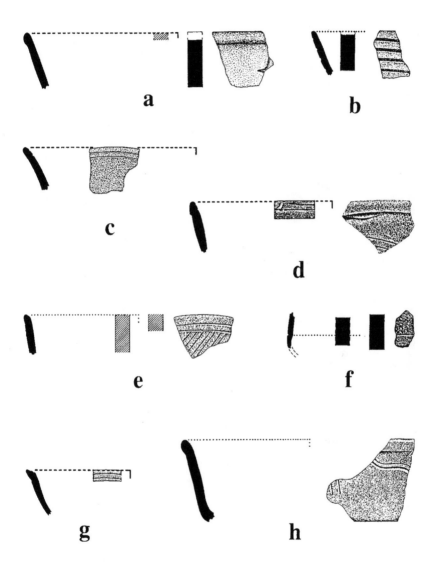

Figure 3.3: Trinidad, Chiuaan phase

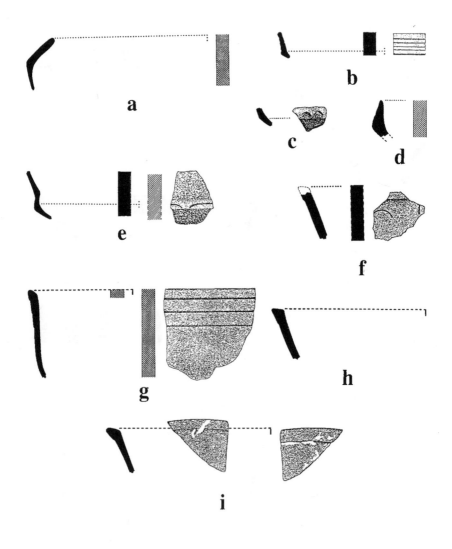

**Figure 3.4: Trinidad Chiuaan phase (a-e);
Bacha phase (f-i)**

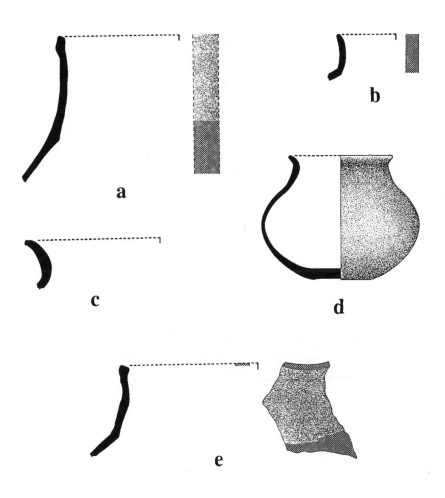

Figure 3.5: Trinidad jars

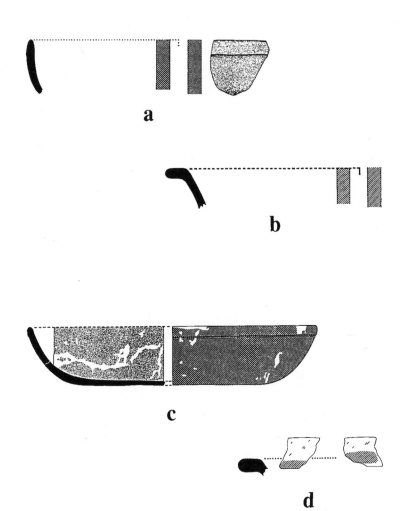

Figure 3.6: Trinidad Xot phase (a, c);
Chacibcan phase (b, d)

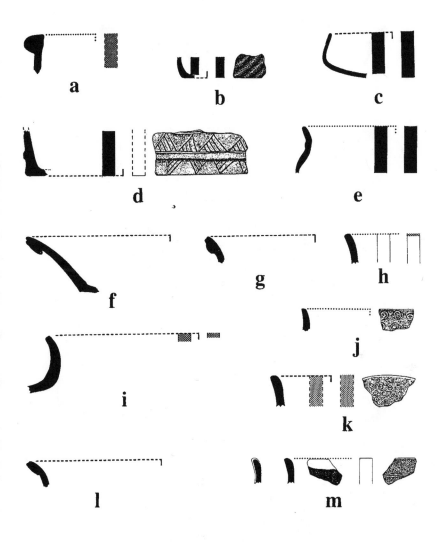

Figure 3.7: Zapatillo (Nueva Esperanza)

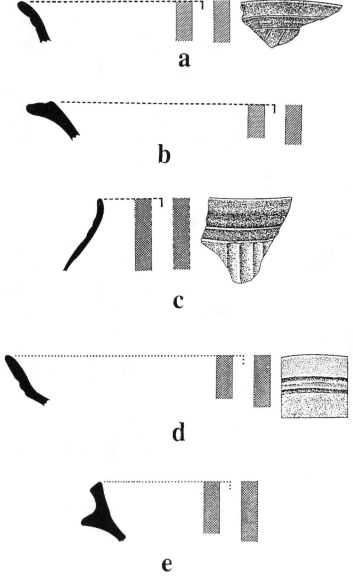

Figure 3.8: Zapatillo

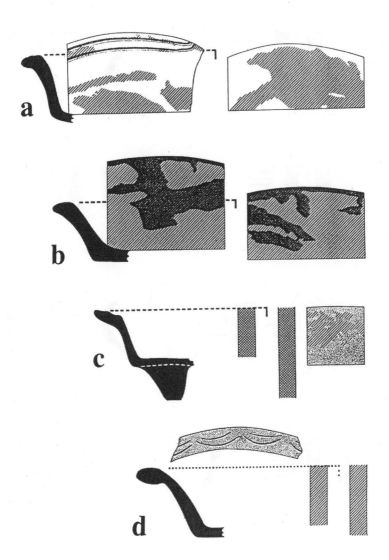

Figure 3.9: Zapatillo

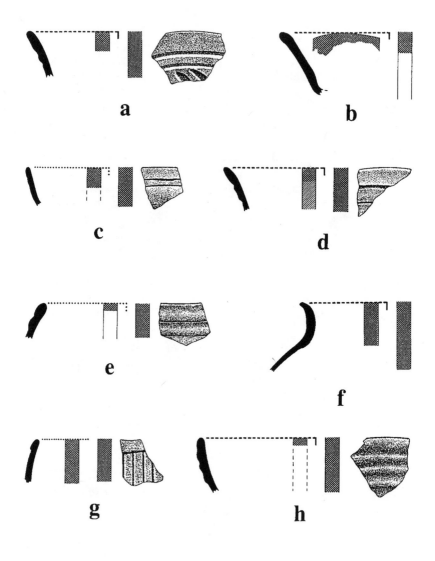

Figure 3.10: Zapatillo Specular Hematite Red (a-g); style of Specular Red (h)

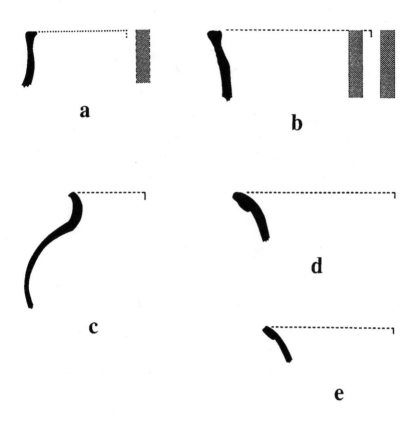

Figure 3.11: Chinikiha

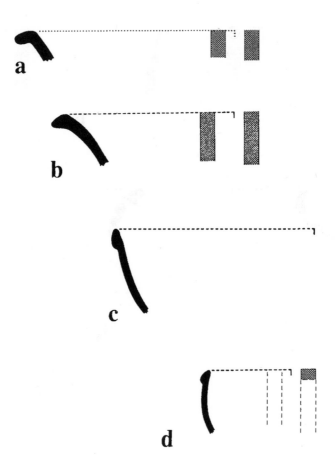

Figure 3.12: Chinikiha

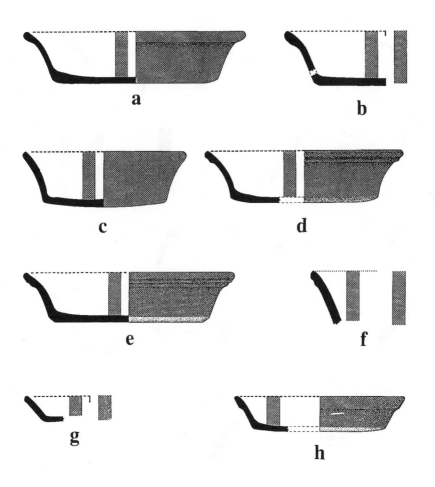

Figure 3.13: Paso Nuevo

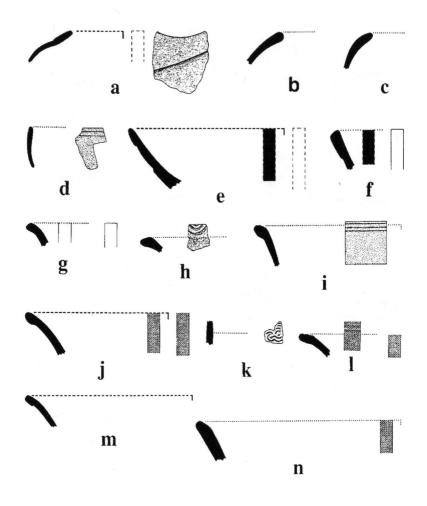

Figure 3.14: Paso Nuevo

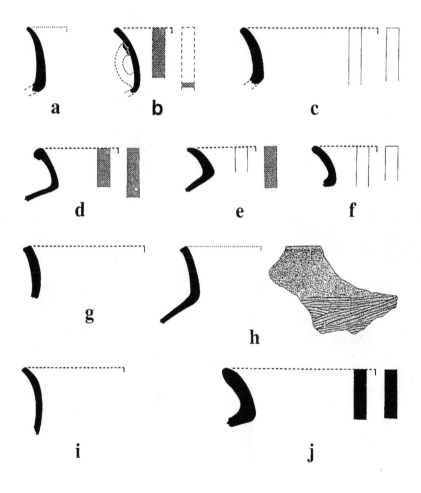

Figure 3.15: Paso Nuevo

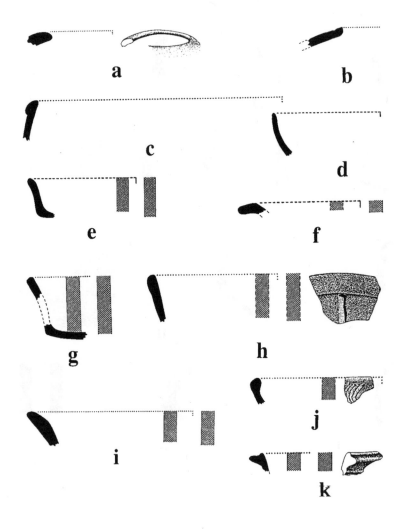

Figure 3.16: Palenque

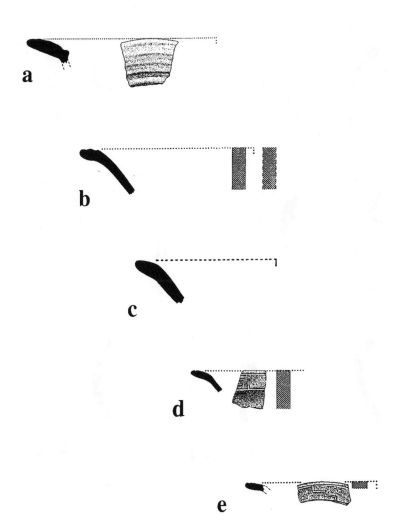

Figure 3.17: Palenque

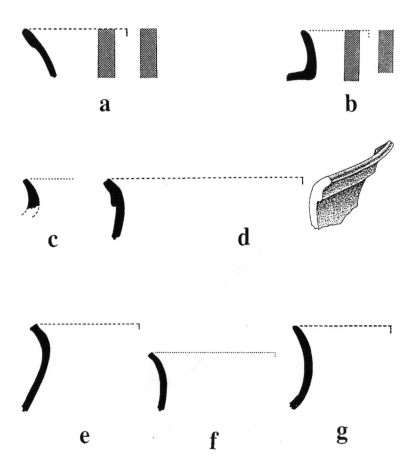

Figure 3.18: Palenque

References

Adams, Richard E. W.
  1971   *The Ceramics of Altar de Sacrificios*. Papers of the Peabody Museum of
          Archaeology and Ethnology, Vol. 63, No. 1. Harvard University, Cambridge,
          MA.

Agrinier, Pierre
  1984   *The Early Olmec Horizon at Mirador, Chiapas, Mexico*. Papers of the New
          World Archaeological Foundation, No. 48. Brigham Young University, Provo,
          UT.

  2000   *Mound 27 and the Middle Preclassic Period at Mirador, Chiapas, Mexico*.
          Papers of the New World Archaeological Foundation, No. 58. Brigham Young
          University, Provo, UT.

Andrews, E. Wyllys V
  1986   Olmec Jades from Chacsinkin, Yucatan, and Maya Ceramics from La Venta,
          Tabasco. In *Research and Reflections in Archaeology and History, Essays
          in Honor of Doris Stone*, edited by E. Wllys Andrews, V, pp. 11-49. Middle
          American Research Institute, Publication 57. Tulane University, New
          Orleans.

  1990   Early Ceramic History of the Lowland Maya. In *Vision and Revision in Maya
          Studies*, edited by Flora S. Clancy and Peter D. Harrison. University of New
          Mexico Press, Albuquerque.

Brady, James E., Joseph W. Ball, Ronald L. Bishop, Duncan C. Pring, Norman Hammond
and Robert A. Housley
  1998   The Lowland Maya "Protoclassic": A Reconsideration of Its Nature and
          Significance. *Ancient Mesoamerica* 9:17-38.

Ceja Tenorio, Jorge Fausto
  1985   Paso de la Amada, an Early Preclassic Site in the Soconusco, Chiapas,
          Mexico. *Papers of the New World Archaeological Foundation*, No. 49.
          Brigham Young University, Provo, UT.

Coe, Michael D.
  1961   *La Victoria, an Early Site on the Pacific Coast of Guatemala*. Papers of the
          Peabody Museum of Archaeology and Ethnology, Vol. 53. Harvard University,
          Cambridge, MA.

Coe, Michael D. and Richard A. Diehl
  1980   *In the Land of the Olmec, Vol. 1; The Archaeology of San Lorenzo Tenochtitlan*.
          University of Texas Press, Austin.

Culbert, T. Patrick
  1993   *The Ceramics of Tikal: Vessels from the Burials, Caches and Problematic
          Deposits*. Tikal Report 25, Part A. The University Museum, University of
          Pennsylvania, Philadelphia.

Culbert, T. Patrick, ed.
  1973   *The Classic Maya Collapse*. School of American Research. University of
          New Mexico Press, Albuquerque.

Cyphers Guillen, Ann
    1987   Ceramics. In *Ancient Chalcatzingo*, edited by David C. Grove, pp. 200-251. University of Texas Press, Austin.

Demarest, Arthur A.
    1976   A Re-evaluation of the Archaeological Sequences of Preclassic Chiapas. In *Studies in Middle American Archaeology*, pp. 75-107, Middle American Research Institute Publication 22. Tulane University, New Orleans.

    1986   *The Archaeology of Santa Leticia and the Rise of Maya Civilization*. Middle American Research Institute Publication 56. Tulane University, New Orleans.

    1989   The Olmec and the Rise of Civilization in Eastern Mesoamerica. In *Regional Perspectives on the Olmec*, edited by Robert J. Sharer and David C. Grove, pp. 303-344. Cambridge University Press, Cambridge.

Demarest, Arthur A. and Robert J. Sharer
    1982   The Origins and Evolution of Usulutan Ceramics. *American Antiquity* 47:810-822.

Drucker, Philip
    1943   *Ceramic Sequences at Tres Zapotes, Veracruz, Mexico*. Bureau of American Ethnology Bulletin 140. Smithsonian Institution, Washington, D.C.

    1952   *La Venta, Tabasco: A Study of Olmec Ceramics and Art*. Bureau of American Ethnology Bulletin 153. Smithsonian Institution, Washington, D.C.

Dunnell, Robert C.
    1978   Style and Function: A Fundamental Dichotomy. *American Antiquity* 43:192-202.

Ekholm, Susanna M.
    1969   *Mound 30a and the Preclassic Ceramic Sequence of Izapa, Chiapas, Mexico*. Papers of the New World Archaeological Foundation No. 25. Brigham Young University, Provo, UT.

Forsyth, Donald W.
    1983   *Investigations at Edzna, Campeche, Mexico: Vol. 2; Ceramics*. Papers of the New World Archaeological Foundation No. 46. Brigham Young University, Provo, UT.

Green, Dee F. and Gareth W. Lowe
    1967   *Altamira and Padre Piedra, Early Preclassic Sites in Chiapas, Mexico*. Papers of the New World Archaeological Foundation No. 20. Brigham Young University, Provo, UT.

Lee, Thomas A.
    1974   *Mound 4 Excavations at San Isidro, Chiapas, Mexico*. Papers of the New World Archaeological Foundation No. 34. Brigham Young University, Provo, UT.

Love, Michael W.
    2002   *Early Complex Society in Pacific Guatemala: Settlements and Chronology of the Rio Naranjo, Guatemala*. Papers of the New World Archaeological Foundation No. 66. Brigham Young University, Provo, UT.

Lowe, Gareth W.
  1977   The Mixe-Zoque as Competing Neighbors of the Early Lowland Maya. In *The Origins of Maya Civilization*, edited by Richard E. W. Adams, pp. 197-248. School of American Research. University of New Mexico Press, Albuquerque.

  1978   Eastern Mesoamerica. In *Chronologies in New World Archaeology*, edited by R. E. Taylor and Clement W. Meighan, pp. 331-393. Academic Press, New York, NY.

  1989   The Heartland Olmec: Evolution of Material Culture. In *Regional Perspectives on the Olmec*, edited by Robert J. Sharer and David C. Grove, pp. 33-67. School of American Research. Cambridge University Press, Cambridge, U.K.

Martin, Simon and Nikolai Grube
  2000   *Chronicles of the Maya Kings and Queens: Deciphering the Dynasties of the Ancient Maya*. Thames & Hudson, London, U.K.

Mason, J. Alden
  1960   *Mound 12, Chiapa de Corzo, Chiapas, Mexico*. Papers of the New World Archaeological Foundation No. 9. Brigham Young University, Provo, UT.

Rands, Robert L.
  1961   Elaboration and Invention in Ceramic Traditions. *American Antiquity* 26:331-340.

  1967   Ceramic Technology and Trade in the Palenque Region, Mexico. In *American Historical Anthropology, Essays in Honor of Leslie Spier*, edited by Carroll L. Riley and Walter W. Taylor, pp. 137-151. Southern Illinois University Press, Carbonale.

  1969   *Mayan Ecology and Trade: 1967-1968*. Mesoamerican Studies, University Museum. Southern Illinois University, Carbondale.

  1974   The Ceramic Sequence at Palenque, Chiapas. In *Mesoamerican Archaeology: New Approaches*, edited by Norman Hammond, pp. 51-76. University of Texas Press, Austin.

  1987   Ceramic Patterns and Traditions in the Palenque Area. In *Maya Ceramics: Papers of the 1985 Maya Ceramic Conference*, edited by Prudence M. Rice and Robert J. Sharer, vol. 1, pp. 203-238. BAR International Series 345. British Archaeological Reports, Oxford.

Rands, Robert L. and Ronald L. Bishop
  2003   The Dish-Plate Tradition at Palenque: Continuity and Change. In *Patterns & Process: A Festschrift in Honor of Dr. Edward V. Sayre*, edited by Lambertus van Zelst, pp. 109-132. Smithsonian Center for Materials Research & Education, Suitland, MD.

Sabloff, Jeremy A.
  1975   *Excavations at Seibal: Ceramics*. Memoirs of the Peabody Museum of Archaeology and Ethnology, Vol. 13, No. 2. Harvard University, Cambridge, MA.

Sharer, Robert J.
 1978   *The Prehistory of Chalchuapa, El Salvador, Vol. 3: Pottery and Conclusions.*
         Museum Monographs, The University Museum. University of Pennsylvania
         Press, Philadelphia.

Sisson, Edward B.
 1976   Survey and Excavation in the Northwestern Chontalpa, Tabasco, Mexico.
         Unpublished Ph.D. dissertation, Department of Anthropology, Harvard
         University, Cambridge, MA.

Smith, Robert E.
 1971   *The Pottery of Mayapan.* Papers of the Peabody Museum of Archaeology and
         Ethnology, Harvard University, Vol. 66, Cambridge, MA.

Weiant, C. W.
 1943   *An Introduction to the Ceramics of Tres Zapotes, Veracruz, Mexico.* Bureau
         of American Ethnology Bulletin 139. Smithsonian Institution, Washington,
         D.C.

Chapter 4

The Construction Chronology of Palenque: Seriation within an Architectural Form

Damien B. Marken

Although Palenque is perhaps most famous for its stone sculpture, large hiero-glyphic corpus, and the impressive tomb of K'inich Janab Pakal I, visitors to the Classic Maya site continuously remark on its architectural beauty. The site boasts a large quantity of intact monumental architecture. Several structures at the site, including those of the Palace, the Temple of the Inscriptions, and the Cross Group structures are extremely well preserved. This large quantity of preserved architec-ture is fertile ground for developing a methodology to architectural dating in the Maya area.

As the most prominent site of the Northwestern Maya architectural regional style (Andrews 1995: 10), Palenque's architecture differs from other regional styles of Maya architecture in several ways. First, the upper façade of buildings at Palenque slope back from the vertical lower walls and façade to form a receding upper façade or mansard roof. The slope of this receding upper façade is nearly parallel to the slope of the interior vaults of the building (Andrews 1975: 173). The upper façades at Palenque are divided from the lower walls by a projecting medial molding which is also sloped, and possibly had the functional use as a drainage system for rain water (Heyden & Gendrop 1975: 132), although this function cannot be confirmed. Both the lower and upper façades were often deco-rated with stucco sculpture. Second, the roofcombs of Palenque consist of two "parallel" walls joined together at shallow angles. Built above the central wall of the structure "so presenting no impediment to the creation of a spacious interior" (Gendrop 1974: 83; Heyden & Gendrop 1975: 141), these walls are pierced by numerous window-like openings, creating a lattice-type roofcomb also seen at Yaxchilan (Pollock 1965: 424) and House A at Tonina (Marquina 1964: 658). These walls are constructed of distinctive cut stones and were embellished with stucco sculpture, possibly serving as identifiers as to function and dedication of a structure (Griffin 1978: 142). Lastly, the ratio of wall thickness to vault span of Palencano structures is much greater than seen at contemporaneous Maya sites of the Peten; in their temple-type and range-type structures, ancient Palencanos used extremely thin walls to support vaults spanning very wide rooms.

Surprisingly, previous construction chronologies of the architecture of Palenque have been largely based on ceramic and hieroglyphic data associated with specific structures (Martin & Grube 2000; Schele 1981, 1986). Unfortunately, numerous Palencano structures are associated with neither ceramic nor hieroglyphic dates. These structures have previously been chronologically placed based on "stylistic" criteria, if not all together excluded from the chronologies. This study seeks to create a relative construction chronology of the temple-type structures at Palenque based on architectural attributes and stratigraphy, independent of ceramic and hieroglyphic dates. This relative architectural construction chronology is intended as a third temporal indicator to be cross-analyzed with Palenque's ceramic and hieroglyphic construction chronologies to create a more complete and refined construction sequence.

Typology of Palencano Temple-Type Structures

In order to create an independent relative architectural construction chronology, a sample of monumental structures was selected to create an architectural typology of Palencano temple-type structures. This typology (and chronology) does not include the range-type structures of the Palace, such as Houses A, B, C, D, or E, nor does it include range-type complexes, as defined by Marken (2002b), such as House L of the Palace, Group IV Structure J1, and Temple XVI. The structures considered in the original sample all consist of two parallel, vaulted galleries connected by three central doorways (with the exception of Temple XIX; Straight, Chapter 10) and pierced in the front by one, three, or five doorways. Thus, certain structures, such as Temples I, III, X, XXa, and the Temple of the Jaguar, which can be classed as temples, as defined by Andrews (1975: 39), have been excluded from the typology, yet included within the chronology using complementary lines of architectural and structural evidence. Further limiting the sample size, only exposed architecture has been considered in the typology, as there exists insufficient documentation of the architectural details of stratigraphically earlier construction styles, methods, and techniques. The stratigraphy of Palenque will be dealt with on a structure by structure basis following the typology. This typology has been presented elsewhere in a concise form (Marken 2002a); given here is a more comprehensive description of the methodology and includes analysis of Palenque's known architectural stratigraphy.

This typology is based on a cross-analysis of five distinct architectural attributes:

1) Structure plans
2) Vault soffit, or vault ceiling shape
3) The presence or absence of cross-vaults
4) Wall construction
5) Mortar

Due to the varying states of architectural preservation at Palenque, certain attributes of particular structures are unknown (namely soffit shape and cross-vaults), and thus cannot be considered. Undocumented restoration likewise occasionally presents problems in subsequent architectural analysis (Porter 1918: 60-61). Structures where these sorts of problems are present are Temples XIII, XV, XX, and XXI.

Structure Plans (Fig. 4.1)

An examination of the plans of the temple-type structures of Palenque revealed four distinct groupings of plan types, labeled Types 1-4. Type 3 plans have been subdivided into two groups, Type 3A and Type 3B, identical except for the presence of a vaulted inner sanctuary in Type 3A plans. Due to the small sample size, statistical analysis was not deemed a viable method of analysis. The plan type groupings are based on similarities in the arrangement of entrances, and the size and arrangement of the central piers in relation to those of the façade.

Type 1 plans consist of solid rear and lateral walls and a façade wall pierced by three doorways. Within the structure are two parallel galleries perpendicular to the lateral walls, connected by three doorways. While this description may appear rudimentary to those familiar with Palencano architecture, Type 1 plans are unique in the arrangement of their piers. The dimensions of the façade piers are nearly identical to those of the central piers which support the two central half-vaults, or double-vault mass (Palenque's famous Y-shaped central support, [see Gendrop 1974: 83]; also called a cantilevered mass [Roys 1934]). The lateral façade piers are likewise mirrored along the central axis of these structures. Examples of this structure plan are the Temple Olvidado (Fig. 4.2a), the Temple of the Count and Temple XX.

Type 2 plans are characterized by a façade pierced by five, instead of three, doorways. Further distinguishing Type 2, the central piers are extended beyond the length of their façade counterparts, as are the lateral central piers. Two partition walls, dividing the rear gallery into three rooms are present as well. Although these partition walls are occasionally present in Type 1 plans, such as in the Temple of the Count, they are omnipresent in Type 2. Unfortunately, only two examples of this plan type are known at Palenque: Temple V (Fig. 4.2b) and the Temple of the Inscriptions.

Type 3 plans all have central piers substantially longer than those of the façade, but eliminate the use of lateral central piers. A trait shared with Type 2 are

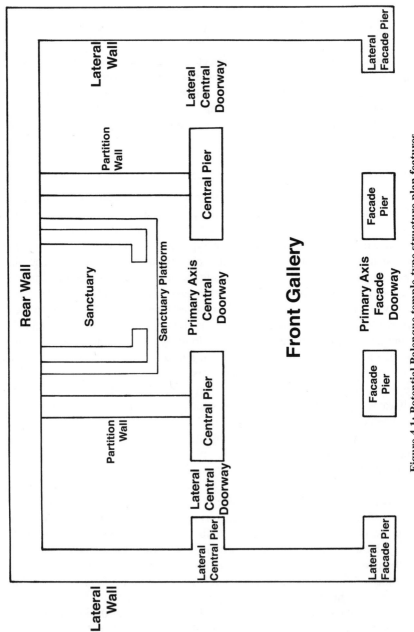

Figure 4.1: Potential Palenque temple-type structure plan features

partition walls dividing the rear gallery into three rooms. Type 3A plans, restricted to the Cross/South Group and generally considered to be the work of Pakal the Great's eldest son, K'inich Kan Bahlam II (Hartung 1992: 16; Schele 1981: 111-112), differ from Type 3B plans by the addition of a vaulted inner sanctuary within the rear primary axis room. Structures with Type 3A plans include the Cross Group buildings, as well as Temples XIV and XVII (Fig. 4.2c). Structures with Type 3B plans are Temples IV, XII (Fig. 4.2d), XIII, XV, XVIII and XVIIIa.

Type 4 plans are the least well known of the Palencano plan types, in that the recent Temples XIX and XXI (Fig. 4.2e) excavations have not been extensively published. Sampling problems aside, Type 4 plans are distinguished by their single façade doorway. In a way, these buildings are constructed inside-out, or more accurately outside-in; the central piers are roughly the same dimensions as the façade piers of other temple-type structures. Although this structural change substantially increases the interior space within the building, it also likely contributed to the premature collapse of Temple XIX (Greene Robertson et al. 1999, 6) and the reduced dimensions of Temple XXI. Reducing the supporting mass along the

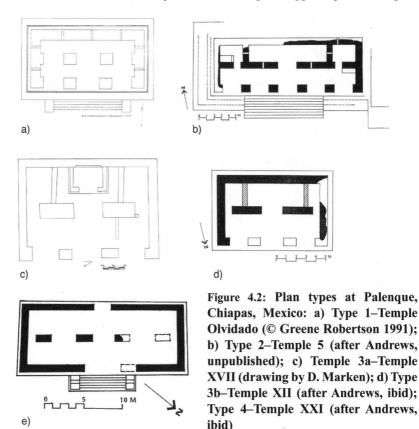

a)

b)

c)

d)

e)

Figure 4.2: Plan types at Palenque, Chiapas, Mexico: a) Type 1–Temple Olvidado (© Greene Robertson 1991); b) Type 2–Temple 5 (after Andrews, unpublished); c) Temple 3a–Temple XVII (drawing by D. Marken); d) Type 3b–Temple XII (after Andrews, ibid); Type 4–Temple XXI (after Andrews, ibid)

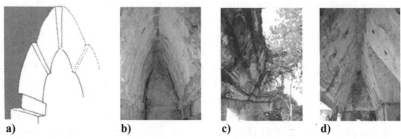

a)　　　　　　　b)　　　　　　　c)　　　　　　　d)

Figure 4.3: Palenque Vault Soffit Shapes: a) Temple Olvidado (drawing © Greene Robertson 1991); b) Temple of the Count; c) Temple V; d) Temple of the Sun (photos by D. Marken)

central transverse axis enhanced the instability of the already unstable Palenque structures (Roys 1934, 38).

Soffit Shape

Although there are several varying vault soffit shapes and sizes at Palenque, they have been divided here into two categories: irregular and straight soffits. Irregular soffits all include a single-member interior medial molding at the vault spring and either a double arc (as seen in the Temple Olvidado; Fig. 4.3a), bottle-shaped (as seen in Temple II and the Temple of the Count; Fig. 4.3b), or stepped soffit (as seen in Temple V; Fig. 4.3c). Straight vault soffits, or vault ceilings, have a 7-15 cm offset at the vault spring and rise in a smooth straight line from the vault spring to the capstone (Fig. 4.3d), and are present in Temple IV, Temple XII, Temple XIV, the Temple of the Inscriptions, the Temple of the Cross, the Temple of the Sun, the Temple of the Foliated Cross, Temple XVII, Temple XVIII, Temple XVIIIa, and Temple XIX (Marken 2002b). Significantly, all the structures of the Palace have straight soffits.

Cross-Vaults

While the ancient Palencanos always used lintels, normally of wood, to span the façade doorways of their monumental structures (Stephens 1969, 312-13), they used three different methods to span central doorways (Fig. 4.4): lintels, cross-vaults, and what have been termed doorway vaults (Marken 2000a, 2000b). These three methods were used interchangeably and two different methods were often utilized within the same structure. While lintels are familiar to most readers, cross-vault is a more obscure term and needs embellishment.

Cross-vaults reduce the weight of the structure roof, but do not change the aesthetics of the central doorways (Schele 1986: 119). A thin vertical wall ran from the capstone to the wooden lintel of the cross-vault, giving the appearance of a lintel-spanned doorway (Blom 1923: 62). With the exception of those of the Temple of the Inscriptions, where they are used to span all three central doorways,

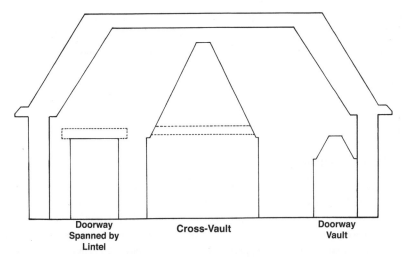

**Figure 4.4: Hypothetical transverse section showing
variable central doorway spanning methods**

cross-vaults at Palenque span only primary axis central doorways. Four types of cross-vaults are present at Palenque, differing in the arrangement of the lintel and thin vertical wall. The first type of cross-vault, is present only in Temple XII (Fig. 4.5a). The vertical wall is absent, and the lintel, located below the vault spring, is the same width as the entire central pier. The second type is present in the Temple of the Inscriptions (Fig. 4.5b). The lintel, also located below the vault spring, is square in cross-section (approximately 30 cm by 30 cm) and placed, along with the vertical dividing wall, at the front of the cross-vault. The third type of cross-vault is the most common at Palenque (Fig. 4.5c). Seen in the Cross Group, Temple XIV and Temple XVII, the lintels (of approximately the same dimensions as those from the Temple of the Inscriptions) of this cross-vault type are placed one course above the vault spring, and with the dividing wall at the rear of the cross-vault. The last type of cross-vault at Palenque is the trilobe, or trifoil, arch

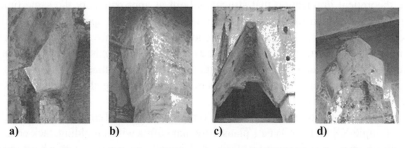

Figure 4.5: Cross-vault types at Palenque: a) Temple IX; b) Temple of the Inscriptions; c) Temple of the Cross; d) The Palace, House A (photos by D. Marken)

seen today in House A of the Palace (Fig. 4.5d). Sections of this double arc cross-vault were also recovered from the rubble of Temple XIX. At present, it is unclear whether or not these varying arrangements of lintels contributed differently to the stability of each cross-vault type as each collapsed structure seems to have fallen for different reasons (see Marken 2002b).

Doorway vaults (Fig. 4.4) are often secondary constructions and reproduce, on a small scale, the larger primary axis cross-vaults and span only lateral central doorways.

Wall Construction

Wall construction at Palenque consists of three general types of masonry: well-faced blocks and slabs with a relatively modest layer of stucco, roughly shaped blocks covered with a thick layer of white stucco, and irregular stone construction covered with a thick layer of grey/white stucco (thick layers of clay with a thin lime wash coat are also present). Irregular stone construction includes the extensive use of spalls, and the seemingly more deliberate placement of longer unshaped "spanning stones." There is slight overlap between the latter two construction types within particular buildings, such as Temple XIV, Temple XVII, and Temple XXI.

Mortar

Mesoamerican mortars, as defined by Littman (1957: 136), fall into three general classes: lime mortar, a lime/clay aggregate, and clay mortar. The classification given is based on Littman's chemical analysis of Palenque mortars (1959: 266), and a visual comparison of these mortars with those unanalyzed.

Typological Groupings

From the distribution of these five attributes: (1) plan type, (2) soffit shape, (3) cross-vaults, (4) wall construction, and (5) mortar, certain groupings of Palencano temple-type structures become readily apparent (Table 4.1). These groupings carry the theoretical implication that structures built at approximately the same time will be more similar to each other than those from different epochs (Loten 1970: xxii). Keeping in mind Spinden's prediction that vault span would increase over time in Maya architecture (Loten 1970: 2) and the line of masonry development proposed by Kubler (1975: 133), beginning with block masonry toward less regular stones covered by thicker layers of stucco, a relative chronology of these structure groupings can be formed.

Group A structures, including the Temple Olvidado, Temple of the Count, and Temple XX all have Type 1 plans, irregular soffits with a molding, lack cross-vaults of any sort, and exhibit well-faced slab wall construction with a hard lime mortar. Their vault spans are among the smallest found at Palenque.

Table 4.1: Palenque Architectural Attributes: Temple-Type Structures

Structures/Attributes:	Plan Type	Prim.Axis/Lateral Doorways	Soffit Shape	Wall Construction	Mortar Type	Vault Span-F/R
T. Olvidado	Type 1	Lintel/Lintel	Curved+Molding	Well-Cut Slabs	Lime Mortar	1.32m/1.28m
T. Count	Type 1	Lintel/Lintel	Curved+Molding	Well-Cut Slabs	Lime Mortar	1.50m/1.40m
T. XX	Type 1	-----------	-----------	Well-Cut Slabs	Lime Mortar	1.80/1.50m
T. II	Type 1/2*	Lintel/Lintel	Curved+Molding	Well-Cut Slabs	Lime Mortar	1.95m/2.20m
T. V	Type 2	Lintel/Lintel	Stepped+Molding	Well-Cut Slabs	Lime/Clay Aggregate	2.29m/2.25m
T. Inscriptions	Type 2	Cross-Vault/Cross-Vault	Straight+Offset	Rough Blocks	Lime Mortar	2.02m/2.05m
T. XII	Type 3B	Cross-Vault/Lintel	Straight+Offset	Rough Blocks	Lime/Clay Aggregate	2.36m/2.38m
T. XIII	Type 3B	-----------	-----------	Rough Blocks	-----------	2.30m/2.25m
T. Cross	Type 3A	Cross-Vault/Doorway Vault	Straight+Offset	Rough Blocks	Lime Mortar	3.30m/2.86m
T. Sun	Type 3A	Cross-Vault/Doorway Vault	Straight+Offset	Rough Blocks	Lime Mortar	2.88m/2.80m
T. Foliated Cross	Type 3A	Cross-Vault/Doorway Vault	Straight+Offset	Rough Blocks	Lime Mortar	3.20m?/3.07m
T. XIV	Type 3A	Cross-Vault/Doorway Vault	Straight+Offset	Rough Blocks**	Lime/Clay Aggregate	2.30m/2.50m
T. XVII	Type 3A	Cross-Vault/Doorway Vault	Straight+Offset	Rough Blocks**	Clay Mortar	2.70m/3.10m
T. IV	Type 3B	Lintel/ Doorway Vault	Straight+Offset	Irregular Stones	Lime/Clay Aggregate	2.50m/2.52m
T. XV	Type 3B	-----------	-----------	Irregular Stones	Clay Mortar	2.50m/2.35m
T. XVIII	Type 3B	-----------/Doorway Vault	-----------	Irregular Stones	Clay Mortar	2.04m/2.08m
T. XVIIIa	Type 3B	Cross-Vault/-----------	-----------	Irregular Stones	Clay Mortar	1.55m?/2.10m
T. XIX	Type 4	Cross-Vault/-----------	Straight+Offset	Irregular Stones	Clay Mortar	3.12m/2.29-3.62m
T. XXI	Type 4	-----------	-----------	Irregular Stones	Clay Mortar	2.98m/3.03m

* Temple II's plan is a Type 1 plan, except that the central piers resemble those of Types 2 and 3

** The construction blocks of these structures are slightly more irregular than those of other structures so labeled

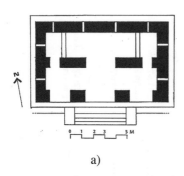 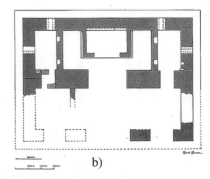

a)   b)

Figure 4.6: Aberrant plans at Palenque: a) Temple II (after Andrews); b) Temple of the Foliated Cross (© Greene Robertson 1991).

Temple II is identical to these structures except that its central piers are one meter longer than their façade counterparts (Fig. 4.6a). Interestingly, the lateral central doorways are one meter shorter than their façade counterparts. For this reason, Temple II has been classed with Group A, as a likely transition structure between Group A and Group B.

Group B includes Temple V, the Temple of the Inscriptions, Temple XII and Temple XIII. This grouping is not as uniform as Group A and is tentative. Temple V matches Group A in all attributes, except in plan type, which is the same as that of the Temple of the Inscriptions. As its vault span seems to be a gradual progression from Temple II, Temple V may represent another transitory structure between Group A and the Temple of the Inscriptions. Temple XII may also pre-date the Temple of the Inscriptions as it lacks doorway vaults, and its cross-vault appears to be a precursor to those of the Temple of the Inscriptions. Temple XIII has been placed at the end of this construction period due to the stratigraphy of the pyramid-platform it shares with Temple XII and the Temple of the Inscriptions; Temple XIII's final phase substructure overlaps that of the Temple of the Inscriptions (personal observation).

Group C includes the Temples of the Cross, the Sun, and the Foliated Cross, Temple XIV, and Temple XVII. These all have Type 3A plans, straight soffits, the same type of cross-vaulting and doorway vaults. There is a progressive deterioration in the quality of masonry and mortar, indicating a gradual transition toward the subsequent architectural group.

The plan of the Temple of the Foliated Cross (Fig. 4.6b) differs slightly from those of Group C. Although its plan most closely resembles Type 3A plans, due to the presence of a vaulted inner sanctuary (including other similarities), lateral central piers, a plan Type 1 and Type 2 feature, are present. However, the lateral central piers of the Temple of the Foliated Cross do not resemble those of plan Types 1 and 2. The lateral central piers of Type 1 match those of the façade piers in dimension, while those of Type 2 are longer than the lateral façade piers. Based on the placement of two remaining bases of the façade piers, the lateral central piers of the Temple of the Foliated Cross appear to have been shorter in length than the lateral façade piers. As the lateral central piers of the structure do not resemble those of any other structure at Palenque, the Temple of the Foliated Cross has been classed with Group C, based on the presence of an inner sanctuary and the similarity of other architectural attributes to other Group C structures.

Group D includes Temples IV, XV, XVIII, and XVIIIa. All consist of irregular stone wall construction, and with the exception of Temple IV, clay mortar. Temples XVIII and XVIIIa, often referred to as "twin-temples," share the same pyramid substructure, and were likely built at the same time. Temple IV lacks a cross-vault, but as doorway vaults, which seem to appear later at Palenque, are present, this difference is possibly an aberration. Little remains of Temple XV, classed here based on plan, wall construction, and mortar, though due to its spatial association with the Cross Group, it could possibly be temporally affiliated with Group C.

Group E includes Temples XIX and XXI. The similarities between these structures are striking. They are the only known examples of Type 4 plans, and share identical types of wall construction and mortar. Further evidence of the close temporal affiliation of these structures is the identical construction method used to build the uppermost façade staircase and substructure platform molding of each building (although the quality of construction differs, see Straight, Chapter 10).

Although Temples XVIII and XVIIIa have significantly different plan types from Temples XIX and XXI, these structures share the same wall construction and mortar, and all likely had cross-vaults and straight soffits. One line of evidence yet mentioned further links these pairs of buildings, separating them from other architectural groups: the construction technique of the stucco panel once on the rear wall of Temple XVIII (Blom & La Farge 1926: 176) matches the technique used for the Temple XIX stucco panel (personal observation). This technique of setting separately modeled glyph blocks into a bed of wet stucco, and stucco sculpture without the use of stone armatures, is not seen elsewhere at Palenque, except in the Temple of the Jaguar (Holmes 1896: 191) and House A of the Palace (Greene Robertson 1985: 9).

Architectural Stratigraphy

At present, architectural stratigraphy of significant depth is little known at Palenque. Extensive excavations have revealed that numerous large structures within the site "core" represent stratigraphically single architectural phases. These include the Temple of the Inscriptions, the Temple of the Cross, the Temple of the Sun, the Temple of the Foliated Cross, the Temple of the Count, Temple XIV, Temple XIX, Temple XXI, and Temple Olvidado.

Due to the separate excavations of Alberto Ruz Lhuillier and Arnoldo González Cruz, the North Group at Palenque is currently the most well-documented case of architectural stratigraphy at Palenque, specifically the substructure shared by Temples I, II, III, IV, and V, otherwise named Temple VIII. The earliest construction of the North Group was Temple V-sub, built on a low substructure platform and measuring 13.20 m by 4.40 m (Tovalín Ahumada & Ceja Manrique 1996: 93). This single gallery superstructure unfortunately lacks associated ceramics (Tovalín Ahumada & Ceja Manrique 1996: 93). After Temple V-sub, Temple II was erected to the east (Ruz 1958b: 192), followed by Temple V (Ruz 1958c: 246). Subsequently, the substructure pyramid of Temple II was extended to the east and west, and Temples I and III constructed, flanking Temple II. Where the substructure extensions of Temple II abut the earlier construction phase is evident after even casual examination. Finally, Temple IV was constructed above the platforms of Temple II and Temple III (Ruz 1958b: 192).

The other elongated substructure supporting multiple superstructures at Palenque is the Inscriptions platform, which supports Temples XII, XIIa, XIII, and the Temple of the Inscriptions. Although the Temple of the Inscriptions is a single-phase construction, which predates the final phase of Temple XIII's substructure, both Temple XII and Temple XIII are built above preceding structures. Excavations by Jorge Acosta encountered a second stucco floor 1.74 m beneath the final stucco floor of Temple XII (1973: 30). Two piers corresponding to this architectural phase indicate that the structure was constructed of stone masonry (Acosta 1973: 31). Further excavations by González Cruz revealed that beneath this penultimate architectural phase was another vaulted structure (Christopher Powell, personal communication 2001). Temple XIII consists of three superimposed vaulted architectural phases as well (González Cruz 1998: 61). The entire stratigraphic sequence has not been fully examined, nor published, so a construction sequence of the Inscriptions platform cannot be postulated at this time.

Lastly, Temple XVIII, Temple XVIIIa, and Temple XX, within the South Group, all consist of two separate architectural phases (Morales C. & Powell 1999: 44; Ruz 1958a: 151; 1962: 59-63). It is interesting to note that the vault mortar of Temple XVIIIa-sub consists of clay mortar (Christopher Powell, personal communication 2002), while that of Temple XX-sub is a white mortar, likely of lime (personal observation). The soffit shape of Temple XX-sub is stepped. Unfortunately, due to the paucity of published photos, and lack of systematic architectural description of all Palencano earlier architectural phases, it is impossible to compare and correlate specific earlier phases to one another architecturally. Thus within the proposed architectural construction chronology, the positioning of these structures is uncertain and tentative (and are thus marked with a question mark in Table 4.2).

**Table 4.2: Proposed Architectural Construction Chronology of
Temple-Type Structures at Palenque**

Structure	Typological Grouping	Structure	Typological Grouping
Temple V-sub		Temple XIII	Group B
Temple XVIII-sub ?		Temple of the Cross	Group C
Temple XVIIIa-sub ?		Temple of the Sun	Group C
		Temple of the Foliated Cross	Group C
Temple XX-sub ?			
		Temple XIV	Group C
Temple XII-sub 2 ?			
Temple XIII-sub 2 ?		Temple XVII	Group C
Temple X ?		Temple XV	Group D
Temple XII-sub 1 ?		Temple of the Jaguar	
Temple XIII-sub 1 ?			
		Temple I	
Temple Olvidado	Group A	Temple III	
Temple of the Count	Group A		
Temple XX	Group A	Temple IV	Group D
Temple II	Group A	Temple XVIII	Group D
		Temple XVIIIa	Group D
Temple V	Group B		
		Temple XIX	Group E
Temple XII	Group B		
		Temple XXI	Group E
Temple of the Inscriptions	Group B		
		Temple Xxa	

Placement of Ungrouped Temple-Type Structures
within the Chronology

The temple-type structures at Palenque excluded from the architectural typology
are Temple I, Temple III, Temple X, Temple XXa, and the Temple of the Jaguar.
These structures were excluded from the typology due to the variation among
their plans. As Temples I and III can been placed within the chronology based on
the stratigraphy of Temple VIII, the North Group platform, this section will concentrate on Temple X, Temple XXa and the Temple of the Jaguar.

Temple X may be the earliest of the exposed temple-type structures at Palenque. Like Temple V-sub, a stratigraphically early structure, Temple X is a single gallery structure, and was once vaulted (Ruz 1958b: 190). Furthermore, the wall construction corresponds to the wall construction of Group A structures. Unfortunately the structure is in ruins, and little else can be said about it architecturally.

Temple XXa is also a single gallery structure, but likely had a perishable roof (González Cruz, personal communication 2001). Unlike Temple X, whose façade is pierced by five doorways, Temple XXa's façade consists of a solid masonry wall pierced by a single doorway. Temples XIX and XXI are the only other temple-type structures at Palenque with a single façade doorway, and share the same type of wall construction as Temple XXa. The thin walls (under a meter) and large interior space of Temple XXa also resembles Group E structures.

The Temple of the Jaguar is the best preserved of the ungrouped temple-type structures at Palenque. The vaulting, wall construction and wall mortar coincide with those of Group C, although the wall construction and mortar seem to be of a lower quality than those of the Cross Group structures. In this regard, the Temple of the Jaguar most resembles Temple XIV. Although the structure's lack of a cross-vault creates some ambiguity in its chronological placement, this is perhaps due to its small size and may not be a temporal indicator. As previously mentioned, the construction technique of the stucco panel matches those of the stucco panels of Temples XVIII and XIX (Blom & La Farge 1926: 176; Holmes 1896: 191). As this technique is rare at Palenque, its use within the Temple of the Jaguar possibly indicates a slight temporal association with late Group D and Group E structures.

Summary of the Architectural Construction Chronology of Palenque

Table 4.2 presents a preliminary construction chronology of the temple-type structures of Palenque based on the architectural typology and Palenque's architectural stratigraphy. This architectural construction sequence is complementary to Palenque's ceramic sequence and hieroglyphic chronology. In selecting five architectural attributes, and examining their differences within the temple-type structures at Palenque, different structure groupings became immediately apparent. Although this sequence is highly linear, the possibility of "renaissance" architectural styles has not been ignored. It is necessary to remember that the exposed architecture at Palenque may only date to a 100-year period (Mathews, Chapter 1; Straight, Chapter 10), somewhat limiting a possible "rebirth" of older construction styles and methods. The extensive excavations within the site "core" have failed to reveal the same stratigraphic architectural depth seen at other prominent Maya sites, such as Tikal (Hammond 1982: 248; Hanson 1998: 50), and Copan (Fash 1998: 227; 2001: 81). At Palenque, there appears to have been little rebuilding directly above earlier structures. Temple-type structures often seem to have been in maintained use (García Moll 1991: 241), rather than leveled and used as fill for a later construction. Instead, a more spatially horizontal stratigraphy may represent Palenque's construction chronology.

Summary of the Ceramic Construction Chronology

Using ceramics to date architecture requires certain factors to insure temporal association. First, structures cannot predate the ceramics contained within the core (Loten 1970: 34). Secondly, ceramics used to give a rough date must come from stratigraphically sealed deposits, such as caches and tombs. At Palenque, numerous sub-floor caches and sub-floor tombs have been used to date construction episodes, especially among the Cross Group structures (Rands 1974b: 66). To reliably associate these caches and tombs with the construction of a structure, the cache or tomb must be incorporated within the original architectural construction (Ruz 1965: 452). Cases where the floor was clearly cut into in order to place a sub-floor cache or tomb cannot serve to date a structure; they indicate only that the structure continued to be in use during that particular ceramic phase. Lastly, the deposition of early ceramics during a later time period always remains a possible problem for the archaeologist as they would thus predate the structure.

Table 4.3: Ceramic Construction Chronology of Palenque

Structure	Ceramic Phase	Approximate Date
Ball Court (Temple IX) ???	Motiepa (fill)	c. A.D. 350-500
Temple XVIIIa-sub	Cascada (vaulted tomb)	c. A.D. 500-620
Plaza Temple of the Count	Cascada (fill)	c. A.D. 500-620
Temple XX-sub	Cascada (vaulted tomb)	c. A.D. 500-620
Temple XV ???	Cascada (tomb)	c. A.D. 500-620
Temple of the Count	Otolum (sub-floor tomb)	c. A.D. 620-700
Temple of the Inscriptions	Otolum (vaulted tomb)	c. A.D. 620-700
Temple of the Cross	Otolum (sub-floor cache)	c. A.D. 620-700
Temple of the Foliated Cross	Murcielagos (sub-floor cache)	c. A.D. 700-750
Temple XV ???	Murcielagos (tomb)	c. A.D. 700-750
Temple XVII	Murcielagos (sub-floor cache)	c. A.D. 700-750
Temples XVIII+XVIIIa	Murcielagos (sub-floor tombs)	c. A.D. 700-750
Temple XIX	Murcielagos (primary deposit)	c. A.D. 700-750
Temples XVIII+XVIIIa	Balunte (refill)	c. A.D. 750-820
Tower	Balunte (sub-floor cache)	c. A.D. 750-820
North Palace Stairway	Balunte (fill)	c. A.D. 750-820

Based on the available ceramic data from Palenque (Rands 1974a, 1974b, 1987, n.d.a, n.d.b; personal communication 2002, 2003), a ceramic construction chronology can be postulated, independent from, yet complementary to, the previous construction chronology based on the distribution of architectural attributes (Table 4.3). As mentioned, the context of ceramic deposits is imperative to constructing both ceramic chronologies, and construction chronologies based on ceramics.

The continued use of Temple XX during Murcielagos times, as evidenced by the presence of Murcielagos ceramics associated with excavated sub-floor tombs, has been excluded from the chronology, as construction dates are the primary concern (Balcells, Chapter 9; see Marken 2002b for further discussion). The double mentioning of Temples XVIII and XVIIIa has been maintained, as the differing ceramics possibly represent overlap between two ceramic complexes. However, the Balunte phase ceramics come from Temple XVIIIa Tomb I, which Berlin believed to have been sacked in prehistoric times and refilled (Ruz 1958c: 260). Thus, a Murcielagos date seems a stronger possibility for construction (Rands, personal communication 2003).

Concerning Temple XV, the large temporal difference between the ceramics of Tomb 1 (Cascada phase) and the other Temple XV tombs (Murcielagos phase) creates ambiguity in the ceramic date of the structure. As the excavation reports do not describe in detail the stratigraphic positions of the tombs, it is unclear whether any of the tombs date to the structure's construction. Due to this uncertainty, and the architectural analysis of Temple XV, a Murcielagos phase construction date seems to be the stronger possibility.

While Motiepa sherds have been found in the core of the Ball Court (Temple IX) at Palenque (Schele 1986: 117) this early date bares closer scrutiny. If secure, this date would make Palenque's ball court one of the earliest in the Maya area. The only known Early Classic ball courts in the Maya area are from Copan (Fash 2001: 78), Río Azul (Adams 1999), a site in Campeche and possibly at Tikal (Eric Taladoire, personal communication 2001). Considering the minor monumental architecture currently known at Palenque from this period, compared to the other sites with Early Classic ball courts, this early date for the Ball Court currently seems unlikely. However, if future investigation in the western sector of the site reveals that Palenque had a substantial Early Classic occupation, the A.D. 350-500 date for the Ball Court would become more acceptable.

One significant change in Table 4.3 to the pre-existing ceramic construction chronology is the designation of the Temple XVIIIa-sub ceramics as Cascada (Rands, personal communication 2003), as opposed to Motiepa as previously noted (Rands 1974a: 36; 1974b: 60). This revision is the result of Rands' reevaluation of existing data, and the incorporation of the additional Cascada phase into the ceramic sequence originally proposed (see Rands 1987: Figs. 2, 7h, k). Also currently included within Cascada phase constructions is the plaza underlying the Temple of the Count, although some earlier material was included as part of the fill (Rands, personal communication 2003).

Temple Olvidado has been associated with ceramics of the Picota complex, contained within a sub-floor tomb (Nieto Calleja & Signoret 1989: 193), but as Rands has not confirmed this classification, neither in the literature nor by personal communication, Temple Olvidado has been excluded within the above chronology. In fact, the vessels published by Nieto Calleja and Signoret are not Picota, as cylindrical forms never occur within the Picota complex (Kirk Straight, personal communication 2002). However, other evidence may link Temple Olvidado to an early ceramic complex. The occupant of Temple Olvidado Tomb 3 was buried with a "ceremonial belt" identical to that of the occupant of the Temple XVIIIa-sub vaulted tomb, except the belt of the Temple Olvidado occupant was made of chert instead of jade (Nieto Calleja & Signoret 1989: 209), indicating a possible temporal affiliation between the two burials. This supplementary line of evidence does not confirm that Temple Olvidado occurs early within the architectural chronology of Palenque, but does support the fact that Temple Olvidado is likely the earliest double-vaulted temple-type structure known from Palenque.

Although not as comprehensive, the construction chronology of temple-type structures at Palenque based on ceramics supports the architectural chronology proposed in Tables 4.1 and 4.2, and helps elucidate the construction chronology of earlier, unexposed structures, such as Temple XVIIIa-sub and Temple XX-sub. Of the structures from Group A, the Temple of the Count is associated with Otolum ceramics, with which the Temple Olvidado ceramics may be eventually included. Within Group B, the Temple of the Inscriptions is associated with Otolum ceramics. The Temple of the Cross and the Temple of the Sun are also associated with this phase. As the other similar structures are associated with the subsequent Murcielagos phase, Group C likely dates to the transition period between the Otolum and Murcielagos phases. Amongst the structures of Group D, Temple XV ceramically seems the earliest, while Temples XVIII and XVIIIa are the latest. The ceramics from the sub-floor tombs of Temple XVIII and XVIIIa are slightly later than expected based on architectural forms, but as evidenced by the differing ceramic complexes recovered from the Cross Group structures, temporal overlap also likely occurs between the Murcielagos and Balunte ceramic complexes (see also Rands & Bishop 2003). As both Murcielagos and Balunte ceramics are strongly associated with Temple XIX (Rands n.d.a; Straight n.d.), there seems to be strong temporal affiliation between Temples XVIII, XVIIIa, and Group E based on both architectural and ceramic data.

Summary of the Hieroglyphic Construction Chronology

Based on the available epigraphic data associated with temple-type structures at Palenque, a hieroglyphic construction chronology can be formed (Table 4.4) (Berlin 1944; Martin & Grube 2000; Mathews & Greene Robertson 1985; Ringle 1996; Schele 1974, 1981, 1986; Stuart, in press). Numerous temple-type structures

Table 4.4: Hieroglyphic Construction Chronology of Temple-Type Structures at Palenque

Structure	Ruler Name	Long Count Date	Gregorian Date
Temple Olvidado	Janab Pakal I	9.10.14.15.0	A.D. 647
Temple of the Inscriptions	Kan Bahlam II		c. A.D. 684
Temple of the Cross	Kan Bahlam II	9.12.19.14.12	A.D. 692
Temple of the Sun	Kan Bahlam II	9.12.19.14.12	A.D. 692
Temple of the Foliated Cross	Kan Bahlam II	9.12.19.14.12	A.D. 692
Temple XVII	Kan Bahlam II		A.D. 695-702 ?
Temple XIV	Kan Bahlam II		
Temple XVIII	Ahkal Mo' Nahb III		A.D. 731
Temple XVIIIa	Ahkal Mo' Nahb III		
Temple XIX	Ahkal Mo' Nahb III	9.15.2.7.16	A.D. 734
Temple III	Ahkal Mo' Nahb III		
Temple IV	Ahkal Mo' Nahb III		
Temple XXI	Ahkal Mo' Nahb III		

can be included within this chronology, even when dedication dates are unknown. Certain structures may not be associated with a Long Count date, yet mention a ruler's name, allowing the structure to be placed chronologically (Mathews 2001; Stuart 2000). While it is important to keep in mind the possibility of later rulers adding their own carved monuments to earlier structures, cross-analysis with the architectural and ceramic construction chronologies should aid in rendering any such discrepancies immediately apparent.

As can be seen, several structures lack associated hieroglyphic dates, but can be attributed to the reign of specific rulers. Table 4.4 places securely dated structures before structures without secure dates, although they may not necessarily predate those structures lacking hieroglyphic dates. Certain rulers, such as K'inich Janab Pakal I, concentrated their construction programs within the Palace, but as those structures are range-type structures, they have been excluded from this chronology.

Conclusion

The cross-analysis of the hieroglyphic data of Palenque with the proposed architectural and ceramic construction chronologies further refines the construction chronology of the temple-type structures of Palenque, while defining the temporal limits of the exposed architecture at the site (Table 4.5).

Unfortunately, no early phase architecture is associated with hieroglyphic dates. As the relationships between separate stratigraphic architectural sets (i.e., the North Group platform and the Inscriptions platform) are unclear, little can be defined regarding Palenque's early construction chronology without associated

Table 4.5: Chronology of Palenque Temple-Type Structures:
Cross-Analysis of Architectural, Ceramic, and Hieroglyphic Chronologies

Structures	Archit. Grouping	Ceramic Phase	Hieroglyphic Date	Ruler
T. V-sub				
T. XVIII-sub ?				
T. XVIIIa-sub		Cascada		
T. XX-sub		Cascada		
T. XII-sub 2 ?				
T. XIII-sub 2 ?				
T. X ?				
T. XII-sub 1 ?				
T. XIII-sub 1 ?				
T. Olvidado	Group A		A.D. 647	Janab Pakal I
T. Count	Group A	Otolum		
T. XX	Group A			
T. II	Group A			
T. V	Group B			
T. XII	Group B			
T. Inscriptions	Group B	Otolum	c. A.D. 684	Kan Bahlam II
T. XIII	Group B			
T. Cross	Group C	Otolum	A.D. 692	Kan Bahlam II
T. Sun	Group C		A.D. 692	Kan Bahlam II
T. Foliated Cross	Group C	Murcielagos	A.D. 692	Kan Bahlam II
T. XIV	Group C			Kan Bahlam II
T. XVII	Group C	Murcielagos	A.D. 695-702?	Kan Bahlam II
T. XV	Group D	Murcielagos		
T. Jaguar				
T. I & T. III				Ahkal Mo' Nahb III
T. IV	Group D			Ahkal Mo' Nahb III
T. XVIII	Group D	Murcielagos/Balunte	A.D. 731	Ahkal Mo' Nahb III
T. XVIIIa	Group D	Murcielagos/Balunte		Ahkal Mo' Nahb III
T. XIX	Group E	Murcielagos/Balunte	A.D. 734	Ahkal Mo' Nahb III
T. XXI	Group E		A.D. 736	Ahkal Mo' Nahb III
T. XXa				

ceramic dates. For example, the positions of Temple XII-sub1 and Temple XIII-sub1 within the chronology are tentative and unconfirmed. At present there is not sufficient data available regarding these structures to place them securely within the chronology. Acosta's description of the piers of Temple XII-sub1 (1973: 30-31) is similar in form to the piers of Temple Olvidado. The thin layer of stucco remaining on these buried piers indicates that the structure was not long in use before the final construction phase of Temple XII. While excavating and restoring the Temple of the Sun, Miguel Fernandez encountered approximately twenty coats of stucco on the walls, stairs, and terraces (García Moll 1991: 166). As the layers of stucco on the Temple of the Sun are rather substantial for a possible one hundred-year occupation period (c. A.D. 692-799?), the approximate period of occupation of Temple XII-sub1 was probably short. No data is available on Temples XII-sub2 and XIII-sub2, although a ceramic date may be available in the future. Their tentative placement is based on their stratigraphic location.

Due to the greater overall amount of available architectural data, the architectural chronology proposed in Tables 4.1 and 4.2 has been largely maintained in Table 4.5, except when ceramic or hieroglyphic data more precisely define the chronological sequence. As hieroglyphic dates define a rough absolute construction chronology for a portion of the Classic Maya occupation period at Palenque, the architectural sequence can thus securely place those structures lacking associated hieroglyphic dates within the overall construction chronology. Ceramic dates help confirm the architectural sequence, and have been used to relatively date separate, well-defined stratigraphic architectural phases, such as Temple XVIIIa-sub and Temple XX-sub. These data can then be cross-analyzed with epigraphic events in an attempt to discern whether specific events may be associated with changes in the archaeological record.

One of the questions raised by this revised chronology relates to changes in construction materials. Why did Late Classic Palencanos abandon the excellent lime mortar used in the construction of the Cross Group structures when building Temples XVIII, XVIIIa, XIX, and XXI? Two possible explanations to the end of lime mortar use in architectural construction are (1) a change in the local environment, and (2) changes in the organization of monumental construction. The first possibility concerns the degradation of the local forest by the Palenque population for both the making of lime mortar and habitation. Large amounts of firewood must be burned to produce high-quality lime for the construction and sculpture so abundant at Palenque. As this lime continued to be used for sculptural decoration until the "abandonment" of Palenque, c. A.D. 800, trees were still available for lime production, but may have become a scarce resource by the reign of K'inich Ahkal Mo' Nahb III. While intriguing, without a detailed study of the Late Classic environment at Palenque this environmental hypothesis cannot be proven, and remains merely conjecture.

At present, the second possibility is more open to analysis. When the shift from lime to clay mortar becomes apparent in the archaeological record, numerous monumental structures are built in an extremely short span of time. Elite residential compounds also appear to increase in number and scale during this period (Marken & González Cruz, Chapter 8). Perhaps the available labor population remained the same from the reigns of K'inich Kan Bahlam II to K'inich Ahkal Mo' Nahb III, but was expected to build more structures during a shorter period of time. In order to fulfill their "quota," laborers may have had to "cut some corners" in production. Thus less time was spent cutting/transporting firewood and burning lime, as well as shaping wall and vault stones, as is evident from the constructions of the period. In contrast to this cost-cutting, more time would have been necessary to arrange wall stones and spalls, but these changes in construction technique likely reflect an overall gain in saved production time. While certain architectural elements, such as vaultspring stones and capstones, were uniformly shaped and appear to have been deemed structurally important to Palencano builders, these elements seem to have been cut in slabs and roughly shaped in the fashion of a time-saving assembly line. Other possible explanations for changes in labor organization during this period are posited elsewhere (Marken & González Cruz, Chapter 8; Straight, Chapter 10). However, it is likely that the changes in construction technique seen at Palenque are due to a combination of several factors.

Although construction continued throughout the site "center" during the Late Classic period (Schele 1981: 111-112), the earliest temple-type constructions seem to have had a wider spatial distribution than those that followed, which were primarily focused around the Cross Group/South Group. The reasons for this concentrated construction activity in one particular part of the site remain unexplained. One possibility is that later Palencano architectural activity was not necessarily spatially focused. The absence of deep architectural stratigraphy at Palenque may instead reflect the intensity of archaeological investigation at the site, largely concentrated around the Palace and South Group. Further excavation outside the ceremonial center could resolve this possibility, as well as help elucidate the architectural development of Palenque as a whole.

References

Acosta, Jorge R.
  1973   Exploraciones y Restauraciones en Palenque (1968-1970). *Anales del INAH.* Epoca 7a. Tom. III:1970-1971, pp. 21-60. INAH, Mexico, D.F.

Adams, Richard E. W.
  1999   *Río Azul: An Ancient Maya City.* University of Oklahoma Press, Norman.

Andrews, George F.
  1975   *Maya Cities: Placemaking and Urbanization.* University of Oklahoma Press, Norman.

  1995   Arquitectura maya. *Arqueología Mexicana* 2(11):4-12.

Berlin, Heinrich
  1944   Un Templo Olvidado en Palenque. In *Revista Mexicana de Estudios Antropologias 6*, pp. 62-90. Sociedad Mexicana de Antropología, Mexico, D.F.

Blom, Franz
  1923   *Las Ruinas de Palenque, Xupá y Finca Encanto.* INAH, Mexico, D.F.

Blom, Franz and Oliver La Farge
1926   *Tribes and Temples: A Record of the Expedition to Middle America Conducted by the Tulane University of Louisiana in 1925, Vols. I & II.* Tulane University of Louisiana, New Orleans, LA.

Fash, William L.
1998   Dynastic Architectural Programs: Intention and Design in Classic Maya Buildings at Copan and Other Sites. In *Function and Meaning in Classic Maya Architecture. A Symposium at Dumbarton Oaks, 7th and 8th October 1994*, edited by Stephen D. Houston, pp. 223-270. Dumbarton Oaks Research Library and Collection, Washington, D.C.

2001   *Scribes, Warriors and Kings: The City of Copan and the Ancient Maya.* Revised Edition. Thames & Hudson, London, U.K.

García Moll, Roberto, ed.
1991   *Palenque 1926-1945.* Antologias. Serie Arqueologia. INAH, Mexico, D.F.

Gendrop, Paul
1974   Consideraciones Sobre la Arquitectura de Palenque. In *The Art, Iconography and Dynastic History of Palenque, Part II. Primera Mesa Redonda de Palenque.* Vol. II, edited by Merle Greene Robertson, pp. 81-88. Robert Lewis Stevenson School, Pebble Beach, CA.

González Cruz, Arnoldo
1998   El Templo de la Reina Roja, Palenque, Chiapas. *Arqueología Mexicana* 5 (30):61.

Greene Robertson, Merle
1985   *The Sculpture of Palenque, Vol. III: The Late Buildings of the Palace.* Princeton University Press, Princeton, NJ.

1991   *The Sculpture of Palenque, Vol. IV: The Cross Group, the North Group, the Olvidado, and Other Pieces.* Princeton University Press, Princeton, NJ.

Greene Robertson, Merle, Alfonso Morales Cleveland, and Christopher Powell
1999   *Projecto Grupo de las Cruces: Informe de Campo (Segundo Año).* PARI/ INAH, Palenque, Chiapas, Mexico, May 1999. Unpublished field report.

Griffin, Gillett G.
1978   Cresterias of Palenque. In *Tercera Mesa Redonda de Palenque.* Vol. IV, edited by Merle Greene Robertson and Donnan Call Jeffers, pp. 139-146. Pre-Columbian Art Research Institute, San Francisco, CA.

Hammond, Norman
1982   *Ancient Maya Civilization.* Cambridge University Press, Cambridge, U.K.

Hansen, Richard D.
1998   Continuity and Disjunction: The Pre-Classic Antecedents of Classic Maya Architecture. In *Function and Meaning in Classic Maya Architecture. A Symposium at Dumbarton Oaks, 7th and 8th October 1994*, edited by Stephen D. Houston, pp. 49-122. Dumbarton Oaks Research Library and Collection, Washington, D.C.

Hartung, Horst
1992   Entre Concepto y Ejecución. Apuntes Sobre lo Creativo en la Arquittectura Maya. *Cuadernos de la Aquittectura Meoamericana* 19:13-21.

Heyden, Doris and Paul Gendrop
  1975   *Pre-Columbian Architecture of Mesoamerica.* Translated by Judith Stanton.
          Harry N. Abrams, Inc., New York, NY.

Holmes, William H.
  1896   *Archaeological Studies Among the Ancient Cities of Mexico. Part II:
          Monuments of Chiapas, Oaxaca and the Valley of Mexico.* Field Columbian
          Museum Publication 16. Vol. I, No. 2. Chicago, IL.

Kubler, George
  1975   *The Art and Architecture of Ancient America.* 2nd edition. Penguin Books,
          Baltimore, MD.

Littman, Edwin R.
  1957   Ancient Mesoamerican Mortars, Plasters, and Stuccos: Comalcalco, Part I.
          American Antiquity 23 (2):135-140.

  1959   Ancient Mesoamerican Mortars, Plasters, and Stuccos: Palenque, Chiapas.
          American Antiquity 25 (2):264-266.

Loten, Stanley H.
  1970   *The Maya Architecture of Tikal, Guatemala: A Preliminary Seriation of
          Vaulted Building Plans.* Unpublished Ph.D. dissertation, University of
          Pennsylvania, Philadelphia.

Marken, Damien B.
  2002a   Palenque Architecture: A Preliminary Chronology. Paper presented at the
          67th Anual Meeting of the Society for American Archaeology in Denver, CO.
          March 2002.

  2002b   *L'Architecture de Palenque: Les Temples.* Unpublished M.A. thesis.
          Université de Paris I: La Sorbonne.

Martin, Simon and Nikolai Grube
  2000   *Chronicle of the Maya Kings and Queens: Deciphering the Dynasties of the
          Ancient Maya.* Thames & Hudson, London, U.K.

Marquina, Ignacio
  1964   *Arquitectura Prehispanica.* INAH, Mexico, D.F.

Mathews, Peter
  2001   The Dates of Tonina and a Dark Horse in Its History. *PARI Journal* II(1):1-6.

Mathews, Peter and Merle Greene Robertson
  1985   Notes on the Olvidado, Palenque, Chiapas, Mexico. In *Fifth Palenque Round
          Table–1983.* Vol. VII, edited by Merle Greene Robertson and Virginia M.
          Fields, pp. 7-18. Pre-Columbian Art Research Institute, San Francisco, CA.

Morales Cleveland, Alfonso and Christopher Powell
  1999   *Annual Field Report, Proyecto de las Cruces. June 1998-April 1999.*
          Unpublished field report.

Nieto Calleja, Rosalba and Humberto J. Schiavon Signoret
  1989   El Templo Olvidado de Palenque, Chiapas. *Arquelogia 5*, pp. 91-210.
          Direccion de Monumentos Prehispanicos. INAH, Mexico, D.F.

80 | Damien B. Marken

Pollock, Harry E. D.
    1965   Architecture of the Maya Lowlands. In *Handbook of Middle American Indians, Vol. 2: Archaeology of Southern Mesoamerica, Part 1*, edited by Robert Wauchope and Gordon R. Willey, pp. 378-440. University of Texas Press, Austin.

Porter, A. Kingsley
    1918 *Beyond Architecture*. Marshall Jones Co., Boston, MA.

Rands, Robert L.
    1974a   A Chronological Framework for Palenque. In *The Art, Iconography and Dynastic History of Palenque, Part I. Primera Mesa Redonda de Palenque.* Vol. I, edited by Merle Greene Robertson, pp. 35-40. Robert Lewis Stevenson School, Pebble Beach, CA.

    1974b   The Ceramic Sequence at Palenque, Chiapas. In *Mesoamerican Archaeology: New Approaches*, edited by Norman Hammond, pp. 51-76. University of Texas Press, Austin.

    1987   Ceramic Patterns and Traditions in the Palenque Area. In *Maya Ceramics. Papers from the 1985 Maya Ceramic Conference*, edited by Prudence M. Rice and Robert J. Sharer, pp. 203-238. BAR International Series 345. Oxford, U.K.

    n.d.a   Phase Focus: Ceramics at Palenque. Unpublished manuscript in the possession of the author.

    n.d.b   Temple XIX: Ceramics. Manuscript in the possession of the author.

Rands, Robert L. and Ronald L. Bishop
    2003   The Dish-Plate Tradition at Palenque: Continuity and Change. In *Patterns & Process: A Festschrift in Honor of Dr. Edward V. Sayre*, edited by Lambertus van Zelst, pp. 109-132. Smithsonian Center for Materials Research & Education, Suitland, MD.

Ringle, William M.
    1996   Birds of a Feather: The Fallen Stucco Inscription of Temple XVIII, Palenque, Chiapas. In *Eighth Palenque Round Table–1993*. Vol. X, edited by Merle Greene Robertson, Martin Macri, and Jan McHargue, pp. 45-62. Pre-Columbian Art Research Institute, San Francisco, CA.

Roys, Lawrence
    1934   The Engineering Knowledge of the Maya. In *Contributions to American Archaeology, Vol. II.* No. 6, pp. 27-105. Carnegie Institution of Washington, Washington, D.C.

Ruz Lhuillier, Alberto
    1958a   Exploraciones en Palenque: 1954. *Anales del Instituto Nacional de Antropologia e Historia*, Tomo X, Núm 39, pp. 117-184. INAH, Mexcio, D.F.

    1958b   Exploraciones en Palenque: 1955. *Anales del Instituto Nacional de Antropologia e Historia*, Tomo X, Núm 39, pp. 185-240. INAH, Mexcio, D.F.

    1958c   Exploraciones en Palenque: 1956. *Anales del Instituto Nacional de Antropologia e Historia*, Tomo X, Núm 39, pp. 241-299. INAH, Mexcio, D.F.

1962   Exploraciones en Palenque: 1957. *Anales del Instituto Nacional de Antropologia e Historia*, Tomo XIV, Núm 43, pp. 35-90. INAH, Mexico, D.F.

1965   Tombs and Funerary Practices of the Maya Lowlands. In *Handbook of Middle American Indians, Vol. 2: Archaeology of Southern Mesoamerica, Part 1*, edited by Robert Wauchope and Gordon R. Willey, pp. 441-461. University of Texas Press, Austin.

Schele, Linda
1974   The Attribution of Monumental Architecture to Specific Rulers at Palenque. Paper presented at the XLI Congreso International de Americanistas. Mexico, D.F.

1981   Sacred Site and World-View at Palenque. In *Mesoamerican Sites and World-Views*, edited by Elizabeth P. Benson, pp. 87-118. Dumbarton Oaks Research Library and Collection, Washington, D.C.

1986   Architectural Development and Political History at Palenque. In *City-States of the Maya: Art and Architecture*. Maya Denver 1986 Conference, edited by Elizabeth P. Benson, pp. 110-137. Rocky Mountain Institute for Pre-Columbian Studies, Denver, CO.

Spinden, Herbert J.
1975   *A Study of Maya Art: Its Subject Matter and Historical Development*. Dover Publications, Inc., New York, NY.

Stephens, John L.
1969   *Incidents of Travel in Central America Chiapas and Yucatan, Vols. I & II*. Dover Publications, Inc., New York. Originally published in 1841, by Harper & Brothers, New York, NY.

Straight, Kirk D.
n.d.   Temple XIX Ceramic Report. Summer 2002. Unpublished manuscript in possession of the author.

Stuart, David S.
2000   Las nuevas inscriptiones del Templo XIX. *Arqueología Mexicana* 8(45):28-30.

In press   *The Hieroglyphic Inscriptions from Temple XIX at Palenque: A Commentary*. Pre-Columbian Art Research Institute, San Francisco, CA.

Tovalin Ahumada, Alejandro and Gabriela Ceja Manrique
1996   Desarrollo Arquitectónico del Grupo Norte de Palenque. In *Eighth Palenque Round Table—1993*. Vol. X, edited by Merle Greene Robertson, Martin Macri, and Jan McHargue, pp. 93-102. Pre-Columbian Art Research Institute, San Francisco, CA.

Part III

SETTLEMENT

Chapter 5

The Problem of Political Integration in the Kingdom of Baak

A Regional Perspective for Settlement Patterns in the Palenque Region

Rodrigo Liendo Stuardo

Introduction

In recent years, the study of the internal functioning of ancient complex societies has received a good deal of attention from archaeologists (Earle 1997; Feinman & Marcus 1998). Specifically, the interest has been focused on the analysis of the diverse strategies of economic and political integration developed in specific social settings. In Maya studies, the nature of this integration remains controversial. Current research shows that the coexistence of a high degree of political and economic stratification, with a marked functional homogeneity, characterizes Pre-Hispanic Maya society. According to this evidence, questions regarding both the nature of the different segments that shaped Maya society and its integrative mechanisms are fundamental to arguments that characterize it as either segmentary, or unitary.

Using data from recent regional settlement pattern studies conducted in the Palenque region, this chapter discusses the general settlement pattern in order to infer aspects of structure and development and the mechanisms that might have held together different social units throughout Palenque's developmental sequence.

Political Integration in the Northwestern Maya Lowlands

Compared to other areas in the Maya lowlands, in the northwestern Classic Maya area little effort has been put into a detailed understanding of political or economic issues from a strictly archaeological point of view. The focus on political integration in the area has primarily been limited to the discussion of epigraphic evidence with reference to the presence and distribution of emblem glyphs (Culbert 1991; Marcus 1976, 1993; Mathews 1991), the identification of minor lords (Schele 1986, 1991; Schele & Freidel 1990), and recorded evidence of events that might indicate subordination between polities: royal visits, presence of paramount leaders at accession ceremonies, exchanges of aristocratic women, etc. (Grube & Martin 1998; Martin & Grube 1995, 2000). From these analyses it has been argued that Palenque emerged as the capital of an influential political unit in the northwestern portion of the Maya lowlands by the end of the Early Classic (following the founding of the Palenque dynasty by K'uk' Bahlam I in A.D. 431). Regardless of the accuracy of these reconstructions, inscriptions, by the nature of the messages they convey (focused mainly on chosen events in the lives of a selected few), are frequently ill-suited to convey information regarding the way households and entire communities were economically and politically integrated to larger political units.

Archaeological research at Palenque has mostly centered on the description and analysis of architectural and sculptural remains at the main site, with a limited interest in other aspects of archaeological evidence (García Moll 1991; Garza 1992; González Cruz 1998; Greene Robertson 1983, 1985a, 1985b, 1991; Kelley 1965; Lounsbury 1974, 1976, 1980, 1985; Mathews & Schele 1974; Morales 1999; Ruz 1952, 1955, 1958, 1962, 1973; Schele 1976, 1978, 1986, 1991). The single most important exception to this trend is Rands' (1967, 1987) successive survey efforts that covered an extensive area of approximately 7,000 km^2 during the 1960s and 1970s. This study established the first ceramic sequence for the region (Rands 1957) and gathered important regional data necessary for the reconstruction of Palenque's settlement pattern. Rands' methodology aimed to deal mainly with the problem of defining the nature of local resource exploitation, manufacture and the consumption of ceramics. Compositional analysis of ceramics from the Palenque area allowed him to infer that only a limited range of specialized ceramic forms (incensario supports) were manufactured in the immediate vicinity of the site core. In general terms, Palenque's "[basic] role in the regional exchange system was that of a consumer" (Rands & Bishop 1980: 42). The conclusions from Rands and Bishop's study of ceramic paste composition (Bishop 1992; Bishop, Rands & Harbottle 1982; Rands & Bishop 1980, 2003) have had an enduring and significant influence on how scholars have perceived the political and economic development of this important site over the years (Marcus 1976; Potter 1993: 291-292; Rice 1987: 77-79; Schele 1991).

Following Rands' pioneering work, several regional survey projects with different aims and theoretical orientations have been conducted in the area (Grave Tirado 1996; Liendo Stuardo 1999; Ochoa 1978). Nevertheless, most surveys have focused on the location of sites with large civic-ceremonial architecture, leaving aside the investigation of the smaller communities located between them. Recent research focused on Palenque's hinterland, provides a more fine-grained description of settlement features in the immediate vicinity of the site (a surveyed area of 37 km²), allowing a more intensive analysis of trends of population control and subsistence strategies (Liendo Stuardo 1999).

Since 1999, the Proyecto Integración Política en el Señorío de Palenque (PIP-SP) has tried to expand the survey area in order to encompass a significant portion of the region that might have been under Palenque's political or economic influence based on epigraphic evidence of political subordination of lesser sites with regard to Palenque (Marcus 1976, 1993; Mathews 1991; Mathews & Schele 1974; Riese 1978; Schele 1986, 1991; Schele & Freidel 1990; Schele & Mathews 1993). At the same time, stratigraphic and extensive excavations have been pursued in a sample of secondary sites in the region including El Lacandón, Nututún, Santa Isabel (Liendo 2001), La Providencia, Lindavista, and Chinikiha (Liendo 2003) in an attempt to establish the dynamics of political integration in the region.

A series of inscriptions might have delineated the limits of the political territory centered at Palenque (Xupá to the south, Tortuguero to the west, and Chinikiha to the east). This region contains also a number of minor sites of relative importance that lack reported inscriptions, but exhibit important architecture and locational relevance to the general settlement system (La Cascada, Santa Isabel, El Lacandón, La Providencia, Sulusum, Lindavista, Reforma, Belisario Dominguez, El Bari, El Aguacate, La Concepción, San Joaquín, and San Juan). It also contains hundreds of small clusters of low platforms that might have constituted the residences for the bulk of the Pre-Hispanic population in the region (Fig. 5.1).

Placing the City of Palenque in a Regional Context

Barnhart's mapping efforts and recent household excavations undertaken as part of the Proyecto Especial Palenque during the seasons of 1992-1994 by the National Institute of Anthropology and History of Mexico at Groups I-II, B, C, and IV (Ceja Manrique 1994; López Bravo 1994, 1995; Barnhart 2001) have shown that during its last occupational moment Palenque covered an area of approximately 3 km². Barnhart's mapping project has identified 1,600 structures at the site core with a probable population range of 6,000 to 8,000 residents. According to this estimate, population densities within city limits were quite high, 2,000 to 2,666 persons/km², a number only comparable to Copan's estimates with 3,000 persons/km².

Like other Mesoamerican cities, Palenque combines a sector with a clear formal architectural layout with unplanned sectors showing a more random distri-

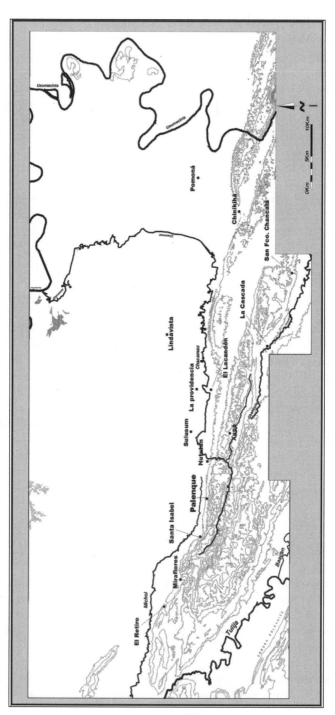

Figure 5.1: Sites mentioned in the text

bution of buildings. The city also shows a modular pattern: building compounds apparently similar in form and function, differing only in scale and in number of buildings. Important aspects of the internal organization of these compounds remain unknown, however. Although a clear idea of the number or extension of these compounds is still lacking, it is quite probable that the limits among residential units were based on topographic limitations. It is fair to say that for the vast majority of ancient city dwellers, these residential compounds might have represented the locus where the main social reproductive activities ("habitus") might have taken place. Incomplete as the available information might be, some residential compounds seem to be structurally similar (see Marken & González Cruz, Chapter 8). The resemblance among residential units has to do with the multifunctional character typical of Pre-Hispanic residential units. When archaeological data from different excavated compounds are compared (such as data from Groups B, C, and IV) several parallels become clear. Within Group C, for example, Structures C2 and C6 are complex buildings with associated domestic activities, whereas Structures C3, C4, and C5 contained three interments and the remains of several composite anthropomorphic censer holders. Within Group B, most of the buildings excavated show evidence of domestic activities, except for Structures B7 and B8 whose central rooms functioned as sanctuaries similar to those located in the Cross Group and House F in the Palace (see Child, Chapter 12). Inside these sanctuaries several incense burners were located.

Structures J1 and J5 limit Group IV's central plaza to the north with Structures J6 and J7 forming the northeastern corner of it. Archaeological data retrieved from the former indicate predominantly domestic functions for these buildings, while the latter had more ceremonial functions, judging from the number of interments and censer burners found within them. This evidence, incomplete in many ways, indicates an interesting pattern of activities associated with residential compounds within the city. The architectural similarities among residential compounds could imply an equivalent set of ritual and economic activities among their inhabitants. Furthermore, while the qualitative (construction materials, façade decoration) and quantitative differences (number of structures, architectonic volume) could reflect natural domestic developmental cycles, or differences in status, rather than significant functional differences among the residential units.

The Regional Context

We still lack critical information regarding the relationship between Palenque and a series of smaller centers located in the greater Palenque region. However, some advances have been made during the past three years in relation to the general structure and distribution of settlements in an area proposed to be under Palenque's direct political control (Berlin 1958; Culbert 1991; Marcus 1976, 1993; Mathews 1991). Our project has recorded a total of 413 sites within an area of 450 km² (see Table 5.1 & Fig. 5.2). The survey area encompasses three environmentally diverse

Table 5.1: Site type distribution in the Palenque region

Structure Type	Number
Platform	1,100
Range Platform	164
Pyramid	50
"L" Platform	42
Group Type	**Number**
Patio Oriented Group	149
Multipatio Group	14
Informal Group	135
Plaza Oriented Group	8
Site Type	**Number**
Complex Civic Ceremonial	8
Discrete Civic Ceremonial	23
Domestic Unit	287
Isolated Platform	130
Total Sites	448

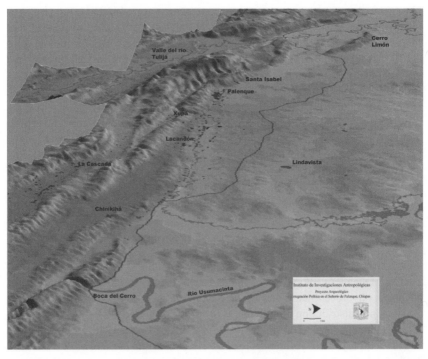

Figure 5.2: Settlement distribution

morphogenetic systems. From north to south these are the Pleistocene fluvial terraces, the Intermediate Plains, and the Tertiary formations of the Sierra de Chiapas (Rands 1973a, 1974; West et al. 1969). The Pleistocene fluvial terraces are
composed mainly of alluvial plains and are Quaternary in age. These Quaternary
deposits become thinner as one moves toward the Tertiary rock formation of the
Sierra de Chiapas. Pleistocene sea-level variations, and the concomitant change
in the level of the drainage systems leading to the Gulf, caused a cyclic erosion
and sedimentation of the alluvial plain (West et al. 1969: 33). Alternating cycles
of sea level drops and rises during glacial and interglacial periods led to processes
of alluviation of river valleys. The latest of these cycles corresponded with the
rising sea level which followed the Woodfordian interglacial (c. 16,000 B.P. to
the present) (West et al. 1969: 33). The fluvial terraces are the product of recent
sedimentation that has left a generally broad surface extending seaward from the
Intermediate Plains. Although the Usumacinta drainage system has eroded large
quantities of the Pleistocene surface, floods caused by the periodic changes in the
river water course have penetrated upstream toward the Tertiary foothills. The
comparatively high settlement densities in this area demonstrate the importance
of this zone during Pre-Hispanic times. Two factors account for the presence of
population concentrations in these areas: transportation and a varied and resource-
rich ecosystem (West et al. 1969).

The Intermediate Plains are the oldest component of the Tabasco Plains. They
are the result of alluviation processes paralleling the Tertiary hills and mountains
of southern Tabasco and northern Chiapas. These Pleistocene Plains are characterized by a smooth sloping surface with a general seaward inclination. The Plains
have been heavily eroded by each of the major drainage systems. The surface is
generally flat near the major flood plains of the principal river systems becoming
progressively higher (50-75 m) toward the base of the Sierra de Chiapas.

The topsoil of the Intermediate Plains is heavily weathered. Within the
eroded level (15 m thick), the vast majority of alluvial material has been replaced
by kaolinitic clays and silica. Soil levels vary noticeably. Stratigraphy generally
has an A-horizon of 7-10 cm composed of a rather yellow/reddish clay and an
intense red iron-manganese B-horizon. In areas covered by high grasses the A-
horizon is composed of a thicker layer of black friable soils grading markedly
into a B-horizon of reddish kaolinitic clay (West et al. 1969). Shallow soils and
poor drainage make the Intermediate Plains a vast area (10,800 km^2) generally not
suited for agriculture.

The Sierra de Chiapas is composed of Tertiary limestones and dolomitic limestones. The stratigraphy of the Sierra de Chiapas varies from medium to coarse
with intense fracture and high levels of dissolution. The nature of this process
has created the karstic topography of the region. The Tertiary is represented by
big thick layers of compact lutite and sand. It seems that the Sierra de Chiapas
afforded the best conditions for site location during Pre-Hispanic times. The vast
majority of sites are located along the first escarpments of the Sierra.

Some of the variability detected during our surveys among site types might be due to variation in subsistence adaptations, but other aspects of settlement variation (population densities, location of civic ceremonial centers, settlement layout) might be the result of historical and social circumstances tied to the development of social inequalities and hierarchical organizations associated with the rise of political complexity in the Palenque region. Although currently under study, some of these historical processes indicate that important changes occurred in the region as a whole with the foundation of the Palenque dynasty in A.D. 431.

Rural Architectural Variability

For the purposes of this research two dimensions of functional variation in ancient architecture were taken into consideration: (1) nonresidential structures indicating functional complexity, and, (2) the distribution, characteristics and number of dwelling structures. Ashmore (1981) suggests 20 m^2 to be the norm for dwelling platforms in the Maya lowlands for the Classic period. Within the study area platform size (excluding those smaller than 8 m^2) ranges from 8 to 748 m^2, averaging 36.4 m^2 (a 10-percent trimmed mean for a sample of 164). This evidence suggests that on average platforms in the Palenque area tended to be larger than those reported by Ashmore and more akin with the evidence for other areas in Mesoamerica (Evans 1988: 26-28; Smith 1992: 307). Two tentative explanations may account for this difference. First, ethnohistorical accounts describing Chol-speaking communities in the Chiapas-Tabasco lowlands give figures of 19 to 25 individuals per structure (Villagutierre, cited in Hellmuth 1977) and Rice (1987) suggests a figure of ten individuals per mound in his study of the Peten district. Bigger coresidential groups in the area under consideration could account for the differences in platform size when compared to other areas in the Maya lowlands and certainly would be an important reason to upscale total population figures for the study region. Platform size and form can also be indicative of differences in wealth and status.

The interpretation of small low platforms as the remains of domestic structures is based on several criteria. First is the "principle of abundance" (Ashmore 1981: 40-41). These are by far the most abundant structure types in the region (a total of 1,306 platforms with a probable residential function were detected during our survey). Second, the formal attributes of such platforms are similar to modern households in the region. Third, the small degree of architectural variation among single platforms composing a patio group is a good indicator of the predominantly domestic function of the majority of platforms. If functional differences were present, then architectural variation would be expected. Fourth, in those cases where test pit excavations were pursued, the characteristics of the artifacts recovered in association with the platforms are the strongest evidence for a domestic function.

Range structures differ from the more common dwelling platforms by their elongated design, by the height of the basal platforms that support them, by the use of well-cut stones in their construction, and by the existence on many occasions of a front staircase. Within the study area 164 range structures were found in association with other platforms and pyramids enclosing a patio area, never in isolation. The probable function of this specific type of building is the subject of debate in current archaeological research in the Maya area. Their closeness to other civic-ceremonial facilities has led to their characterization as special elite residences with civic functions (de Montmollin 1989: 51)

Pyramids were easy to distinguish from domestic structures based on several formal attributes: a square ground plan, a basal area usually larger than 120 m^2, height more than 5 m, better quality construction material, and an architectural layout tending to form rather standardized plaza contexts. Fifty pyramids were found always in association with other architectural components (ball courts, plazas, and platforms) denoting a civic-ceremonial function. The restricted floor space (less than 8 m^2) of several platforms found makes it very unlikely that these structures were dwellings. Their tendency to be located at the corners of patio groups also suggests that these structures may not have been residences, but served other functions such as storehouses, kitchens, or altars. However, accurate identification will need to await further investigation.

Rural Site Variability

Within the study area several sites (Palenque, Nututún, Santa Isabel, Xupá, El Lacandón, Sulusum, La Providencia, La Cascada, San Juan, Reforma de Ocampo, Lindavista, Belisario Dominguez, and Chinikihá) stand out as larger and more internally complex than any of the surrounding undifferentiated habitation sites in the regional system. All these sites present clear evidence that elite residences are closely associated with features of ceremonial-civic functions. They represent nodes of political and economic activities in the regional system "serving political and ceremonial needs of a group larger than the household" (de Montmollin 1988: 43). They were labeled as "civic-ceremonial centers," and differ quantitatively and qualitatively from "civic-ceremonial sites," which may have only one civic-ceremonial structure.

Sites were classified using formal criteria in the following manner:

Single platform. The habitational function of all single platform sites is not absolutely certain. In those cases where surface collection was possible or where test pits were excavated, single platforms yielded materials that can be associated with habitational functions (N = 130) They could be interpreted as temporary residences associated with agricultural activities. However, more evidence is needed to test this hypothesis.

Informal group. These constitute the second most abundant site type in the region (N = 135). Their major formal characteristic is the absence of a central patio. Structures are located randomly in relation to each other. The number of structures in these groups ranges from two to four. The small number of structures per site and the lack of a central patio could be considered evidence for a late foundation for this type of site (Tourtellot 1983: 97-121).

Patio-oriented group. One hundred forty-nine patio-oriented groups were found within the study area. These have three or four platforms oriented toward a central patio. Patio groups are the most common and best understood unit of settlement analysis in Maya studies (Ashmore 1981; Ashmore & Wilk 1988; Tourtellot 1983). According to de Montmollin (1988: 43) they represent "the material correlate of a household level unit of sociopolitical organization."

Multipatio group. Fourteen multipatio groups were found. They correspond to the next higher level of settlement complexity above the patio group within the surveyed area. A multipatio group is a cluster of several patio groups separated by less than 100 m from each other and by more than 100 m of vacant terrain from other patio groups. The number of patios composing a multipatio group varies from two to five, and the number of structures from seven to sixteen.

It is uncertain whether all sites classified under the same label are functionally equivalent, especially when considering chronologically distant periods. By the same token, we cannot always be certain that sites classified under different labels represent significantly different kinds of settlements. This problem stems principally from the fact that we have limited control over variability in the distribution of ceramic and lithic artifacts on the ground surface and a small number of excavated contexts. Yet, the classification system allows a more reliable classification of certain aspects of the general settlement pattern. It distinguishes, for example, between large, nucleated sites, on the one hand, and small dispersed ones, on the other. To some degree it also accounts for the differential distribution of an important array of architectural remains ranging from simple domestic residences to buildings with a more evident civic-ceremonial function.

Following these criteria thirty-one groups with a probable civic-ceremonial function can be suggested. These are clusters characterized by the presence of high construction volumes and by the existence of architectural types (pyramids, ball courts, civic-plazas, and range structures) that could represent the nodes of important social activities for whole communities. Although the size of the ancient city of Palenque is similar to other middle-size lowland Maya urban centers, most

Table 5.2: Comparative population table

Site	% Population Living at the Main Site	Site Area (km²)	% Population Living in Rural Area	Rural area (km²)	Source
Palenque	92.0	3.0	8.0	37	Liendo
Copan	44.8	0.6	55.2	23.4	Gonlin
Seibal	17.0	1.6	83.0	13.6	Tourtellot
Tikal	22.5	16.0	77.5	104.0	Culbert et.al.
Tayasal	48.5	8.0	51.5	18	Chase

striking are the differences in terms of the sheer number and density of structures present within the site core compared to its immediate surroundings (Table 5.2).

From an emic perspective, it might have been quite clear to anybody entering the city that it was characterized as qualitatively different. During the Balunte period (A.D. 750-820) the immediate city hinterland (approximately 37 km^2 delimited by the secondary sites of Nututún to the east, Santa Isabel to the west, and the system of low hills paralleling the Sierra to the north) was a region with an extremely low population density (25 persons/km^2). The vast majority of settlements located in this area correspond to single patio compounds. Among them a tiny fraction has more than one patio, perhaps indicating the presence of more than one nuclear family. Without exception, these groups date to the Otolum or Murcielagos periods (A.D. 620-750) (Table 5.2).

Since very early in its occupational sequence, the narrow valley to the north of the city was probably used as an agricultural sector. Nevertheless, only for Otolum times can we securely identify the first settlements in this area (sixteen discrete groups have been identified for this period). Contemporaneously, there is evidence for the development of intensive agricultural fields in the same area. This evidence seems to indicate that the Otolum and Murcielagos periods witnessed an important development of the city's system of agricultural production (Fig. 5.3). The results of this study show a high degree of population nucleation at Palenque with very low sustaining rural populations. Increased agricultural production through intensification of agricultural fields during the Otolum and Murcielagos periods possibly stemmed from the necessity of supporting the strong demographic concentration at Palenque. This evidence indicates in a rather indirect way that important demographic processes were part of the development of political and economic complexity in the region. These demographic processes might have involved the movement of people from the hinterlands to Palenque proper (from voluntaristic to compulsory mechanisms). The Balunte period marks a shift of settlement organization within Palenque's immediate hinterland (Fig. 5.4). Nine new intensive agricultural fields can be securely dated to this period and eighty-eight new settlements are founded. The Balunte period settlement pattern around Palenque is one where small house groups tend to be located on or close to their agricultural fields producing a more dispersed pattern than the Otolum or Murcielagos periods.

In general terms, there is a trend up to the Balunte period attesting to a change in the correlation between population at Palenque and the overall population evident in the hinterland. This change has been explained elsewhere (Liendo 2003: 119) as an attempt by individual farmers residing in Palenque to assert individual control over land. There is a greater presence of Tabasco Plain pottery at Palenque and at sites to the east along the Chacamax River during Late Murcielagos and Balunte periods attesting important changes in the settlement system at large. Although several explanations ranging from population pressure arguments (Rands 1973, 1977: 163) to those with a more political focus (Bishop 1994: 35).

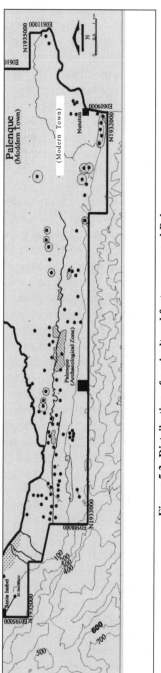

Figure 5.3: Distribution of agricultural features around Palenque

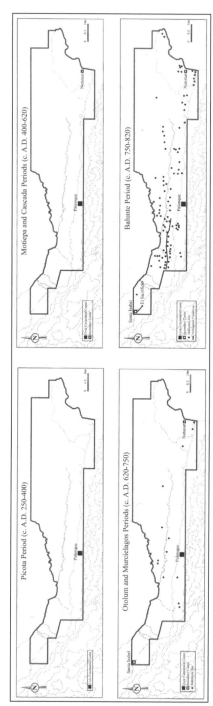

Figure 5.4: Settlement development at Palenque regional core

The preliminary results from this study also demonstrate the existence during Balunte times of several sub-regions outside Palenque's immediate hinterland (40 km²). These sub-regions can be defined by their different occupation histories, multiple subsets of population densities, architectural variation, causeways connecting micro-regions with the larger region, and the existence of a clearly defined set of frontier zones. These micro-zones might be indicative of the existence of potential socio-political groups larger than single communities, but smaller than a polity (districts or provinces). Five micro-regions could be defined in these terms: the Palenque regional core, El Lacandón-Nututún subregion, the Chancalá Valley, the Llanuras Intermedias sub-region and, the Sierras sub-region.

The first, the Palenque regional core, is the area delimited by the sites of Nututún to the east, Santa Isabel to the west, and the low hills paralleling the Sierra to the north, totaling approximately 37 km². This lightly settled sub-region (25 persons/km²) is characterized by its simplicity in terms of the number of architectural and settlement types. With few exceptions, sites correspond to single patio groups composed of low platforms, with twenty-eight corresponding to single mound sites. The distribution of rural house groups within Palenque's immediate hinterland cannot be fully explained as a direct result of ecological factors impinging upon farmers' decisions on where to settle. Hence, a more political framework is needed to elucidate in a more satisfactory way those processes leading to political centralization in the region.

A series of sites located on the southern bank of the river Chacamax conform the El Lacandón-Nututún subregion (delimited to the west by the site of Nututún, El Lacandón to the east, and the river Chacamax to the north). El Lacandón is a small community (16 ha) with a civic-ceremonial area of 3 ha. This central area includes several buildings with clear residential, administrative, and ceremonial functions. In 1999, seventy-four structures were surveyed. El Lacandón is an important site for the understanding of early settlement dynamics. Important Late Preclassic-Early Classic ceramic assemblages were found during excavations in 2000 (López Bravo, personal communication 2003), a characteristic shared with Nututún and Paso Nuevo (Rands, Chapter 3). Within this region (25 km²) 480 structures distributed in forty-five discrete groups were detected. This area also shows a higher structure density per km² than the one observed in the Palenque regional core (19 structures per km² compared to 9.6). The settlement clusters seem also to be more evenly distributed across the region when compared to the settlements around Palenque.

The Chankalá Valley is formed by two narrow valleys behind the first line of hills of the Sierra de Chiapas. One hundred twenty-four sites were located in 80 km² during the survey season of 2002. Of these, five sites correspond to civic-ceremonial sites showing a more complex architectural layout and higher indexes of construction volume than the rest (Xupá, La Cascada, Chancalá, San Juan Chancalaíto, and Reforma de Ocampo). Interestingly, the Chankala Valley seems to have been the setting for two differentiated settlement systems that correspond to the natural division of the terrain into two separate river basins: the Ashipa river basin and the Chankalá river basin. Our survey detected a broad 15-km zone with no evidence of settlements, maybe indicating the existence of a political frontier. This "frontier" corresponds neatly with the distribution of two settlement clusters: one centered on the civic-ceremonial site of Xupá and the other gravitating around three major sites (two of which, La Cascada and San Juan Chancalaíto, are connected by a sacbe).

The cluster centered around Xupá is composed of twenty small architectonic groups without major differences among them. Xupá itself is a site of 10.5 ha. With a concentration of important buildings with good preservation. Fourteen buildings delimit an ample plaza. Both inscriptions (Blom 1926) and the abundant ceramic assemblage found at the site seem to indicate a late date for the settlement of the site. Xupá shares with a number of other sites in the region a very late occupation date (Murcielagos and Balunte periods). Its location close to a passage through the Sierra indicates its association to the El Lacandón-Nututún sub-region settlement system.

To the east, the second site cluster shows a different settlement dynamic when compared to the former. The three principal centers of the Chankalá river basin (La Cascada, 8 ha, 21 structures; San Juan Chancalaíto, 13 ha, 40 structures; and Reforma de Ocampo, 19 ha, 57 structures) probably functioned as nodal points for the eighty-five undifferentiated platform groups that occupied the valley. These three civic-ceremonial centers present complex architectonic layouts coupled with the presence of ball courts (San Juan Chancalaito and La Cascada), plazas, and more elaborate building facilities.

The Llanuras Intermedias sub-region has been the subject of successive surveys through the years (Ochoa 1978; Rands 1973a, 1973b, 1977). The archaeological evidence gathered so far seems to indicate a settlement development with an architectural pattern that departs from the one that characterizes the former two sub-regions. The sites that make up this area (La Siria, Belisario Domínguez, El Barí, Cinco de Mayo, El Aguacate, Francisco Madero, Lindavista, and San Joaquín) form a rather homogeneous group in terms of their chronology. All of them present ceramic assemblages belonging to Late Classic Otolum, Murcielagos, and Balunte phases with close ties to Palencano ceramic types. They also share a common building technique (earthen mounds) and a dispersed settlement pattern with the presence of monumental architecture. They conform to a very regular pattern with sites located 4 km away from each other and connecting the Sierras region to the Balancán area to the north. The sites in the Llanuras Intermedias sub-region form discrete population clusters congregated around settings where monumental architecture is present.

The sites located in the Llanuras Intermedias seems to indicate a settlement dynamic based on the distribution of a rather dispersed population around nuclei of monumental architecture localized discretely and regularly across the landscape. The architectural core present at these sites shows a clear modular layout:

ball courts, pyramids, and platform groups forming quadrangles. The settlement regularity and the rather short and late ceramic sequence might indicate a strategy aimed toward the development of an important route connecting Palenque to the Lower Usumacinta region.

The Sierras subregion (from El Lacandón to Chinikiha in the east and the southern bank of river Chacamax to the north) is characterized by the presence of a continuous line of settlements from Palenque to Chinikiha (located 37 km to the east). Although evidence of early occupations dating to the Late Preclassic period have been detected at Paso Nuevo, El Lacandón, and Chinikiha, this area witnessed a population burst during the Late Classic period with the founding of numerous settlements connecting these three sites demonstrating longer occupation histories. During Murcielagos-Balunte times (A.D. 700-820) a continuous string of settlements connected Palenque and Chinikiha along the Sierra. These settlements are associated with a causeway running east-west beginning in the vicinity of Chinikiha and ending close to the site of El Lacandón. In general, the population figures for the Sierras sub-region seem higher than those proposed for the Llanuras Intermedias region. The population distribution in the Sierras is continuous and corresponds mainly to small platform groups with probable habitational functions. There is a salient absence of civic-ceremonial compounds in the area (with the exception of Chinikiha), with a tendency for several platform groups to cluster around groups with higher construction volumes, though lacking architectural components denoting clear civic-ceremonial functions (Fig. 5.5).

Assessing Settlement Dynamic Trends

Although the ceramic analysis is still in progress, most of the sites localized within settlement survey limits can be tentatively assigned to the Late Classic Balunte

Figure 5.5: Wide view of *sacbe*

Figure 5.6: Detailed view of *sacbe*

period (A.D. 750-820). Exceptions are Paso Nuevo and Chinikiha, where Robert Rands has extensively reported the finding of Sierra Rojo ceramics, diagnostic of Late Formative and Early Classic assemblages (Rands, Chapter 3), and El Lacandón where an important early settlement has been explored (López Bravo, personal communication 2003). Small quantities of Sierra Rojo assemblages have also been found at La Cascada, San Juan Chancalaíto, and Chancala. Without a doubt, the presence of clear Preclassic and Early Classic deposits in a sample of sites along the first escarpments of the Sierra de Chiapas attest to the importance of pursuing new regional investigations focused on these poorly known early periods. In those cases where no associated surface sherds could be found or test pits excavated, a clear chronological assessment remains controversial at best, nevertheless, three moments are evident in the regional archaeological record and worthy of further analysis. The first moment (Picota-Motiepa ceramic periods, c. A.D. 250-500) is characterized by the development of political centralization with the founding of the ruling dynasty at Palenque and an increase of population figures within city limits.

At the same time, the development of a regional settlement hierarchy can be inferred. Although the relationship between smaller sites, such as Nututún or El Lacandón, with Palenque during early times remains unclear, the presence of similar ceramic types and their proximity to the main site might indicate the areal extension of the interaction sphere centered at Palenque.

The second transformation of Palenque's urban landscape (Otolum-Murcielagos, c. A.D. 600-750) corresponds to the moment of greatest political expansion of the site in the region. Population figures increases exponentially and the city reaches its maximum extension. The majority of securely dated buildings in the main zone date to this moment (Marken, Chapter 4). Intensive agricultural fields also date to the same period. This development surely had as its main goal to sustain the increasing site core population. New sites were founded in the region: Xupá and Santa Isabel. Another, El Lacandón, was abandoned. The third transformation (Balunte, c. A.D. 750-820) is characterized by the settling of the territory previously vacant between minor nucleated centers in the region.

Concluding Remarks

The chronological, settlement structure, and architectural patterns allowing the division of the rural region into settlement sub-regions casts doubt on the possibility of approaching rural settlement dynamics as a single regional phenomenon. Rural populations within the Palenque area might not have constituted a homogeneous unitary sociopolitical unit responding in similar ways to strictly top-down mechanisms impinging upon them. In this regard, the impact of the three moments in regional settlement changes described above on individual rural communities or subregions remains an important area of future research. On the other hand, the evidence presented thus far seems to indicate a high level of redundancy among the components of Palenque's urban and rural landscapes. The residential compounds in the city show significant formal, and probably functional, similarities among them. The most evident differences have to do with scale and possible differences of status. The size, density, and architectural complexity present at Palenque exceeds in several orders of magnitude all other archaeological remains in the region. This fact alone bespeaks the disproportionate importance that Palenque might have held in practically every single aspect of daily life for the rural population in the region regardless of social status or settlement type residence.

Nevertheless, it would be a mistake to deny the existence of strong local networks of social obligations that integrated rural populations into socially discrete units. An understanding of the possible ways available to the myriad of small and middle-size communities for integration within the greater Palenque polity must be contextualized and viewed from several scales of analysis (the household, the community, and the subregion). Most likely our main mistake is to cast the problem in terms of "either-or" scenarios, trying to understand the problem of ancient Maya political integration as either segmentary or unitary. By definition, the problem of integration is a matter of degree. It is not measured by the mere size of nucleated centers, nor by population density, but by the level of specialization of the system components.

Acknowledgments

This research has been sponsored in different parts of its development by grants provided by the National Science Foundation, the Wenner Gren and Heinz Foundations, and CONACyT.

References

Ashmore, Wendy
    1981   Some Issues of Method and Theory in Lowland Maya Settlement Archaeology. In *Lowland Maya Settlement Patterns*, edited by Wendy Ashmore, pp. 37-69. University of New Mexico Press, Albuquerque.

    1988   Household and Community at Classic Quiriguá. In *Household and Community in the Mesoamerican Past*, edited by Richard R. Wilk and Wendy Ashmore, pp. 153-169. University of New Mexico Press, Albuquerque.

Ashmore, Wendy and Richard R. Wilk
    1988   Household and Community in the Mesoamerican Past. In *Household and Community in the Mesoamerican Past,* edited by Richard R. Wilk and Wendy Ashmore, pp. 1-27, University of New Mexico Press, Albuquerque.

Barnhart, Edwin L.
    2001   *Palenque Mapping Project: Settlement and Urbanism at an Ancient Maya City.* Unpublished Ph.D. dissertation. University of Texas, Austin.

Berlin, Heinrich
  1958   El glifo emblema en las inscripciones mayas. *Journal de la Societé de Américanistes* 47:111-119.

Bishop, Ronald L.
  1992   Instrumentation and the Future of Archaeology. In *Quandries and Quests: Visions of Archaeology's Future*, edited by LuAnn Wandsnider, pp. 160-169. Center of Archaeological Investigations Occasional Paper No. 20, Southern Illinois University, Carbondale.

  1994   PreColumbian Pottery: Research in the Maya Region. In *Archaeometry of PreColumbian Sites*, edited by David A. Scott and Pieter Meyers, pp. 15-66. The Getty Conservation Institute, Los Angeles, CA.

Blom, Franz
  1926   *Tribes and Temples. A Record of the Expedition to Middle America Conducted by the Tulane University of Louisiana.* Tulane University, New Orleans, LA.

Ceja Manrique, Maria Gabriela
  1994   *Excavaciones Arqueologicas en los Grupos I y II, Palenque, Chiapas.* Manuscript on file, Proyecto Palenque, INAH, Mexico, D.F.

Chase, Arlen F.
  1990   Maya Archaeology and Population Estimates in the Tayasal-Paxcoman Zone, Peten, Guatemala. In *Precolumbian Population History in the Maya Lowlands*, edited by T. Patrick Colbert and Don S. Rice, pp. 149-166. University of New Mexico Press, Albuquerque.

Culbert, T. Patrick, ed.
  1973   *The Classic Maya Collapse.* University of New Mexico Press, Albuquerque.

  1991   *Classic Maya Political History.* Cambridge University Press, Cambridge, U.K.

Culbert, T. Patrick, Laura J. Kosakowsky, Robert E. Fry, and William A. Haviland
  1990   The Population of Tikal Guatemala. In *Precolumbian Population History in the Maya Lowlands*, edited by T. Patrick Colbert and Don S. Rice, pp. 103-122. University of New Mexico Press, Albuquerque.

de Montmollin, Olivier
  1988   Settlement Scale and Theory in Maya Archaeology. In *Recent Studies in PreColumbian Archaeology,* edited by Nicholus J. Saunders and Olivier de Montmollin, pp. 63-101. BAR International Series 421, Oxford, U.K.

  1989   *The Archeology of Political Structure.* Cambridge University Press, Cambridge, U.K.

Earle, Timothy
  1997   *How Chiefs Come to Power: The Political Economy in Prehistory.* Stanford University Press, Stanford, CA.

Evans, Susan T.
  1988   *Excavations at Cihuatecpan.* Vanderbilt University Publications in Anthropology, Vol. 36, Nashville, TN.

Feinman, Gary M. and Joyce Marcus, eds.
  1998   *Archaic States.* School of American Research Press, Santa Fe, NM.

García Moll, Roberto, ed.
1991   *Palenque. 1926-1945.* INAH, México, D.F.

Garza, Mercedes de la
1992   *Palenque.* Gobierno del Estado de Chiapas, Tuxtla Gutiérrez.

Gonlin, Nancy
1993   *Rural Household Archaeology at Copán, Honduras.* Unpublished Ph.D. dissertation, Pennsylvania State University, University Park.

González Cruz, Arnoldo
1998   *Informe de Actividades del Proyecto Especial Palenque: 1992-1994* Manuscript on file, Centro INAH Chiapas, Tuxtla Gutiérrez.

Grave Tirado, Luis Alfonso
1996   *Patrón de Asentamiento en la Región de Palenque, Chiapas.* B.A. thesis, Escuela Nacional de Antropología e Historia, Mexico, D.F.

Greene Robertson, Merle
1983   *The Sculpture of Palenque, Vol. 1: The Temple of the Inscriptions.* Princeton University Press, Princeton, NJ.

1985a   *The Sculpture of Palenque, Vol. 2: The Early Buildings of the Palace and the Wall Paintings.* Princeton University Press, Princeton, NJ.

1985b   *The Sculpture of Palenque, Vol. 3: The Late Buildings of the Palace.* Princeton University Press, Princeton, NJ.

1991   *The Sculpture of Palenque, Vol. 4: The Cross Group, the North Group, the Olvidado, and Other Pieces.* Princeton Univesity Press, Princeton, NJ.

Grube, Nikolai and Simon Martin
1998   Politica Clasica Maya dentro de una tradicion mesoamericana: un modelo geografico de organizacion politica hegemonica. In *Modelos de entidades politicas Mayas*, edited by Silvia Trejo, pp. 131-146. INAH, Mexico, D.F.

Hellmuth, Nicholus
1977   Cholti-Lacandon Chiapas and Peten Itza Agriculture, Settlement Pattern, and Population. In *Maya Prehistory: Studies in Memory of Sir Eric Thomson*, edited by Norman Hammond, pp. 421-448. Academic Press, London.

Kelley, David
1965   The Birth of the Gods at Palenque. *Estudios de Cultura Maya* 5:93-134.

Liendo Stuardo, Rodrigo
1999   *The Organization of Agricultural Production at a Classic Maya Center: Settlement Patterns in the Palenque Region, Chiapas, Mexico.* Unpublished Ph.D. dissertation, University of Pittsburgh, Pittsburgh, PA.

2001   Palenque y su área de sustentación: Patrón de asentamiento y organización política en un centro Maya del Clásico. *Mexicon,* Vol. XXIII.

2002   Organización social y producción agrícola en Palenque. In *La Organización Social Entre los Mayas. Memoria de la Tercera Mesa Redonda de Palenque, Vol. I*, edited by V. Tiesler Blos, R. Cobos, and M. Greene Robertson, pp. 307-327. Conaculta–INAH, Mexico, D.F.

2003   *The Organization of Agricultural Production at a Maya Center. Settlement Patterns in the Palenque Region, Chiapas, Mexico.* Serie Arqueología de México. University of Pittsburgh Latin American Archaeological Publications/ INAH, Pittsburgh, PA and Mexico, D.F.

López Bravo, Roberto
  1994   Exploraciones Arqueologicas en el Grupo C de Palenque. In *Cuarto Foro de Arqueologia de Chiapas*. Instituto Chiapaneco de Cultura, Tuxtla Gutiérrez.
  1995   *El Grupo B, Palenque, Chiapas. Una Unidad Habitacional Maya del Clasico Tardio*. B.A. thesis, ENAH, Mexico.

Lounsbury, Floyd G.
  1974   The Inscription of the Sarcophagus Lid at Palenque. In *Primera Mesa Redonda de Palenque, Part II*, edited by Merle Greene Robertson, pp. 5-20. Robert Louis Stevenson School, Peeble Beach, CA.
  1976   A Rationale for the Initial Date of the Temple of the Cross at Palenque. In *The Art, Iconography, and Dynastic History of Palenque, Part III: Proceedings of the Segunda Mesa Redonda de Palenque*, edited by Merle Greene Robertson, pp. 211-224. Robert Louis Stevenson School, Pebble Beach, CA.
  1980   Some Problems in the Interpretation of the Mythological Portion of the Hieroglyphic Text of the Temple of the Cross at Palenque. In *Third Palenque Round Table–1978, Part 2*, edited by Merle Greene Robertson, pp. 99-115. University of Texas Press, Austin.
  1985   The Identities of the Mythological Figures in the "Cross Group" of Inscriptions at Palenque. In *Fourth Round Table of Palenque–1980*, edited by Merle Greene Robertson & Elizabeth Benson, pp. 45-58. Pre-Columbian Art Research Institute, San Francisco, CA.

Marcus, Joyce
  1976   *Emblem and State in the Classic Maya Lowlands*. Dumbarton Oaks Research Library and Collection, Washington, D.C.
  1993   Ancient Maya Political Organization. In *Lowland Maya Civilization in the Eighth Century*, edited by Jeremy A. Sabloff & John S. Henderson, pp. 111-184. Dumbarton Oaks Research Library and Collection, Washington, D.C.

Martin, Simon and Nikolai Grube
  1995   Maya Superstates. *Archaeology* 48 (6):41-43.
  2000   *Chronicle of the Maya Kings and Queens. Deciphering the Dynasties of the Ancient Maya*. Thames & Hudson, New York.

Mathews, Peter
  1991   Classic Maya Emblem Glyphs. In *Classic Maya Political History. Hieroglyphic and Archaeological Evidence,* edited by T. Patrick Culbert, pp. 19-29. Cambridge University Press, Cambridge, U.K.

Mathews, Peter and Linda Schele
  1974   Lords of Palenque—The Glyphic Evidence. In *Primera Mesa Redonda de Palenque, Part I,* edited by Merle Greene Robertson, pp. 63-75. Robert Louis Stevenson School, Pebble Beach, CA.

Morales Cleveland, Alfonso
  1999   Palenque Cross Group Project: Ongoing Excavations Update. *Pre-Columbian Art Research Institute Newsletter* 27:1-3.

Ochoa, Lorenzo, ed.
  1978   *Estudios Preliminares sobre los Mayas de las Tierras Bajas Noroccidentales*. UNAM, Mexico, D.F.

Potter, Daniel R.
    1993   Analytical Approaches to Late Classic Maya Lithic Industries. In *Lowland Maya Civilization in the Eighth Century A.D.*, edited by Jeremy A. Sabloff and John S. Henderson, pp. 273-298. Dumbarton Oaks Research Library and Collection, Washington, D.C.

Rands, Robert L.
    1967   Ceramic Technology and Trade in the Palenque Region, Mexico. In *American Historical Anthropology, Essays in Honor of Leslie Spier*, edited by C. L Riley and W. W. Taylor, pp. 137-151. Southern Illinois University Press, Carbondale.

    1973a   The Classic Maya Collapse: Usumacinta Zone and the Northwestern Periphery. In *The Classic Maya Collapse*, edited by T.P. Culbert, pp. 165-205. University of New Mexico Press, Albuquerque.

    1973b   The Classic Maya Collapse in the Southern Maya Lowlands: Chronology. In *The Classic Maya Collapse*, edited by T. P. Culbert, pp. 43-62. University of New Mexico Press, Albuquerque.

    1974   The Ceramic Sequence at Palenque, Chiapas. In *Mesoamerican Archaeology: New Approaches*, edited by Norman Hammond, pp. 51-75. University of Texas Press, Austin.

    1977   The Rise of Classic Maya Civilization in the Northwestern Zone: Isolation and Integration. In *The Origins of Maya Civilization*, edited by R. E. W. Adams, pp. 159-180. University of New Mexico Press, Albuquerque.

    1987   Ceramic Patterns and Traditions in the Palenque Area. In *Maya Ceramics: Papers of the 1985 Maya Ceramic Conference, Part I*, edited by Prudence M. Rice and Robert J. Sharer, pp. 203-238. BAR International Series 345, Oxford, U.K.

Rands, Robert L. and Barbara C. Rands
    1957   The Ceramic Position of Palenque, Chiapas. *American Antiquity* 23:140-150.

    1959   The Incensario Complex of Palenque, Chipas. *American Antiquity* 25:225-236.

Rands, Barbara C. and Robert L. Rands
    1961   Excavations in a Cemetery at Palenque. *Estudios de Cultura Maya* 1:87-106.

Rands, Robert L. and Ronald L. Bishop
    1980   Resource Procurement Zones and Patterns of Ceramic Exchange in the Palenque Region, Mexico. In *Models and Methods in Regional Exchange*, edited by Robert Fry, pp. 19-46. Society for American Archaeology Papers 1, Washington, D.C.

    2003   The Dish-Plate Tradition at Palenque: Continuity and Change. In *Patterns & Process: A Festschrift in Honor of Dr. Edward V. Sayre*, edited by Lambertus van Zelst, pp. 109-132. Smithsonian Center for Materials Research & Education, Suitland, MD.

Rice, Prudence M.
    1987   Lowland Maya Pottery Production in the Late Classic Period. In *Maya Ceramics: Papers from the 1985 Ceramic Conference, Part II*, edited by Prudence M. Rice and Robert J. Sharer, pp. 76-85. BAR International Series 345, Oxford, U.K.

Riese, Berthold
 1978   La inscripción del Monumento 6 de Tortuguero. *Estudios de Cultura Maya* 11:187-198.

Ruz Lhuillier, Alberto
 1952   Exploraciones en Palenque: 1950-1951. *Anales del INAH* 5:25-66 .
 1955   Exploraciones en Palenque: 1952. *Anales del INAH* 6:79-110.
 1958   Exploraciones Arqueológicas en Palenque: 1953-1956. *Anales del INAH* 10:69-299.
 1962   Exploraciones Arqueológicas en Palenque: 1957. *Anales del INAH* 14:35-90.
 1973   *El Templo de las Inscripciones*. INAH, Mexico, D.F.

Schele, Linda
 1976   Accession Iconography of Chan-Bahlum in the Group of the Cross at Palenque. In *The Art, Iconography, and Dynastic History of Palenque, Part III. Proceedings of the Segunda Mesa Redonda de Palenque*, edited by Merle Greene Robertson, pp. 9-34. Robert Louis Stevenson School, Pebble Beach, CA.

 1978   Genealogical Documentation in the Tri-Figure Panels at Palenque. *Tercera Mesa Redonda de Palenque*, edited by Merle Greene Robertson, pp. 41-70. Pre-Columbian Art Research Institute, Pebble Beach, CA.

 1986   Architectural Development and Political History at Palenque. In *City-States of the Maya: Art and Architecture*, edited by Elizabeth P. Benson, pp. 110-138. Rocky Mountain Institute for Pre-Columbian Studies, Denver, CO.

 1991   An Epigraphic History of the Western Maya Region. In *Classic Maya Political History: Hieroglyphic and Archaeological Evidence*, edited by T. Patrick Culbert, pp. 72-101. Cambridge University Press, Cambridge, U.K.

Schele, Linda and David A. Freidel
 1990   *A Forest of Kings: The Untold Story of the Ancient Maya*. William Morrow, New York.

Schele, Linda and Peter Mathews
 1993   *The Dynastic History of Palenque. The Proceedings of the Maya Hieroglyphic Workshop*. Transcribed by P. Wanyerka, University of Texas, Austin.
 1998   *The Code of Kings*. Scribner's, New York.

Smith, Michael E.
 1992   *Archaeological Research at Aztec-Period Rural Sites in Morelos, Mexico, Vol. I*. University of Pittsburgh Memoirs in Latin American Archaeology No. 4, Pittsburgh, PA.

Tourtellot, Gair
 1983   An Assessment of Classic Maya Household Composition. In *Prehistoric Settlement Patterns,* edited by Evon Z. Vogt and Richard M. Leventhal, pp. 35-54. University of New Mexico Press, Albuquerque, NM.

 1990   Population Estimates for Preclassic and Classic Seibal, Peten. In *Precolumbian Population History in the Maya Lowlands*, edited by T. Patrick Colbert and Don S. Rice, pp. 83-102. University of New Mexico Press, Albuquerque.

West, R.C., et al.
 1969   *The Tabasco Lowlands of Southern Mexico*. Coastal Studies Series 27, Lousiana State University, Baton Rouge.

Chapter 6

Indicators of Urbanism at Palenque

Edwin L. Barnhart

In their 1989 paper "The Mesoamerican Urban Tradition," William Sanders and David Webster drew distinctions between Maya and Central Mexican cities, identifying the former as "regal-ritual" centers and the later as "administrative" centers (classification system after Fox [1977]). In a rebuttal paper, Chase, Chase, and Haviland (1989) used data from Tikal and Caracol to argue that Sanders and Webster had underestimated the urban qualities of Classic Maya centers. Despite a solo article in which Webster conceded that Classic Maya society seemed composed of autonomous city-states (Webster 1997), Webster and Sanders published a new paper in 2001 that continued their original stance in the debate. There, they took their distinctions a step further, comparing Copan against Tenochtitlan and ultimately suggesting that the Central Mexican cities were so far advanced beyond their Maya counterparts that they "should probably never have applied the word city even in a qualified sense" to the centers of the ancient Maya (Webster & Sanders 2001). On the one hand, they are correct in claiming that Central Mexican cities were much more urbanized than those built by the Maya. On the other hand, their assertion that Classic Maya centers should not be called cities is overstated. That the ancient Maya did not reach the same degree of urbanization as Central Mexico is insufficient justification to remove their centers from the category of city. Central Mexico's level of urbanism was more intense; that point Webster and Sanders have abundantly proved. Their approach to this question, however, has turned what should be a debate about differences in social organization into a challenge for Mayanists to prove that urbanism existed among the ancient Maya.

Despite what Central Mexico may have achieved above and beyond the Maya, Chase, Chase, and Haviland (1989) successfully demonstrated that both Tikal and Caracol had urban qualities. Studies like Smyth and Dore's 1994 publication

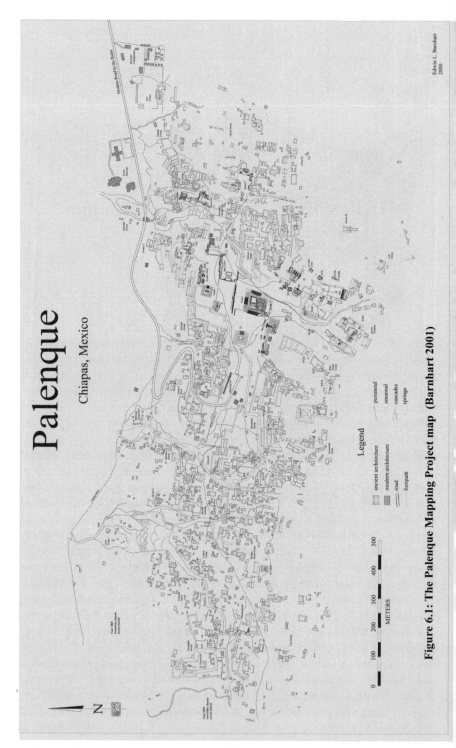

Palenque

Chiapas, Mexico

Legend

ancient architecture
modern architecture
road
footpath

perennial
seasonal
cascades
springs

METERS
0   100   200   300   400   500

Edwin L. Barnhart
2000

Figure 6.1: The Palenque Mapping Project map (Barnhart 2001)

108

"Maya Urbanism" have since continued to show urbanism existed among the Maya. Even before the 1990s debate had begun scholars had argued the case of Maya urbanism (Andrews 1975; Marcus 1983). Whether one defines urbanism by the most basic criteria first suggested by Wirth (1938)—(1) large population size, (2) dense population nucleation, and (3) high internal heterogeneity—or by Childe's (1950) expanded criteria list including items like intensive agriculture, monumental architecture, trade and writing, or even by the additional criteria suggested in Webster and Sanders' most recent paper, the major Classic Maya centers clearly exhibit urban qualities, albeit to varying degrees.

This chapter seeks to demonstrate that Palenque's settlement exhibits urban qualities and by proxy is best defined as a "city." Using a combination of data collected by the recently completed Palenque Mapping Project (Barnhart 2001) and that of various Palenque excavation projects, some of the more common characteristics used to define urbanism will be reviewed for their presence or absence at the site. Data from other well-documented Maya centers will then be compared as a way to assess the relative intensity of the urbanism that existed at Palenque. The following will demonstrate that Palenque was one of the most urbanized cities built by ancient Maya and that it possessed some of the urban characteristics argued by Webster and Sanders (2001) to have been exclusive in Mesoamerica to Central Mexican centers.

Settlement Density/Nucleation

The Palenque Mapping Project (PMP) recorded 1,481 structures and sixteen linear kilometers of terracing in a 2.2-km^2 area (Fig. 6.1). The area covered by the PMP should be considered Palenque's site core, not the core and periphery combined for the site's total settlement area. Even more so than Tikal's core bounded by bajos and earthworks (Haviland 1970) or Copan's alluvial valley floor (Willey et al. 1978), Palenque's plateau location provides a clear boundary for its site core area. However, unlike Tikal and Copan whose peripheral settlement drops, but is still significant, Palenque's immediate periphery has an extremely low settlement density, almost negligible compared to its core settlement area (Liendo, Chapter 5).

The mountainsides surrounding Palenque were too steep for building and the plains to the north were seasonally inundated (Fig. 6.2). Blom and La Farge (1926-27) estimated the site's settlement to extend 16 km^2 around its center. While it is true that ruined structures are found at a distance from the center, they are so infrequent and isolated that it would be misleading to compare them to the peripheral settlements of Tikal or Copan. The PMP map and informal reconnaissance further indicate that Palenque is at most 3 km^2 of site core surrounded by small pockets of peripheral settlement. There was simply a lack of habitable land around Palenque's center, a circumstance Carneiro (1970) termed "geographic circumscription" in his treatise on the origins of the state. Attracted by a rich resource

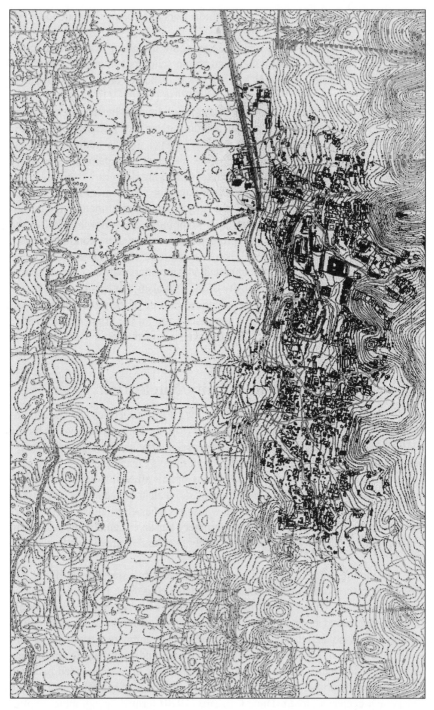

Figure 6.2: Area topography map, overlaid by the PMP map

Table 6.1
Core Area Urban Settlement Densities at Selected Classic Maya Sites
(Adapted from Sharer 1994 and Rice and Culbert 1990)

site	core area (km²)	Structures / km²
Copan	0.6	1,449
Palenque	2.2	673
Dzibilchaltun	19.0	442
Caracol	2.2	300
Siebal	1.6	275
Tikal	9.0	235
Becan	3.0	222
Sayil	2.4	220
Quirigua	3.0	128
Belize Valley	5.0	118
Uaxactun	2.0	112
Nohmul	4.0	58

base (to be discussed in later sections) Palenque's inhabitants densely settled the limited land area of the plateau. The scale of Palenque's settlement density, with almost no separation between buildings, could not have been achieved without economic coordination and overarching political organization.

While much work remains to be done on the chronology of Palenque's construction sequence, most excavation evidence to date suggests that Palenque, similar to many Classic sites, reached its population peak in the Late Classic period. For the purposes of this discussion, we will assume that the majority of Palenque's structures were occupied during that time period. Table 6.1 compares an estimated Palenque Late Classic maximum settlement density with data reported from contemporary centers. The results indicate Palenque was second only to Copan in degree of community nucleation.

Table 6.2
Comparison of Population Estimates at Selected Classic Maya Sites
(adapted from Sharer 1994 and Rice & Culbert 1990)

site	core area (km²)	peak population	population/km²
Copan	0.6	5,797 - 9,464	9,662 -15,773
Sayil	3.4	8,148 - 9,900	2,396 - 2,912
Palenque	2.2	4,147 - 6,220	1,885 - 2,827
Komchen	2.0	2,500 - 3,000	1,250 - 1,500
Siebal	1.6	1,644 - 1,028	
Santa Rita	5.0	4,958 - 8,722	992 - 1,744
Tikal	9.0	8,300 - 922	
Tayasal	8.0	6,861 -10,400	858 - 1,300
Caracol	2.2	1,200 - 1,600	545 - 727

Population Size

Palenque's site core population density appears to have been quite high (Table 6.2). However, the lack of substantial peripheral settlement renders its overall population size small compared to other major Classic period centers. Current evidence of core settlement at Palenque supports no more than 6220 people at its population apex. Although continued survey of Palenque's scant periphery could increase that number, Palenque's overall population never attained the levels estimated for sites like Tikal and Caracol. Small population size has traditionally been one of the key attributes used to refute the existence of urbanism among the Classic Maya (Sanders & Webster 1989; Webster & Sanders 2001). Even Copan's dense surrounding population is not considered urban because its small, 1-km^2 coverage falls short of what is deemed urban. However, if the criterion of settlement density were accepted, one could not interpret many ancient Sumerian settlements as urban city either. As Andrews (1975) points out, Sumerian cities typically had populations ranging between 7,000–20,000 people. Based on this cross-cultural comparison, I would argue that while community size intensifies urbanism, nucleation and social diversity are better criteria for judging its presence or absence within ancient settlements.

Social Diversity

Social diversity is a key component of the urban setting but can be difficult to detect in an abandoned community. Archaeologists typically look for differences in housing types and burial goods, as well as evidence of occupational specialization through the presence of craft workshops. In Palenque, the great variation in building sizes and patio arrangements supports generalized assumptions of Classic Maya social diversity (Adams 1970; Becker 1973; Haviland & Moholy-Nagy 1992). The many burials excavated by Blom in the 1920s showed great diversity in accompanying goods (Blom & La Farge 1926-1927). As for craft workshops, however, only two documented areas have been thus far detected archaeologically; an incensario workshop area found by Rands (1974) approximately one kilometer east of the Palace and a possible masonry workshop found in Group H during the 1998 season of the PMP. A third example may have existed at Temple XVI where INAH excavations found figurine molds and unfinished figurines (Marken & González, Chapter 8; Rands, personal communication 2002). Indeed this is a valid point of the Webster and Sanders argument; there is little evidence of craft production within the larger Classic Maya centers. At Tikal only two ceramic workshops (Chase et al. 1989) have been documented. At Sayil, only one ceramic workshop was found (Smyth & Dore 1994). Webster and Sanders (2001) cite Copan specifically as an example of a site that has been intensively surveyed and yet produced very little evidence for craft specialization. A possible explanation for this pattern is presented in the conclusion of this chapter.

Subsistence

As Webster and Sanders correctly qualify, a community with a significant portion of its population separated from farming activities needs the support of an intensive agricultural system. Rodrigo Liendo (1999, Chapter 5) has identified substantial areas of irrigation canals and agricultural terracing in the plains directly below Palenque's plateau. Some of those terraces, such as the ones within and to the east of the present-day Mayabell Campground, were mapped during the PMP survey

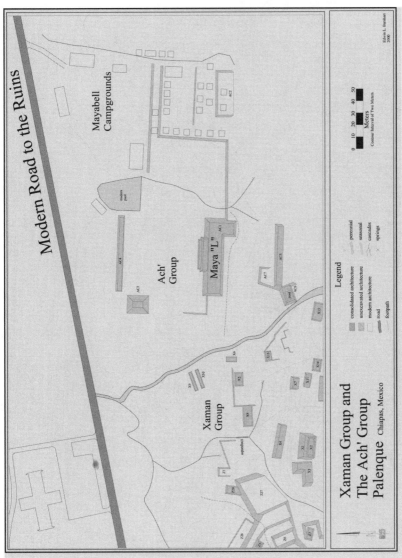

Figure 6.3: The Ach' Group and connected terracing

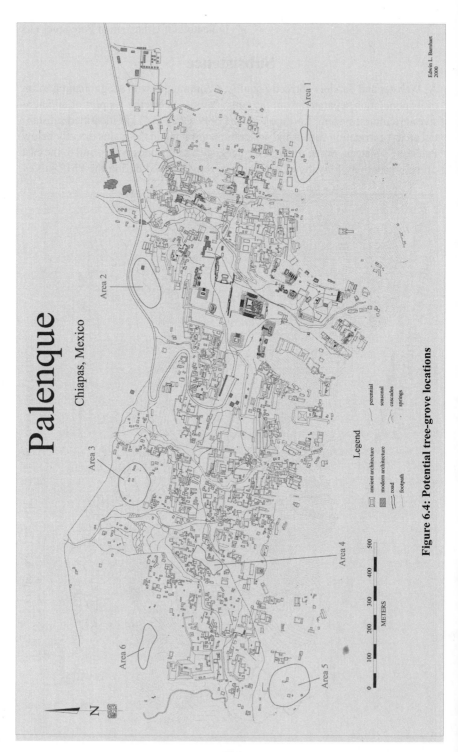

Palenque

Chiapas, Mexico

Area 1

Area 2

Area 3

Area 4

Area 5

Area 6

N

Legend

▨ ancient architecture
▨ modern architecture
〜 road
〜 footpath

— perennial
▨ seasonal
〜 cascades
○ springs

0 100 200 300 400 500
METERS

Edwin L. Barnhart
2000

Figure 6.4: Potential tree-grove locations

114

Figure 6.5: Reconstruction of the "Maya L" (drawing by H. Hurst)

(Fig. 6.3). The terraces are wide, gently sloped and do not have structures built upon them. They also connect to the only off-plateau public plaza at Palenque, the Ach' Group. The "Maya L", the dominant structure of that 80 m by 80 m plaza, has a distinctly public architectural form (see Fig. 6.5).

This building has a 30 m wide staircase that leads 6 m up to a 50 m long, L-shaped superstructure. The front face had fourteen entry points into the structure. Fifty column stubs are still visible on the superstructure surface. Its direct association with agricultural terracing and irrigation canals makes it logical to assume it was involved in subsistence activities as well. Its form and placement at the transition zone between the intensively cultivated plains and the core settlement area suggests a farmers market, a co-op, or perhaps even a surplus redistribution center. This latter function would have been needed to support a large, socially diverse community separated from the responsibilities of agricultural production. There is also reason to believe that tree groves were cultivated within Palenque's core settlement. In modern and historic times, Tabasco and northern Chiapas have been centers for the arboriculture industry. The region is known for cacao production in particular. At Tikal, Haviland (1970) proposed that breadfruit trees grown within and around patio groups supplemented its inhabitant's diets. At Sayil, Smyth and Dore (1994) used soil analysis and aerial excavation techniques to detect what they called "in-fields" or large garden plots within the core settlement. It is proposed here that a similar subsistence strategy was employed at Palenque. Fig. 6.4 demonstrates six areas free of ancient structures. As noted during the course of the PMP survey, these same areas have sporadic tree groves within their boundaries. Although we cannot know whether the same groves have been there since antiquity, but it is clear that the area can support groves.

Palenque's ancient name was *Lakam Ha'* meaning "Big Water." The glyph translated as **LAKAM**, however, is actually an iconographic representation of a tree (Fig. 6.6). Its translation is based on phonetic substitutions found at other sites (Stuart 1996). If Palenque, as hypothesized here, was using fruiting trees for subsistence and as trade items then it might give rise to a rethinking of why the hieroglyph **LAKAM**, meaning "big" is iconographically represented as a bent over tree.

LAKAM-HA'

**Figure 6.6:
Palenque's toponym for
its central precinct**

Wrapping around Pakal's sarcophagus are relief carvings representing a sequence of hieroglyphically named royal ancestors that had come before him (Fig. 6.7). Each ancestor is depicted emerging from a fruiting tree, trees with leaves very much like the **LAKAM** of Palenque's toponym. As noted by Merle Greene Robertson (1983) and McAnany (1995), each tree has a different kind of fruit. In McAnany's interpretation the trees symbolize the longevity of the royal lineage. Perhaps the trees, while symbolizing the lineage, also emphasize one of Palenque's most valuable resources, fruiting tree groves. Fruit, a renewable and to many regions exotic resource, could have been a major source of wealth and its perishable nature would make it virtually undetectable in the archaeological record. In fact, all conquest period accounts of Mesoamerican markets list agricultural and perishable products as the majority of traded items.

Public Works

Typically in the Maya region terracing encountered outside major Maya centers is determined to be agricultural in function. Caracol's terracing is perhaps the Maya world's most expansive example (Chase et al. 1989). At Palenque, the majority of terracing appears instead to have been employed to stabilize hillside residential sectors. Residential complexes both east and west of Palenque's ceremonial center contain residential terracing. Most complexes contain multiple terraces running over 100 m in length. In total, over sixteen linear kilometers of terraces have been documented at Palenque. Interestingly, hundreds of terraces were neither ritual nor agricultural in function; they were built to facilitate residential settlement of Palenque's hillsides and to protect structures on the plateau from soil erosion.

© M. Greene Robertson

**Figure 6.7: The west side of Pakal's sarcophagus
(drawing by M. Greene Robertson 1983)**

In other words, major community labor and material resources were spent to increase habitable land so that a sizable population could live within the site core.

The Xinil Pa' Group alone contains over a kilometer of interconnected terracing (Fig. 6.8). The scale of these terraces required the supervision of skilled architects, engineers, and surveyors as well as an organized labor force of a size

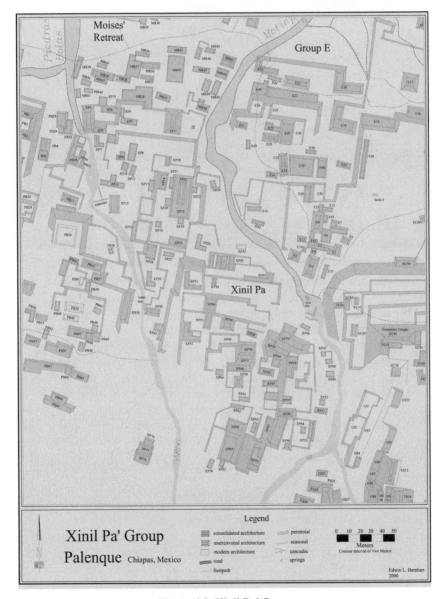

Figure 6.8: Xinil Pa' Group

Figure 6.9: Intact terrace segment in the Encantado Group

beyond that of a single extended family. The effectiveness of their erosion control and the sophistication of their building techniques are testified by the fact that the terraces have survived despite a millennium of rainy seasons (Fig. 6.9). Palenque's terraces had to withstand the forces of intense rainy season water flow down the hillsides as well as direct the water away from habitation zones.

Another aspect of Palenque's settlement zone that should be termed "public works" is its intensive water management system, found not only in the central precinct but in the outlying neighborhoods as well. This elaborate system of drains, canals, and aqueducts was designed to prevent flooding on the plateau while simultaneously providing running water to residential zones and a year-round supply of water to the agricultural land in the plains below (see French, Chapter 7).

Conclusion

Webster and Sanders (2001) assert that Teotihuacan and Tenochtitlan were able to build urban infrastructure and monumental city centers through an accumulation of wealth generated by production and commerce. If Palenque did not have these elements, how then did it accumulate its obvious wealth? The answer may lie in its available natural resources. At Teotihuacan, stone products were the most abundant resources. The workshops recorded manufactured mostly stone, jewelry, and ceramic products (Millon 1974). The evidence from the Tenochtitlan market comes primarily from conquest period accounts and the few surviving native texts, not from archaeological research. Without written accounts, there would be no proof of perishable food products in Atzec markets that made up the majority of Tenochtitlan's traded goods, as Webster and Sanders note. Palenque had a lush, tropical environment that offered mainly perishable items, flora and fauna based resources. If Palenque's primary trade items were perishable, what would one expect to find archaeologically? The answer is at best organic residues, detectable only through in-depth soil testing. Colha, a Classic Maya site in Belize, is situated near a considerably large deposit of chert. As a result, there exists evidence of the massive commercial production of stone tools (Hester & Shafer 1984). Why would we expect durable product workshops in areas that had few durable resources? Palenque's primary wealth generators were likely perishable goods, things not detectable through traditional archaeological excavation.

In their conclusion, Webster and Sanders (2001) state that one of the key urban characteristics lacking in Maya centers is evidence of city planning. They cite Tenochtitlan as having actively recruited inhabitants from surrounding regions and accommodated them by building urban infrastructure in the form of streets, markets, canals, aqueducts, dikes, and wetland field systems. Copan is then cited as the counterexample, having no urban infrastructure or intensive agricultural systems and hence no ability to recruit population to its settlement core. Palenque, in the form of its "public works," exhibits exactly the kind of recruitment-oriented urban infrastructure Webster and Sanders did not find in Copan. Sixteen linear kilometers of terracing were put in place with the express purpose of opening more habitable land within the city's core. Major communal resources were expended well outside of the central precinct in primarily residential areas of the site denoting a civic-mindedness rarely evidenced among the Classic period Maya. Extensive water management features not only contained Palenque's six perennial streams but also redistributed a precious resource throughout the community. The agricultural terraces and canal systems in the plains below the Palenque were clearly efforts to intensify agricultural production and the Maya L appears dedicated to connecting that production zone to the densely settled plateau above.

In sum, Palenque had a moderately large population that, despite an abundant local resource base, chose to settle in an extremely nucleated pattern. Community leaders facilitated that settlement density by building on extensive urban infrastructure. By at least the Late Classic period, Palenque's plateau was almost completely covered by settlement and evidence suggests a population supported by an intensive agricultural system maintained in the fertile plains below. Considering all these urban characteristics, added to its massive central precinct and over 300-year written history, it seems implausible to call Palenque anything less than a city.

References

Adams, Richard E. W.
  1970   Suggested Classic period occupational specialization in the Southern Maya Lowlands. In *Monographs & Papers in Maya Archaeology* 61, edited by William R. Bullard, pp. 487-502. Peabody Museum of Archaeology & Ethnography, Cambridge, MA.

Andrews, George F.
  1975   *Maya Cities: Placemaking and Urbanization.* University of Oklahoma Press, Norman.

Barnhart, Edwin L.
  2001   The Palenque Mapping Project: Settlement and Urbanism at an Ancient Maya City. Unpublished Ph.D. dissertation, University of Texas, Austin.

Becker, Marshall J.
  1973   Archaeological Evidence for Occupational Specialization among the Classic Period Maya at Tikal, Guatemala. *American Antiquity* 38(4):396-406.

Blom, Franz and O. La Farge
  1926-27 *Tribes and Temples: A Record of the Expedition to Middle America Conducted by the Tulane University of Louisiana in 1925, Vols. I & II.* Tulane University of Louisiana, New Orleans, LA.

Carniero, Robert
  1970   A Theory of the Origin of the State. *Science*, Vol. 169:733-783.

Chase, Diane Z., Arlen F. Chase, and William A. Haviland
  1989   The Classic Maya City: Reconsidering the Mesoamerican Urban Tradition. *American Anthropologist* 91(3):499-506.

Childe, V. Gordon
  1950   *The Urban Revolution. Town Planning Review*, Vol. XXI, pp. 3-17.

Fox, Richard
  1977   *Urban Anthropology.* Prentice Hall, Englewood Cliffs, NJ.

Greene Robertson, Merle
  1983   *The Sculpture of Palenque, Vol. 1: The Temple of the Inscriptions.* Princeton University Press, Princeton, NJ.

Haviland, William
  1970   Tikal, Guatemala and Mesoamerican Urbanism. *World Archaeology* 2:186-198.

Haviland, William A. and Hattula Moholy-Nagy
  1992   Distinguishing the High and Mighty from the Hoi Polloi at Tikal, Guatemala. In *Mesoamerican Elites: An Archaeological Assessment*, edited by Diane Z. Chase and Arlen F. Chase, pp. 50-60. University of Oklahoma Press, Norman.

Hester, Thomas and Harry Shafer
  1984   Exploitation of Chert Resources by the Ancient Maya of Northern Belize. *World Archaeology* 16(2):157-173.

Liendo Stuardo, Rodrigo
  1999   The Organization of Agricultural Production at a Maya Center, Settlement Patterns in the Palenque Region, Chiapas, Mexico. Unpublished Ph.D. dissertation, University of Pittsburgh, PA.

Marcus, Joyce
1983 On the Nature of the Mesoamerican City. In *Prehistoric Settlement Patterns*, edited by Evan Z.Vogt and Richard M. Leventhal, pp. 195-242. University of New Mexico Press and Peabody Museum of Archaeology and Ethnology, Harvard University, Cambridge, MA.

McAnany, Patricia A.
1995 *Living with the Ancestors: Kinship and Kingship in Ancient Maya Society.* University of Texas Press, Austin.

Millon, Rene
1974 *The Study of Urbanism at Teotihuacan, Mexico, Vol. 1.* University of Texas Press, Austin.

Rands, Robert L.
1974 The Ceramic Sequence at Palenque, Chiapas. In *Mesoamerican Archaeology, New Approaches*, edited by Norman Hammond, pp. 51-76. University of Texas Press, Austin.

Rice, Don S. and T. Patrick Culbert
1990 Historical Contexts for Population Reconstruction in the Maya Lowlands. In *Precolumbian Population History in the Maya Lowlands*, edited by T. Patrick Culbert and Don S. Rice, pp. 1-36. University of New Mexico Press, Albuquerque.

Sanders, William T. and David Webster
1989 The Mesoamerican Urban Tradition. *American Anthropologist* 90:521-546.

Sharer, Robert
1994 *The Ancient Maya.* 5th Ed. Stanford University Press, Palo Alto, CA.

Smyth, Michael and Christopher Dore
1994 Maya Urbanism. *National Geographic Research & Exploration*, 10(1):38-55.

Stuart, David
1996 *Kings of Stone: A Consideration of Stelae in Maya Ritual and Representation.* RES 29/30:149-171.

Webster, David
1997 City-States of the Maya. In *The Archaeology of City-States*, edited by Deborah L. Nichols and Thomas H. Charlton, pp. 135-154. Smithsonian Institute Press, Washington, D.C.

Webster, David and William T. Sanders
2001 La Antigua Ciudad Mesoamericana: Teoria y Concepto. In *Reconstruyendo la Cuidad Maya: El Urbanismo en Las Sociedades Antiguas*, edited by Andreas Cuidad Ruiz, M. Josefa Iglesias Ponce De Leon, and M. Carmen Martinez Martinez, pp. 34-64. Sociedad Espanola De Estudios Mayas, Pub. 6, Madrid.

Willey, Gordon R., Richard Leventhal, and William L. Fash
1978 Maya Settlement in the Copan Valley. *Archaeology* 31(4):32-43

Wirth, Louis
1938 Urbanism as a Way of Life. *American Journal of Sociology* 44:3-24.

Chapter 7

Creating Space through Water Management at the Classic Maya Site of Palenque, Chiapas

Kirk D. French

Many water management features were identified during the survey conducted by the Palenque Mapping Project, directed by Edwin Barnhart and under the auspices of Mexico's Instituto Nacional de Antropología e Historia (INAH), the Foundation for the Advancement of Mesoamerican Studies, Inc. (FAMSI), and the Pre-Columbian Art Research Institute (PARI). These features included aqueducts, bridges, dams, drains, walled channels, and pools. The Maya built such features in order to manage the perennial waterways located throughout the site. With nine separate watercourses found in Palenque, we can say that water was widely incorporated into the city plan. The presence of such copious rushing water enabled the Palencanos to create a unique system of water management anomalous to that of other Maya lowland sites (French 2000, 2001; Scarborough & Gallopin 1991).

The focus of this chapter is to reveal the elaborate water management system found in Palenque. What functions did features such as the subterranean aqueducts serve? I shall demonstrate that many of Palenque's water management features were multifunctional and highly sophisticated.

Flood and erosion control are two of the functions performed by the aqueducts. As water descended from the steep mountains and entered the level plaza, flooding along with erosion would have been common. Maudslay (1889-1902) visited Palenque in the dry season, prior to the refurbishing of the Palace aqueduct's entrance, and stated that the main plaza completely flooded three times during his stay. Today, with the maintenance of the aqueduct system, the main plaza is unlikely to flood even during the rainy season. By forcing the stream below the plaza floor, the aqueducts act as storm drains.

Built on a narrow escarpment surrounded by steep hills, sheer cliffs, and deep streams, Palenque suffered a scarcity of livable terrain. The flat topography that did exist in the site was often burdened with natural waterways. In response, the residents of Palenque constructed several subterranean aqueducts and covered preexisting streams. By doing so, they increased the size of their plazas and were able to create surface areas large enough to maintain normal civic life within a major Maya center.

The importance of the Pre-Columbian plaza is revealed through a comprehensive examination of plazas, both archaeologically and ethnographically (Low 2000). The ethnographic information supplies an ethnoarchaeological foundation by demonstrating the importance of plazas today in Latin American communities. This chapter exemplifies a method of interpreting the past by combining water management issues with architectural functions within an ancient Maya community.

Flood Control

Flood control was one function performed by the aqueducts at Palenque. From August to November, Palenque receives 45 percent (977 mm) of its annual rainfall (SARA 1999) (Fig. 7.1). This substantial concentration in precipitation causes the streams in the mountains to expand in size as they rush swiftly downhill toward the level escarpment. The abrupt change in declination causes the streams to slow, forcing the water level to rise and flood the plaza and residential areas. As stated earlier, Maudslay (1889-1902) noted the frequency of plaza flooding at Palenque during the dry season, prior to the current maintenance of the Palace aqueduct (OT-A1) (Figs. 7.2 & 7.3). His fieldwork was conducted between February and April, when the average rainfall reaches only 159 mm. Prior to 1950, the entrance to the Palace aqueduct was completely collapsed, causing the Otolum to flow a few meters to the east in a new streambed. Maudslay's account, along with the damaged entrance, provides a view of how the Main Plaza would function during heavy rains without the assistance of the aqueduct. By forcing the flowing water of the streams below the surface of the plaza, the city planners were able to decrease the risks of plaza and residential flooding.

Erosion

Another problem Palenque's city planners must have faced, along with seasonal flooding, was erosion. Without proper water control features in place, erosion would have been a crisis, not just for the elite but also for the larger number of urban residents living outside the city's center. In order to minimize land loss and residential disruption from erosion, a partial canalization of all nine waterways was implemented. Construction of these walled channels and/or aqueducts outside of the center suggests what Barnhart (2001, Chapter 6) refers to as "public works." These public works encompass all monumental constructions that served the needs of the general populous or the community at large. The sophistication of

Month	mm of Rainfall
Jan	88.9
Feb	55.6
Mar	55.6
Apr	48.1
May	185.2
Jun	307
Jul	188.9
Aug	244.4
Sep	440.7
Oct	292.6
Nov	144.4
Dec	114.8
TOTAL	2166.2

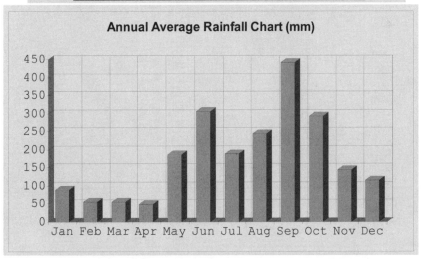

Figure 7.1: Palenque's Annual Average Rainfall Charts 1985-1995

the water management features is evidenced by the fact that the majority of them are still intact and functioning after more than a millenium of rainy seasons.

Creating Space

Palenque's control of nine separate waterways, generated from fifty-six recorded springs, provided an ample supply of water for an expanding population. With this great quantity of water came an unforgiving landscape consisting of steep hills, sheer cliffs, and deep streams posing challenges for city growth. Thus, the obstacle for the city planners of Palenque would not be water insufficiency, but rather a paucity of habitable terrain. This adversity of inhospitable land led the ancient Palencanos to develop the second most densely populated city in the Maya

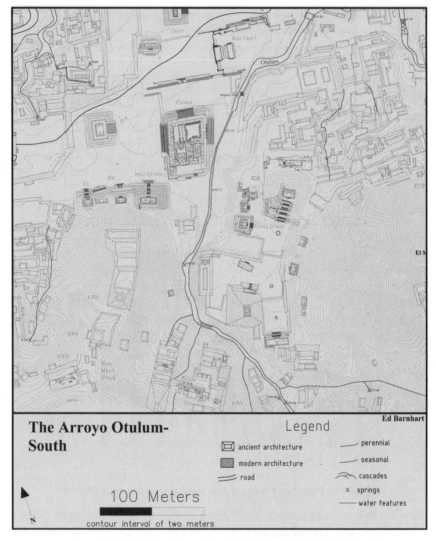

Figure 7.2: The south Otolum stream
(courtesy Edwin L. Barnhart and the Palenque Mapping Project)

region (Barnhart 2001, Chapter 6), along with a phenomenal subterranean aqueduct system.

Although many of the site's residential groups were constructed on the terraced hillsides, the plazas and public centers were created atop a narrow limestone escarpment measuring approximately 1.7 km east-west by 260 m north-south. While the escarpment does continue further to the west, evidence of Pre-Hispanic settlement declines abruptly. The constricted limestone shelf provided limited

**Figure 7.3: An interior view of Palenque's best-preserved aqueduct, OT-A1
(photo by K. P. French)**

space for such occasions as religious or political ceremonies, public markets, or city expansion.

The majority of civic activities in Mesoamerica occurred in large, level, open spaces located within the city's center—plazas. These areas were designed for public use and provided a setting for everyday urban life where daily interactions, economic exchange, and informal conversations occurred, and created a socially meaningful space within the city (Low 2000). These communal interplays are thought to be the threads that create the natural "human whole" (Arensberg 1961; Redfield 1955) that serves as a society's principal unit of biological and cultural reproduction (Yaeger & Canuto 2000: 2). Murdock (1949) also strongly emphasized the importance of interaction among community members, claiming it as a necessary condition of the community's existence.

The modern Latin American plaza can provide insight into the Pre-Columbian plaza via ethnoarchaeology. Many scholars share the belief that the grid-plan town with a central plaza found throughout Latin America is a European creation, but Low (2000) presents suggestive evidence that counters this assumption. She explains that the redesign of Spanish cities in grid-plan during the mid-sixteenth century under the rule of Philip II was in part stimulated by the urban-design experiments of the New World. By overlooking the Pre-Columbian architectural and archaeological record, many historians have constructed a Eurocentric view of the evolution of the New World urban form. Town centers of European cities such as Córdoba and Madrid, rebuilt many years after the colonization process began, mimic the design of the newly created plazas of the Spanish-American New World. Low's implication that the colonial plaza and grid-plan design found in Latin America was more an indigenous than Spanish creation only adds validity to the ethnographic research of plazas as ethnoarchaeological data.

Today, throughout Latin America, plazas are locations within cities where communal activities take place. The church as well as the government offices of a city are typically found on the borders of the plaza, where the majority of public religious and political gatherings occur. The design of most Mesoamerican plazas exhibits a similar layout, where the grandest temples coupled with a palace or elite residential structure characteristically create the borders of the plaza.

At Palenque, contributing to the dilemma of building on its confined plateau were the spring-fed streams that naturally marred and divided the landscape. Andrews (1975) claimed that this irregular natural terrain caused many problems for the city's builders, who were forced to do a considerable amount of reshaping of the existing ground form to maintain a semblance of visual order in the overall layout of the city. To simultaneously control flooding and erosion and also bridge the divided areas to expand civic space, the Maya of Palenque covered portions of the pre-existing streams by constructing elaborate subterranean aqueducts that guided the stream beneath plaza floors. The two plazas of concern here are the Picota Plaza (Figs. 7.4 & 7.5) and the Main Plaza.

The Picota Plaza, located 1 km due west of the site center, contains approximately 1,477 m^2 of surface area and houses the Picota stream beneath its floor. In order to estimate how much surface space was gained by channeling the stream underground, the average width of the Picota stream was calculated by systematically measuring its width where canalization was absent; an average width of 7.23 m was established. This figure was then multiplied by 47 m, the length of the Picota aqueduct (P-A1) (Fig. 7.6), to arrive at an estimate of 340 m^2 of surface area created by covering the stream (Fig. 7.7). The construction of P-A1 allowed the Maya of Palenque to increase their plaza size by 23 percent (Figs. 7.4 & 7.5). Apart from plaza expansion, the absence of the aqueduct would have prevented the construction of the structure and staircase built on the south side.

Main plazas are one of the most important elements of a Maya center. The counterweight to mass is void, and the Maya valued the plazas as much as the structures that surrounded them (Andrews 1975; Miller 1999: 23). Larger buildings demand larger plazas, so the plazas required expansion as a city grew and

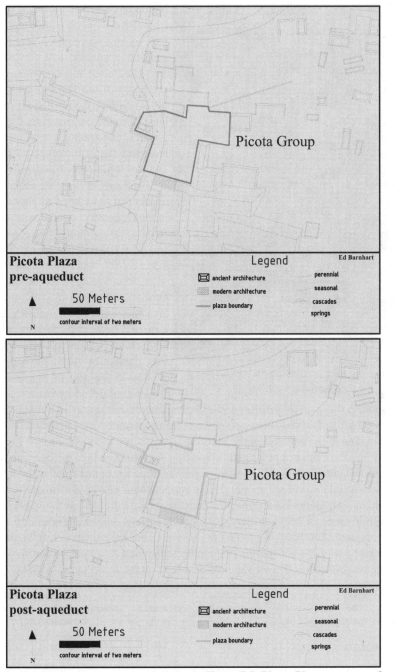

Figure 7.4: Picota Plaza, preaqueduct (top) Figure 7.5: Picota Plaza, post aquaduct
(courtesy Barnhart and the PMP)

Figure 7.6: A view of P-A1's exit (photo by K. French)

buildings became larger. Due to the irregularities of Palenque's topography, expansion required inventiveness.

The Palace was constructed on the banks of the Otolum stream in order to utilize the open space on its west side. On the east side, the city planners constructed a subterranean aqueduct beneath the plaza floor. Due to variations in materials and architectural styles, the aqueduct appears to have been implemented in four separate stages, with each stage creating more space to the south side of the plaza (Figs. 7.8 & 7.9).

By covering 155 m of the Otolum, only 971 m² of surface area was actually created, which is a mere 3 percent of the total plaza size. But 6,547 m² of surface area was gained by bridging together the area to the east of the Otolum. The land produced by the aqueduct, along with the level terrain east of the Otolum, increased the size of the Main Plaza by 23 percent. Today, Palenque's Main Plaza is partially divided by the Otolum stream, due to the collapse of the Palace aqueduct's southern portion.

From the evidence presented here, it appears that the Maya of Palenque constructed a unique water management system in order to control erosion and flooding while simultaneously creating more surface area. The cost of implementing a system such as the subterranean aqueducts speaks volumes on the importance of public space in Maya society. Palenque's water management is in dire need of more attention. Next, we intend to pursue further investigation into the water systems by way of a test-pitting program in and around Palenque's water features. An endeavor such as this would only shed light on the subject.

plaza	plaza size (m²)	average arroya width (m)	aqueduct length (m)	land generated (m²}	% increase	land gained opposite streamside (m²)	total % gained
Picota	1,477	7.23	47	340	23	na	23
Main	33,421	6.27	154	971	3	6,547	23

Figure 7.7: Plaza expansion calculations

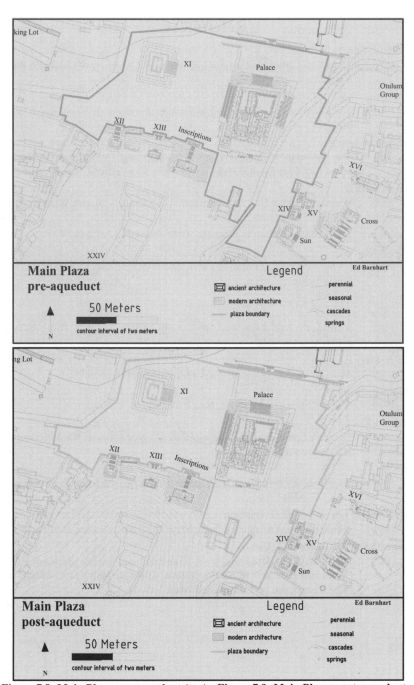

Figure 7.8: Main Plaza, preaqueduct (top). Figure 7.9: Main Plaza, post-aqueduct (courtesy Barnhart and the PMP)

References

Andrews, George F.
1975   *Maya Cities: Placemaking and Urbanization.* University of Oklahoma Press, Norman.

Arensberg, C. M.
1961   The Community as Object and as Sample. *American Anthropologist* 63:241-64.

Barnhart, Edwin L.
2001   *The Palenque Mapping Project: Settlement and Urbanism at an Ancient Maya City.* Unpublished Ph.D. dissertation, University of Texas, Austin.

French, Kirk D.
2000   Managing Lakam Ha': An Exploration of Palenque's Diverse Water Systems. *PARI Journal* I(1):21-22.

2001   The Precious Otolum of Palenque. *PARI Journal* II(2):12-16.

Low, Sethra M.
2000   *On the Plaza: The Politics of Public Space and Culture.* University of Texas Press, Austin.

Maudslay, Alfred P.
1889-

1902   *Biologia Centrali-Americana: Archaeology.* 4 Volumes. R. H. Porter & Dulau & Co., London, U.K.

Miller, Mary E.
1999   *Maya Art and Architecture.* Thames & Hudson, Ltd., London, U.K.

Murdock, George P.
1949   *Social Structure.* Macmillan, New York, NY.

Redfield, Robert
1955   *The Little Community: Viewpoints for the Study of a Human Whole.* University of Chicago Press, Chicago, IL.

SARA
1999   *Secretaría de Agricultura y Recursos Hidráulicos del Estado de Chiapas,* Tuxtla Gutiérrez, Mexico.

Scarborough, Vernon L., and G. Gallopin
1991   A Water Storage Adaptation in the Maya Lowlands. *Science* 251:658-662.

Yaeger, Jason and Marcello A. Canuto
2000   Introducing an Archaeology of Communities. In *The Archaeology of Communities: A New World Perspective,* edited by Marcello A. Canuto and Jason Yaeger, pp. 1-15. Routledge Press, New York.

Part IV

ARCHITECTURE AND EXCAVATION

Chapter 8

Elite Residential Compounds
at Late Classic Palenque

Damien B. Marken and
Arnoldo González Cruz

Archaeological investigations at Palenque have historically concentrated on the well-preserved and impressive monumental architecture of the site's ceremonial center. Little is actually known about how many people lived within the site core and what their economic/social status was. While much research remains to be undertaken at Palenque in regard to residential groups of all sizes, there is sufficient available data to make certain generalizations about elite settlement within, and near, the site ceremonial center. Assessment of the spatial layouts and, to a lesser extent, the inferred functions of these compounds can shed light on organizational aspects of elite culture at Classic Palenque.

Investigation of possible elite residences at Palenque began in 1949 with Alberto Ruz Lhuillier's excavations of Groups I, II, III, and IV, located to the north of the North Group. These excavations uncovered numerous multiroomed structures exhibiting possible residential functions (Ruz 1949, 1952). The proximity of these residential groups to the royal center of Palenque, the pervasiveness of vaulted architecture within these groups, and the recovered grave furniture, all support the interpretation of these groups as subregnal elite residential compounds. Similar criteria have been used to identify elite compounds at other Maya sites (Chase & Chase 1992: 4; Tourtellot 1983: 41). Further excavation conducted by the junior author of Group IV and Groups B and C in the early 1990s has significantly increased the available information on elite residences at Palenque (González Cruz 1993).[1] This chapter seeks to discern similarities and differences between these three groups to establish a basis for comparison of Palencano elite residential compounds with other such architectural ensembles at Palenque and other Maya sites. Two of these groups, Group IV and C, share numerous similarities in layout and structural forms. Spatially, Group B/Murcielagos differs primarily due to topography, but architectural analysis and excavation data indicate habitation by a non-familial residential unit. Trends seen in these subregnal elite compounds allow comparison with the architectural layout and functionality of the Palace, traditionally viewed as the center of the Palencano royal court.

The Palenque Site Core

Frequent summations of the Palenque "site core" limit this epicentral area to the portion of the site currently visible today by visitors. The classification of the Palace, Temple of the Inscriptions, Cross/South Group, North Group, and associated plazas as the site core (Andrews 1975) fails to adequately appreciate the full size and extent of the site.[2] As revealed by the work of the Palenque Mapping Project (PMP), the actual site core of Palenque encompasses all structures located on an approximately 3 km by 1 km modified escarpment (Barnhart 2001). This escarpment effectively circumscribes the site from the surrounding area. Terracing at Palenque (Barnhart, Chapter 6), and other space creation techniques (French, Chapter 7), create and delineate space for administrative, ritual, and residential functions and/or needs. These techniques may be reminiscent of hilltop sites in Oaxaca, where extensive residential terraces delimit settlement extent (Kowalewski et al. 1992: 267). Furthermore, these "public works" alter and define space for more restricted residential/administrative/ceremonial areas within the site core itself. It should not be ignored that in many ways, these "public works," while modifying the local landscape (to maximize available space), were limited in extent by the natural topography of the site core.

Despite internal divisions (as well as natural ones in the form of streams and rivers), we view the Palenque escarpment as a single, large settlement unit, much as William Fash considers El Bosque, Salamar/Comedero, Las Sepulturas, and the Main Group at Copan, Honduras, as a single unit (1983: 286). Barnhart (Chapter 6) feels the settlement map indicates that Palenque was an urban center, as opposed to a ritual-regal center following Sanders and Webster's (1988; Webster 1997) classification of Classic Maya centers. Although the overall Palenque core population does not achieve the high numbers required by Sanders and Webster's administrative center designation, Barnhart considers Palenque's population density indicative of an urban settlement.

Relevant here is the nature of the site core settlement at Palenque: a high proportion of the groups mapped by Barnhart and his colleagues would fall into Willey and Leventhal's (1979) Type 3 or 4 site category for settlement within the Copan pocket. Type 3 and 4 sites at Copan are found at the upper end of a settlement hierarchy defined by the scale and quality of stone masonry construction of the largest structure within sites outlying the Main Group at Copan. Sites in the Type 3 and 4 categories have largely been interpreted as elite compounds, while Type 1 and 2 sites are considered to have housed humbler folk (Hendon 1991;

Stomper 2001; Webster 1989; Willey & Leventhal 1979). Excavated examples of Type 3 and 4 groups at Palenque are discussed below, while unexcavated examples include the Encantado Group, the Xupil Group, and Moises' Retreat (see Barnhart, Chapter 6: Fig. 6.1). The structures of these groups do not resemble Palencano monumental architecture, though most are built entirely of stone masonry. Furthermore, the abundance of vaulted architecture within these groups supports their elite nature. If stone masonry is indeed indicative of elite residence, as appears to be the case in the Maya area (Haviland & Moholy-Nagy 1992: 51; Tourtellot 1993), then preliminary assessments lean toward a high elite population within the Palenque site core (proportional to the overall population).

High concentrations of elites, with a proportionately low overall population, are characteristic of central places throughout Postclassic Mesoamerica, such as the Tarascan capital Tzintzuntzan (Pollard 1980: 683). Other examples include several Quichean centers in highland Guatemala (Fox 1991), Maní, Yucatan, and Cholula, Pueblo (Marcus 1993). Archaeological research in the southern lowlands indicates that Classic Maya sites also exhibited elite nucleation (Chase & Chase 1987; Chase et al. 1989; Fash 2001; Sanders & Webster 1988). The preliminary data from Palenque seems to follow this general Mesoamerican trend.

Elite Compounds and Groups at Palenque

While many of the excavated structures at Palenque, such as the Cross Group structures, likely served some sort of ceremonial/ritual function (Baudez 1996a; Houston 1996), the exact functions of range structures and range-complexes (see below for the definition of the term "range-complex") in the Maya area are difficult to define and remain unclear. Extensive excavations in the site core by several INAH projects, directed by the junior author since 1989, have uncovered several distinct architectural groups just outside what is generally considered Palenque's ceremonial center. Many of these groups appear to have served as residential compounds for the Palencano elite.

The data from the Group IV, Group C, Group B, and Murcielagos Group excavations indicate that some of their residents during the Late Classic were of elite status. People of differing social strata resided within Maya elite residential compounds, such as servants, retainers, etc., as well as differentially ranked elites (Hendon 1991; Inomata 2001). While further investigation is necessary to confirm this at Palenque, excavations at comparable elite compounds elsewhere, such as Groups 10L-2 and 9N-8 at Copan (Andrews et al. 2003; Webster 1989), the Causeway Group at Aguateca (Inomata & Triadan 2003), and Group 7F-1 at Tikal (Haviland 1981), demonstrate this "mixing" of social strata to be typical of Late Classic Maya elite compounds. As at least three levels of elite ranking are evident from Palenque's burial data (Marken 2003), it seems reasonable to assume intra-compound social distinctions existed at Palenque as at other large Maya sites.

Group IV

Located about 2 km to the west of the Palace plaza, Group IV consists of roughly thirteen structures, four of which have been partially excavated. Included in Barnhart's Group J (2001), Group IV is demarcated within Group J and from other nearby architectural groups by artificial terraces on the north, south, and east, and by the road currently leading to the site on the west (Fig. 8.1). Structures J1, J2, J4, J6, J7, and J11 are all spatially associated with the same irregularly-shaped plaza (referred to here as the Group IV main plaza). Structures J13, J14, and J15 are built upon a slightly raised platform to the northeast of the main plaza. These smaller, unexcavated structures are reminiscent auxiliary structures in elite compounds at Copan (Hendon 1991; Webster 1989) and Aguateca (Inomata 2001: 43), possibly serving as kitchens, storage structures, or the residences of elite dependents. Certainly the open platform upon which these structures are built could have served as a work area, however the function of these structures is speculative at present.

The southwest corner of the Group IV main plaza is circumscribed by a 1.50 m high (from the plaza) terrace wall that runs into the south side of Structure J1. Much of the west side of this terrace is covered by a 2.70 m wide stairway leading to the top of the terrace. Structure J3 is located on the west edge of this terrace platform. Covered in dirt and overgrowth, little can be discerned at present

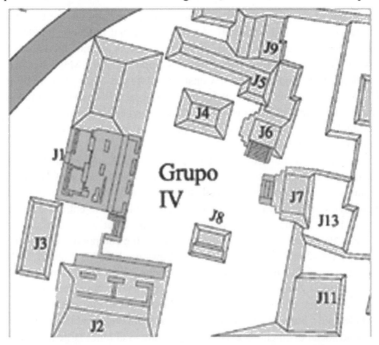

Figure 8.1: Map of Group IV, Palenque (courtesy of Edwin L. Barnhart)

regarding this structure, except that its basal platform was constructed of small-sized, roughly shaped blocks and spalls. Also built upon this terrace platform is Structure J2, a partially excavated vaulted masonry structure approximately 3.56 m high (Fig. 8.2). The façade of Structure J2 is pierced by two doorway vaults accessed (from the terrace platform) by two 25 cm high steps. The vault stones of the doorway vaults are faced at an angle, indicating specialized construction techniques (Roys 1934). Above these doorways are "vault niches" that are now open to the exterior due to the partial collapse of the façade. Prior to collapse, these niches may have served some sort of storage function. Although Structure J2 exhibits irregular-block wall construction with a high amount of spalls, mid-sized, faced, cut slabs were used at the vault spring and corners. This construction technique, and the presence of specialized vault stones and a high quality, white lime mortar, dates the construction of Structure J2 to around the reign of K'inich Kan Bahlam II (c. A.D. 680-710).

Structures J6 and J7 are identical structures consisting of approximately 2.80 m high stepped pyramid substructures, with inset corners, and unpreserved super-structures likely of perishable materials. Steep stairways ascend from the plaza to the pyramid summits. In front of the stairway of Structure J7 a burial was placed beneath the plaza floor along the primary axis (González Cruz 1993) and another was placed within the substructure itself (López Bravo 2004). Within the substructure of Structure J6 a vaulted tomb was constructed (Schele 1991). While

Figure 8.2: Structure J2, Group IV, Palenque (photo by Damien B. Marken)

the looted tomb was without preserved burial remains, recovered ceramics date to the Murcielagos phase (A.D. 700-750; Rands, personal communication 2003). Their height and pyramidal form, and location on the east side of the main plaza, indicate that both structures possibly served some sort of ritual, or shrine, function. These eastern shrine structures mark Group IV's main plaza as a Plaza Plan 2, first identified at Tikal (Becker 1999), and seen in the Northern Courtyard of the Murciélagos Palace at Dos Pilas (Demarest et al. 2003: 138), Tikal Group 7F-1 (Haviland 1981: Fig. 5.5), as well as other Maya sites (Tourtellot 1983: 40-41).

Between the southeast corner of Structure J6 and the northwest corner of Structure J7, excavations by Barbara and Robert Rands encountered numerous, superimposed burials. The arrangement and high variation between the burials revealed that "the cemetery was in use over a considerable period of time, or that burial traditions were subject to profound shifts" (Rands & Rands 1961: 104). Subsequent chronological analysis of the ceramics from the cemetery supports the first of these suppositions (Rands, personal communication 2003). Based on ceramic and stratigraphic evidence the occupation of Group IV began prior to Otolum times (A.D. 620-700) and continued until Balunte (A.D. 750-820; Rands & Rands 1961: Figs. 11 & 12).

Although these interments were not as finely constructed as the subfloor tombs of the ceremonial center (Marken 2003), Burial 11, an early burial containing the remains of a subadult male, was the largest and best-constructed crypt within the cemetery indicating conferred hereditary status (Rands & Rands 1961: 97-99). However, later burials show an increased presence of Palencano "elite" grave goods, including ceramic vessels, compared to early burials, and the presence of sacrificial victims within burials also has a later occurrence. Two later burials (Burials 3 and 5), one with a female adult skull, contained bone needles along with other indicators of elite status (shell pendant, ceramic vessels, perforated monkey teeth, and snail shells; Rands & Rands 1961: 95). The association of bone needles with an elite female interment hints that the female residents of Group IV engaged in textile weaving, an activity connected with females throughout Mesoamerica (McAnany & Plank 2001: 96).

Structure J1 was the largest and most prominent structure within Group IV. Composed of two stories, the half-excavated Structure J1 was built entirely of stone masonry and is preserved to a height of 4.75 m from the main plaza floor. While the upper-story vaults have collapsed, the lower level vaults remain intact, with the exception of the eastern-most (front) gallery. The wall construction of both stories consists of some large and smaller roughly shaped blocks, with a high number of spalls, mirroring the wall construction of Temple XIX. Likewise, the wall stucco and mortar of Structure J1, with a high amount of pea-gravel and limestone chip inclusions, is near identical to that of Temple XIX, indicating a possible Late Classic construction (c. 720-800).

Structure J1 is a typical example of the range-complex architectural class seen elsewhere at Palenque, including part of Temple XVI, Group C Structure

C2, and Murcielagos Group Structure MC1 (Marken 2002). These range-complexes at Palenque do exhibit a certain degree of variation amongst one another, but all include multiple parallel galleries and vaulted staircases leading to an upper level. Generally speaking, the spatial arrangements of range-complexes are not as symmetrically planned as Palencano monumental architecture. The lower level of Structure J1 consists of three main parallel vaulted galleries (one of which is collapsed), with another short parallel gallery offset between the second and third galleries (Fig. 8.3). Another vaulted gallery runs perpendicular from the end of the third gallery, before turning a short corner and ending. At the southern end of the third gallery a vaulted and "winding" staircase provides access to the upper story. Access to most of these galleries was restricted. The first gallery was accessed via three doorways originally, until a secondary dividing wall was built to turn the southern end of the gallery into a separate room with a single doorway and a stone bench. A single doorway vault provided access to the second gallery from the first, and from the second to the third gallery. The vaults of J1's lower level are low in comparison to the vaults of the monumental architecture at Palenque; none exceed 3 m (gallery 3) in height. One row of vault beams is present in both the second and third galleries, and was likely present in the now collapsed first gallery.

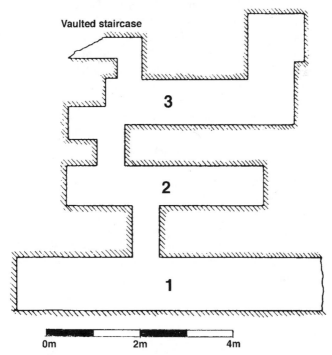

**Figure 8.3: Plan of the ground floor of Structure J1, Group IV, Palenque
(after García Moll 1991)**

The top floor of Structure J1 is a range-type structure composed of two parallel galleries. The walls are preserved to a maximum height of 1.74 m and there is good evidence that both galleries were vaulted and entirely constructed of stone masonry. Originally, the excavated portions of the galleries were connected by three doorways, and eventually sealed by thin secondary walls. There is no trace of benches or other architectural features within the structure. The east gallery opened up to the main plaza of Group IV by means of at least three doorways, but could only be accessed (once the central doorways were blocked) by a doorway at the south end of the gallery. It is unlikely that a third gallery existed further east, as a basal molding is evident around the east face of the upper-level structure. Furthermore, the small east façade piers would have provided a poor central support for a stone vault. The west façade is pierced by a single doorway—reached by a poorly preserved stairway. Eventually, the southwest portion of the west gallery was entirely closed off by secondary dividing walls. This room could then only be accessed from the galleries below by ascending the vaulted staircase.

Within the east gallery of the upper story of Structure J1, Alberto Ruz Lhuillier uncovered the Tablet of the Slaves against the secondary wall blocking the central doorway (Ruz 1952). While the iconographic scene of this carved limestone panel depicts the Palencano ruler K'inich Ahkal Mo' Nahb III (Wald 1997), the text (also mentioning the accession of K'inich Ahkal Mo' Nahb III) describes events in the life of an individual named Chak Sutz'. This individual, born on 9.11.18.9.17 (A.D. 668), carries several different titles, including that of *sajal* (a high-ranking title, often held by regional "sub-lords" in the western Maya area [see Schele & Mathews 1991]). Based on the text of the Tablet of the Slaves, Chak Sutz' has largely been interpreted as the lineal head of the Group IV compound (Schele 1991).

That the portrait of K'inich Ahkal Mo' Nahb III dominates Tablet of the Slaves scene does not lessen the importance of Chak Sutz' as the lineal head of the Group IV compound. Claude Baudez has convincingly argued that while central sculpture of the front façade of the House of Bacabs at Copan (Str. 9N-82) depicted the contemporary Copaneco ruler, Yax Pasaj, the dominant individual of Group 9N-8 was one of his subordinates (1989: 75). The fact that an aged Chak Sutz' (the monument celebrates his 60th birthday) was able to erect monuments commemorating events in his life, represents a recognition of his power and influence. Yet even a successful lord and lineage head such as Chak Sutz' would still need to demonstrate his subordination to the contemporary Palenque *k'uhul ajaw* ("holy lord") on his own sculpted monuments.

Group C

Group C is located to the east of the Palace, on a flat area just above the east bank of the Murcielagos River (see Barnhart, Chapter 6: Fig. 6.1). Discussion centers on the six excavated structures (Structures C1, C2, C3, C4, C5, and C6) arranged around the group's largest plaza, here called the main plaza of Group C

(Fig. 8.4). A small staircase leads south up a natural slope from this plaza to a ter-raced platform where several unexcavated structures were built. However, the most impressive structures of Group C face upon the main plaza, and likely played im-portant functional roles within the group (López Bravo 2004). It appears that Group C was accessed from the Palenque ceremonial center by a stone bridge crossing the Murcielagos River, and a large series of terraces and stairways, implying the promi-nence of its residents (Fig. 8.5). The construction methods of these structures, as well as associated ceramics, date to the end of the Late Classic period at Palenque (c. A.D. 720-800).

Located in the southwest corner of the main plaza facing north, Structure C1 consisted of a stepped pyramid substructure (approximately 3 m high), composed of three terraces, and a perishable superstructure. The superstructure was accessed by a wide, four-to-five step, stone stairway.

While the eastern edge of the main plaza is marked by a large stairway, a 2.15 m high terrace wall built on bedrock delineates its southeast corner. Upon the raised platform created by this stairway and terrace wall was built Structure C2 to the south, and Structures C3, C4, and C5 to the east. Structures C3 and C5 are 4.70 m and 6.20 m high, respectively, stepped masonry pyramids with inset corners—identical in form to Structures J6 and J7 mentioned above. Between these two earlier structures Structure C4 was built overlapping their substructures. Perishable buildings accessed by steep stairways on the west substructure faces were likely located at the summit of all three structures. As has been surmised for

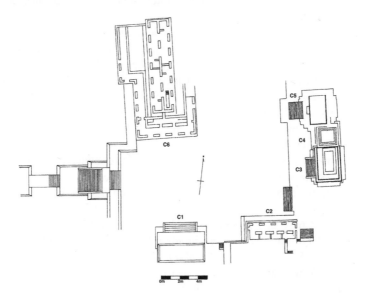

Figure 8.4: Plan drawing of Group C, Palenque. (drawing by Alonso Mendez)

**Figure 8.5: Reconstruction drawing of Group C, Palenque
(drawing by Alonso Mendez)**

Structures J6 and J7, these three buildings likely served as lineage shrines for the residents of Group C.

Structure C2 (Fig. 8.6) is a rather simple range-complex in comparison to Group IV Structure J1. The lower story consists of two parallel galleries built on a 0.41 m high basal platform. Once vaulted to a height of 3.60 m, most of the roof has since collapsed along with much of the west end of the structure. Secondary construction walls divide each gallery into four rooms. Though four doorways pierce the façade of Structure C2, the northeast room could also be accessed by a small doorway on the east. The two galleries are connected by four doorways spanned by low cross-vaults without lintels, though the east rooms were connected by a doorway vault that was later sealed. From the southeast room, a vaulted passage and staircase lead to an upper story, constructed of perishable materials. A stairway to the east of Structure C2 likewise ascends to the level of the upper story.

Structure C6 is another range-complex associated with the main plaza of Group C. A large multi-chambered building, Structure C6 is constructed on a basal platform 25 cm above the main plaza. The southern section of Structure C6 is composed of two parallel vaulted galleries, now collapsed, running east-west. The southern façade of the structure is pierced by four doorways. Two doorways lead up a 35 cm step from the southern gallery to that of the north. A large stone bench is located in the northwest corner of this rear gallery. At the east and west

Figure 8.6: Structure C2, Group C, Palenque. (photo by Damien B. Marken)

ends of these double galleries, separate galleries ran perpendicularly to the north, although the gallery to the west is poorly preserved. Along roughly the primary axis of the southern section of Structure C6 a vaulted staircase ascended to an upper-story seemingly built over solid fill. This poorly preserved upper level consists of two parallel galleries divided into a series of small private chambers, many of which contain small stone benches. The architectural parallels between this structure and the so-called "dormitory residences" at Copan (Webster 1989) and other Maya sites are striking.

Although carved monuments and architectural sculpture are absent (or unpreserved) from the excavated structures within Group C, the structures bounding the main plaza are architecturally similar to several Group IV structures. The presence of Structures C3, C4, and C5 on the east side of the main plaza marks the plaza as a Plaza Plan 2 (PP2) (Becker 1999). Both Group IV and Group C seem to conform to a regional PP2 layout. While PP2 residential groups cut across social hierarchies at Tikal (Becker 1999: 137), the overall similarities between Group IV and Group C at Palenque indicate that both groups housed people of similar status. The architecture from both groups suggests that some of the residents were elites (unexcavated non-elite PP2 groups may exist at Palenque). Structures C2 and C6 are both range-complexes, though of differing size and architectural complexity. Structure C2 appears to be a scaled-down version of Structure J1, minus second story masonry walls. Structure C6 is a much larger range-complex than either Structure C2 or J1. The benches within several second-story rooms give the impression of residential quarters, although the rooms may have served a variety of functions.

Group B and Murcielagos Group

Group B and the Murcielagos Group are located on a series of terraces modifying the natural topography between the Otolum and Murcielagos Rivers below and to the northeast of Palenque's ceremonial center. Designated as separate groups, their spatial proximity allows them to be discussed as a whole (see Barnhart, Chapter 6: Fig. 6.1). The largest architectural constructions of Group B are associated with a series of plazas, connected by wide stairways, descending toward Structure MC1 (Figs. 8.7 & 8.8). The structures considered here are

Structures B2, B7, B8, B9, and MC1. Several unexcavated buildings present within each group have been excluded from this discussion.

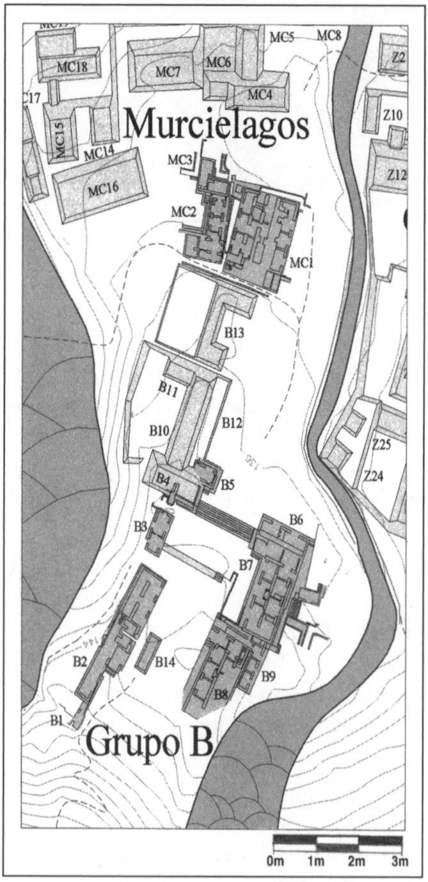

Structure B2, constructed of irregularly shaped blocks and a high quantity of spalls, is built upon a 1 m high (from plaza) substructure platform and faces east. The central section of the structure, with its low vaults and entrance, was a functional sweatbath (Child, Chapter 12; González Cruz 1993). As is evidenced by sweatbaths elsewhere in the Maya area, the rooms to the north and south perhaps served as changing/preparation rooms for the sweatbath.

Facing Structure B2, Structure B8 is a range-structure with two parallel galleries running north-south, and a single east-west gallery extension on the north. The west gallery, facing the plaza, is divided into four rooms, each accessed by a single doorway. The northern of the two center rooms contains the remains of a small sanctuary of limestone construction, in kind to the monumental sanctuaries in the Cross Group structures and Temples XIV and XVII that

Figure 8.7: Map of Group B and Murcielagos Group, Palenque (courtesy of Edwin L. Barnhart)

served as symbolic sweatbaths (Child, Chapter 12; Houston 1996). Positioned directly across the plaza from the functional sweatbath of Structure B2, the symbolic sweatbath of Structure B8 likely fulfilled the same ritual purpose as the monumental sanctuaries of the Cross Group. Furthermore, within and in front of this sanctuary, as well as the one within Structure B7, several ceramic "tier-of-heads" variant incensarios were recovered (González Cruz 1993; López Bravo 2004). This incensario variant is generally only associated at Palenque with the Cross Group structures (Bishop, Rands & Harbottle 1982: Fig. 2a; Rands, Bishop & Harbottle 1978: 22; Rands & Rands 1959), the only buildings with the symbolic sweatbath architectural feature. However, the location and architecture of Group B suggest much more private ritual use than seen within the Cross Group.

Within the northern gallery of Structure B8, which was eventually closed off from the perpendicular galleries to the south, a vaulted staircase leads down to a vaulted corridor providing access to two vaulted tombs beneath the plaza level (González Cruz 1993). This corridor could be entered from the east through Structure B9, a series of three private chambers built behind and below Structure B8, and from the north by an unpreserved doorway between Structures B7 and B8.

Though slightly larger, with more spacious rooms, Structure B7 is similar in plan to Structure B8. Two of the five rooms on the eastern half of the structure

Figure 8.8: Reconstruction drawing of Group B, Palenque
(drawing by Alonso Mendez)

contain stone benches as primary architectural features. Beneath the floor of the sanctuary room is a vaulted tomb containing the remains of two adult elite females, as indicated by skeletal remains and grave furniture consisting of several ceramic figurines and vessels (López Bravo 2000: 40). Attached to the north of Structure B7 at the level of the lower plaza is Structure B6, a small two-room structure (similar to Structure B9), one of which contains a bench.

Structure MC1 is a large, two-story range-complex built of masonry walls. It is unclear if the second story was vaulted. The lower story consists of three parallel, vaulted galleries connected by numerous cross-vaulted doorways. The western-most gallery opens west toward Structure MC2, and its vault has since collapsed. Secondary construction walls divide each gallery into at least three rooms (Fig. 8.9). Secondary walls also serve to close some doorways connecting galleries. From the southern room of the middle gallery a vaulted staircase leads to the second story. The eastern-most of these three galleries leads (from north to south) to a vaulted funerary chamber (Ruz 1952: 34). Added to the east side of the structure, is a secondary construction vaulted gallery divided into three rooms, resembling possible retainer quarters, due to the presence of a bench in the northern-most room.

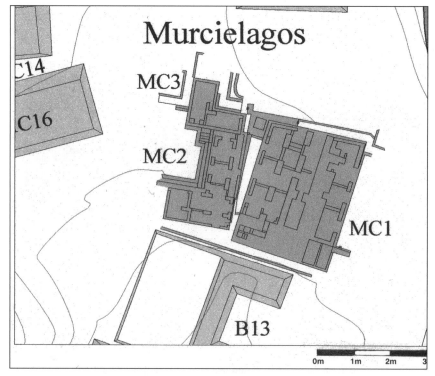

Figure 8.9: Map of Murcielagos Group, Palenque. (courtesy of Edwin L. Barnhart)

Wall construction appears to be of a better quality than that seen in previously discussed range-complexes (Structures J1, C2, and C6), consisting of roughly shaped blocks and slabs with some spalls. The vaults (2.40-2.66 m in height) are constructed of small, thin slabs (1-4 cm thick), with longer and wider slab vault-spring stones. Capstones are extremely regular in form, resembling possible "assembly line" production (Straight, Chapter 10). One row of vault beams is present providing additional vault support. The vault soffit shape of Structure MC1 is almost unique at Palenque; "double-offsets" are present below the vaultspring (Fig. 8.10). These "double-offsets" are also seen in the North Subterraneos of the Palace. Both walls and vaults are heavily stuccoed, with a low-quality stucco (high amount of inclusions), and a clay mortar was used in construction. The overall architectural data indicate a rather late construction date (c. 750-800) consistent with associated Balunte ceramics, one carrying an A.D. 799 hieroglyphic date (Ruz 1952: Fig. 14).

While the actual association of Structure MC1 with Group B remains slightly ambiguous, the buildings of Group B were not likely permanent residences. Owing to the clearly ritualistic nature of the architecture of Structures B2, B7, and B8, in association with Palenque's sweatbath cult, it seems unlikely that the inhabitants of Group B resided there as a familial unit. The evidence for domestic activities uncovered during excavation (López Bravo 2000: 40) more likely represents the use of the compound as a residence for members of a ritual group, much like the "dormitories" seen at Tikal (Harrison 1970) and Copan (Cheeks & Spink 1986; Webster 1989), or the "boys houses" of Yucatan described by Landa (Tozzer 1941: 124). Like other range-complexes, Structure MC1 may have been a residence for Palencano elites, possibly those of the lineage of Six Kimi Pakal named in the inscription on the aforementioned carved black vessel found within the structure (Martin & Grube 2000: 175; Ruz 1952: Fig. 14).

Figure 8.10: Double offset. Structure MC1 vaulted gallery, Murcielagos Group, Palenque (photo by Damien B. Marken)

Comparison and Conclusions

Elite residential compounds in the Maya area have been demonstrated to have served a variety of functions (Adams 1970; Becker 1973; Christie 2003), and likely housed people of differing social statuses besides elites, such as servants, retainers, or slaves (Inomata 2001; Webster 1989). The architectural layouts of Group IV and Group C, and associated artifacts, coincide with these interpretations. Although Group B likely served ritual/dormitory functions, Palencano elites resided in the nearby Structure MC1. What then, were the similarities and differences between these elite residences, and those of Palenque's ruling family?

Since John Lloyd Stephens stayed there during his 1840 visit to the site, the Palace has been generally considered as the residence of the Palenque royal household (Stephens 1969). Part of the difficulty in identifying structure functions within the Palace is that few artifacts have been excavated in situ to support the residential interpretation. This is the norm in the Maya area; elite residences were probably kept clean and free of floor trash (Adams 1977: 146). Further compounding the problem is "the frequent construction by the Maya of repetitive, modular spaces, most of which had no functionally revealing, durable, built-in features" (Webster 2001: 149). In his architectural comparison of the Palace at Palenque and the Central Acropolis at Tikal, George Andrews (1980) concluded that the Palace was a multi-functional set of buildings, which he termed a palace-complex. Based on architectural form, layout, and differential access to rooms, Andrews classified the rooms of the Palace into fourteen functional groupings (Andrews 1980: 16-22). While we agree with some of Andrew's classifications, more precise definitions of certain spaces may be possible.

Like Andrews, we view the northern section (Houses A, AD, C, and D in its final form) of the Palace as fulfilling a public administrative, or "courtly," role, with galleries facing outward toward "more public" surrounding plazas, and facing inward on more private, but still "open," inner sunken courtyards (Andrews 1980: 20). The spatial layout and architectural decoration of these structures, including carved stone depictions of captives in the East Court, can be interpreted as possible ritual locations (the outer galleries), and as places to receive prestigious visitors to the Palace (the inner courtyards).

Several other functions of various Palace structures have been argued since Andrews presented his classifications. Claude Baudez (1996b) has demonstrated that Houses E and K and the South Subterraneos formed part of a procession for ritual enthronement. House E also likely served as a throne room and the inscription from the Tablet of the 96 Glyphs names it as a place of accession for several Palenque rulers (Berlin 1970). In fact, the Tower Court seems to be the center of the Late Classic Palencano royal court; both House E and the courtyard itself were constantly remodeled and renovated by the succession of rulers following K'inich Janab Pakal I (r. A.D. 612-683). A functional sweatbath has been identified behind House I (Child, Chapter 12), and a symbolic sweatbath is located within House F across the southeast court from House E.

David Webster has suggested that the term "court-complex" may be better suited to describe "palace-complexes" throughout the Maya area (Webster 2001: 141). In using this term, Webster integrates two conceptualizations of the Maya royal court: (1) the architectural complexes that gave the court its spatial definition, and (2) the network of individuals that defined the makeup and social aspects of Maya courtly life. However, an entire court-complex may not be definable at the Palace at Palenque, and could be expanded to include other structures within the ceremonial center (as well as most temple structures), namely the Ball Court, Temple XVI, Temple XXc and Temple XXII. Excavations of Temple XVI encountered a possible ceramic figurine workshop (indicated by the recovery of "new" figurines and molds [Fig. 8.11]), and several recovered manos yielded traces of ground pigments used in paints, as well as possible habitation areas within the complex. Extensive painted stucco sculpture adorned the exteriors of buildings within this complex (Fig. 8.12), and various rulers placed multiple carved limestone panels within different component structures. Temple XXc, a perishable, L-shaped structure located directly behind Temple XX, appears to have also served some residential function, possibly a food preparation area, as evidenced by the extensive midden excavated between Temples XX and XXc. This structure is spatially associated with Temple XXII, a range-complex currently under excavation.

The household represented by this expanded "court-complex" exhibits aspects and functions not seen within the other residential compounds examined. Clearly, Maya royal household administration at Palenque functioned differently than that of lower-ranking elite households (Sanders 1992: 281). The greatest difference, and the most easily identifiable, is one of scale and embellishment. The structures of the royal court-complex are larger and somewhat disbursed among ritual/ mortuary monumental structures throughout the ceremonial center. Although Structure J1 contained a carved limestone tablet (the Tablet of the Slaves), the exteriors of subregnal elite structures do not seem to have been crowned with the elaborate stucco sculpture for which Palenque is famous.

Yet, the sweatbath cult, defined by Child (Chapter 12), appears to have been important to both dynastic and subregnal elites at Palenque. Both Group B and the Palace had functional and symbolic sweatbaths in essentially "private" spaces for elite use. Meanwhile, the Cross Group served as the spatial forum (as part of the royal court-complex) from which this elite cult activity could be brought, symbolically, to a more public audience by the royal dynasty.

Recent investigations into ancient Maya court networks (Inomata & Houston 2001) have raised the possible comparability of royal and non-royal court settings. Webster cites possible meeting places within the homes of subregnal elites at Copan (Webster 2001: 146). At Palenque, the placement of the Tablet of the Slaves on the second story of Structure J1 is the best evidence for such a non-royal "throne room" or presentation area. Structure J1, and the range-complexes C2 and MC1 all have parallel layouts; this sharing of architectural attributes that indicates

Figure 8.11: Figurine mold recovered from Temple XVI (photo by Alfonso Morales Cleveland)

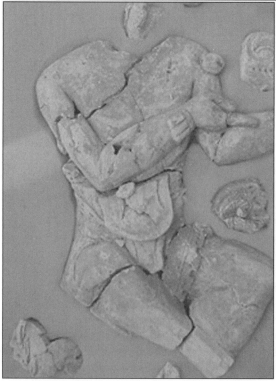

Figure 8.12: High-relief stucco sculpture recovered from Temple XVI (photo by Damien B. Marken)

these structures shared similar sets of functions. This possible "receiving area" architectural form differs from other such interpreted structures elsewhere in the Maya area. Subregnal throne rooms from Copan (Webster 1989), and Aguateca (Inomata & Triadan 2003), are generally tandem/transverse structures as seen by Peter Harrison in the Central Acropolis at Tikal (1970, 2003). Little remains of the architecture of the second floors of Structures C2 and MC1, but that of Structure J1 is a range structure (no-tandem/transverse) like those of the Palace at Palenque. This difference likely marks regional variation as opposed to functional or hierarchical differences. The plan of the throne room of Yax Pasaj, the final ruler of Copan, is similar to those of his sublords (compare Andrews et al. 2003: Fig. 3.2, and Webster 2001: Fig. 5.7). To a degree, royal and subregnal residence plans at Tikal also match (Haviland 1981: 100). At Palenque, the two-storied range-complex layout of Structure J1 also matches the multi-level configuration of House E and the South Subterraneos, the royal Palencano accession building, and throne room.

Jessica Christie (2003: 325) has recently described House E as the home of K'inich Janab Pakal I. Although she raises some valid points, Christie fails to consider the formalization of Palencano courts through the standardization of their central architectural spaces and the use of carved monuments, like the Oval Palace Tablet, and painted texts to legitimize such courtly forums. Erected to celebrate K'inich Janab Pakal I's accession in A.D. 612, the Oval Palace Tablet remained in place throughout Palenque's subsequent dynastic history. Since following rulers did not remove, nor replace, this earlier monument, it must have been conceived as a prestige enhancer, or legitimizing heirloom. When K'inich K'an Joy Chitam II placed an inscribed throne beneath the Oval Palace Tablet, and when K'inich Ahkal Mo' Nahb III added the painted inscription above it (Greene Robertson 1985), they were imbuing House E with further ideological and political meaning for themselves and their successors. Thus later individuals were able to use the monuments of their predecessors as social status markers. In Group IV, the image of K'inich Ahkal Mo' Nahb' III on the Tablet of the Slaves gave royal sanction to the subregnal receiving area within Structure J1. Even after the death of Chak Sutz', the continued presence of this image and accompanying text would serve as a reminder of the importance of his lineage to future visitors.

Final Comments

From a chronological standpoint, the subregnal elite compounds discussed above further differ from the royal court-complex in terms of continuity and time depth. Groups B, C, and Murcielagos all date, ceramically and architecturally, to near the end of the dynastic history of Palenque (c. A.D. 720–800). While Group IV enjoyed a comparatively longer occupation sequence, much of the existent architecture within that group likely dates only to the end of the Late Classic period, following an apparent rise in the fortunes and prestige of its inhabitants. In fact, nearly all the range-complexes at Palenque date to this period, during which the construction of temple structures halts (Marken, Chapter 4). The Palace (Greene Robertson 1985) and Temple XVI (González Cruz & Bernal Romero 2000) on the other hand, were architectural accretions, developed over several generations. What we then see at Palenque is a late shift in construction labor from monumental temple structures to range-complexes, and the formation of several subregnal elite groups, while the expansion and elaboration of the royal court-complex continued.

This shift appears to begin during the reign of K'inich Ahkal Mo' Nahb III (r. 721-c.740), when fundamental changes occur in the ceramics, architecture, and iconography of Palenque (see Marken 2002: 92-98, 2003). These changes and the shift in labor focus (from temples to range-complexes) may be reflected in the scene from the Temple XXI bench panel (hieroglyphically dated to A.D. 736), recently discovered by the junior author (see González Cruz & Bernal Romero 2003, 2004). The scene depicts three titled human individuals (from left to right): (1) the Palenque k'uhul ajaw, K'inich Ahkal Mo' Nahb III, (2) the deceased ruler K'inich Janab Pakal I impersonating a mythological founder (David Stuart, personal communication 2002), (3) and an individual named Upakal K'inich, carrying the title of ba-ch'ok ("first-prince"), followed by the k'uhul ajaw title and the Palenque emblem glyph. What was the role of this "first-prince-lord of Palenque?" Are we witnessing a switch to some form of dual rulership at Palenque?

The implications of this monument have yet to be fully explored, but an intriguing possibility is one of decentralized rulership at Palenque during the reign of K'inich Ahkal Mo' Nahb III, with subregnal elites beginning to exert greater control of their own lineage labor to build their own compounds. A breakdown in the centralized control of labor is reflected in the construction of larger elite compounds and is preceded by the dynastic sharing of iconographic space with subregnal lords. The Temple XIX monuments depict K'inich Ahkal Mo' Nahb III with numerous of his sublords, whose support was necessary for him to accede to the throne (Straight, Chapter 10; Stuart, Chapter 11). While the possibility of duel rulership at Palenque, as implied by the Temple XXI bench inscription is, at best, an unsubstantiated guess, it seems likely that during this period some Palencano subregnal elites, such as Chak Sutz', began to extend their network of influence into the domain of site politics.

Notes

1. Structure names used in this chapter follow the designations of the Palenque Mapping Project (Barnhart 2001), and differ from those previously used by Ruz Lhuillier (1949, 1952), and the junior author (1993). For example, Group IV structure J6 is labeled as Structure C by Ruz and as Structure 4 by the junior author. Another example is Ruz Group III, here named Group Murcielagos Structure MC1. The reasons for using Barnhart's designations are twofold: (1) the Barnhart labels easily differentiate structures between various groups throughout the site, and (2) to maintain continuity within the present volume.

2. In this chapter the term "ceremonial center" at Palenque is used in reference to the Palace and surrounding structures (i.e., the North Group and the South/Cross Group).

References

Adams, Richard E. W.
 1970 Suggested Classic Period Occupational Specialization in the Southern Maya Lowlands. In *Monographs & Papers in Maya Archaeology* 61, edited by William R. Bullard, pp. 487-502. Peabody Museum of Archaeology & Ethnography, Cambridge, MA.

 1977 *Prehistoric Mesoamerica*. Little, Brown & Co., New York, NY.

Andrews, E. Wyllys V, Jodi L. Johnson, William F. Doonan, Gloria E. Everson, Kathryn E. Sampeck, and Harold E. Starratt
 2003 A Multipurpose Structure in the Late Classic Palace at Copan. In *Maya Palaces and Elite Residences*, edited by Jessica J. Chistie, pp. 69-97. University of Texas Press, Austin.

Andrews, George F.
 1975 *Maya Cities: Placemaking and Urbanization*. University of Oklahoma Press, Norman.

 1980 Palace Complexes and the Maya Elite: Palenque and Tikal. Paper presented at the Cuarta Mesa Redonda de Palenque. Palenque, Chiapas, Mexico, June 8-14, 1980.

Barnhart, Edwin L.
 2001 *The Palenque Mapping Project: Settlement and Urbanism at an Ancient Maya City*. Unpublished Ph.D. dissertation. University of Texas, Austin.

Baudez, Claude F.
 1989 House of the Bacabs: An Iconographic Analysis. In *House of the Bacabs, Copan, Honduras*, edited by David Webster, pp. 73-81. Dumbarton Oaks Research Library and Collection, Washington, D.C.

 1996a The Cross Group at Palenque. In *Eighth Palenque Round Table–1993*. Vol. X, edited by Merle Greene Robertson, Martin Macri, and Jan McHargue, pp. 121-128. Pre-Columbian Art Research Institute, San Francisco, CA.

 1996b Arquitectura y escenografía en Palenque: un ritual de entronizacíon. *RES 29/30*:172-179.

Becker, Marshall J.
 1973 Archaeological Evidence for Occupational Specialization Among the Classic Period Maya at Tikal, Guatemala. *American Antiquity* 38(4): 396-406.

 1999 *Excavations in Residential Areas of Tikal: Groups with Shrines*. Tikal Report 21. University Museum, University of Pennsylvania, Philadelphia.

Berlin, Henrich
 1970 The Tablet of the 96 Glyphs at Palenque, Chiapas, Mexico. *Archaeological Studies in Middle America*. pp. 135-149. Middle American Research Institute, Pub. 26, Tulane University, New Orleans, LA.

Bishop, Ronald L., Robert L. Rands, and Garman Harbottle
 1982 A Ceramic Compositional Interpretation of Incense-Burner Trade in the Palenque Area, Mexico. In *Nuclear and Chemical Dating Techniques*, edited by L. A. Currie, pp. 411-440. ACS Symposium Series 176. American Chemical Society, Washington, D.C.

Chase, Arlen F. and Diane Z. Chase
   1987   *Investigations at the Classic Maya Center of Caracol, Belize: 1985-1987.*
          Pre-Columbian Art Research Institute Monograph 3, San Francisco, CA.
   1992   Mesoamerican Elites: Assumptions, Definitions, and Models. In *Mesoamerican
          Elites: An Archaeological Assessment*, edited by Diane Z. Chase and Arlen F.
          Chase, pp. 3-17. University of Oklahoma Press, Norman.

Chase, Dianne Z., Arlen F. Chase, and William A. Haviland
   1989   The Mesoamerican Urban Tradition: A Reconsideration. *American Anthro-
          pologist* 91(3): 499-506.

Cheek, Charles D. and Marly L. Spink
   1986   Excavaciones en el Grupo 3 Estructura 223 (Operación VII). In *Excavaciones
          en el área urbana de Copan. Vol. 1*, edited by William T. Sanders. Secretaría
          de Cultura y Turismo, Instituto Hondureño de Antropología e Historia,
          Tegucigalpa.

Christie, Jessica J., ed.
   2003   *Maya Palaces and Elite Residences: An Interdisciplinary Approach.*
          University of Texas Press, Austin.

Demarest, Arthur, Kim Morgan, Claudia Wolley, and Héctor Escobedo
   2003   The Political Acquistion of Sacred Geography: The Murciélagos Complex at
          Dos Pilas. In *Maya Palaces and Elite Residences*, edited by Jessica J. Chistie,
          pp. 120-153. University of Texas Press, Austin.

Fash, William L.
   1983   Deducing Social Organization from Classic Maya Settlement Pattern: A Case
          Study from the Copan Valley. In *Civilization in the Ancient Americas*, edited
          by Richard M. Leventhal and Alan L. Kolata, pp. 261-288. University of
          New Mexico Press and Peabody Museum of Archaeology and Ethnography,
          Cambridge, MA.
   2001   *Scribes, Warriors and Kings: The City of Copan and the Ancient Maya.*
          Revised Edition. Thames & Hudson, London.

Fox, John W.
   1991   On the Rise and Fall of *Tuláns* and Maya Segmentary States. *American An-
          thropologist* 91(3): 656-681.

Fox, Richard
   1977   *Urban Anthropology.* Prentice-Hall, Englewood Cliffs, NJ.

García Moll, Roberto, ed.
   1991   *Palenque. 1926-1945.* INAH, México, D.F.

González Cruz, Arnoldo
   1993   *Trabajo Arqueologicos en Palenque, Chiapas: Informe de Campo. VI
          Temporada.* Volumen VII. Serie Informes de Campo 6. Projecto Arqueologico
          Palenque. INAH, Mexico, D.F.

González Cruz, Arnoldo and Guillermo Bernal Romero
   2000   Grupo XVI de Palenque: Conjunto arquitectónico de la nobleza provincial.
          Arqueología Mexicana VIII(45): 20-25.
   2003   *The Throne of Ahkal Mo' Nahb' III: A Unique Finding at Palenque.* INAH/
          Nestlé, Mexico, D.F.

2004   The Throne Panel of Temple 21 at Palenque. In *Courtly Art of the Ancient Maya*, edited by Mary E. Miller and Simon Martin, pp. 264-267. Thames & Hudson/Fine Arts Museums of San Francisco, San Francisco, CA.

Greene Robertson, Merle
1985   *The Sculpture of Palenque Vol. II: The Early Buildings of the Palace and Wall Paintings*. Princeton University Press, Princeton, NJ.

Harrison, Peter D.
1970   *The Central Acropolis, Tikal, Guatemala: A Preliminary Study of the Functions of Its Central Components during the Late Classic Period*. Ph.D. dissertation. University of Pennsylvania, Philadelphia.

2003   Palaces of the Royal Court at Tikal. In *Maya Palaces and Elite Residences*, edited by Jessica J. Chistie, pp. 98-119. University of Texas Press, Austin.

Haviland, William A.
1981   Dower Houses and Minor Centers at Tikal, Guatemala: An Investigation into the Identification of Valid Units in Settlement Hierarchies. In *Lowland Maya Settlement Patterns*, edited by Wendy Ashmore, pp. 89-120. School of American Research, University of New Mexico Press, Albuquerque.

Haviland, William A. and Hattula Moholy-Nagy
1992   Distinguishing the High & Mighty from the Hoi Polloi at Tikal, Guatemala. In *Mesoamerican Elites: An Archaeological Assessment*, edited by Diane Z. Chase and Arlen F. Chase, pp. 50-60. University of Oklahoma Press, Norman.

Hendon, Julia A.
1991   Status and Power in Classic Maya Society: An Archaeological Study. *American Anthropologist* 93(4): 894-918.

Houston, Stephen D.
1996   Symbolic Sweatbaths of the Maya: Architectural Meaning in the Cross Group at Palenque, Mexico. *Latin American Antiquity* 7(2): 132-151.

Inomata, Takeshi
2001   King's People: Classic Maya Courtiers in a Comparative Study. In *Royal Courts of the Ancient Maya, Vol. 1*, edited by Takeshi Inomata and Stephen D. Houston, pp. 27-53. Westview Press, Boulder, CO.

Inomata, Takeshi and Stephen D. Houston, eds.
2001   *Royal Courts of the Ancient Maya, Vols. 1 & 2*, edited by Takeshi Inomata and Stephen D. Houston. Westview Press, Boulder, CO.

Inomata, Takeshi and Daniela Triadan
2003   Where Did Elites Live? Identifying Elite Residences at Aguateca, Guatemala. In *Maya Palaces and Elite Residences*, edited by Jessica J. Chistie, pp. 154-183. University of Texas Press, Austin.

Kowalewski, Stephen A., Gary M. Feinman, and Laura Finsten
1992   "The Elite" and Assessment of Social Stratification in Mesoamerican Archaeology. In *Mesoamerican Elites: An Archaeological Assessment*, edited by Diane Z. Chase and Arlen F. Chase, pp. 259-277. University of Oklahoma Press, Norman.

López Bravo, Roberto
    2000   La Vereración de los Ancestros en Palenque. *Arqueología Mexicana* VIII(45): 38-43.

    2004   State and Domestic Cult in Palenque Censer Stands. In *Courtly Art of the Ancient Maya*, edited by Mary E. Miller and Simon Martin, pp. 256-258. Thames & Hudson/Fine Arts Museums of San Francisco, San Francisco, CA.

Marcus, Joyce
    1993   Ancient Maya Political Organization. In *Lowland Maya Civilization in the 8th Century A.D.*, edited by Jeremy A. Sabloff and John S. Henderson, pp. 111-184. Dumbarton Oaks Research Library & Collection, Washington, D.C.

Marken, Damien B.
    2002   *L'Architecture de Palenque: Les Temples*. Unpublished M.A. thesis, Université de Paris I: La Sorbonne.

    2003   Elite Political Structure at Late Classic Palenque, Chiapas, Mexico. Paper presented at the 5th World Archaeology Congress, Washington, D.C. June 23rd, 2003.

Martin, Simon and Nikolai Grube
    2000   *Chronicles of the Maya Kings and Queens: Deciphering the Dynasties of the Ancient Maya*. Thames & Hudson, London, U.K.

McAnany, Patricia A. and Shannon Plank
    2001   Perspectives on Actors, Gender Roles, and Architecture at Classic Maya Courts and Households. In *Royal Courts of the Ancient Maya, Vol. 1*, edited by Takeshi Inomata and Stephen D. Houston, pp. 84-129. Westview Press, Boulder, CO.

Pollard, Helen P.
    1980   Central Places and Cities: A Consideration of the Protohistoric Tarascan State. *American Antiquity* 45:677-696.

Rands, Barbara C. and Robert L. Rands
    1961   Excavations in a Cemetery at Palenque. *Estudios de Cultura Maya, Vol. I*, pp. 87-106. UNAM, Mexico, D.F.

Rands, Robert L.
    1987   Ceramic Patterns and Traditions in the Palenque Area. In *Maya Ceramics. Papers from the 1985 Maya Ceramic Conference*, edited by Prudence M. Rice and Robert J. Sharer, pp. 203-238. BAR International Series 345(i), Oxford, U.K.

Rands, Robert L., Ronald L. Bishop, and Garman Harbottle
    1978   Thematic and Compositional Variation in Palenque Region Incensarios. In *Tercera Mesa Redonda de Palenque*. Vol. IV, edited by Merle Greene Robertson and Donnan Call Jeffers, pp. 19-30. Pre-Columbian Art Research Institute, San Francisco, CA.

Rands, Robert L. and Barbara C. Rands
    1959   The Incensario Complex of Palenque, Chiapas. *American Antiquity* 25(2): 225-236.

Roys, Lawrence
  1934   The Engineering Knowledge of the Maya. *Contributions to American Archaeology,* Vol. II. No. 6. pp. 27-105. Carnegie Institution of Washington, Washington, D.C.

Ruz Lhuillier, Alberto
  1949   *Exploraciones Arqueológicas en Palenque: 1949.* Informe Inédito. Archivo del Instituto Nacional de Antropologia y Historia. Mexico, D.F.

  1952   Exploraciones en Palenque: 1950. *Anales del Instituto Nacional de Antropologia e Historia,* Tomo V, Núm 33, pp. 25-45. INAH, Mexico, D.F.

Sanders, William T.
  1992   Ranking and Stratification in Pre-Hispanic Mesoamerica. In *Mesoamerican Elites: An Archaeological Assessment,* edited by Diane Z. Chase and Arlen F. Chase, pp. 278-291. University of Oklahoma Press, Norman.

Sanders, William T. and David Webster
  1988   The Mesoamerican Urban Tradition. *American Anthropologist* 90(3): 521-546.

Schele, Linda
  1991   The Demotion of Chac–Zutz': Lineage Compounds and Subsidiary Lords at Palenque. In *6th Palenque Round Table, 1986,* edited by Merle Greene Robertson and Virginia M. Fields, pp. 6-11. Univeristy of Oklahoma Press, Norman.

Schele, Linda and Peter Mathews
  1991   Royal Visits and other Intersite Relationships among the Classic Maya. In *Classic Maya Political History: Hieroglyphic and Archaeological Evidence,* edited by T. Patrick Culbert, pp. 226-252. University of Cambridge Press, Cambridge, U.K.

Stephens, John L.
  1969   *Incidents of Travel in Central America Chiapas and Yucatan, Vol. I & II.* Dover Publications, Inc., New York. Originally published in 1841, by Harper & Brothers, New York, NY.

Stomper, Jeffrey A.
  2001   A Model for Late Classic Community Structure at Copan, Honduras. In *Landscape and Power in Ancient Mesoamerica,* edited by Rex Koontz, Kathryn Reese-Taylor, and Annabeth Headrick, pp. 197-230. Westview Press, Boulder, CO.

Tourtellot, Gair
  1983   An Assessment of Classic Maya Household Composition. In *Prehistoric Settlement Patterns,* edited by Evon Z. Vogt and Richard M. Leventhal, pp. 35-54. University of New Mexico Press & Peabody Museum of Archaeology and Ethnography, Cambridge, MA.

  1993   A View of Ancient Maya Settlement Patterns in the 8th-Century. In *Lowland Maya Civilization in the 8th Century A.D.,* edited by Jeremy A. Sabloff and John S. Henderson, pp. 219-241. Dumbarton Oaks Research Library & Collection, Washington, D.C.

Tozzer, Alfred M.
    1941   *Landa's Relacion de las Cosas de Yucatan.* Papers of the Peabody Museum of American Archaeology and Ethnology 18. Peabody Museum of American Archaeology & Ethnology, Cambridge, MA.

Wald, Robert F.
    1997   The Politics of Art and History at Palenque: The Interplay of Text and Iconography on the Tablet of the Slaves. Paper in the possession of the author.

Webster, David
    1989   The House of the Bacabs: Its Social Context. In *House of the Bacabs, Copan, Honduras*, edited by David Webster, pp. 5-40. Dumbarton Oaks Research Library and Collection, Washington, D.C.

    1997   City-States of the Maya. In *The Archaeology of City-States*, edited by Deborah L. Nichols and Thomas H. Charlton, pp. 135-154. Smithsonian Institution Press, Washington, D.C.

    2001   Spatial Dimensions of Maya Courtly Life: Problems and Issues. In *Royal Courts of the Ancient Maya, Vol. 1*, edited by Takeshi Inomata and Stephen D. Houston, pp. 130-167. Westview Press, Boulder, CO.

Willey, Gordon R. and Richard M. Leventhal
    1979   Prehistoric Settlement at Copan. In *Maya Archaeology and Ethnohistory*, edited by Norman Hammond and Gordon R. Willey, pp. 75-102. University of Texas Press, Austin.

Chapter 9

Following the Traces of Temple XX: Proyecto Grupo de las Cruces 2002 Excavations

Joshua A. Balcells González

The objective of this brief chapter is to illustrate the general characteristics of Temple XX from a purely archaeological perspective to further understand the structure within the temporal framework of Palenque. Clearly some issues about the nature of Temple XX remain unresolved, and the information presented here, derived from two field seasons of the Proyecto Grupo de las Cruces (PGC), represents only preliminary interpretations.

Temple XX is a pyramidal structure located within the South Group at Palenque. The South Group is composed of three main rectilinear plazas—Stephens Plaza, Plaza B, and Plaza C—bounded by numerous pyramidal structures (Fig. 9.1). Temple XX is located at the southwest end of Plaza B and faces onto this open space. Plaza B also extends to the west, around the northeast corner of Temple XX's substructure, toward Temples XXa, XXI, and XXII. The structure is thus bounded by an open plaza to the east, by Temple XXa, a later annex structure, to the north, by Temple XXc, a low L-shaped platform, to the west, and finally, by the Otolum River directly to the south.

Although Temple XX had been minimally explored in previous years during small-scale excavations, the PGC, directed by Alfonso Morales Cleveland, began excavations in 2001, focused on revealing the architectural features of Temple XX. One of the principal concerns of the project was to document and conserve the structural features, including the funeral chamber containing painted murals, which is located inside the substructure of the temple.

Promptly during the 2001-2002 excavations we realized that Temple XX is one of the most problematic structures at the site, primarily as a result of its extremely decayed and eroded state, the paucity of associated ceramic artifacts, and the total absence of associated hieroglyphic information. Notwithstanding,

Figure 9.1: Reconstruction of South Group as seen from Temple XIX
(drawn by Joe Balley)

we decided to confront this enigma, and because of our efforts during two field seasons, we have been able to learn a great deal more about the architecture of Palenque. The project has never lacked human resources, and equipment and materials needed to study Temple XX were, and continue to be, generously provided by the project. Finally, we employed a rigorous system of recording the architectural restoration, the artifacts, and the geo-radar scanning techniques used to document the structure.

Architecture: Description of the Structure

Excavation made clear that the Temple XX superstructure was situated on top of a natural bedrock mound, composed of limestone typical of the Palenque area. The Pre-Hispanic architects and laborers who built the structure took advantage of the natural shape and volume of the bedrock, in some places simply covering the natural limestone with a thin layer of construction stones. This contributed to the high level of structural collapse and destruction that characterizes the building; the damage is such that in places up to three formerly separate walls have been found fallen and resting together on the same spot (Fig. 9.2).

The superstructure (Fig. 9.3) is composed of three stepped levels enclosing four pillars, two at the front and two toward the middle of the temple; each of these pillars are mirrored by respective lateral piers connected to the inside of the north and south walls, only two of which are preserved.

The remains of two walls in the southwest portion suggest that the temple had two side rooms that flanked a central room, and, judging from remains found, the floors of the rooms were most likely stuccoed. The dividing walls forming these rooms do not seem to be part of the original structure design, but were instead later additions. Other buildings at Palenque with a similar floor plan are the Temple Olvidado, Temple of the Count, and to a lesser degree Temple II of the North Group (Marken, Chapter 4).

On the front (east) side of Temple XX there were most likely five structural terraces, *talud* in form, with a central staircase giving access to the temple superstructure. This staircase foundation partly rests on the bedrock of the highest level of the current south plaza, providing access to Temple XX.

These conclusions are strengthened by the discovery of two groups of steps that were perpendicularly aligned to intersect each other. One is composed of nine steps oriented east-west, and provided access to the highest level of the plaza on which Temple XX was founded; the other group is constructed in the same manner with nine steps oriented north-south. The groups of steps rise from a stucco floor, with treads and risers measuring 30 cm by 30 cm.

As stated previously, the riser of the seventh step oriented north-south functions as a base for the steps of the final construction phase of Temple XX. Interestingly, there are two more steps, behind those already mentioned, which are covered by the construction fill of the final phase; this suggests an architectural

Figure 9.2: Collapse about walls on the south side of Temple XX (below)

Figure 9.3: Plan view of superstructure (drawing by Joshua Balcells Gonzales)

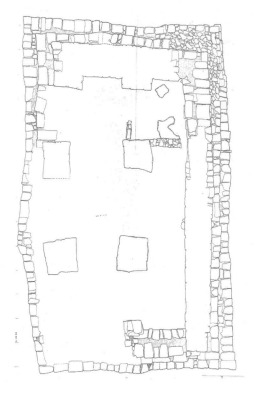

overlap or reuse of the older steps. For this reason, I hypothezise that at one time they served as a means of direct access between the plaza and an earlier phase of Temple XX, and that they were reutilized following modification of the plaza level and the substructure.

At least two platforms were built up from the plaza level to the west, behind Temple XX, separated from the temple by a passageway approximately 1.50 m in width. This space, oriented north-south, at least in part, served to drain the heavy runoff during the rainy season.

On the west side of the building, there are at least five visible *talud* terrace walls, and according to our architectural projections, three more such terrace walls must have been raised before the full height of the upper structure was attained. In all there were eight structural terraces with an approximately 60 degree sloped *talud*. The masonry is of faced, but irregular construction stones, and in some parts totally unworked stones were put in place simply to give shape to the wall. The limestone bedrock also extrudes in several places on this side of the structure. According to our calculations, it is likely the building reached a total height of around 27 m above the west plaza. The east plaza has a difference in height from the west plaza that varies more or less between 6 m and 9 m in elevation.

As stated previously, at least two platforms rise from the west plaza level, both constructed directly on the bedrock, and a natural passageway formed by a bedrock outcrop separates them. The platforms are not attached to Temple XX, and are separated by a passageway oriented north-south, in which the remains of a poorly preserved stucco floor have been found. The back wall of the platform and the first talud wall of Temple XX remain separated by a distance varying from 1 m in the northern part of the passageway to 1.50 m in the southern part.

During the excavation of Trenches 2 and 3 (on the west side) significant quantities of apparently domestic refuse were found in the passage, including remains of obsidian blades, plates, cups, censers, figurines, and manos. This suggests a residential function for the platform, and these portions of the passageway could represent small domestic refuse areas.

Also, from what we were able to observe of Temple XX-sub, on the east side we found a centrally located stairway with two *alfardas* from which two asymmetrical walls extend.

It is important to mention that the Temple XX superstructure was not built directly atop the earlier construction phase superstructure. From our excavations we know that Temple XX-sub, like other temples at Palenque, was situated on the highest and most central part of a bedrock mound; when Temple XX was constructed, the temple platform was placed toward the north, filling in the area not covered by remains of Temple XX-sub. Test pits in the interior of Temple XX, where the majority of collapsed material from the roof and other parts of the structure were recovered, demonstrate this. The northern part of the temple was the most affected by tectonic activity; it was filled in with well-cut stones, but enough space was left in between them to allow the temple to collapse.

Tombs

Geophysical survey techniques of geo-radar and magnetometry were used to verify the existence of subsurface archaeological remains under Temples XX and XIX. Dr. Jose Ortega (INAH) carried out the electromagnetic and magnetometric testing, using a geo-radar with two penetration antennas (900 and 300 mghz) and a magnetometer-gradiometer, to detect subsurface voids created by substructures, tombs, or other types of cavities that register as anomalies.

One of the goals of the 2001 field season was to excavate the interior of Temple XX in order to document the stratigraphic levels corresponding to different construction phases, while simultaneously correlating this with data from the geo-radar surveys. Working in this manner, Ortega detected an anomaly 57 cm below the surface in the southwest part of the structure (Fig. 9.4).

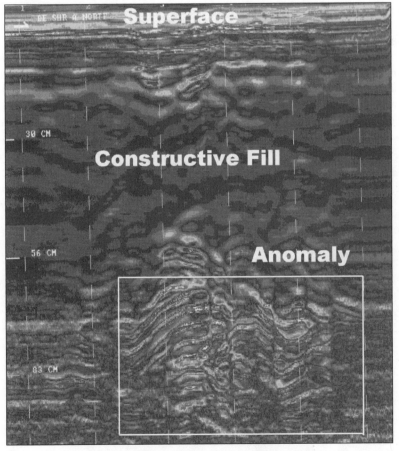

**Figure 9.4: Anomaly detected in the southwest part of the structure
at 57 cm below the surface**

The southwest area of Temple XX is composed of a room, approximately 2.40 m by 2.20 m. The remains of a stucco floor are still preserved. To the north this area is bordered by a stone alignment and by one of the piers; the interior wall of the structure lies to the south, as well as lateral piers parallel to the middle piers. The east side the room is bordered by another alignment of stones similar to the one on the north side, and evidence suggests that the east alignment did not completely block the room, but simply restricted access to one part. Finally, the internal wall forms the west side of the room.

With this in mind, and according to the geo-radar data, excavations were conducted in the room, and at a depth of approximately 50 cm we encountered an alignment of elongated construction stones. These covered a series of flattened slabs which in turn covered a rectangular stone box approximately 1.60 m long by 80 cm wide, and 45 cm high. This "box" had a 20 cm opening on its east side with a small rectangular slab serving as a lintel for the aperture. Likewise, a niche was present on the interior west face, medially aligned opposite the aforementioned opening (Fig. 9.5).

Upon uncovering this feature, our first impression was to consider it a slab-lined funerary cist, or possibly a small secondary burial chamber. We drew this initial conclusion because according to Arnoldo González Cruz (personal communication 2001), it is common at Palenque to find two or more small burials alongside a large, more elaborate interment. However, after probing with a small

Figure 9.5: Stone box, possible tomb opened at Pre-Hispanic times

digital camera we realized that there was absolutely nothing inside this "slab-lined box" but a stone floor and traces of rubble.

The immediate absence of burial evidence gave rise to more a priori assumptions about the stone box, namely that it was a bench pertaining to an earlier construction phase or a niche for placing offerings. However, upon full excavation of this feature, the evidence strongly suggested that it was indeed a funerary crypt, and the conclusion was no longer speculative. The floor was composed of stone slab fragments painted with cinnabar, and surprisingly, in the north part of the feature eleven jade beads were found along with two jade earplugs (Tomb 1; Fig. 9.6). Skeletal remains were absent apart from some poorly preserved dental enamel, and no associated ceramic artifacts were found.

Considering the similarities with Temple XVIII, where three aligned tombs were found, and the spatial proximity between the two temples, we anticipated the presence of another tomb inside the structure, oriented along the same axis as the tomb just described. We then opened another unit 1.50 m from the stone box (Tomb 1), and another crypt was found at a depth of approximately 40 cm from the temple floor (Fig. 9.7). Inside we found disturbed skeletal remains, poorly preserved, including four teeth with jade incrustations (Fig. 9.8), as well as a small jade head (Fig. 9.9).

To the south, outside of this crypt, a rectangular ceramic vessel and a cup were found, both in pieces, but well preserved. Preliminary analysis indicates

**Figure 9.6: Jade beads found inside the stone box
below southwest room of Temple XX**

Figure 9.7: Alfonso Morales Cleveland and Joshua Balcells Gonzales excavating the cist

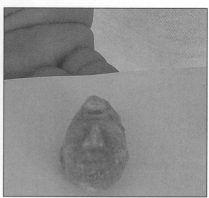

Figure 9.8:
Teeth with jade incrustation

Figure 9.9:
A small jade head found inside cist

that they date to the Murcielagos phase, between A.D. 700-750 (Robert Rands, personal communication 2002).

Following the Traces of Temple XX: Preliminary Considerations

Situating Temple XX within the known chronology of Palenque is a problematic undertaking: the absence of glyphs associated with the architecture, the scarcity of ceramics in clear contexts, and the almost complete destruction of the architectural features, present the main challenges to archaeological interpretation.

On the plus side, however, we can document two definite, partially preserved construction phases at the temple. The first, Temple XX-sub, includes a vaulted funerary chamber with painted murals and eleven ceramic vessels (Fig. 9.10). In regards to the second construction phase, Temple XX, at our disposal we have one funerary crypt with associated ceramics, sherds from the construction fill, and a well-defined architectural plan for this final construction phase.

I will now try to integrate Temple XX into the long history of Palenque by describing the material and features listed above. The architectural style, ceramic remains, and the three tombs located thus far in Temple XX suggest a long

Figure 9.10:
Inside the tomb, we can see some vessels and numerous jade beads
(PGC Database Photography)

Figure 9.11:
Part of the wall murals inside the tomb
(PGC Database Photography)

occupation for the structure, and this information will help us to understand the different structural modifications and additions that were carried out there.

The funerary chamber with painted murals (Fig. 9.11) lies within an earlier construction phase, Temple XX-sub, that is notable for its perfectly faced construction stones, sometimes extremely rectangular and thin in form, but always

Figure 9.12: Steps uncovered in the east plaza

Figure 9.13: Steps uncovered, east plaza

Figure 9.14: *Alfardas* **and their respective steps**

very smoothly finished. Also, the walls and accompanying moldings of the sub-structure are all covered with stucco. Remains from this period are contemporaneous with the steps uncovered in the east plaza (Extensions of Trench 3 Op.6.5, 2001 [Figs. 9.12 & 9.13]), the *alfardas* and their respective steps leading to the structure (Extensions between Trench 2 and 3 Op. 6.5, 2001 [Fig. 9.14]), and the stuccoed wall in the northeast corner (Extensions of Trench 4 Op. 6.5, 2002). The wall encountered behind Temple XXa (Trench 3 Unit 0, Op. 6.10, 2002), the architectural platforms found in the units of Op. 6.8 in the upper southwest corner of the structure (2001), and various reused corners in the northwest part of the structure (Trenches 1 and 2 Op. 6.10, 2002) are also contemporaneous with the aforementioned features of the substructure.

The most recent construction phase, Temple XX, is related to the use of a rougher and more solid type of stone, in some cases well faced, and in others completely amorphous, and at times applied without the use of mortar. This phase can be dated more or less to the same phase as the funerary cist found the previous season (2001) at 25 cm below the surface of the superstructure. The ceramics found in this burial belong to the Murcielagos phase, placing the final renovation of Temple XX from A.D. 700-750.

During the summer of 2002, while discussing the architectural and ceramic aspects of the excavation with colleagues from the project, we became more aware of the long time span of the occupation of Temple XX. We concluded that it corresponds to the beginning of the known construction sequence at Palenque, around

A.D. 660, based on architectural forms (Marken, Chapter 4), and remained in use through Murcielagos times (A.D. 700-750) because the ceramics are related to those of Temples XIX, XVIII, and possibly XXI, Group IV, and others.

The argument supporting such a long occupation for Temple XX is derived principally from the painted tomb located in Temple XX-sub, where the eleven ceramic vessels date to the Cascada phase, from A.D. 500-620 (Robert Rands, personal communication 2002). The ceramics recovered from the refuse middens of the west platforms, the northeast corner, and the looted funerary cist inside the structure primarily date to the Murcielagos and Balunte phases (approximately A.D. 700-820), and suggest an occupation lasting for at least 200 years. Some sherds found in Temple XX indicate that the structure was also used during the Otolum and Balunte phases (Kirk Straight, personal communication 2002).

As shown by the work of Damien Marken (Chapter 4) and Kirk Straight (Chapter 10), Temple XX displays architectural and ceramic attributes that span from relatively early periods until the Late Classic, contemporaneous with various structures of the South Group, and with other groups such as Group IV and the Palace. The similarity in architectural plans also indicate contemporaneity with the Temple of the Count and the Temple Olvidado.

After excavating at Temple XX, I can personally confirm that it is a very odd and enigmatic structure, and it poses multiple challenges for both architectural interpretation and the subsequent restoration process. One partial explanation for this complexity is that, due to the long occupation of the structure and the fragility of the materials used in the first construction phase, the structure was subjected to multiple modifications during at least three principle construction phases.

Not only have we ascertained the contemporaneity of this structure with others, but we have also learned how different techniques and technologies can be employed to archaeological studies, and how to better interpret the variability in form and depth of the architecture at Palenque. There still remains much to learn about Temple XX, the South Group and the entire site in general. But with continued efforts like those put forth by the entire PGC team, we will no doubt continue to provide answers to these diverse questions, and hopefully the politics and conditions outside of the investigation will allow knowledge to triumph in Palenque.

Acknowledgments

I deeply thank Damien Marken for inviting me to participate in this volume, *gracias amigo*. I would especially like to thank Alfonso Morales and Julia Miller for guiding the PGC down a good path, Kirk Straight for aiding in the ceramic analysis, Dr. Jose Ortega y Ulises with the geo-radar, Rogelio Rivero and the entire group of Tzeltales and Choles who worked with us each day in the field.

Chapter 10

A House of Cards:
Construction, Proportion and Form
at Temple XIX, Palenque, Chiapas, Mexico
Kirk D. Straight

Introduction

The construction of Temple XIX falls within an interval when, presumably, multiple architectural projects occurred simultaneously throughout the growing Late Classic center of Palenque. The most obvious securely dated development which can be traced is in the monumental buildings of the South Group. The twin temples, XVIII and XVIIIa, constructed in A.D. 731, present different floor plans and proportions (yet comparable construction technique) than those encountered at Temple XIX, dated to A.D. 734. This sudden shift in architecture form appears to be a point of divergence which may have significance for understanding the social or political environment of the Late Classic Palenque Maya inhabitants. This shift in building form or type occurs in the midreign of the ruler K'inich Ahkal Mo' Nahb III, a time of increasingly complex interregional exchange in both ceramics and captives among Palenque and neighboring centers, according to epigraphic and ceramic compositional data (Martin and Grube 2000; Martin et al. 2002; Rands 1967, 1974, 1988; Rands & Bishop 2003).

The comparison of the layout and dimensions of Temple XIX versus those of other structures at the site provides an initial basis for interpretation of change. These numbers also have implications concerning the precarious structure proportions (wall width to gallery span to height) encountered at Temple XIX. Furthermore, the preparation of construction block and mortar (as well as the constructed form of buildings) seems to shift through time at Palenque (see Marken, Chapter 4), reinforcing the idea of an interrelated continuum of proportion, form, and technical adaptations. This however does not imply continuous improvement, in fact, the numbers will show that proportions do not get significantly greater (the limits are reached early in the short observable sequence), and in fact construction techniques decline in quality, implying a complex evolution of architectural development rather than a linear progression of improvement.

Setting

Temple XIX is, in fact, unique. Yet it is situated within a structure arrangement in the South Group or South Acropolis which is rebuilt over the Temple XVIIIa and Temple XX tombs and substructures. It appears that this portion of the center was a focus of architectural growth and continuous habitation from Early Classic through Late Classic times, as attested by an unbroken ceramic sequence from Cascada into Balunte times (Straight n.d.). The physical location of this group of structures is also meaningful in respect to site layout, as the three elevated plazas which extend south from the Cross Group are adjacent to the Otolum stream which initiates south of Temple XIX and flows just to the west on its course through the aqueduct east of the Palace. The corbelled ceiling of the aqueduct physically joins the South Group to the Palace and Inscriptions platform which would otherwise be separated by the stream (French, Chapter 7). Much has been said about the Cross Group's position in the shadow of the Mirador hill with the Otolum stream to the west and the Murcielagos stream to the east. Stephen Houston (1996: 133) has suggested that the city core of Palenque, referred to by the glyphic toponym *Lakam Ha'* ("Banner Water"), was taken by the ancient inhabitants from the name of the Otolum stream. The position of Temple XIX at the extreme south of the extended Cross Group/South Group configuration, near the issuance of the Otolum stream and in an area of the site built over earlier structures with elite/royal burials, points to the possible ritual importance the structure may have held during its Classic functioning days.

The Cross Group/South Group architectural arrangement closely follows the natural topography of this sector of the center. The two most prominent hills were modified into substructures (at different times) in order to support the Temple of the Cross and Temple XX; both restricted by verticality and single access stairways facing inward on adjoining lower space, artificially raised and leveled to form rectangular plazas. Lacking the tightly spaced convoluted architecture and absolute traffic control of the Palace at Palenque or the Central Acropolis at Tikal, the Cross Group/South Group conforms to more of an "amphitheater" arrangement (see Kubler 1985: 252), with large vaulted structures spaced around connecting plazas, perched atop architectural terraces. Plaza B (halfway between the Temple of the Cross and Temple XIX) opens up this amphitheater setting by extending west around the base of Temple XX's superstructure, delimited to the west by Temple XXII raised above the bank of the Otolum stream, and to the north by a high architectural terrace which supports Temple XXI. This western portion of Plaza B contains a multiple room ranged structure or "palace" (Temple XXII) as well as several low platforms behind Temple XX, assumed to have supported perishable structures (Balcells González, Chapter 9). These structures conform more to domestic space than to the majority of non-residential temples in the area, although their precise functions and construction dates are not known.

Background

Ceramic seriation (Rands 1967, 1974, 1987) and epigraphy (Berlin 1965; Lounsbury 1991; Mathews 1974; Schele 1992) directly associated with monumental architecture have led to dating possibilities for epicentral buildings at Palenque. These and other "style data" have been used as the basis for seriation schemes of Late Classic architectural developments at the site (Proskouriakoff 1950; Schele 1981). Working only with temple-type structures, Damien Marken (Chapter 4) has recently proposed a modal analysis of architectural attributes in order to place them in chronologic order; providing an alternative and complementary relative dating technique for Palenque. In this chapter, I will not assume a "logical" or linear progression of increasing quality of construction or advancing proportions, but instead, rely on ceramics, architectural style, and epigraphy for dating.

The dynastic history of Palenque, as reconstructed by epigraphers, ranges from A.D. 387 to 799, while epicentral architecture dated by ceramics, epigraphy, and art were constructed exclusively during Late Otolum to Murcielagos times (A.D. 640-740). Construction of Temple XIX was epigraphically recorded as a temple dedication (*och' otot, och' k'ak'*), on three carved stone monuments originally attached to the temple itself (Stuart, in press). This makes Temple XIX the latest epigraphically dated structure (9.15.2.7.16, A.D. 734) in the sequence. The earliest dated temple structure, located in the western precinct, was named the *Olvidado* by Heinrich Berlin (1944). Though partially collapsed, the Temple Olvidado remains intact enough to discern that it has two narrow corbel vaulted galleries, an inclined façade, or mansard-style roof, with roof comb elements and stucco sculptured interior and exterior piers. With all the hallmarks of a classic Palenque-style temple and blessed with a high degree of preservation, the Olvidado has provided secure data for comparison with epicentral structures. It has been dated to 9.10.14.5.10 (A.D. 647) by a reconstructed glyphic inscription modeled in stucco (Berlin 1944; Mathews & Greene Robertson 1985).

Various epicentral structures were built over earlier structures and Early Classic ceramics were recovered from under the floor of the tomb within the Inscriptions Temple, in the fill of the Temple of the Count (Temple VII, North Group) and in the core of the ball court structures (Schele 1986). Substructures have been reported from excavations into the platform cores of Temple XVIIIa (Ruz 1958), Temple XX (Greene Robertson et al. 1999), Temple V (Tovalín Ahumada & Ceje Manrique 1996), and the Palace (Schele 1986). While Early Classic materials are present, all latest phase architecture in the epicenter relates to Late Classic times. The possibility also exists that earlier temple structures remain unexcavated in other areas of the site, or completely razed by the Maya in antiquity.

From the construction of the Temple Olvidado in A.D. 647 to Temple XIX in A.D 734, all epicentral architecture seen at the site today can be bracketed within a ninety-year period. The Tower has been dated to post-A.D. 770 in some architectural seriations, possibly extending this sequence, though the exact date of construction of this unique structure may be closer to A.D. 700, based on its construction technique which is roughly analogous to the Cross Group temples. Ceramics at other parts of the site (González Cruz 1993) seem to indicate occupation beyond A.D. 734, though securely dating architecture to this period, c. A.D. 740-800, is difficult, and may represent a shift in construction efforts from temples to elite residential compounds outside the epicenter (see Marken, Chapter 4; Marken & González Cruz, Chapter 8).

Construction Techniques

Although evidently well planned from its inception, the Temple XIX architects utilized mostly non-trimmed, single-faced limestone blocks for wall/pier facing stones, interspersed with a range of 1 cm to 15 cm chinking stones, or spalls, evidently laid in a weak mortar mixed with a high percent of clay. Construction blocks were laid somewhat haphazardly to form two faced walls and piers with dry rubble cores consisting of unworked, fragmented limestone and light brown clay fill. This filler clay or mortar appears as light brown fine particle earth which powders when dry and can easily be balled up when wet, and was evidently not a strong binding agent (especially when vaulting over wide galleries). A thin interior stucco covering was applied, providing no structural support, and a 10 cm thick exterior *concrete* application completed the roof, possibly providing some structural support after setting up. The roof vault was formed without the use of a strong lime based mortar with sideways placed short limestone "tongue-shaped" tenons and roughly rectangular blocks or slabs, which required little or no preparation beyond quarrying to provide the minimal hearting required to hold the vault in place.

Springline stones and capstones from the vault of Temple XIX were trimmed into rectangles averaging 1.8 m by 0.5 m by 0.1 m. These "specialty stones" are quite uniform medium hard limestone which were trimmed on four sides after being removed in slabs of a uniform thickness; springline stones were drilled at one end to produce the exterior "curtain holder" effect on the medial molding of temples like those of the Cross Group. Non-load bearing stucco applications were originally applied over the exterior of all walls, and a unique multistep stucco formation was employed in spanning the 3.58 m slightly off centered axial cross-vault with a trifoil, trilobe, or keyhole arch.

The carefully trimmed springline stones of uniform dimension were originally laid atop the built-up walls and piers of Temple XIX. The overhang created by the placement of these stones produced both the exterior medial molding and the interior springline of the corbelled roof soffit. In this manner, the level, uniform layer of springline stones evenly dispersed the weight of the roof construction above. The vault was capped with well-trimmed capstones and the remainder of the roof construction above provided weight to stabilize the entire structure. As Roys (1934: 73) notes, in regard to the "dead weight" of this roof mass:

> This layer therefore sets heavily and firmly upon the walls and vault sides and holds them in place, just as the flat roof of a house built of playing cards holds the cardboard sides from falling inward and is an important strength-giving part of this miniature building.

Roys' analogy to the house of cards' roof providing stability to hold the structure together is of note in light of the construction techniques evident at Temple XIX. In addition to the leveling stonework described, excavations produced large slab stones covered with the exterior roof coating. This 10-12 cm layer of lime aggregate or lime concrete contained a large percent of limestone pebbles and river gravel embedded in a grey stucco matrix. Fragments of this thick homogenous layer which once sealed the roof exterior were the strongest, most cohesive samples of stucco encountered at Temple XIX. Blocks of this lime cement proved to be as durable as limestone blocks of comparable thickness. Interestingly, no uniformly cut (of identical dimension) blocks used in the construction of roof combs on other structures were recovered from the interior, substructure, or rear of Temple XIX. Although some alternate form of roof comb construction cannot definitively be ruled out, it appears reasonable that Temple XIX never had one.

The substructure terraces were formed with single-faced limestone blocks set against the built-up dry fill core overlaying bedrock. Excavations down to bedrock revealed large limestone boulders set in dark dense clay, evidently as a ballast or preparatory layer to increase stability. This effect was not diligently repeated while the successive layers of the substructure terraces were randomly laid with little attempt to organize or level the fill. The construction blocks utilized show minimal evidence of trimming prior to being laid as "facing" or wall stones and all exteriors were evidently covered over with stucco.

Stucco

Few systematic or technological studies of stucco preparation, use, or maintenance have actually been conducted and reported.[1] This is regrettable because stucco is one of the four components (stucco, stone, mud, and wood) used by the ancient Maya in constructing monumental architecture. Stucco or lime mortar is probably the key factor in attaining a coherent monolithic mass (Roys 1934: 38) and sustained stability over time in constructing Maya corbelled vaulted structures (Roys 1934: 42-43, 55). Furthermore, the majority of published reports on stucco concern only laboratory work toward defining their composition, while the broader context of the production of this material and its cultural and ecological implications have gone virtually ignored (Schreiner 2001: 2-3).

Stucco, in a quality lime-based form, is found in multiple contexts at Temple XIX, however it was not used as a mortar or binding agent in the construction of the substructure, basal platform, superstructure walls/piers, or the roof vault. In a strong, well-prepared form, stucco was utilized to prepare a ballast layer some 20-cm thick, to accept the trimmed limestone slabs which formed the temple floor. Quality stucco was also employed to seal the joins of the stone slab floor and to connect the throne panels to each other and to this floor. Moving from east to west within the superstructure, the stone slab floor ends just west of the fifth pier, the remaining floor space being composed of a polished stucco surface. This stucco surface appears to have functioned as the formal floor in the western portion of the building, although the reasons for this division remain unresolved.

A polychrome modeled stucco panel was formed over the east face of the "central" pier, with preformed glyphic blocks set into the curing panel (Fig. 10.1). Stucco fragments from this panel were the purest samples of lime stucco, lacking any visible inclusions and appearing as white chalk in cross-section. Stucco sculptural elements were recovered from the uppermost terrace supporting the Temple XIX superstructure, east and west of the entrance, running the entire length of the building and continuing around the sides. Though in a decayed and fragmented state, the quantity of these remains indicate that an elaborate sculptural program once adorned the exterior of the structure. Stucco elements were attached with

hand-snapped, grooved limestone armature bars, similar to those recovered from other structures at the site, including the Temple of the Inscriptions (Greene Robertson 1985).

Figure 10.1:
Modeled stucco
polychrome panel,
Temple XIX

The mortar used at Temple XIX is a "mud mortar" (see Schele 1986: 118) or "clay mortar" (Marken 2002a, 2002b). This mortar was used as a bed to accept stones of construction, and in forming the core of random rubble. The mortar seems to be closest to that described and analyzed by Littman (1959: sample 16) from the Temple of the Jaguar, dated by Linda Schele (1981: 112) to 9.15.0.0.0.+/- 10 tuns. It is of note that this sample contained 24 percent calcium carbonate, and probably represents a specific recipe (albeit a poor one) like all other mortars at the site. While the inclusion of inert material in stucco provides stability and reduces shrinking and cracking of the final product, the use of clay would not be optimum.

Another use of stucco at Temple XIX involved the application of successive layers of stucco in the formation and capping of the trefoil arch which spanned the "central" interior axis of Temple XIX. This type of construction is known from House A of the Palace (Fig. 10.2) and was identified for Temple XIX by Christopher Powell and Joe Balley from material recovered from specific context during excavations of Temple XIX. Littman describes a stucco sample recovered from Comalcalco which exhibited three distinct layers, differentiated by color and hardness. In his chemical analysis, Littman could find no reason to account for the differing properties of the layers in this sample (1958: 296). The samples recovered at Temple XIX (Fig. 10.3) show a similar multi-stage forming technique, whereby the trefoil arch form was created through successive modeling phases

over the stone soffit of the axial cross-vault. The fragments recovered not only provide evidence of the trefoil form of the fallen cross vault of Temple XIX, they also denote a fairly developed technical knowledge of stucco preparation.

Figure 10.2:
Trilobed, trefoil, or keyhole
style arch modeled in stucco,
House A of the Palace

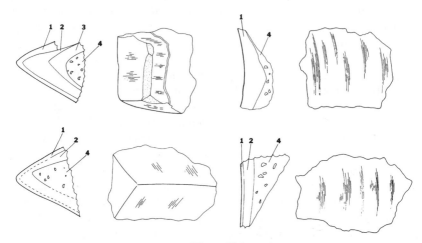

Figure 10.3:
Stucco from the keyhole arch at Temple XIX showing consecutive modeling stages:
1) polished fine white stucco "finishing" layer,
2) less fine white stucco with few inclusions (same as 3),
3) less fine white stucco with few inclusions (same as 2),
4) grey stucco "primer" with high percent of gravel and other inclusions

Stone

Trimmed and formed slabs and blocks of limestone were utilized for aesthetic value more often than for maintaining structural integrity in the construction of the 33-m long superstructure of Temple XIX. The following categories of limestone construction block were recovered:

A. Wall Stones—generally irregular, with an inclination toward rectangles, sizes ranging from to 20 cm to over a meter in length and averaging 40-60 cm in depth

B. Soffit Stones—unhewn "tongue-shaped" tenons and roughly rectangular blocks

C. Capstone—1.8 m by 0.5 m trimmed limestone slabs averaging 9 cm in thickness

D. Springline Stones—1.8 m by 0.5 m trimmed limestone slabs identical to capstones, with the addition of angled "cord-holder" biconically drilled holes at one end

E. Floorslabs—averaging 4-7 cm in thickness, large, mostly rectangular trimmed limestone slabs up to 2 m-long, laid in a bed of mortar as a final floor surface

Compared to earlier architecture at the site, the wall stones and soffit stones used at Temple XIX seem sloppily prepared and inadequate, while trimmed slabs (C, D, E) were used simultaneously in specific positions of structural importance.

Spalls, or small limestone pieces wedged between construction blocks, typically provide stability points while fresh stucco sets up; however at Temple XIX, the great number of spalls used in wall/pier construction suggests use as additional bonding points as they would act in a dry laid wall. The crude stone work of Temple XIX would benefit from this practice, being prone to crushing from uneven and overburdened wall construction. In this manner, the Temple XIX architects generously chinked the stonework in an attempt to steady the irregular stone blocks set in weak mortar. This is not a perfect solution, rather an option or alternative to using well-squared construction blocks or a strong mortar. A drawing of a load-bearing support pier from Temple XIX (Fig. 10.4) illustrates how this practice was taken to extremes, or rather, that the optimum effect was surpassed to the point of diminishing quality. Areas large enough to be taken up by single construction stones are instead filled in with a multitude of spalls. This is most precarious in combination with a very weak mortar, especially in the lower portion of the walls which once held the heavy load of the massive construction above.

Furthermore, carved limestone cord holder elements were set along the superior landing (four to a side) into cut limestone slabs of the skirt,[2] which was then stuccoed over. Carved panels, the limestone coverslab of the throne platform, the formal entrance steps, and the *alfarda* panel boxes all represent non-structural stone work. In short, Temple XIX had all the fine finishing touches, yet little effort

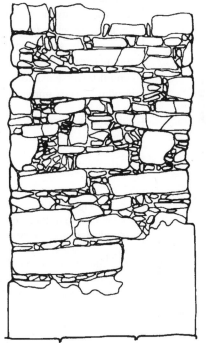

was made to trim, and hence improve the structural *durability* of important soffit stones or wall/pier construction blocks. This situation is paralleled in the use of stucco, where the elaborately modeled keyhole vault and polychrome panel are "unnecessary" items in a pragmatic sense, while this quality stucco when used as a mortar would have improved the structural durability, and by extension, structural *stability* (lessen settling) of the building.

Figure 10.4:
Elevation drawing of central pier
face showing excessive "spalling" and
generally poor construction technique,
Temple XIX

Architectural Form

The terms house and temple are not logical classes, but convenient labels which have been adopted based on form and proportion of structures, context within the overall site, and information gleaned from iconography and epigraphy. The terms have been applied with varying discretion by nearly all Mayanist researchers and are imbedded in the literature no matter what evocation they bring to the reader.

George Andrews (1975: 39) defines temple-type structures as small buildings of ritual or ceremonial function, restricted from everyday life raised on pyramidal substructures above connecting open plaza spaces. This description accords well with most "temples" at Palenque, and like most other temple-type structures at the site, Temple XIX was built as a double vaulted gallery structure with a single axis facing inward toward a large plaza. Nonetheless, the structure exhibits very wide galleries in proportion to thin walls and interior support piers and is far larger than any other temple at the site with a dissimilar constructed form focused on a large, enclosed, and uninterrupted interior space.

The constructed form of Temple XIX (and Temple XXI) diverged from the near ubiquitous Palenque form having three or five entrances produced by two or four exterior support piers (Fig. 10.5). At Temple XIX, a single 5.3 m axial entrance must have been spanned by a wooden lintel, while seven interior rectangular support piers were widely spaced, non-symmetrically, through the central traverse axis of the building. The amount of

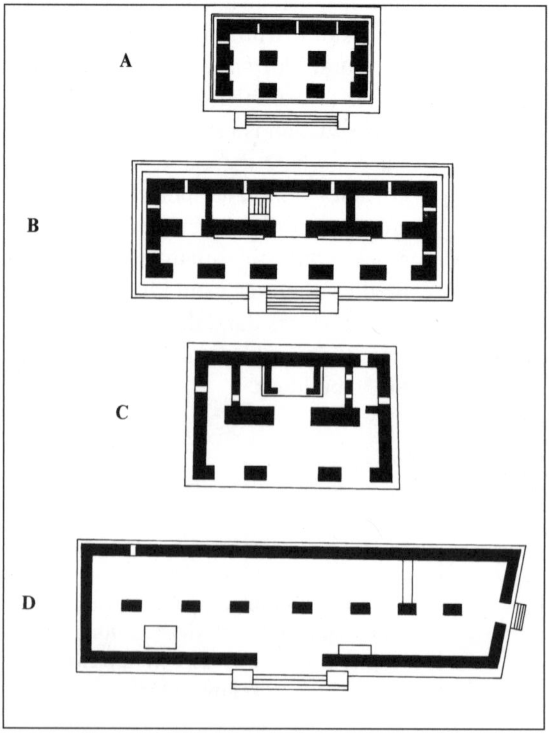

Figure 10.5:
Comparison of Palenque temple floorplans at equal scale:
a) Temple of the Count (VII);
b) Temple of the Inscriptions;
c) Temple of the Cross;
d) Temple XIX

space captured within the 33 m long Temple XIX superstructure was not diminished by curtain walls, inner sanctums or other permanent traffic screens. The only structural features encountered during excavation were a small plain bench inside the west front gallery, and an elaborate formal platform also within the front gallery, to the east (Fig. 10.6).

The lack of any interior room divisions or inner sanctums at Temple XIX, suggest that the structure was not utilized for domestic functions in the same way proposed for "palaces," but rather served for the meeting of groups of individuals,

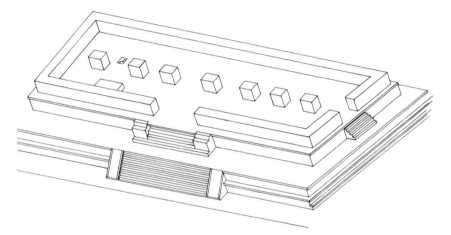

Figure 10.6: Isometric reconstruction of Temple XIX floorplan

possibly in conjunction with storage. The east side of the structure interior is focused on a 1.68 m by 2.50 m platform, 56 cm in height, centered between the two easternmost interior support piers. The platform was originally finely constructed with carved limestone panels containing long incised hieroglyphic texts, fronting the west and south sides. These panels portray multiple lords from Palenque (including K'inich Ahkal Mo' Nahb III) and neighboring sites (Stuart, Chapter 11) involved in court activity. Postholes strategically cut through the stone slab floor attest that the platform or throne was probably originally canopied (Fig. 10.7). One is immediately reminded of Late Classic polychrome vase scenes showing opulent lords sitting within structures upon flat platforms beneath curtains, admiring themselves in mirrors, receiving tribute, or engaging in other activities with a cast of court characters or royal visitors. The Temple XIX platform faces south into the rear gallery, providing ample space to address an assembly within the structure. A single small window shaft pierces the south structure wall and would have provided little in the way of light. If activities occurred within Temple XIX, they were certainly aided by torch or lamp light, or else conducted in near total darkness.

Temple XIX and Temple XXI are the only epicentral vaulted double gallery structures at Palenque which exhibit the following characteristics simultaneously:

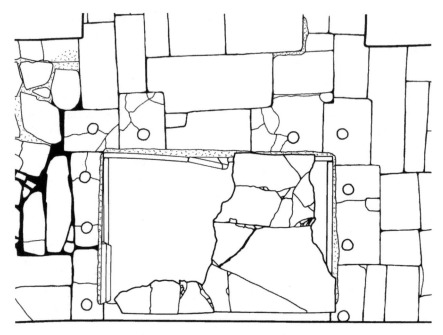

Figure 10.7: Plan drawing of Temple XIX platform and postholes cut through stone slab floor (presumably for a perishable canopy)

(1) a single axial entrance, (2) hieroglyphic platform (throne), (3) no non-load bearing curtain walls, and (4) an orientation facing north.

Interestingly, Temple XXI seems to have been built with several improvements in construction technique and form, though with identical proportions as Temple XIX.

The Temple XXI superstructure is shorter in overall length than Temple XIX with fewer interior support piers, though with the same proportions in cross-section. This actually gives Temple XXI a greater ratio of bearing wall to vaulted space, decreasing the crushing pressure per square meter. Efforts were also made to bolster the corners of Temple XXI by using megalithic squared stone blocks, both in the basal platform and in the superstructure. This effort was complemented with the use of enormous, thick, well-trimmed limestone blocks to form the two perfect courses of the basal molding. By contrast, the basal molding at Temple XIX was formed with much smaller, unevenly coursed, softer limestone blocks which have decayed and shifted, whereas Temple XXI's basal molding remains in superior condition and alignment. Temple XIX and Temple XXI have near identical wall construction, weak "clay mortar," sub-floor chambers constructed into their basal platforms (neither containing mortuary remains), free standing "altar" or "throne" platforms with elaborate iconography and glyphic inscriptions, stone slab floors, and "box-like" slab construction entrance stairs (Straight 1999).

Glyphic texts from both structures bear identical dedication dates (González Cruz & Bernal Romero 2003; also see Stuart, Chapter 11).

Epigraphy and Iconography

Any discussion of Temple XIX would be incomplete without mention of the wealth of information provided by the associated monuments. Although space does not permit a full discussion of these monuments, certain aspects of the epigraphic and iconographic content are particularly insightful for discussion of the construction and use of Temple XIX.

The dedication or *och' k'ak'* ("fire enters") event is recorded at 9.15.2.17.16 (A.D. 734) on three carved limestone monuments from Temple XIX: the Lápida de los Ayudantes, the west platform panel and the west *alfarda* tablet. The latest date recorded at Temple XIX is 9.15.5.0.0 (A.D. 736), a *hotun* ending from the west platform panel, just 924 days after the initial dedication. A stucco panel bearing the retrospective calendar round dates for 9.13.17.9.0, 9.14.0.0.0, and 9.14.2.9.0 may have been erected post-9.15.5.0.0 according to Bernal Romero (2002) and Martin and Grube (2000), but not after 9.15.10.10.13, in accordance with the dates of the K'an Tok' Tablet from Temple XVI. Straight and Marken (2002) have argued that a 9.15.2.9.0 installation of the stucco panel is the best possibility, viewing this as a katun anniversary of the Temple XVIII jamb event enacted by K'inich Ahkal Mo' Nahb III, and a katun earlier than the Temple XIX structure dedication. Either possibility produces a short, 2.5 to 7.5 year, secure use-life for Temple XIX.

The *alfarda* tablet from the west side of the formal entrance stairs contains a reference to the type or functional class of the structure as perceived by the Palencanos. The possessed glyphic compound *u - ? - pi? - ji - li* structurally and contextually equates with the term *upibnaahil* or "oven-house" recorded on the *alfarda* tablets from the Cross Group temples (Houston 1996; Stuart 2000a, 2000b). In the case of the Cross Group temples, the structures are "owned" by the Triad gods; Temple XIX may as well have been "owned" by a person or more probably a "god." The glyphic compound *u - ? - pi? - ji - li* is unknown in the corpus of inscriptions at Palenque. Although other glyphic compounds from the Temple XIX inscriptions are unique (such as the "fish in beak" glyph), this particular reference, when compared to other contextually similar references, implies that Temple XIX was of a functional class of structures discriminated by the Palencanos themselves. In some manner, Temple XIX is referenced to as a *kind* of structure, such as *pibnaahil* ("sweatbaths") in the parallel scenario present at the Cross Group temples.

It should be noted that Houston (1996) and Child (Chapter 12) evaluate several glyphic compounds from the Cross Group inscriptions which are somehow equivalent, or alternate ways of referring to *pibnaahil* or "sweatbaths" (probably with implied nuances of meaning); none of these correlate with the *u - ? - pi? - ji*

-il compound from the Temple XIX *alfarda* tablet. Though undeciphered, this glyphic compound indicates that Temple XIX was a specific type of structure, different from all others known from Palenque.

A glyphic compound representing the proper name of the structure also appears on the *alfarda* tablet, and three times in conjunction with the names of the Palenque triad deities on the west panel of the platform from the structure interior. David Stuart (2000b, in press) has read this glyphic compound as **CHAK - ? - NAAH - hi** for *chak-?-naah* or "red-?-house." Without digressing into the semantics of color designations, the term *chak*, for "red" or "great," is in stark contrast to *sak nuk naah*, or "white-?-house," the proposed glyphic name for House E of the Palace. House E is reported (on the Tablet of the 96 Glyphs) as the structure where several Late Classic rulers, including K'inich Ahkal Mo' Nahb III, acceded to the office of *kuh'ul ajaw*. Viewed in conjunction with the unique architectural layout of the structure, these glyphic references strongly suggest that Temple XIX represents a distinct building type, one that appears late in the known architectural sequence at Palenque. The south panel of the Temple XIX platform probably "names" the structure with other glyphic "titles" as well, possibly extending or augmenting the functional designation or personal "name" of the structure and enforcing its importance in a typically prolix Classic Mayan fashion. Recording *what* Temple XIX was seems to have been of utmost concern.

Multiple individuals are portrayed and named on the Temple XIX monuments. The individual named **yo - OK - ? - TAL**, holding the rank of *yahaw k'ak'*, is named on the west *alfarda* tablet, the Lápida de los Ayudantes and on the south platform panel. In the latter two instances, his name and title appear with a full portrait situated to the left of K'inich Ahkal Mo' Nahb III. This individual is not known from any other inscriptions at the site. The individual named Chak Sutz', known to have held the rank of *yahaw k'ak'* during the reign of K'inich Ahkal Mo' Nahb III, is conspicuously absent from the inscriptions of Temple XIX. The "replacement" of one *yahaw k'ak'* by another suggests that Chak Sutz' died and was supplanted by **yo - OK - ? - TAL**, or that the latter individual was in some fashion intimately associated with Temple XIX, perhaps as a ritual specialist, caretaker, or prominent government or court officer. The last date associated with Chak Sutz' (from the Tablet of the Slaves, Group IV) falls a couple of years before the 9.15.2.7.16 dedication of Temple XIX, at which time he would have been sixty-two years old. There are no known portraits of Chak Sutz', either accompanying the ruler K'inich Ahkal Mo' Nahb III, or in any other context.

The south platform panel portrays six individuals, three to either side of K'inich Ahkal Mo' Nahb III, who appear to be Palencano "lords," each with a private "name-tag." The west platform panel portrays three more individuals of unknown origin, the central figure bearing the epitaph *aj ux te' kuh'*. Ux Te' Kuh' is presumed to be a site in the Tabasco plains, and is mentioned in the texts of Palenque (Temple of the Sun, Temple XXI) and Tortuguero (Monument 6). The inscriptions from Temple XXI state that K'inich Ahkal Mo' Nahb III's mother was from the site of Ux Te' Kuh'. No overt mention of warfare or "vassalship-overlordship" appears in the Temple XIX inscriptions.

Premature Collapse and Termination

Analysis of the distribution of artifacts from the floor of Temple XIX presented a special interpretation problem for investigators. I have concluded that the fragmented monuments, ceramics, lithics, and sundry other materials recovered probably pertain to a final "expiry rite," and may not reflect the formal usage of the structure during its active days. Temple XIX's stucco and stone panels were victims of systematic mayhem, pottery vessels were "quartered" with pieces deposited in both sides (and the exterior terrace) of the structure, and stone floor slabs were removed (and never recovered) in order to retrieve or deposit (or both) materials within the basal platform. The formal platform, altar or "throne" from the west side of the structure was smashed, entered, refilled, and then thrashed again by slamming a huge stone slab into the image of K'inich Ahkal Mo' Nab III's head, through the center of the south panel.

While the "termination" or "ritual killing" of structures has been documented in the Maya area, the reconstructed final activities performed within Temple XIX are particularly disturbing. The carved platform panels appeared "brand new," the south panel retaining most of its hematite wash and "blown" cinnabar appliqués. The Lápida de los Ayudantes was evidently in a similar pristine state, before being dismembered, its pieces left to rest in various configurations inside and outside the structure. Portions of the polychrome stucco panel were surgically removed, some heaped in a pile in the western end of the front gallery, others buried below floor level on central axis, in the rear gallery. Even more puzzling were patches of the interior roof or wall stucco found lying on the stone slab floor with finished side down. The largest slab of fallen interior stucco was recovered from below the main fragment of the Lápida de los Ayudantes, which had been placed in front of the carved platform. One corner of the "kill-stone" which smashed the south platform panel was still in contact with this monument fragment, where it had been carefully set down and then pivoted forward with enough force to partially powder the carved facing stone of the platform, crushing through the central figure's head and snapping the panel into four pieces.

Why were patches of interior stucco found below the floor deposits? Had Temple XIX been left to deteriorate and then re-entered for a "termination ritual," or did some calamitous shift dislodge the stucco coating, prompting an immediate and dramatic "killing" of the entire building once structural failure was imminent? After much consideration, I have concluded that the totality of physical and contextual evidence supports the latter conclusion more consistently than the first; after a partial loss of structural integrity, Temple XIX was disemboweled, if you will, permanently relieved of the power it was once imbued with.

The Fall of the Max

Temple XIX went up without incident, was decorated, dedicated, and used for *at least 900 days*. How and when it fell are hinted at, more the former than the latter. The facts show that Temple XIX was a structural feat of some planning, preparation, engineering, and labor. The uses of materials show a knowledge of their properties to some extent, and further that the Maya pushed these limits in their manipulation of engineering practices when constructing buildings.

   Nonetheless, the construction of Temple XIX did not benefit from decent bonding of surfaces between construction stones, deep hearting of facing stones, or efforts to evenly lay stones in uniform courses; nor was any great effort made to alternate breaking joints between stones, avoiding stress lines in the walls and piers.

   Although these "oversites" did not produce the finest crafted building at the site, the implications for structural integrity are that if it stood for 900 days, then the vault would not overturn due to precarious proportions, half vaults could be constructed, and a roof held by the support walls. In 900 days the mortar would dry somewhat, though it was inherently weak, and wooden beams would still have been in place to stop the sagging of the vault.

   Temple XIX may have served perfectly for several years after its erection until the previously mentioned shortcomings in construction and design threatened stability. Settling of the stonework, encouraged by the use of a weak mortar and irregular-shaped construction blocks, would eventually lead to the collapse of Temple XIX. The structure would also have been seriously compromised when the wooden lintel which once spanned the 5.3 m entrance rotted out. We do not know at what time the Temple XIX superstructure collapsed, though it was clearly abandoned during Classic times at Palenque. If the structure did suffer a loss of structural integrity after the first few years of use, the most probable reasons, given the proportions and construction quality of the edifice, were either settling of stones and mortar of the temple superstructure itself or of the basement matrix which was laid more haphazardly.

   Premature failure of the wooden entrance lintel is unlikely considering the quality of wood available to the ancient Maya, and their skill in employing it. Though requiring a considerable effort in preparation, local hardwoods like Chico Sapote could have provided a single beam of substantial strength. This beam would have focused weight on the support jambs of the entrance, which, if they collapsed, would have brought down the wooden beam and the central portion of the roof rising from it. This scenario is more properly viewed as a specific stress on the wall construction where excessive pressure was exerted through the wooden beam, rather than failure of the wooden member itself.

   The corbelled vault dispersing the entire weight of the roof over the support walls and piers translates into a crushing pressure felt down through the building structure. All bearing walls and piers must resist this compression strength applied by the roof construction above. Mortar or stone (whichever is weaker) will crack under this crushing pressure distributed down through the architectural frame of the building. In short, the increased chance of crushing failure at Temple XIX was exacerbated by the massive roof being focused on a small percent of bearing wall/pier. These bearing supports were not particularly well grounded into a level surface.

Comparative Construction

Why was a lime based durable stucco not used as a mortar between stones of the superstructure walls and vaults as was previously done at Temples II, V, XX, or the Cross Group temples? The Cross Group temples have a different quality (hardness) stone and a durable lime mortar, comparable in *quality* to the finest stucco recovered at Temple XIX, where it was used primarily for decorative and non-structural elements. Though not completely hewn to fine surfaces, most of the construction blocks used in the Cross Group temples maintain solid cohesion to this day, held in place by a durable lime based mortar.

Architecture from the first third of the Late Classic sequence observable at Palenque (c. A.D. 647-677) displays a meticulous nature in the preparation of stone construction blocks and stucco mortar, as well as the perfect coursing with which these uniform blocks were set (Fig. 10.8). Carefully hewn limestone blocks were peck-faced on all six sides with a percussion technique. Even faces hearted into walls or piers where they do not provide an exterior surface are carefully trimmed (Temple V, Temple XX). These stones were laid in an excellent quality pure white lime based mortar, producing a cohesive monolithic mass. Substructure terrace walls are also constructed with uniform coursing of hewn block at this time (Fig. 10.9).

The carefully trimmed limestone blocks of Temples V, X, and XX are far superior to the quickly quarried construction stones of Temple XIX, and yet carefully trimmed and formed limestone slabs were used by the Temple XIX architects in non-essential contexts like the throne, the floor slabs, the entrance stairs and the superior landing "skirt." The well-trimmed springline stones (drilled) and capstones of Temple XIX are instances where the improved stones would have fit together tightly, and being uniform in thickness, produce more of a monolithic unit under the weight of the roof above. However, most if not all of the corbelled soffit stones were unmodified, and in a weak mortar would have been prone to settling. This entire load was also held by precariously thin walls of uncoursed, irregular stone blocks laid in the same weak mortar, balanced on a constructed platform of questionable foundation quality.

Compared to other vaults still standing at the site, the vault stones recovered from Temple XIX seem ill-suited for the job. Just outside the immediate epicenter, at Structure MC1 in the Murcielagos compound, vaults were constructed entirely of well-trimmed limestone slabs (Fig. 10.10). These vaults required more effort in

Figure 10.8: Interior of central axial doorway (facing east), Temple V, North Group

Figure 10.9: Substructure wall, Temple V, North Group

preparation and continue to stand today. Structure J1 in Group IV, although in a considerable state of decay, was once vaulted in a similar fashion to that proposed for Temple XIX, where, untrimmed tenon stones were tightly laid to form the vault soffit (Fig. 10.11). These tenons rise from a uniform springline formed of sideways laid "stretcher" slabs.

At Palenque, the vaulted double gallery structures set atop the Palace platform are all referred to as houses. The earliest dated "house," House E, is iconographically presented as a perishable structure writ in stone. The awnings are carved in imitation of thatch, and no roof comb was constructed (Greene Robertson 1985). No other houses feature thatch representations, and the term house as applied to

Figure 10.10:
Slab vault construction, Structure MC1,
Murcielagos Group (above)

Figure 10.11:
Structure J1, Group IV—note three preserved
courses of vault construction still intact

all the structures in one isolated local does not imply any uniformity of function or recognized structure type. Some houses, like House C, have low vault angles (61 degrees) producing a non-temple appearance, while others, like House E, have higher, 69 degree vault angles, within the range of temple constructions. Further distinctions in internal layout and proportions probably represent differences of function among this group of structures.

The outer ring of houses (A, A.D., D) is composed of three long double gallery structures, more than four times as long as wide which have exterior piers forming a "U" around the perimeter of the Palace. These structures all share a near continuous center bearing wall, though broken by simple and corbelled cross vaults. The Palace provides exterior "public" space, as well as interior "private" or "restricted" areas, completely removed from the general public view. These interior spaces include vaulted structures of various configurations (House E, B, C), as well as open sunken courtyards. Some spaces, like the Tower and the "Lavatories" to its west, certainly have specific functions (be they astronomical or utilitarian), different from all other structures or areas of the Palace complex.

George Andrews (1980), employing comparative trait analysis, grouped the structures of the Palace into fifteen categories representing distinct building, or activity areas, which he felt related to function. Andrews further proposed that in comparison to the Central Arcopolis at Tikal, and to European palaces, the range of structure types identified for the Palenque Palace indicate that it acted as a multifunctioning complex, though the designation of specific functions of structures is difficult to make in the absence of perishable material associated with the structures or appropriate ethnographic analogies explaining Classic Maya architectural needs.

The proportions of the houses when compared to each other or to double vaulted "temple" structures outside the Palace do not group together into simple categories. A range of proportions is encountered among wall width to gallery span, vault angles, and overall width to length of superstructure. The inner houses like E, B, and C are shorter like temples, yet Houses E and C have configurations which suggest they were actively utilized, not vacant buildings of primarily religious or ritual function.

The Temple of the Cross, Temple of the Foliated Cross, Temple of the Sun, Temple XVII, Temple XVIII, Temple XVIIIa, and Temple XX all conform to a fundamental "temple" or shrine structure form. These structures (save perhaps Temple XX) have restricted central rear chambers: the three Cross Group temples and Temple XVII have the addition of a free standing inner sanctuary structure within. Elaborate iconographic and glyphic stone or stucco sculptures have been recovered from the Cross Group temples, Temple XVII, Temple XVIII, Temple XIX, and Temple XXI; those associated with the Cross Group temples and Temple XVII are attributed to the ruler K'inich Kan Bahlam II, those of Temple XVIII, Temple XIX, and Temple XXI with K'inich Ahkal Mo' Nahb III.

Construction of Temple XVIII predates that of Temples XIX and XXI. Analysis of the art and inscriptions from Temple XVIII has led William Ringle to propose that this structure acted as a lineage temple for the *Mat* group of royal individuals. The rear wall stucco panel portrays the three sons of Pakal the Great: K'inich Kan Bahlam II, K'inich K'an Joy Chitam II, and Tiwol Chan Mat, the father of K'inich Ahkal Mo' Nahb III (Ringle 1996: 55-56). The carved glyphic limestone jamb panels of Temple XVIII focus on events in the life of K'inich Ahkal Mo' Nahb III, including birth, preaccession rituals, and his seating as ruler (*kuh'ul ajaw*) in A.D. 721. Taken together, these texts preserve the order of accession of Palenque rulers associated with the *Mat* glyphic compound, which has been exclusively associated with a putative bloodline extending from the ruler Ah Ne Ohl Mat, who's accession is recorded as 9.8.11.9.10 8 Ok 18 Muwaan (A.D. 605) with the inclusion of the "olmec period ruler" or "diety" U K'ix Chan (Ringle 1996: 56).

Temples XIX and XXI, as discussed already, have markedly different constructed forms than other buildings of the Cross Group/South Group and the rest of the known site. I also hesitantly add a somewhat similar form in Temple XXa, a very wide (3.5 m) single gallery structure added to the north side of the Temple XX superstructure which does not appear to have been vaulted (Marken 2000b). The most striking distinctions which set these three buildings apart from the temple-type structures of the Cross Group/South Group are amount of continuous interior space, northward facing axis, and the presence of low flat rectangular platforms in the eastern interior. While the simple slab platform of Temple XXa is not as elaborate as those recovered from Temples XIX and XXI, the structure does share the more important features of the former which act to set the three apart from temple-type or range-type structures at Palenque as a whole. Perhaps the term gallery-type structure is most appropriate to this set of architecture.

Function from Form

Very few identified structure forms can be associated with specific functions or activities performed within. The most reliable indicator of structure usage is the recovered material associated with that structure. After directly associated artifacts, constructed form and position within the overall site suggest how a structure may have been used in Classic times. In certain cases, specific traits of structures can be cross-analyzed to group those with similar features together. Once separated into categories, ethnohistoric analogy, analysis of traffic control, or distribution studies may provide support for the functional identification of these structures. This type of comparison has identified certain very specific function type structures, as well as providing broader interpretation of larger complexes.

A Maya sweatbath, as archaeologically excavated at Palenque and at neighboring Piedras Negras, portrays a suite of characteristics which are readily observable in the constructed stone form of the building. These include a water channel, low doorway, small vaulted chamber, firebox, and often subsidiary rooms. These features identify such structures at functioning sweatbaths, known in generally the same form from ethnohistoric documents (Child, Chapter 12). Maya ball courts are another example of a specific architectural form which is immediately identifiable, even without excavation. Two parallel long structures running north-south create the "playing alley" of the ball court, recognized at many Maya epicenters.

While sweatbaths and ball courts are exceptions to the vast amounts of anonymous architecture of unknown function, comparative trait analysis has also been employed to group structure types in an attempt to determine the range of possible functions within a group of structures. From the earliest days of investigation, the major distinction cited in monumental architecture has been between temples and palaces. This continues to this day where the main distinction made between epicentral architecture is that between temples, with steep stairs leading to small restricted chambers with no direct signs of living, to multiroom "range structures" associated with suspected residential, utilitarian, or production material. Comparing the architectural traits of grouped structures at the Central Acropolis at Tikal (Andrews 1980; Harrison 1986) and the Palace at Palenque (Andrews 1980) led researchers to conclude that these complexes contained varied facilities, though of uncertain function. The Palace at Palenque is a unique compound at the center of the ancient settlement, and fulfills most requirements for a central administrative/royal court complex.

William Fash associates several structures at Copan with specific "houses" mentioned in the Quiche ethnohistoric document, the *Popol Vuh*. Based primarily on iconography, these structures are viewed as reconstructions of ritual/mythical edifices and may have served in a range of actual function. The identification of a *popol nah* or council house was also made, based on archaeology, epigraphy, and ethnographic analogy (Fash 1991).

How any structure was used by the ancient Maya is a matter of speculation; relating buildings with elaborate iconographic programs to specific Maya practices is difficult. Any identification of function will likely be rooted in a specific model of Maya society. In the Copan example, the construction of a *popol nah* or council house is viewed as a desperate attempt to unite a fragmenting society following the decapitation of the thirteenth Copan ruler at the hands of the rival city of Quiriqua (Fash 1991). Whether in reaction to this or other pressures, the *popol pah* (dated to 9.15.15.0.0, A.D. 731) was constructed during the reign of the fourteenth Copan ruler, and it seems that Late Classic society at Copan did initiate some "shared" form of government. During the same time period, "brothers" of the ruler erected benches with dedicatory texts claiming authority derived from relation to the king. However, this is not necessarily evidence of discord or social unrest and may simply represent evolving political relations between the dynastic ruler and subregional elites (Bardsley 1996).

As a reaction to a weakened dynastic hold or simply in response to a burgeoning population of increasing complexity, the *popol nah* at Copan provides one example where a structure's former function has been inferred. Though the exact activities performed within are not known, the idea is that the structure itself was dedicated to activities of a governmental nature, involving a group of elites gathered from various locals throughout the site.

Researchers have speculated for decades on the function and meaning of the three temples which have collectively become known as the Cross Group at Palenque: the Temple of the Cross, the Temple of the Sun, and the Temple of the Foliated Cross. These three temples contain a wealth of iconographic, epigraphic, and architectural information which make them of particular interest to Mayanists. Based on setting, form, and iconography, Claude Baudez (1996) posited that the three temple grouping was actually used by the Palenque king or elites as a perambulation route during ritual reenactments. Based on specific iconographic markers, combined with the physical location of each structure at three distinct levels oriented in three different cardinal directions, Baudez suggests the king moved from one to the next structure while physically acting out ceremonial routines. While this hypothesis again contextualizes how the temples may have acted as purely ceremonial edifices within the central precinct of Palenque, no direct function of the individual structures was proposed.

From the information available on the Cross Temples, Stephen Houston (1996) has hypothesized that these structures are in fact ritual sweatbaths of the Triad gods. This conclusion comes on the basis of identifying the traits of a Maya sweatbath with the inner sanctuary architecture present within the Cross Group temples combined with evaluation of the associated iconography and epigraphy. Carved monuments originally mounted to the structures name each temple (or sanctuary) in relation to one of the three Triad gods. Each temple is also named functionally as a *pibnaahil*, or sweatbath, again "owned" by the Triad gods. The structures are not actually functioning sweatbaths, rather ceremonial structures built in the form of the prenatal sweatbaths of the Triad gods. The small inner chambers of the Cross Group temples may well have held wooden statues or litters, the subsidiary rooms housing elaborate costumes or other religious paraphernalia related to their actual usage in Classic times. However, in the absence of such direct evidence of function, the form, setting, and imagery of the Cross Group temples suggest these structures were in fact wholly religious/ceremonial buildings rather than living spaces.

By comparison, Temple XIX is an elevated structure oriented inward on a large plaza which, like the Cross Group temples, has a small altar platform centrally placed on axis with the structure. With much more inner space unfettered by curtain walls or an inner sanctuary, the platform or throne in the east side of the building must have been the focus of the structure interior. Also, the layout of the piers suggests a traffic route, which may have been reinforced by perishable curtains or traffic screens.[3] The gross amount of interior space achieved with the construction of Temple XIX removes the building from the temple category, while its constructed form, lacking room divisions, separates it from palaces or range structures by definition. It appears that Temple XIX was not a structure divided into spaces for multiple simultaneous functions, it was meant to house multiple individuals at the same function. The iconography of the platform panels reinforces this meeting house idea.

Proportion

The comparison of the proportions of Palenque structures, when put into a chronologic order, reveals several trends (see Fig. 10.5). The South Subterraneos and houses of the Palace have larger room spans than contemporaneous temple-type structures, like the Temple of the Count, or Temple of the Inscriptions. In fact, the proportions of wall thickness to vault span produced at the South Subterraneos and House E represent the most precarious ratios known at the site before the construction of Temple XIX. House C, perhaps constructed c. A.D. 663, has proportions which closely approximate those of the Cross Group temples, which postdate House C's construction by thirty years. It is clear from these examples that proportions do not increase over time; the earliest dated structures of the sequence were built with the greatest ratios of thin walls to wide galleries (vault span).

Table 10.1: Representative Preserved Structures from Palenque

STRUCTURE	GALLERY WIDTH	ave. WALL THICKNESS	TOTAL HEIGHT	FLOOR to SPRING	SPRING to CAPSTONE	VAULT ANGLE	WALL WIDTH to SPAN:HEIGHT
Olvidado	127 124-130	100	435	200	235	71.5	1 : 1.3 : 4.3
S. Subterraneos	235	78.5 53	303	177	126	43	1 : 3 : 3.9 1 : 3.5 : 4.6
T. Count	145	110	470	250	220	curved	1 : 1.3 : 4.3
T. V	227	99	396	220	176	stepped	1 : 2.3 : 4
House E	238	64-outer 74-central	479	259	220	69	1 : 3.7 : 7.4
House C	275	86.5	492	300	192	61	1 : 3.2 : 5.7
House F	250	62	328	216	112	59	1 : 4 : 5.3
Inscriptions	202	118	600	307	293	75	1 : 1.7 : 5.1
T. Cross	308 F330/R286	98	646	325	321	68	1 : 3.1 : 6.6
T. Sun	284 F330/R286	102	650	323	327	71	1 : 2.8 : 6.4
T. Foliated Cross	313 F330/R286	106	620	320	300	70	1 : 3 : 5.8
T. XVIII	206 F330/R286	79.5		250			1 : 2.5 : ?
T. XIX	320 F330/R286	86	[688]	344*	[344]	70-72	1 : 3.7 : 8
T. XXI	303	86		300+			1. 3.5 : [>6]

Temple-type structures, if isolated from houses or ranged buildings, *do* show a linear progression of increasing proportions of wall thickness to vault span to overall structure height.[4] The exception noted on Table 10.1 is Temple V, which parallels the Temple of the Inscriptions in floor plan. At A.D. 692 (9.13.0.0.0) the completion of the three Cross Group temples represent the epitome in design and construction at Palenque. The Cross Group temples also represent an abrupt increase of proportions within the temple-type structure category.

The proportions of Temple XIX and of Temple XXI show an increase from those of the Cross Group temples, but not in direct succession. Before the construction of the "sister" temples, XIX and XXI, a decrease in proportion is evident at Temple XIV, Temple XVII, and the "twin" temples, XVIII and XVIIIa. Further complicating the interpretation of these numbers, Temple XIX and Temple XXI have divergent architectural plans, or forms; they cannot be assigned to temple-type or range-type building categories.

Final Thoughts

In summary, the precarious proportions combined with the poor construction quality of Temple XIX do not support any theory of dysfunction or social unrest. If I had to attribute the "failure" of Temple XIX to any single factor, I would have to say that the use of a weak mortar would be at the top of the list. The reader is also reminded that the structure may have effectively fulfilled its intended purpose; any decrease in construction quality was probably not noticed by the ancient Palencanos as it is by archaeologists. As detailed, all interior and exterior surfaces were covered with stucco, except for the stone slab floor and formal entrance steps, which received exceptional care in construction. The exterior sculpture program and carved monuments would only have added to the sense of grandeur of this completed edifice. Temple XIX would have appeared of the same or superior quality as earlier buildings at the site until cracks appeared from settling or a sudden shift from a partial collapse reverberated through the structure, detaching stucco work or collapsing part of the roof soffit.

While building projects in general have sometimes been interpreted as an elite stress on Maya society, "by drawing more resources and people from agriculture and by encouraging warfare (through city competition)" (Sabloff 1994), other researchers have convincingly argued that, properly timed and coordinated, construction did not necessarily require an excessive amount of labor (Abrams 1994; Webster 1985). The burning of wood for lime production during large construction efforts has also been cited as a factor contributing to deforestation (and ensuing erosion and climatic changes) leading to an ecological atrocity which the Maya wrought upon themselves (Schreiner 2001; Abrams & Rue 1988). In evaluating the validity of such conclusions, it is important to carefully consider the construction programs at specific sites within a broader context of the region where they occurred. Energetic and resource stresses can only be evaluated properly through specific concordance studies weighing simultaneous construction efforts, population size, and the natural environment. The organization of building projects may also bear on their "costs" beyond direct volumetric or extrapolated energetic data. Availability of suitable fuel wood for lime production or stone for construction blocks as well as the organization and timing in acquiring these should be evaluated within the context of the total system. Lime must be produced and aged before construction begins; uniform springline stones may be preformed by skilled stoneworkers in an assembly line fashion in advance while untrimmed construction blocks are quarried and transported later by less skilled individuals. Only through the meticulous reconstruction of the timing, process, quality, and quantity of building construction within the larger framework of demographics, environment, and social organization will archaeologists be able to evaluate larger questions of stress and decline or reorganization on a societal level.

Notes

[1] It should be noted that Hyman's 1973 paper presented at the 38th meetings of the Society of American Anthropologists and Littman's series of articles published in the late 1950's are still the best pioneering works on the subject of Maya stucco. Unfortunately this type of work has not received the continued attention which it deserves (however, see Schreiner 2001).

[2] I have used the term "skirt" in reference to the line of well-trimmed rectangular limestone slabs which the Temple XIX architects placed abutting the basal platform and running east-west down the superior landing. These stones were carefully prepared, though their function appears to have been solely as a ballast to accept a stucco covering. Again we are faced with the most labor intensive construction stones serving no apparent utility.

[3] Excavations in 1998-1999 produced drilled interior springline stones at the base of the two most central piers. Following the "curtain" hypothesis, it appears logical that some form of interior divisioning of space was created with perishable screens.

[4] The table presented here does not include all the preserved structures known from Palenque; it is a representative sample meant to describe a trend. Dr. Robert Sharer kindly pointed out that a larger sample should have been used for a more comprehensive analysis. I agree in full, unfortunately time restrictions on the publishing of this volume have precluded a reanalysis with a fuller sample, which will have to wait for a subsequent publication.

References

Abrams, Elliot M.
    1994   *How the Maya Built Their World.* University of Texas Press, Austin.
Abrams, Elliot M. and David Rue
    1988   The causes and consequences of deforestation among the prehistoric Maya. *Human Ecology* 14:377-395.

Andrews, George F.
1975   *Maya Cities: Placemaking and Urbanization*. University of Oklahoma Press, Norman.

1980   Palace Complexes and the Maya Elite: Palenque and Tikal. Paper presented at the Cuarta Mesa Redonda de Palenque, Chiapas, Mexico, June 8-14, 1980.

Bardsley, Sandra
1996   Benches, Brothers, and Lineage Lords of Copan. In *Eighth Palenque Round Table–1993*. Vol. X, edited by Merle Greene Robertson, Martin Macri, and Jan McHargue, pp. 195-201. Pre-Columbian Art Research Institute, San Francisco, CA.

Baudez, Claude F.
1996   The Cross Group at Palenque. In *Eighth Palenque Round Table–1993*. Vol. X, edited by Merle Greene Robertson, Martin Macri, and Jan McHargue, pp. 121-128. Pre-Columbian Art Research Institute, San Francisco, CA.

Berlin, Heinrich
1944   Un Templo Olvidado en Palenque. *Revista Mexicana de Estudios Antropologias* 6:62-90.

1965   The Inscription of the Temple of the Cross at Palenque. *American Antiquity* 30:330-342.

Bernal Romero, Guillermo
2002   Análisis epigráfico del Tablero de K'an Tok, Palenque, Chiapas. In *La Organización Social Entre los Mayas. Memoria de la Tercera Mesa Redonda de Palenque, Vol. I*, edited by V. Tiesler Blos, R. Cobos, & M. Greene Robertson, pp. 307-327. Conaculta-INAH, Mexico, D.F.

Blom, Franz and Oliver La Farge
1926   *Tribes and Temples: A Record of the Expedition to Middle America Conducted by the Tulane University of Louisiana in 1925, Vols. I & II*. Tulane University of Louisiana, New Orleans, LA.

Fash, William L.
1991   *Scribes, Warriors and Kings*. Thames & Hudson Inc., New York, NY.

González Cruz, Arnoldo
1993   *Trabajo Arqueologicos en Palenque, Chiapas: Informe de Campo VI Temporada*. Volumen VII. Serie Informes de Campo 6. Projecto Arqueologico Palenque. INAH, Mexico, D.F.

González Cruz, Arnoldo and Guillermo Bernal Romero
2003   *The Throne of Ahkal Mo' Nahb' III: A Unique Finding at Palenque*. INAH/Nestlé, Mexico, D.F.

Greene Robertson, Merle
1985   *The Sculpture of Palenque, Vol. III: The Late Buildings of the Palace*. Princeton University Press, Princeton, NJ.

Greene Robertson, Merle, Alfonso Morales Cleveland and Christopher Powell
1999   *Projecto Grupo de las Cruces: Informe de Campo (Segundo Año)*. PARI/INAH, Palenque, Chiapas, Mexico, Mayo 1999. Unpublished field report.

Harrison, Peter D.
  1986   Tikal: Selected Topics. In *City-States of the Maya: Art and Architecture*, edited by E. P. Benson, pp. 45-71. Rocky Mountain Institute for Pre-Columbian Studies, Denver, CO.

Houston, Stephen D.
  1996   Symbolic Sweatbaths of the Maya: Architectural Meaning in the Cross Group at Palenque, Mexico. *Latin American Antiquity* 7(2): 132-151.

Hyman, David S.
  1973   Pre-Hispanic Mesoamerican Building Cements. Paper presented at the 38th Annual Meeting of the Society for American Archaeology. San Francisco, California. May 3, 1973.

Kubler, George
  1985   *Studies in Ancient American and European Art:The Collected Essays of George Kubler*, edited by Thomas F. Reese. Yale University Press, New Haven, CT.

Littman, Edwin R.
  1957   Ancient Mesoamerican Mortars, Plasters and Stuccos: Comalcalco, Part I. *American Antiquity* 23(2):135-140.

  1958   Ancient Mesoamerican Mortars, Plasters and Stuccos: Comalcalco, Part II. *American Antiquity* 23(3):292-296.

  1959   Ancient Mesoamerican Mortars, Plasters and Stuccos: Palenque, Chiapas. *American Antiquity* 25(2):264-266.

Lounsbury, Floyd G.
  1991   Recent Work in the Decipherment of Palenque's Hieroglyphic Inscriptions. *American Anthropologist* 93:809-825.

Marken, Damien B.
  2002a   Palenque Architecture: A Preliminary Chronology. Paper presented at the 67th Annual Meeting of the Society for American Archaeology, Denver, CO. March 2002.

  2002b   L'Architecture de Palenque: Les Temples. Unpublished M.A. thesis. Université de Paris I: La Sorbonne.

Martin, Simon and Nikolai Grube
  2000   *Chronicles of the Maya Kings and Queens: Deciphering the Dynasties of the Ancient Mayas*. Thames & Hudson, London, U.K.

Martin, Simon, Marc Zender, and Nikolai Grube
  2002   Palenque and Its Neighbors. *Notebook for the XXVIth Maya Hieroglyphic Forum at Texas*, Austin.

Mathews, Peter and Linda Schele
  1974   The Lords of Palenque: The Glyphic Evidence. In *Primera Mesa Redonda de Palenque, part I.* ed. by Merle Greene Robertson, pp.63-76. Robert Louis Stevenson School, Pebble Beach, CA.

Mathews, Peter and Merle Greene Robertson
  1985   Notes on the Olvidado, Palenque, Chiapas, Mexico. In *Fifth Palenque Round Table–1983*. Vol. VII, edited by Merle Greene Robertson and Virginia M.

Fields, pp. 7-18. Pre-Columbian Art Research Institute, San Francisco, CA.

Proskouriakoff, Tatiana
1950   *A Study of Classic Maya Sculpture.* Carnegie Institute of Washington, Publication 593. Washington, D.C.

Rands, Robert L.
1967   Ceramic Technology and Trade in the Palenque Region, Mexico. In *American Historical Anthropology: Essays in Honor of Leslie Spier*, edited by C. L. Riley & W. W. Taylor, pp. 137-151. University of Southern Illinois Press. Carbondale, IL.

1974   The Ceramic Sequence at Palenque, Chiapas. In *Mesoamerican Archaeology: New Approaches*, edited by Norman Hammond, pp. 51-76. University of Texas Press, Austin.

1987   Ceramic Patterns and Traditions in the Palenque Area. In *Maya Ceramics. Papers from the 1985 Maya Ceramic Conference*, edited by Prudence M. Rice and Robert J. Sharer, pp. 203-238. BAR International Series 345(i). Hadrian Books Ltd., Oxford, U.K.

1988   Least-Cost and Function-Optimizing Interpretations of Ceramic Production: An Archaeological Perspective. In *Ceramic Ecology Revisited, 1987: The Technology and Socioeconomics of Pottery*, edited by Charles C. Kolb, pp. 165-198. BAR International Series 436(ii). Hadrian Books Ltd., Oxford, U.K.

Rands, Robert L. and Ronald L. Bishop
2003   The Dish-Plate Tradition at Palenque: Continuity and Change. In *Patterns & Process: A Festschrift in Honor of Dr. Edward V. Sayre*, edited by Lambertus van Zelst, pp. 109-132. Smithsonian Center for Materials Research & Education, Suitland, MD.

Ringle, William M.
1996   Birds of a Feather: The Fallen Stucco Inscription of Temple XVIII, Palenque, Chiapas. In *Eighth Palenque Round Table–1993*. Vol. X, edited by Merle Greene Robertson, Martin Macri, and Jan McHargue, pp. 45-62. Pre-Columbian Art Research Institute, San Francisco, CA.

Roys, Lawrence
1934   The Engineering Knowledge of the Maya. In *Contributions to American Archaeology, Vol. II*. No. 6, pp. 27-105. Carnegie Institution of Washington, Washington, D.C.

Ruz Lhuillier, Alberto
1958c   Exploraciones en Palenque: 1956. *Anales del Instituto Nacional de Antropologia e Historia*, Tomo X, Núm 39, pp. 241-299. INAH, Mexcio, D.F.

Sabloff, Jeremy A.
1994   *The New Archaeology and the Ancient Maya.* Scientific American Library, New York, NY.

Schele, Linda
1981   Sacred Site and World View at Palenque. In *Mesoamerican Sites and World Views*, edited by E. P. Benson, pp. 87-118. Dumbarton Oaks Research Library and Collections, Washington, D.C.

1986   Architectural Development and Political History at Palenque. In *City-States of the Maya: Art and Architecture*, edited by E. P. Benson, pp. 110-137. Rocky Mountain Institute for Pre-Columbian Studies, Denver, CO.

1992   A New Look at the Dynastic History of Palenque. In *Handbook of Middle American Indians, Supplement 5: Epigraphy*, edited by Victoria Bricker, pp. 82-109. University of Texas Press, Austin.

Schreiner, Thomas P.

2001   *Traditional Maya Lime Production: Environmental and Cultural Implications of a Native Technology*. Unpublished Ph.D. dissertation, University of California, Berkeley.

Straight, Kirk D.

1999   A Preliminary Analysis of Construction Technique and Architectural Form at Temple XIX, Palenque, Chiapas. Paper presented at the Tercera Mesa Redonda de Palenque, Palenque, Chiapas, Mexico, June 27- July 1, 1999.

n.d.   Preliminary Report of the Ceramics from Temple XIX, Palenque, Chiapas, Mexico. Manuscript in possession of the author.

Straight, Kirk D. and Damien B. Marken

2002   U-Pakal K'inich at Palenque and Its Use as a Pre-Accession Name. *PARI Journal* II(4)/III(1): 1-3.

Stuart, David

2000a   Ritual and History in the Stucco Inscription from Temple XIX at Palenque. *PARI Journal* I(1): 13-19.

2000b   Las Nuevas Inscripciones del Templo XIX. *Arqueología Mexicana* 8(45):28-33.

In press *The Hieroglyphic Inscriptions from Temple XIX at Palenque: A Commentary*. Pre-Columbian Art Research Institute, San Francisco, CA.

Tovalín Ahumada, Alejandro and Gabriela Ceja Manrique

1996   Desarrollo Arquitectonico del Grupo Norte de Palenque. In *Eighth Palenque Round Table–1993*. Vol. X, edited by Merle Greene Robertson, Martin Macri, and Jan McHargue, pp. 93-102. Pre-Columbian Art Research Institute, San Francisco, CA.

Webster, David

1985   Surplus, Labor, and Stress in Late Classic Maya Society. *Journal of Anthropological Research* 41(4):375-389.

Part V

RELIGION AND RITUAL SPACES

Chapter 11

Gods and Histories:
Mythology and Dynastic Succession at
Temples XIX and XXI at Palenque
David Stuart

Introduction

The sculptures and inscriptions unearthed at Temples XIX and XXI rank among the most important discoveries in the long and rich history of Palenque archaeology. Beyond their clear place as high points of Maya sculptural art, the texts and figural scenes in stone and stucco provide significant new information about the Palenque's dynasty during a time, a generation or so before the final gasps of the ruling line, that was previously murky to students of Palenque archaeology and epigraphy. A handful of novel facts of Palenque's interrelated mythology and history are contained within the new inscriptions, but perhaps even more interesting are the insights they give into how one king, the Late Classic ruler K'inich Ahkal Mo' Nahb III,[1] went to remarkable lengths to express his own deep historical and mythological pedigree. The grandson of the celebrated K'inich Janab Pakal I[2] inherited his office through unusual means and during unstable times. This historical setting offers a valuable backdrop for understanding his unusually "personal" connection to the patron god GI, portrayed as Palenque's "Ur-king." The interconnected representation of history and cosmology in these temples is complex and multilayered, but I know of no other Classic Maya narrative that is so clear and explicit in interweaving stories of gods with the destinies of divine rulers. For this reason alone the texts of Temples XIX and XXI, like others at Palenque, emerge as powerful examples of ancient Maya epic literature.

Temples XIX and XXI are located in the southeastern area of the ruins, just to the south of the three main temples of the Cross Group (the Temples of the Cross, the Foliated Cross, and the Sun) (Fig. 11.1).[3] Indeed, as the map suggests, it is perhaps best that we consider Temples XIX and XXI, and even their neighboring

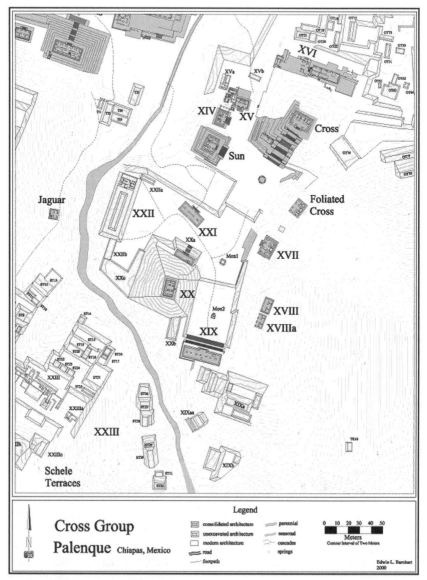

Figure 11.1: Map of the South/Cross Group (from survey by Edwin Barnhart)

structures, as part of a "greater" Cross Group/South Group built along the base of the large hill called *Yemal K'uk' Lakam Witz*, "Descending Quetzal Big Hill." Temple XIX is at the extreme southern end of this group, facing north over a series of stepped courtyards and toward the main central plaza in front of the Temple of the Cross, the dominant pyramid of the area (both temples, as we will see, are thematically linked). Even Temple XXI, a smaller and lower structure located to the northwest of XIX, is skewed in its orientation so that it directly faces the Temple of the Cross. When the ruler K'inich Ahkal Mo' Nahb III dedicated these two structures he clearly meant for them to be seen as expansions on the three-part architectural grouping built some decades earlier by his uncle, K'inich Kan Bahlam II.

Excavations in Temple XIX beginning in 1998 revealed a number of inscription fragments in both stone and stucco. Inscribed *alfardas* adorned the exterior upper stairway, bearing the main dedication date of the building: 9.15.2.7.16 9 Kib 19 K'ayab, or January 14, A.D. 734. In the building's interior, a massive central pier was adorned with a stone panel bearing a portrait of a richly dressed K'inich Ahkal Mo' Nahb III and two kneeling attendants. The same pier also bore a stucco panel on its left side, showing a striding portrait of a man named Upakal K'inich, a mysterious yet important historical figure who may have been K'inich Ahkal Mo' Nahb III's brother. The greatest find from Temple XIX was a low interior platform decorated on two faces with superbly and delicately carved panels bearing figural scenes and hieroglyphic texts. In 2002 a very similar monument, seemingly carved by the same hands, was found in Temple XXI. They are examples of a monumental form otherwise unknown at Palenque, and the original function of the platform type—seemingly called an *okib* or "pedestal" by the Maya—is still a mystery.

The south, or front, side of the Temple XIX platform is clearly the more important of the two panels, displaying an elaborate scene of seven seated figures, all named with captions and framed by a lengthy hieroglyphic text (Fig. 11.2a). In the center of the large assembly we find K'inich Ahkal Mo' Nahb III, shown seated on a jaguar pillow-throne. The west or side panel, by contrast, shows only three named figures and has a shorter inscription (Fig. 11.2b). Interestingly, the format and design of each panel is highly symmetrical, with a central image of a person and flanking portraits and text panels. In many respects this presentation continues the traditional scheme established by earlier Palenque panels, such as the well-known examples of the nearby Cross Group, as well as the Palace Tablet.

Temple XXI's smaller platform is similar in design and conception, and looks to have been carved by the same artisans (Fig. 11.3). It shows a central seated figure as well, this time K'inich Janab Pakal I (clearly in a posthumous portrait), flanked by symmetrical images of lords facing elaborately dressed cats (at first glance one wonders how "historical" such a scene could be!). The person at left is K'inich Ahkal Mo' Nahb III, and at right is his possibly younger brother, Upakal K'inich. Only one side of the platform was decorated, along with the horizontal edge of the upper slab, above the platform's face.

Both temples emphasize an integrated view of mythology and history—certainly not a new theme for Palenque's inscriptions. The principal tablets of the three Cross Group temples, dedicated near the middle of K'inch Kan Bahlam II's reign do much the same thing, presenting a narrative of royal accessions that

Figure 11.2: The platform from Temple XIX: a) south face; b) west face (drawings by David Stuart)

originated with the supernatural births of the Triad in primordial time (Kelley 1965). Temples XIX and XXI served to connect the Triad gods with the next generation of Palenque's kings (K'inich Ahkal Mo' Nahb III and Upakal K'inich) but in a different and, I argue, far more direct and personal way.

K'inich Ahkal Mo' Nahb in Palenque History

K'inich Ahkal Mo' Nahb III came to power in the year A.D. 721, on the day 9.14.10.4.2 9 Ik' 5 K'ayab (Berlin 1968; Mathews & Schele 1974). He succeeded his elderly uncle K'inich K'an Joy Chitam II (see Table 11.1), who had been captured in battle a few years earlier by the ruler of Tonina, only to be mysteriously "returned" to the Palenque throne at sometime soon thereafter (Stuart 2003). After this unstable period, K'inich Ahkal Mo' Nahb III did much to revive the fortunes of the kingdom. Over the course of a reign lasting some fifteen or twenty years he oversaw an impressive and widespread array of monuments and architectural projects throughout the ancient city. The southern sector of the Cross Group seems to hold more of his buildings, including Temples XVIII (possibly his father's funerary monument) and possibly XVIIIa. Within the Palace, K'inich Ahkal Mo' Nahb III appears to have been responsible for modifications in House E, the *Saknuknaah* or "White Great House" originally built by his grandfather K'inich Janab Pakal I. In the courtyard before this structure, at the base of the famous tower of the Palace, the Tablets of the Scribe and Orator cite the name of K'inich Ahkal Mo' Nahb III.

Figure 11.3: The Temple XXI platform (photograph by Alfonso Morales Cleveland)

Table 11.1: The Late Classic Dynasty of Palenque

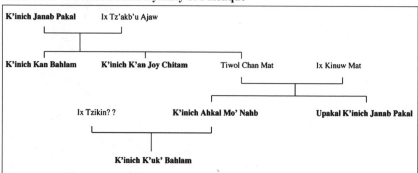

In the North Group, stucco glyphs from Temples III and IV include portions of his name, and a "tomb" glyph also excavated from Temple III strongly indicates this building was a funerary structure. One immediately wonders if this was the burial place of K'inich Ahkal Mo' Nahb III, but this cannot be confirmed until further excavation takes place.

As briefly noted above, K'inich Ahkal Mo' Nahb III was probably the grandson of the great ruler K'inich Janab Pakal I (often known to scholars and others simply as "Pakal"). Following the historical reconstructions first outlined by Ringle (1996) it now seems that Pakal's third son, Tiwol Chan Mat, never assumed the throne, having died in A.D. 680, during the reign of his father. K'inich Ahkal Mo' Nahb III was a very young child at the time of his father's death, but apparently took office not terribly long after the death of his uncle. The complex family history and the unusual chain of royal succession during this period (brother-to-brother, then uncle-to-nephew) helps to explain why K'inich Ahkal Mo' Nahb III went to unusually elaborate and creative lengths to establish his family pedigree and his claim to rule.

The Temple XIX and XXI histories feature another important historical figure named Upakal K'inich (Bernal Romero 2002). He would come to succeed K'inich Ahkal Mo' Nahb III as ruler, but the relationship between the two men remains cloudy.[4] Upakal K'inich is portrayed on the stucco frieze of the Temple XIX pier, as well as on the platform face of Temple XXI, and I lean toward the view that the two were brothers (not father and son), existing for a time at least as close peers within the royal court. Indeed, it is striking that Upakal K'inich is named in the Temple XXI scene as the *b'aah ch'ok K'uhul Baakal Ajaw*, or "the heir, the Holy Baakal Lord." It is highly unusual to have two "Holy Lords" at a given time, but here we seem to have a window on the subtle hierarchies and complex structures within the office(s) of Maya kingship. Clearly both men worked in close conjunction in the design and expression of their status in these two temples.

The written history surrounding K'inich Ahkal Mo' Nahb III seems to always feature his accession date, 9.14.10.4.2 9 Ik' 5 K'ayab, and it continually draws attention to the connection of this date with other significant days of Palenque

Figure 11.4: Passage from the doorjamb of Temple XVIII, linking the accession of K'inich Ahkal Mo' Nahb III with an ancestral deity. (drawing by Hipólito Sanchez)

mythology. On the jambs of Temple XVIII, for example, this is directly connected to the mythological "first seating" of the god or goddess known widely as "Lady Beastie" (Fig. 11.4). This deity was the creator of the Palenque Triad gods GI, GII, and GIII, and assumed office on 2.0.0.10.2 9 Ik' Seating of Sak. Obviously the common 9 Ik' day was a highly significant parallel for the king to emphasize, but this was by no means the end of the numerological and calendrical parallels linking this one king to primordial mythology and the very origins of the gods. Lounsbury (1976) demonstrated that the number of days between the accessions of the Triad creator and K'inich Ahkal Mo' Nahb III not only is evenly divisible by 260 days, but also by 780 (the Mars period), 2,392 (the Palenque 81-moon constant) and 11,960 (the eclipse cycle of the Dresden Codex). Clearly the priests were exceedingly careful to make the distant mythological past mirror the historical present. We will see that the Temple XIX platform includes this same association as part of a much wider network of mythological and historical connections among gods and kings.

The Temple XIX Platform Inscription

On the Temple XIX platform, K'inich Ahkal Mo' Nahb III is shown seated at the center of the south or front panel, surrounded by attendants (Fig. 11.5). The scene is one of accession to rule. The new king's pose and gesture repeat other royal portraits at Palenque shown receiving symbols and accoutrements of office, and this is clearly another example in the tradition. Before him another nobleman holds out a cloth headband, the "crown" of Maya rulership and the essential symbol of the status *ajaw*, "ruler." The presenter of the headband

Figure 11.5: The central scene of the Temple XIX platform
(detail of photograph by Jorge Perez de Lara)

is named Janab Ajaw, whom we know from the K'an Tok Panel inscription to have also been a grandson of K'inich Janab Pakal I, perhaps through a daughter as yet undocumented. The two men facing one another are therefore cousins or perhaps even brothers or half-brothers. Each of the other figures on the platform south panel are shown through individual portraits and they are named with hieroglyphic captions. Few of them are known from the other historical records at Palenque. One exception is the lord seated directly behind the king, next to the headdress placed on its stand. He is the priest (*yajaw k'ahk'*) mentioned and depicted on two other sculptures from Temple XIX; it seems reasonable to suppose that this noble (his name, *yo-ko-?-TAL*, is not completely readable) had some special association with the temple, perhaps as a "resident" official.

The lengthy inscription that surrounds the scene presents far more than a simple record or description of the king's inauguration. Rather, it serves to establish a complex mythological context for understanding the deep historical and cosmological significance of the inauguration event in Palenque's history. The inscription opens (Fig. 11.6) with the Long Count date 12.10.1.13.2, corresponding to March 10, 3309 B.C., a date far earlier than others previously known from Palenque's mythological record in the Cross Group. The event is "sat in the rulership" (*chumlaj ta ajawlel*), in reference to the inauguration of the familiar deity GI, the most prominent member of the set of three sibling gods known as the Palenque Triad (Berlin 1963; Kelley 1965). GI is celebrated throughout Palenque's inscriptions, of course, and his much later birth, on the day 9 Ik' ("Nine Wind") is prominent in several texts of the Temple of the Cross.

Before the discovery of this text we had no knowledge of GI's accession to office, nor any indication that the god was considered a "ruler" in his own right. As we continue reading this passage, we then find that the accession event was

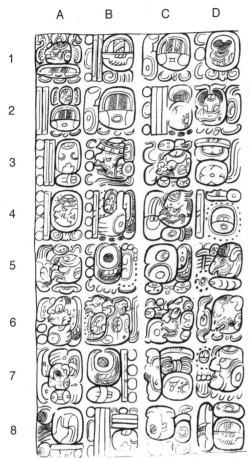

Figure 11.6:
Opening passage of the Temple XIX platform
(drawing by David Stuart)

overseen or sanctioned by another god, Itzamnah, and that the occasion took place "in the sky." This is an extraordinary statement, for Itzamnah is a well-known god who was in Classic times considered a ruler of the heavens. He is often depicted enthroned atop a sky-band design in portraits on Maya pottery (Fig. 11.7). Evidently, this supernatural monarch established Palenque's GI as a ruler, much like powerful kings of large Maya polities, such as Calakmul, "oversaw" the placement of lesser rulers in office. The language is precisely the same, suggesting that among the ancient gods there existed a sort of political hierarchy that reflected the realities of Late Classic geo-politics.

The text on the platform continues with an intriguing record of a sacrifice by decapitation, occurring about eleven years after GI's accession to office (Fig. 11.8). The passage describing this event is long but challenging to read. For example, it is difficult to know who was decapitated on this day—the two glyphs that follow the "axe" each include the sign of a crocodile with deer attributes and star signs in its eyes. This "starry deer crocodile" is a supernatural entity that was probably equated with the Milky Way. Intriguingly, the sacrifice of a crocodile is a widespread and old element of Mesoamerican Creation mythology. It seems to be a Classic Maya variation on a widespread and old story, where a primordial watery creature is killed in order to create the surface of the world.[5] One such narrative is related in the Books of Chilam Balam from Yucatan, where we read of the great reptilian Itzam Cab Ain:

> [Ah Mesencab] turned the sky and the Peten upside down, and Bolon ti Ku raised up Itzam Cab Ain; there was a great cataclysm, and the ages ended with a flood. The 18 Bak

Figure 11.7:
Itzamnah on a celestial throne,
from a polychrome vase (K3056)
(drawing by Persis Clarkson)

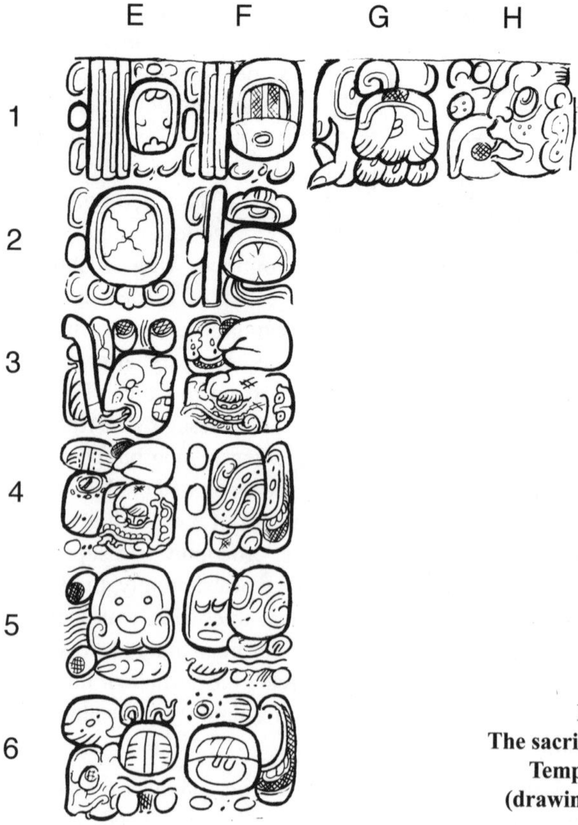

	E	F	G	H
1				
2				
3				
4				
5				
6				

Figure 11.8:
The sacrifice passage from the
Temple XIX platform
(drawing by David Stuart)

Katun was being counted and in its seventeenth part. Bolon ti Ku refused to permit Itzam Cab Ain to take the Peten and to destroy the things of the world, so he cut the throat of Itzam Cab Ain and with his body formed the surface of the Peten (Craine and Reindorp 1978:117-118).[6]

Itzam Cab Ain is, as Taube (1989) has shown, the Yucatec name for the crocodile so widely depicted in Classic art, including its Starry Deer-Crocodile aspect mentioned at Palenque. This story is of course a variation on a similar narrative well known from Central Mexican mythology, wherein Quetzalcoatl and Tezcatlipoca kill the Earth Monster (a zoomorphic aspect of Tlalteuctli) and create the earth from his dismembered body parts (Taube 1993: 69-70). Karl Taube (personal communication, 2003) has recently pointed out to me a clear representation of this event in a Late Postclassic mural excavated at Mayapan in Structure Q. 95 (Barrera Rubio & Peraza Lope 2001) (Fig. 11.9). The crocodile has been speared rather than decapitated, and the human figure above the reptile displays the distinctive shell pectoral of Quetzalcoatl. If we assume GI is indeed the actor behind the crocodile sacrifice recorded in Temple XIX, we can point to another strong parallel between these two deities named Nine Wind, so removed from one

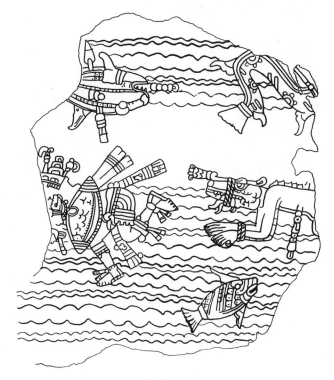

**Figure 11.9: Mural from Structure Q. 95 at Mayapan
(drawing by Karl Taube)**

another in time and space.

The next passage from the Temple XIX platform inscription links this sacrifice record to more familiar mythological history of Palenque. Counting forward over nine centuries, we come to the birth dates of the Palenque Triad (Fig. 11.10), in the proper order GI, GIII, and GII (this birth order is different from the order in

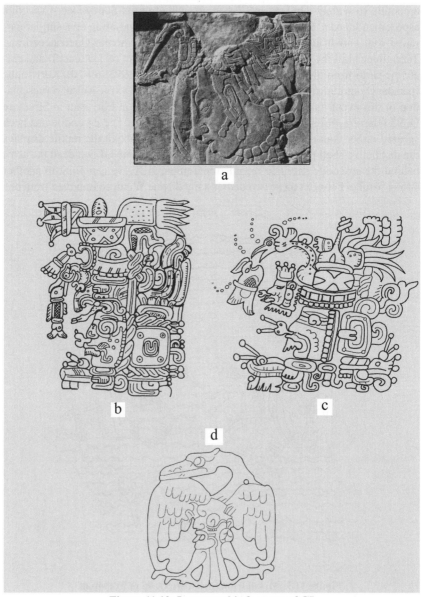

Figure 11.10: Iconographic features of GI

which the gods are always named, which Berlin used for his numerical designations). Their births are the major events celebrated in the Temples of the Cross (GI), Sun (GII), and Foliated Cross (GIII), as first identified by David Kelley (1965). Just as in the Cross temples, the Temple XIX inscription records the births with the metaphorical statement *u-tal?-kab' Matwil*, or "it is his earth-touching at Matwil." Matwil was a "place of origin" for Palenque's patron gods, and also a supernatural locale constantly evoked in the title for historical kings of Palenque during the Classic era, "the Holy Matwil Lord."

The narrative as presented so far raises an obvious and puzzling question: how could the deity GI be born some 960 years after his own accession to office? There can be no question about the chronology of the inscription, nor about the nature of the inauguration and birth glyphs, so we are forced to account for a seemingly backward course of events in some other way. The explanation lies, I believe, in how the births of the Palenque gods was an event of local significance; no records of these births are present at other Maya centers, many of which had their own specific sets of patron deities connected to the regional dynasty. GI, however, was celebrated throughout the lowlands in the Classic period, and his accession date under the auspices of Itzamnah is presented in the Temple XIX as a cosmic happening, "in the sky." The birth, or rebirth, of GI, after 13.0.0.0.0 4 Ajaw 8 Kumk'u was the redefinition of GI as a distinctively Palenque god.

A New Look at GI

Just who was GI? Despite his importance at Palenque and in much of Maya iconography overall, his "meaning" as a god or cosmological entity is largely obscure. Part of the mystery arises from the lack of any clear counterpart among the principal gods of the Postclassic period (Taube 1992). Nevertheless, the symbols we find associated with him and information from the Palenque texts themselves offer a few valuable clues. He is without doubt a god associated with water, as indicated by the fish-fins on his cheek and the heron bird that often merges from his head (Fig. 11.10). There are also good indications that he has stong connections with the sun god, and in one portrait he even has a *k'in* ("sun") sign on his face (Fig. 11.10c). The so-called quadripartite badge element is a common feature of GI as well (Greene Robertson 1974), which displays a *k'in* sign within a large sacrificial bowl. Since the only other setting for the *k'in* bowl is as the glyph **EL** (*elk'in*), I speculate that GI might be the "aquatic sun" who inhabits the eastern world, possibly before sunrise.

The most important, and problematic, textual source for understanding GI is the lengthy mythological portions of the inscription on the Tablet of the Cross. The chronology of the tablet has long presented problems for epigraphers. The interpretations have been discussed in several venues for over a century, but new evidence from the Temple XIX text offer some indirect evidence that might move us toward a final resolution of these long-posed and much-debated questions, and

ultimately to a better understanding of who GI was.

The discussions by Lounsbury (1980) and others have centered on one particularly troubling passage near the beginning of the Tablet of the Cross text (Fig. 11.11). A Distance Number at D1 and C2 records the interval 8.5.0, and precedes a "birth" event at D2 marked in the past tense (*sih-aj-iiy*). The tense marker on the birth verb would suggest it is the earlier of two linked events, or the beginning point of the temporal reckoning. A second verb or event comes at C3, apparently a version of an event found in other Palenque inscriptions showing a "deer hoof" sign (read confidently as **MAY**) above a human hand. This in turn precedes a notation of the date 4 Ajaw 8 Kumk'u, or 13.0.0.0.0, which Lounsbury and others have taken to be the end-point of the calculation.

The question surrounding this passage centers on the Distance Number. The Cross Tablet opens in the immediately preceding glyphs with a record of the birth of the "Triad Progenitor," and it seems natural to see the birth at D2 to be a repetition of this event ("it was so much time from the birth . . . "). However, if we add the Distance Number to the established birth date, we do not reach 4 Ajaw 8 Kumk'u. Instead, the calculation gives:

12.19.13. 4. 0 8 Ajaw 18 Tzek

8. 5. 0

(13. 0. 1. 9. 0 11 Ajaw 18 Mol)

The resulting date is not recorded in the Cross text. Lounsbury, however, followed earlier analysts (e.g., Goodman 1897) in stressing that 4 Ajaw 8 Kumk'u was the end-point of the calculation, resulting in an unexpressed earlier date:

(12.19.11.13. 0 1 Ajaw 8 Muwan)

    <u>8. 5. 0</u>

13. 0. 0. 0. 0 4 Ajaw 8 Kumk'u

This scheme necessitates the existence of two birth episodes, begging the question asked by Lounsbury (1980: 103): "whose birth?" Because the next cited protagonist on the Cross Tablet inscription is GI (at C8 and D8), Lounsbury surmised that the implied birth event pertained to an earlier GI, or "GI'," who shared the name of the more familiar Triad member. He suggested that the first GI, seemingly born on 12.19.11.13.0, was the spouse of "Lady Beastie," whom here I call the Triad Progenitor (the glyphic name is not completely readable). It seemed natural to propose that this couple were the mythic parents of the Palenque Triad. As Schele and Freidel (1990: 244-245) summarize this widely accepted interpretation:

> The First Mother was Lady Beastie [who was] the mother of the gods and the Creatrix in the Maya version of the cosmos . . . [T]he Palencanos saw her operate in their lives through her spirit counterpart, the moon. Her husband and the father of her children is called GI' (G-one-prime) by modern scholars. He established the order of time and space just after the fourth version of the cosmos was created on 4 Ahau 8 Cumku. Both the Creatrix and her husband were born during the previous manifestation of creation, but their children were born 754 years into this one.

Despite standing today as the standard version of Palenque mythology, this story is based on questionable readings. We must look more carefully at the Tablet of the Cross inscription and its troubling passage to begin to see where the problematic issues lie.

Lounsbury's suggestion that we have two separate birth events—and therefore two deities named GI—looks to be an excessively complex reading of the passage. The date 4 Ajaw 8 Kumk'u, at D3 and C4, need not be linked with the "deer hoof" event, as Lounsbury and others long assumed must be the case. It is equally plausible that the date for the "deer hoof" episode was left unexpressed, and that the Distance Number is in fact reckoned from the opening birth event of the inscription. This, after all, seems the natural way to approach the birth glyph at D2 if one were unaware of the supposed ambiguities soon to come. The first calculation given above, leading to an unexpressed date 13.0.1.9.0 11 Ajaw 18 Mol, may well be the correct date for the "deer hoof" event. The "era" date has its own verbal statement at D4 and C5, "13 Bak'tuns are finished."[7]

No matter how we interpret this passage from the Tablet of the Cross, we are still faced with the conundrum that GI existed centuries before his stated birth. So much is clear from the reading the south face of the Temple XIX platform, which states that the god's accession to rulership occurred roughly two centuries before his supposed birth. Let us review the major events involving him, as they are recorded at Palenque:

- GI assumed rulership "in the heavens" on 12.10.1.13.2 9 Ik' 5 Mol under the auspices of Yax Naah Itzamnah. Any previous birth event of this GI remains unknown.
- According to the Temple XIX platform, GI seems to be a major participant in a sacrificial beheading or "axing" of the cosmological entity called the "Starry Deer Crocodile," or two aspects of this creature, on 12.10.12.14.18 1 Etz'nab 6 Yaxk'in.
- GI is cited on the Tablet of the Cross as a participant in a house dedication event in the "north" on 13.0.1.9.2 13 Ik' End of Mol.
- GI is the protagonist of an event described on the west tablet of the Temple of the Inscriptions, where the Death God "was thrown into the center of the sea from the hand of GI." This occurred on 13.4.12.3.6 1 Kimi 19 Pax.
- GI, now as a member of the Palenque Triad, is "born" on 1.18.5.3.2 9 Ik' 15 Keh, apparently as a "creation" of the Triad Progenitor.

That GI's birth closes this chain of events would seem to support Lounsbury's contention that there existed two GIs. But there is no reason why we must consider the "ruling" GI cited in the opening passage of the platform and the first-born of the Triad to be separate entities. The identical forms of the name and shared importance of the day 9 Ik' suggest that they are the same character, or in some way "aspects" of a single deity. The essential sameness of the two is perhaps best seen in a passage from the Tablet of the Cross, where GI's birth is recorded at C17 through F4 (Fig. 11.12). There, we read (starting at the bottom of columns C and D) "he arrives at Matwil (on) 9 Ik' 15 Keh. He touches (?) the earth at Matwil . . ." But throughout this passage we do not find GI's name. As is customary in Classic Mayan syntax—especially in this inscription—the subject's name has been omitted because it is understood from a citation of the previous episode, where GI is named at C16-D16. The subject of that earlier event is the "preborn" GI, yet this god is equated syntactically with the deity who is born eight centuries later.

I suggest, therefore, that the creation of the Triad gods entailed a "rebirth" of a previously existing GI into a new, more localized order of existence (see Table 11.2). The GI who took office under Itzamnah "in the sky" seems a deity of wide cosmological significance, whereas the GI of the Palenque Triad seems a far more limited aspect of the god, intimately tied to the Palenque dynasty.

Sacred Landscape at Lakam Ha'

After a span of 5,880 years the Temple XIX platform text carries us to the time of contemporary history, to an event that was thematically and calendrically linked to the mythology recorded earlier on the platform (Fig. 11.13). The event is the inauguration of the ruler K'inich Ahkal Mo' Nahb III, and the "seating" event is identical to that used for the god in the previous passage. Clearly the date and the verb phrase are meant to evoke a strong connection between the two dates.

Table 11.2: A Proposed Revision to the Palenque Triad Mythology

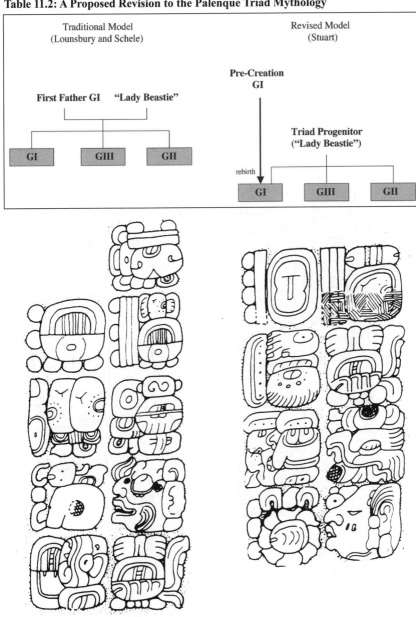

**Figure 11.12: Record of GI's birth from the Tablet of the Cross
(drawing by Linda Schele)**

The word *okib*, "pedestal," names the location of the inauguration or seating ceremony.

The inscription goes on to finally record this ruler's first *k'altun* or "stone binding" ceremony some two years later, on the period ending 9.14.13.0.0, ending the epic narrative of gods and rulers (Fig. 11.14). Like many other Palenque texts, the inscription ends with a formal phrase that emphasizes the location and environmental setting of the tablet and the temple containing it. Here the phrase reads *ut-iiy tan ch'een Lakam Ha'*, or "it happened in front of the well at Lakam Ha." The place name *Lakam Ha'*, "Wide Waters," was the ancient name of Palenque (with no relation to the site today called Lakanha, near Bonampak). Arguably, this was the name given to the Otolum River that runs through the center of the site and falls as wide pools and cascades and on the

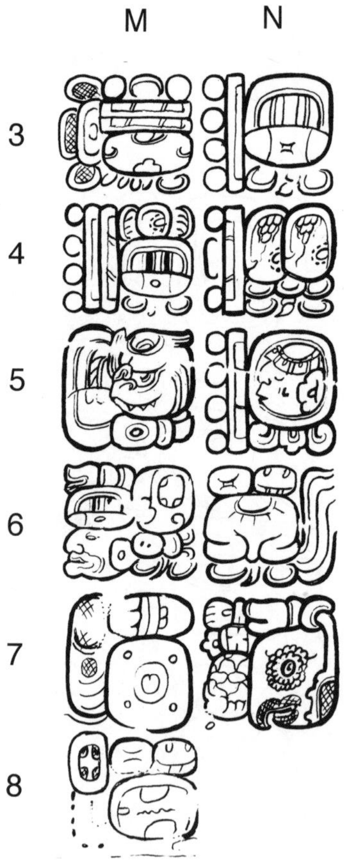

Figure 11.13:
Inauguration record of
K'inich Ahkal Mo' Nahb III
from the Temple XIX platform
(drawing by David Stuart)

Figure 11.14:
The "rope-taking" event recorded
on the west face of the
Temple XIX platform
(drawing by David Stuart)

hillside below the ruins. The "well of Lakam Ha" can only be the spring located on the mountainside directly behind Temple XIX from which the Otolum flows. This must have been one of the most sacred locations in the urban landscape of Palenque. Not only is Temple XIX located in front of it, but the earlier Temple of the Cross—the most imposing structure of the Cross Group—seems to directly face the spring (see Fig. 11.1). Springs and caves were of course major ritual locations in Maya and Mesoamerican religion, and we know of many examples of temple pyramids having direct relationship to such natural features. Perhaps the most familiar case is the Temple of K'uk'ulkan at Chichen Itza, connected by a causeway to the great cenote. Palenque's river, emerging from the mountain spring, offers an ideal Maya example of what the Mexica Aztec called the *altepetl*, "the water-mountain," which became a powerful symbol of state and community. In this way the spring anciently called Lakam Ha' provided an ideal locale for the construction of a major ceremonial complex known today as the Cross Group.

The Deified King

The inscription of the south platform panel presents a narrative linking events in the very distant mythological past to others occurring shortly before the inscription was carved. The design and presentation of the information is extremely careful and deliberate, juxtaposing events and setting them forth as thematically related or even as repetitions of history. Notice for example the episodes of the inscription that fell on the day "9 Ik'" (9 Wind): (1) the opening record of GI's "seating as ruler," (2) the birth, or perhaps rebirth, of this same GI as a member of the Palenque Triad, (3) the accession to office of the Triad creator deity, and (4) finally, the accession to office of the Palenque king. The three inaugurations have clearly been established as complimentary to one another, and they likely held an even stronger significance in Maya thought as interconnected "like in kind" events, much as we know exists in the historical records of the Mexica Aztec. The text opens with GI's accession to office and closes shortly after a record of the king's own inauguration, also on the day "9 Ik'," thus bracketing the narrative contained within.

The desire to forge some sort of equivalence between the accessions of GI and of the king—events separated by nearly four thousand years—was not simply a literary device of the scribe. It is made even more explicit in the scene accompanying the text, where we see K'inich Ahkal Mo' Nahb III leaning forward to receive the headband emblem of his office from a court attendant. In the hieroglyphic captions of these men, we find not only their proper names, but also explicit records that they are "impersonators" of deities. Maya kings and other elite figures apparently often took on ceremonial roles as "embodiments" or active manifestations of certain gods, a phenomenon not unlike the better-known Aztec concept of *ixiptla* (Hvitfeldt 1958). Here, the ruler is named as the impersonator of none other than GI. The nobleman who faces the king with the headband, named

Janab Ajaw, is named as the impersonator of Yax Nah Itzamnah. The historical accession of K'inich Ahkal Mo' Nahb III is not simply harkening back to mythical symbolism, but truly becomes a re-creation of that earlier event, where one god installed another in office. When viewed in the context of the inscription that surrounds it, the "crowning" scene on the new Palenque platform becomes one of the most explicit representations of divine rulership known in Maya art.

The west face of the platform has a long text and a figural scene, but both are smaller than found on the front. The inscription is again difficult to read in places, but it concerns mainly the dedication of an *okib*, a possible Classic Mayan term for the platform itself, meaning "pedestal." The history recounted in this inscription does not concern distant mythological times, but instead begins with a reference to the early Palenque ruler K'an Joy Chitam I, who is said to have built an *okib* in 561 A.D. We then jump forward to the reign of K'inich Ahkal Mo' Nahb III and mention of the ritual dedication of three shrines or temples associated with each of the Triad gods. Temple XIX seems to have been one of these three structures named in the inscription, dedicated to the god GI on 9.15.2.7.16 9 Kib 19 K'ayab, or January 14, A.D. 734. The very same date is featured in two other texts from the building: the outer *alfarda* and also the beautiful Lápida de los Ayudantes that decorated the central interior pier of the temple. The prominence of GI in Temple XIX's writings is interesting in light of the temple's orientation toward the Temple of the Cross, also devoted to this deity.

The scene on the west face of the Temple XIX platform surely depicts an event described in the accompanying text as "rope-taking" (Fig. 11.14), taking place only a short time after the Temple XIX dedication. The main figure is named Sajal B'olon, and he is shown cradling a massive bundle of coiled rope, the function of which is not entirely clear. Three inscriptions from Temple XIX feature this "rope-taking" ritual in connection with two different but related dates: 9.14.2.9.0 9 Ajaw 18 Tzek (recorded on the stucco panel) and 9.15.2.9.0 7 Ajaw 3 Wayeb (recorded on the west side of the platform). Both fall at the precise half-point of the initial hotun (5 Tun) portion of the K'atun period.

Temple XXI

The inscriptions on the Temple XIX and XXI platform cite two building dedication dates: 9.15.2.9.16 9 Kib 19 K'ayab and 9.15.4.15.17 6 Kaban 5 Yaxk'in. The first of these is Temple XIX's own dedication, and the inscription clearly states that it is a "house" of GI (that date is prominently displayed on the *alfarda* of XIX). The second date, falling some two years later, is given as the day on which structures or spaces associated with GII and GIII were dedicated, seemingly to complete the set begun with Temple XIX. But where might these other structures be located? The question could not be answered until 2002, when excavations at Temple XXI, overseen by Arnoldo González Cruz, revealed a clear "partner" to Temple XIX. Temple XXI had been superficially investigated in 1955 (Ruz

Lhuillier 1958), resulting in the discovery of a small beautiful fragment of a text citing a distinctive date found also on the stucco pier of Temple XIX (Schele & Mathews 1979: no. 553; Stuart 2000a). The recent INAH excavations found this fragment to be part of the elaborately decorated platform very similar in design and execution to the platform of Temple XIX (see Fig. 11.3). It then seems likely that Temple XXI was the "house" of GII and/or GIII, in the same way that GI occupied (physically or spiritually) the larger building. Given that the spaces for the two lesser gods were dedicated on the same day, I feel they could easily have been associated with this single structure.[8]

The featured date of Temple XXI is 9.13.17.9.0 3 Ajaw 3 Yaxk'in (June 18, A.D. 709), written as the Initial Series in the text running above the platform's scene. This is another "half hotun" period ending, and interestingly occurs very close to the summer solstice. The date falls within the reign of K'inich K'an Joy Chitam II and far earlier than the time of the carving. The A.D. 709 date may well correspond to the scene, in which case K'inich Ahkal Mo' Nahb III would have been thirty years old (Upakal K'inich was presumably a younger individual, but we lack his birth date). With the absence of the main verb in the text, portions of which remain missing, the occasion is difficult to interpret or understand, but it seems to have been an important dynastic event. The same day is mentioned on the Temple XIX stucco text, where it is said to have been the first of a series of three episodes described by a "heron-with-fish" sign that remains undeciphered. Surviving portions of the initial Temple XXI passage notes that on this day Upakal K'inich "stood up" in the office or status of the "heron-with-fish." No where else is this mentioned in the corpus of Maya inscriptions at Palenque or elsewhere, and I am at a loss to explain its meaning. There is a good possibility, however, that the "heron-with-fish" is closely connected to the scene on the Temple XIX stucco panel (Fig. 11.15), where Upakal K'inich is shown striding in a large bird's head costume, with a fish dangling from its upper beak.

Somewhat surprisingly, the central figure on the Temple XXI platform is the ancestor K'inich Janab Pakal I, who had been dead for several decades by the time Temple XXI was dedicated. Impersonation of ancestors is again a theme of the Temple XXI panel. Interestingly he wears a headband decorated with the names of two early Palenque kings, apparently in an unusual example of a "double impersonation." The headgear and the accompanying text caption both indicate that K'inich Janab Pakal I is "fused" with a king we know of as "Casper" (a nickname coined by Linda Schele) as well as a figure name "Snake's Stingray Spine" (Fig. 11.16). This last name we know from the Tablet of the Cross (in passage F15-Q3) as a "quasi-historical" ruler who assumed office in 967 B.C. "Casper" is also named on the Cross Tablet, in connection with the beginning of Bak'tun 9 in the Early Classic, but here on Temple XXI the reference is somewhat more complicated. According to the final passage of the platform's inscription, "Casper" was also the name of an earlier Palenque Holy Lord who took office on 7.5.3.10.17 10 Kaban 5 Muwan, or July 21, 252 B.C. Pakal, as the impersonator of these two

Figure 11.15:
The stucco panel
from Temple XIX
(photograph by
Jorge Perez de Lara)

figures from proto-history, thus becomes something of an "uber-ancestor," and his wielding of the defied blood letter in his right hand thus becomes an even more powerful image of ancestry and its associations with sacrifice and political office.

Although the specific messages of the XXI platform's complex composition are very hard to discern—the felines are, to my knowledge, unique in Maya art—the overall sense of the tablet is that K'inich Janab Pakal I still continued to exert a powerful symbolic influence on the political life of Palenque, even two generations after his demise. After a time of uncertainty and dynastic instability in the kingdom, K'inich Ahkal Mo' Nahb III and Upakal K'inich sought to connect themselves to their illustrious grandfather and, through him, to the distant historical and mythological origins of the dynasty.

Conclusion

Temple XIX's hieroglyphic inscriptions present some of the most complex and compelling information on Classic Maya mythology and kingship, and the relationship between them. K'inich Ahkal Mo' Nahb III took

**Figure 11.16:
Detail of the
Temple XXI platform,
showing the headdress of
K'inich Janab Pakal
(photograph by
David Stuart)**

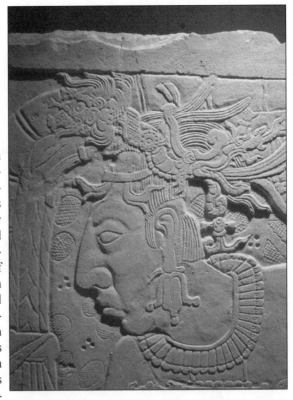

great pains to establish his role as an embodiment of the god GI, going so far as to have his inauguration ceremony occur on a date that could be mathematically represented as a repetition of GI's own accession "in the sky" in primordial times. The mythical origins of Palenque's own political identity perhaps came with the creation or re-birth of GI and his two siblings by a mythical founder, the first to be seated as a "Palenque" king. Only decades before the eventual collapse of Palenque, K'inich Ahkal Mo' Nahb III presented himself in these tablets as a culmination and living symbol of all of these interrelated events, perhaps striving to resurrect Palenque's glory and religious status after its defeat by Tonina.

Many more aspects of the Temple XIX and XXI inscriptions will require discussion at another time, and clearly decades of work on the materials lie ahead. One of several major and fascinating questions to still consider is the larger significance of the day 9 Ik' or 9 Wind, cited four times in the main text of the platform. When David Kelley first recognized this as the birthday of GI in the Temple of the Cross he pondered its relationship to the wider significance of 9 Wind in Mesoamerican religion, especially as a name for Ehecatl-Quetzalcoatl. Was GI truly a Classic Maya counterpart to this famed deity, as Kelley first considered? Although difficult to prove at this stage, I suspect that this and other issues raised by the newest Palenque discoveries will eventually strengthen the connections we are otherwise hesitant to trace among the cultures of ancient Mesoamerica. They are already reviving our study of religion and kingship just within Palenque and the Maya area.

Acknowledgments

I would especially like to thank Merle Greene Robertson and Alfonso Morales Cleveland for their invitation to work with the Temple XIX texts. My on going work with these texts has benefited from insights and help of many individuals who deserve great thanks, including Karen Bassie-Sweet, Guillermo Bernal Romero, Alfonso Lacadena, Damien Marken, Simon Martin, Werner Nahm, Christopher Powell, John Robertson, Stanley Guenter, Stephen Houston, Jorge Perez de Lara, Joel Skidmore, Karl Taube, Erik Velásquez García, and Marc Zender. Portions of this paper echo a few points discussed elsewhere (Stuart 2000b) and summarize discussions from a much more lengthy work on the inscriptions of Temple XIX (Stuart, in press)

Notes

[1] The king's name contains the common honorific prefix *K'inich*, "Great Sun," before Ahkal Mo', "Turtle Macaw" and *Nahb*, "Pool" (this reasonably certain analysis of the name revises earlier designations, including "Chaacal III" or "Akul Anab III"). Scribes at Palenque, as was often the case, wrote many different-looking versions of this royal name, but they are structurally identical.

[2] I transliterate the name using *Janab* in place of the common alternative *Janahb* for the simple reason that the intended lexeme is unknown, and cannot be reconstructed historically at present. The spelling convention **ja-na-bi** might cue one of several possible forms, so for now I use the most neutral (unmarked) representation.

[3] In this essay I must focus on the more extensive texts from Temple XIX (Stuart, in press), but I will necessarily draw upon several parallels between this building and the valuable materials recently discovered by Arnoldo González Cruz of INAH in Temple XXI, and expertly analyzed by Guillermo Bernal Romero. Moreover, it must be said that as of this writing (Fall 2003) the full range of the Temple XXI inscriptions have yet to be circulated or made available to the author.

[4] The one firmly established date of his reign is 9.15.10.10.13 13 Muluk 2 K'ayab, recorded on the so-called K'an Tok Panel, which names this ruler as Upakal K'inich K'inich Janab Pakal. This came just five years after K'inich Ahkal Mo' Nahb III's last known date (9.15.5.0.0) mentioned in Temple XIX. It should be noted that not all researchers accept that Upakal K'inich and K'inich Janab Pakal II are the same individual.

[5] I would like to acknowledge the fine work of Erik Velásquez García (n.d., personal communication 2003) in bringing many of these mythological sources together, and independently relating them to the sacrifice event in the Temple XIX narrative.

[6] The passage from the Tizimin which describes the sacrifice (Edmonson 1982: 41) reads *ca ix xot I cal Itzam Kab Ain ca I ch'aah u petenil u pach*, which Edmonson translates as "and then will be cut the throat of Itzam Kab Ain, who bears the country on his back." In Yucatec, *xot* is "cut, slice" and *cal* (*kal*) is "throat, neck" (Bricker, Po'ot Yah, and Dzul de Po'ot 1998). The Tizimin passage could therefore just as easily describe a complete beheading as a throat cutting.

[7] Support for this revision comes from other citations of the "deer hoof" (*k'al mayij*) event in Palenque's inscriptions. In the text of the Palace Tablet, we find it cited as an early ritual event associated with the seven-year-old K'inich K'an Joy Chitam II. On the jamb of Temple XVIII,

as we have seen, it is also a youth event involving the K'inich Ahkal Mo' Nahb III, who was about six years old at the time. In each instance these events are reckoned from a birth event, precisely as we find in the Tablet of the Cross. The natural conclusion is that the Tablet of the Cross records a similar "deer hoof" event for the eight- year-old Triad Progenitor. Logically, then, GI, or a predecessor with the same name, need not be a participant in this event.
[8] Hopefully the publication of other text fragments reportedly found in Temple XXI will help to clarify the connection of the temple to GII and GIII, which remain somewhat speculative.

Bibliography

Barrera Rubio, Alfredo and Carlos Peraza Lope
  2001   La pintura mural de Mayapán. In *La pintura mural prehispánica en México II: Area Maya, Tomo IV, Estudios*, pp. 419-446. Instituto de Investigaciones Esteticas, UNAM, México, D.F.

Berlin, Heinrich
  1963   The Palenque Triad. *Journal de la Société des Américanistes* [n.s.] 52:91-99.

  1965   The Inscription of the Temple of the Cross at Palenque. *American Antiquity* 30:330-342.

  1968   The Tablet of the 96 Glyphs at Palenque, Chiapas, Mexico. In *Archaeological Studies in Middle America*. Middle American Research Institute, Publication 26, pp. 135-149. MARI, Tulane University, New Orleans.

Bernal Romero, Guillermo
  2002   U Pakal K'inich Janahb' Pakal, el Nuevo gobernador de Palenque. *Lakam Ha'* 1(4): 4-9.

Bricker, Victoria, Eleuterio Po'ot Yah, and Ofelia Dzul de Po'ot
  1998   *A Dictionary of the Maya Language as Spoken in Hocabá, Yucatán*. University of Utah Press, Salt Lake City.

Craine, Eugene R. and Reginald C. Reindorp, eds.
  1978   *Codex Pérez and the Book of Chilam Balam of Maní*. University of Oklahoma Press, Norman.

Edmonson, Munro S., trans.
  1982   *The Ancient Future of the Itza: The Book of Chilam Balam of Tizimin*. University of Texas Press, Austin.

Goodman, J. T.
  1897   The Archaic Maya Inscriptions. Appendix to A. P. Maudslay, *Biologia Centrali Americana: Archaeology*. London, U.K.

Greene Robertson, Merle
  1974   The Quadripartite Badge–A Badge of Rulership. In *Primera Mesa Redonda de Palenque, Part I*, edited by Merle Greene Robertson, pp. 77-94. Robert Louis Stevenson School, Pebble Beach, CA.

Hvitfeldt, Arlid
  1958   *Teotl and *Ixiptlatli: Some Central Conceptions in Ancient Central Mexican Religion*. Munksgaard, Copenhagen.

Kelley, David H.
  1965   Birth of the Gods at Palenque. *Estudios de Cultura Maya 5*, pp. 93-134. UNAM, Mexico.

Lounsbury, Floyd G.
1976   A Rationale for the Initial Date of the Temple of the Cross at Palenque. In *The Art, Iconography & Dynastic History of Palenque, Part III: The Proceedings of the Segunda Mesa Redonda de Palenque*, edited by Merle Greene Robertson, pp. 211-222. Robert Louis Stevenson School, Pebble Beach, CA.

1980   Some Problems in the Interpretation of the Mythological Portion of the Hieroglyphic Text of the Temple of the Cross at Palenque. In *Third Palenque Round Table–1978*, edited by Merle Greene Robertson, pp. 99-115. University of Texas Press, Austin.

1985   The Identities of the Mythological Figures in the Cross Group Inscriptions of Palenque. In *Fourth Palenque Round Tablet–1980*, edited by Merle Greene Robertson and Elizabeth P. Benson, pp. 45-58. Pre-Columbian Art Research Institute, San Francisco, CA

Mathews, Peter and Linda Schele
1974   The Lords of Palenque: The Glyphic Evidence. In *Primera Mesa Redonda de Palenque, Part 1*, edited by Merle Greene Robertson, pp. 63-76. Robert Louis Stevenson School, Pebble Beach, CA.

Ringle, William M.
1996   Birds of a Feather: The Fallen Stucco Inscription of Temple XVIII, Palenque, Chiapas. In *Eighth Palenque Round Table–1993*, edited by Merle Greene Robertson, Martin Macri, and Jan McHargue, pp. 45-61. Pre-Columbian Art Research Institute, San Francisco.

Ruz Lhuillier, Alberto
1958   Exploraciones arqueológicas en Palenque, 1954. *Anales de Instituto Nacional de Antropología e Historia*, Tomo X, Núm 39, pp. 117-184. INAH, Mexico, D.F.

Schele, Linda and David Freidel
1990   *A Forest of Kings*. William Morrow, New York, NY.

Schele, Linda and Peter Mathews
1979   *The* Bodega *of Palenque, Chiapas, Mexico*. Dumbarton Oaks, Washington, D.C.

Stuart, David
2000a   Ritual and History in the Stucco Inscription from Temple XIX at Palenque. *PARI Journal* I(1): 13-19.

2000b   Nuevas inscripciones del Templo XIX. *Arqueología Mexicana* 8(45): 28-33.

2003   Longer Lives the King: The Premature Demise of K'inich Ahkal Mo' Nahb. *PARI Journal* IV(1): 1-4.

In press   *The Inscriptions from Temple XIX at Palenque: A Commentary*. Pre-Columbian Art Research Institute, San Francisco, CA.

Taube, Karl
1989   Itzani cab ain: Caimans, Cosmology, and Calendrics in Postclassic Yucatan. *Research Reports on Ancient Maya Writing 26*. Center for Maya Research, Washington, D.C.

1992   *The Major Gods of Ancient Yucatan*. Dumbarton Oaks, Washington, D.C.

Chapter 12

Ritual Purification and
the Ancient Maya Sweatbath at Palenque

Mark B. Child

Introduction

The widespread use of the sweatbath can be seen in many of the indigenous communities of Mesoamerica today (Gage 1969; Lopatin 1960; Pihó 1989). Most of these regions have a long-standing tradition of sweatbath use that can be traced back thousands of years in the archaeological record (Alcina Franch et al. 1982). Within the Maya region, sweatbaths date from the Preclassic to the Postclassic time periods, attesting to their extensive use throughout both the highlands and lowlands (Table 12.1; Fig. 12.1). The importance of this ancient practice can be seen through the degree of its monumentality, which is not only found at the majority of Maya political centers during the Classic period (A.D. 250-900), but also revealed at many of the ceremonial centers throughout Mesoamerica, such as Tenochtitlan, Tula, Teotihuacan, Chichen Itza, Xochicalco, El Tajin, Monte Alban, and Chiapa de Corzo. However, nowhere is the grandeur of this monumentality more evident than at the Classic Maya centers of Palenque and Piedras Negras. These sites have an abundant sample of monumental works based on the sweatbath, such as ceremonial architecture, iconography, and epigraphy, which assists in the interpretation of this ancient practice. Moreover, recent investigations at the sites of Palenque and Piedras Negras have revealed patterns that aid in the reconstruction of its ideological aspects, in terms of the cosmological symbolism, religious philosophy, and ritual practices of the sweatbath. Thus, this chapter will analyze the various elements of the sweatbath at Palenque, in light of an ethnographic and ethnohistorical framework, to better understand the ideological elements of this ritual practice.

Table 12.1: Identified Maya Sweatbaths in the Archaeological Record

Period	Location	Number	Structure(s)	Reference
Formative				
	Cuello	1	- Str. ?	(Hammond & Bauer 2001: 21)
	Dzibilchaltun	1	- Str. 605	(Andrews & Andrews 1980: 31-33)
Classic				
	Becan	2	- Str. 10	(INAH)
	Calakmul	1	- Str. 2b	(Folan 1996: Fig. 12)
	Ceren	1	- Str. 9	(Mckee 1990: Fig. 2; Sheets 1992:98-102)
	Chiapa de Corzo	1	- Str. 1-J1a	(Lowe & Agrinier 1960: 34-36)
	Comalcalco	2	- Temp. IV&V	(Andrews 1989: 67-72,73-78)
	Copan	1	- Str. 10L-223	(Cheek & Spink 1986: 27-154)
	Edzna	1	- Acropolis	(INAH)
	El Chile	1	- Str. 1	(Satterthwaite 1952: 25-26)
	Malpasito	1	- Str. 18	(Cuevas Reyes 1997: 4-5)
	Nakum	1	- Palace	(IDAEH)
	Palenque	2	- Str. B2 & Palace	(Greene Robertson 1985: 79-80; Ruz 1952: Fig. 3)
	Piedras Negras	8	- Str. P7,N1,S2,S4, R13,O4,J17,S19	(Child 1997-2002 & Satterthwaite 1952)
	Quirigua	2	- Str. 2 & 3	(Morley 1935: 135-138, 139-142)
	San Antonio	1	- Str. 1	(Agrinier 1966: 29-30)
	Tikal	2	- Str. 5E-22, North Gp.	(Jones 1996: 75-77)
	Tonina	1	- Str. ?	(Taladoire 1975)
	Uaxactun	2	- Str. A-V:R7-8, R23	(Smith 1950:20, Fig. 60, 30, Fig. 67)
	Yaxchilan	2	- Str. 17 & 48	(Tate 1992:179,259)
	Zacualpa	1	- Str. 3	(Wauchope 1938: 137)
Postclassic				
	Agua Tibia	1	- Str. 1	(Alcina Franch et al. 1982)
	Chichen Itza	2	- Str. 3C15 & 3E3	(Ruppert 1935: 270, 1952: 56; Morley 1936: 121)
	El Paraiso	1	- Mound 1	(Kidder and Shook 1959: 70-74)
	Iximché	1	- Str. ?	(Ichon 1977: 204)
	Los Cimientos	1	- Str.B-12	(Ichon 1977: 203-209)

Sweatbath Background

The sweatbath serves as a place of healing and ritual in modern Maya communities today (Groark 1997). These tightly sealed structures contain a fire hearth where heated stones are sprinkled with water to produce steam. The treatment by moist heat generates therapeutic properties that purge toxins from the body through profuse sweating (Katz 1990; Orellana 1977). It is believed that sweating

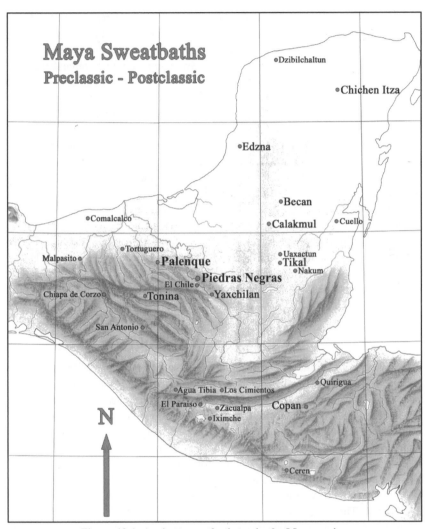

Figure 12.1: Ancient sweatbath use in the Maya region

from intense heat purifies the body from imbalanced corporal and spiritual equilibrium (Logan 1977; Orellana 1987). The sweatbath is especially important to midwives and their patients before, during, and after childbirth (Cosminsky 1972; Moedano 1977; Wagley 1949). In addition, the process of retreating to the sweatbath is seen as a pinnacle of ritual purification where an individual can emerge as if reborn from the earth (Corona 1960; López Austin 1988).

While there is a great deal of variety in the construction of sweatbaths (Servain 1983, 1986), their function remains the same because all sweatbaths share three basic characteristics (Arreola 1936; Carrasco 1946; Cresson 1938; Mason 1935). The first characteristic is the hearth area, which generates the intense heat. This feature is where the hot rocks are sprinkled with water to produce steam. The second characteristic is a tightly sealed sweat chamber that contains the heat. These small rooms have roofs or vaults that are much lower than normal for the purpose of intensifying the heat. The third characteristic is a low and narrow entrance, which minimizes heat loss. The dimensions of these entrances are well below the architectural standards for typical doorways.

Although the aforementioned characteristics are the most important features for recognizing the sweatbath at Palenque, monumental works, such as hieroglyphic writing and iconographic symbolism, also aid in the identification of its ideological aspects. In an article that focused on architectural meaning through metaphorical and semantic data, Stephen Houston (1996) was the first to address the ideological aspects of the Palenque sweatbath. More recently, investigations have revealed new data that not only builds upon his research, but also gives further insights that focus on certain elements that his article did not address. Thus, to provide a comprehensive view of the Palenque sweatbath, I will give a synthesis of his arguments below and later expound upon other ideological aspects of the Palenque sweatbath.

Birth and the Sweatbath

Ethnographic and ethnohistorical literature reveals that the use of the sweatbath for birthing and midwifery throughout Mesoamerica is extremely widespread and plays several roles during the birthing process. First, the sweatbath is used before childbirth to seek out a midwife through consultation and supplication (Sahagún 1969: 149). In addition, the sweatbath serves the purpose of purifying the pregnant woman because of indigenous beliefs that a woman should be free of sin and filth before delivery (Bunzel 1967: 96; Rodríguez 1969: 60). Second, midwives use the sweatbath during childbirth to heat the abdomen of pregnant women, in order for the fetus to be massaged to a preferred position for delivery (Sahagún 1969: 155). The sweatbath is also used during childbirth to help relax and calm the nerves of pregnant women to assist in an easier delivery (Sahagún 1969: 159). And finally, the sweatbath was used after delivery to aid in the recovery of the mother by restoring her bodily equilibrium that was thrown off in delivery and purifying her breast milk (Sahagún 1963: 191). In addition, some indigenous groups maintain that when a woman is fertile she is considered "hot" and if she does not take a sweatbath after childbirth, it is believed that she will turn "cold" and loose her fertility (Katz 1990: 182).

Because the sweatbath has functioned as a place of birth for individuals in Mesoamerican society, the assumption was made that their ancestors must have also been born in these sacred structures; hence, the gods were born in sweatbaths. One reason the Aztecs considered the sweatbath goddess Toci to be the mother of

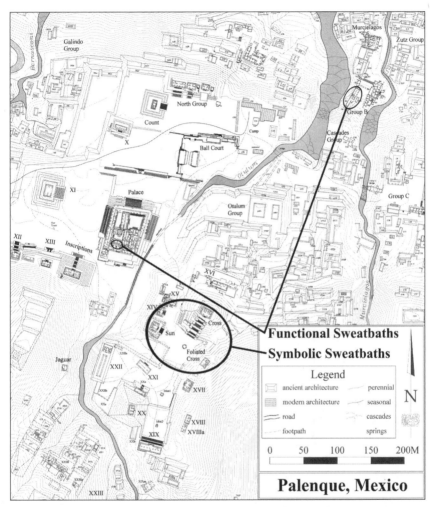

Figure 12.2: Main ceremonial precinct of Palenque (map by Ed Barnhart 2000)

the gods was due to their belief that the gods were born in her sweatbath (Duran 1971: 229; Sahagún 1969: 153-155). This view was not only held by the Aztecs, but also has been identified in ancient Maya mythology. Houston (1996: 145) has shown through architectural and hieroglyphic data that the Cross Group temples at Palenque functioned as "symbolic versions" of the sweatbath, which served as the natal sweatbaths of the patron deities of K'inich Kan Bahlam II (Fig. 12.2).

He supports this premise with the following arguments. First, the hieroglyphic texts from the *alfardas* of these temples refer to their interior sanctuaries as *pib-naahs* (Fig. 12.3), which epigraphers have deciphered as sweatbaths (Stuart 1987: 38; Houston 1996: 136). This lexical translation is taken from the Motul Maya

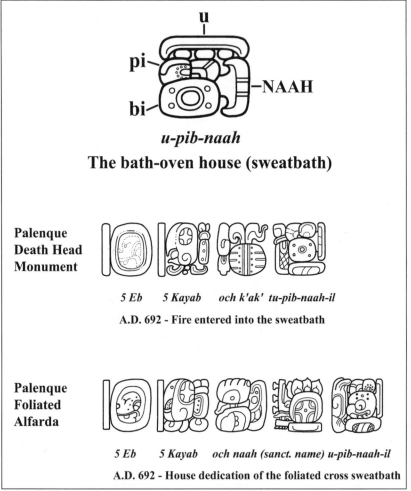

u
pi–
bi–
–NAAH

u-pib-naah
The bath-oven house (sweatbath)

Palenque
Death Head
Monument

5 Eb   *5 Kayab*   *och k'ak' tu-pib-naah-il*
A.D. 692 - Fire entered into the sweatbath

Palenque
Foliated
Alfarda

5 Eb   *5 Kayab*   *och naah (sanct. name) u-pib-naah-il*
A.D. 692 - House dedication of the foliated cross sweatbath

Figure 12.3: Death Head text (© Greene Robertson 1991: fig. 286).
Foliated *alfarda* text (© Greene Robertson 1991: fig. 13e).

dictionary, which states that the word *Pib* is a "very hot bath for postpartum women and other sick persons" (Barrera Vásquez 1980: 651). Second, the hieroglyphic texts from the sanctuary tablets of these temples refer to the birth of three gods in mythological time, otherwise known as the Palenque Triad; Houston (1996: 145) argues that they symbolically represent "the natal sweatbaths" of Kan Bahlam's respective gods, where each sanctuary has a separate name (Stuart & Houston 1994: 86, 89). This symbolic interpretation is supported by many ethnographic and ethnohistorical sources that reveal the use of the sweatbath in midwifery for birthing. Third, Houston (1996: 134) contends that the architectural occurrence of inner sanctuary buildings is not unique to Palenque, but occurs elsewhere during the Classic and Postclassic time periods. Although hieroglyphic texts link the sweatbath to the inner sanctum temple at Palenque, Houston (1996: 145-146) links these two elements at the site of San Miguel on Cozumel through an iconographic argument of birthing, where Ix Chel is the "aged goddess of birth." Fourth, although the architectural layouts of the temples of the Cross Group are similar to the sweat chambers of functioning sweatbaths, Houston (1996: 145) maintains that "the differences are far greater and more striking" because these structures lack the architectural characteristics that suggest bathing. He also points out the symbolic nature of these temples within the hieroglyphic texts by stating that the "heat being generated in the Palenque sweatbaths was of an entirely figurative sort" (Houston 1996: 145).

Thus, Houston has effectively shown that the temples of the Cross Group served only as symbolic sweatbaths. These sanctuaries were built by the Classic Maya to represent the birth houses or natal sweatbaths of their patron deities, otherwise known as the Palenque Triad. Now that the Cross Group architecture has been linked to the supernatural sweatbath, I will focus on other ideological aspects that have not yet been fully addressed.

Springs and the Sweatbath

The ideological aspect of springs is crucial for understanding the cosmological symbolism of the sweatbath. The importance of springs is expressed mostly by the symbolism of fertility through the flow of water. Ethnohistorical accounts reveal that the Aztecs believed that their ancestors lived within the waters of the earth and could be summoned through ritual practices of the sweatbath (Sahagún 1963: 277). In addition, the Aztecs associated their fertility with the sweatbath and "paid honor to the waters" (Sahagún 1970: 22). This fertility is recognizable in the Codex Borbonicus, which portrays the Aztec goddess of birth, Chalchiuhtlique, with the flow of water from her womb. It is interesting to note that the headdress of Toci is depicted with this water symbolism, further suggesting the fertile nature of the sweatbath. This fertility is also symbolized in several of the codices that portray sweatbaths through the flow of water. The Aztec Codex Mendoza (Fig. 12.4), for instance, has stated above it the word Temazcalapan, or "the place of the sweatbath" (Berdan & Anawalt 1992: 3:50). Other Central Mexican codices, such as the Borgia, Vaticanus B, and Florentine, also depict water flowing from the sweatbaths (Sahagún 1963; Seler 1963: 3:13; Códice Vaticano 1972: 32). Moreover, Mixtec codices use water to symbolize the fertility of the sweatbath, such as those depicted in the Codex Vindobonensis (Bellas 2000; Furst 1978).

The concept of springs playing a primary role in the cosmological symbolism of the sweatbath is evident in the founding of the Aztec capital of Tenochtitlan in A.D. 1325. Ethnohistorical documents reveal that the first thing the Aztecs did after crossing the waters of Lake Texcoco to the uninhabited island, was build a sweatbath where everyone could bathe (Duran 1967: II: 43-44; Alvarado Tezozómoc 1975: 61; Chimalpahin 1965: 77; Alva Ixtlilxóchitl 1975: I: 376). In addition, Duran (1964: 29) writes that after the Aztecs searched the island for a place that would be suitable for a permanent home, they founded their city of Tenochtitlan with the erection of another sweatbath at the place where water flowed near the prickly pear cactus.

This Aztec example associated with the founding of a center near a spring is not unique in ancient Mesoamerica. Hieroglyphic texts from the western Maya lowlands reveal the importance of this practice during the Classic period. Monument 6 from Tortuguero was erected in A.D. 669 and records a *pib-naah* associated with the founding of this site in A.D. 510, which is the earliest sweatbath data for the Palenque region (Fig. 12.2). The main event is a burning ritual with some sort of house dedication, which is inscribed as the positional verb *i-ek-wan*, possibly meaning to darken, obscure, cover up, or set in place of (Barrera Vásquez 1980: 149). This same verb is used to describe the *pib-naah* event that took place in A.D. 510, but this time describes the house as a sweatbath. It is interesting to note that the text of Monument 6 refers to the dedication of this sweatbath near a spring. The glyph for spring is prefaced with the adjective *nah-k'an*, meaning "first-precious." Lexical entries from the Maya dictionary refer to jal as a noun, meaning a "fontanela," which is a spring or a place abounding in springs (Barrera Vásquez 1980: 174). Thus this text records: **u-ti-ya 8 CHUWEN 9 MAK e-ke-wa-ni-ya NAH-K'AN-na ja-la u-pi-bi-NAAH a-ku-la K'UK'**, *uht-iiy 8 Chuwen 9 Mak, ek-wan-iiy, nah-k'an jal, u-pib-naah, Ahkal K'uk'*, or loosely paraphrased, "It happened, in A.D. 510, the sweatbath is set in place on the first precious spring, by Ahkal K'uk" (Fig. 12.4).

Although the site of Tortuguero was settled in an ideal location that allowed for the utilization of lacustrine resources to the north and the protection of a hill to the south (Riese 1980), it may have also been settled at the base of this large hill to exploit the springs that flowed forth to create a sacred water mountain. The Spanish adjective that is used in the Motul Maya dictionary to describe the type of spring "*jal*" is a fontanela frontoparietal, which means "a spring that flows forth from the front-side of a hill or cavity." Additional evidence that the noun *jal* signifies a spring comes from the verb *jal*, which means "to create, to root out from the earth, or to extract from the source of something" (Barrera Vásquez 1980: 174).

The fact that sweatbaths are associated with springs could account for the abundance of sweatbath data at Palenque. The place name for this site, *Lakam Ha'* has been given several similar readings, such as "Banner Water" (Houston 1996: 133), "Big Water" (Schele & Mathews 1998: 23), and "Wide Water" (Stuart 2000: 31), which all clearly derive its name from the abundant springs in the surrounding hillsides. Although there are fifty-six known springs that supply nine separate watercourses that move through the site core (French 2001: 12), the main spring where the ceremonial center is located is the Otolum, which continues to flow in modern times. Thus, the argument has been made that the Palenque place name of *Lakam Ha'* stems from the Otolum spring (Stuart & Houston 1994:

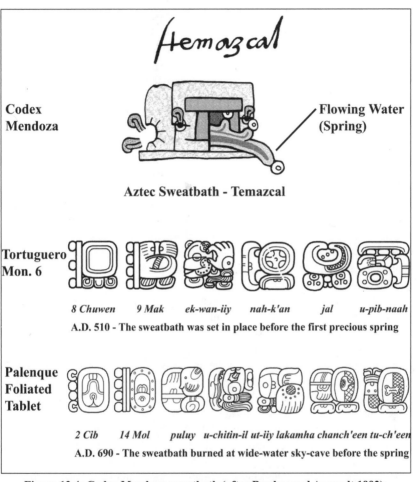

Figure 12.4: Codex Mendoza sweatbath (after Berdan and Anawalt 1992);
Tortuguero text (after Graham 2002: fig. 153);
Foliated Cross text (© Greene Robertson 1991: fig. 153)

31). Hieroglyphic texts of the Cross Group and Temple XIX contain events that end with the final phrase of, *ut-iiy tan ch'een Lakam Ha'*, or paraphrased as, "It happened before the spring of *Lakam Ha'*" (Stuart 2000: 31; Fig. 4). Scholars have argued that the "impinged bone" sign of **CH'EEN** has the reading of "cave, well, or spring" (Stuart 1998). In addition, Stuart has concluded that, "the cave of *Lakam Ha'* could only mean the spring that is in the area, directly below Temple XIX" (Stuart 2000: 31, Fig. 2, see Chapter 11).

Although a few functional sweatbaths have been discovered at Palenque thus far, none have been identified around the Cross Group or at the source of the Otolum spring. Nonetheless, the closest known sweatbath to the Otolum source would be the three symbolic sweatbaths of the Cross Group. The fact that the temples of the Cross Group did not serve as functioning sweatbaths does not detract from their association with springs and the abundance of water at the site.

Caves and the Sweatbath

Houston (1996: 142) first mentions the connection between caves and sweatbaths. This ideological element is crucial for understanding the cosmological symbolism of the sweatbath, because it is associated with the inner sanctum buildings at Palenque, Comalcalco, and San Miguel. The current section will discuss new data on the cosmological symbolism of caves and sweatbaths, in addition to where architectural enshrinement may have originated.

In indigenous communities today, sweatbaths are symbolically viewed as caves or entrances to the underworld (Bricker 1973: 114; Taube 1988: 295-296). The reverse is true as well for the Tzutujil Maya, where caves are sometimes viewed as sweatbaths (Tarn & Prechtel 1986: 184). As Sahagún (1963: 277) states, "the cave, also means place of the dead. Our mothers, our fathers have gone; they have gone to rest in the water, in the cave." Caves were not only viewed as places of the dead, but also were seen as places where newborns came from; hence, the notion of the natal sweatbath (Wagley 1949). The cave symbolism of the Mesoamerican sweatbath not only signified an entrance to the underworld, but also represented the animistic nature of the human body. Many communities that continue to use the sweatbath today believe it is a body where one would enter the womb, purify oneself, and emerge as if reborn (Corona 1960; Katz 1990: 182; López Austin 1988). In addition, the Mixteca of Oaxaca give the names of the following body parts to architectural features of their sweatbaths: head–entrance, foot–back side, back–above, womb–inside, mouth–firebox hole (Katz 1990: 176). Several ethnohistorical descriptions of the sweatbath disclose that it is viewed as a living entity that has "a navel-like opening" (Sahagún 1963: 275). Many of the Aztec codices, including the Magliabechiano, Tudela, and Florentine, portray the exterior facades of their sweatbaths as animistic (Fig. 12.5).

The ancient Mesoamerican sweatbath also portrays the cosmological symbolism of the cave through two architectural elements. The first is the presence of animistic forms on the exterior façade, generally depicting the eyes and mouth of the sweatbath (Códice Tudela 1980). This animistic architecture extends as far back as the Classic period for both functional and symbolic sweatbaths of the Maya. An example of this can be seen on the functional sweatbath known as Structure P7 at Piedras Negras, which is still standing after thirteen hundred years (Child & Child 2001). Its exterior façade represents an animistic being: two niches above the doorway of this structure represent the eyes of the living entity, and the entrance symbolizes the mouth of the cave (Fig. 12.5). This animistic architecture is also expressed on the surviving façades of Palenque's symbolic sweatbaths. The roof entablatures from both the sanctuary and the vestibule of the Temple

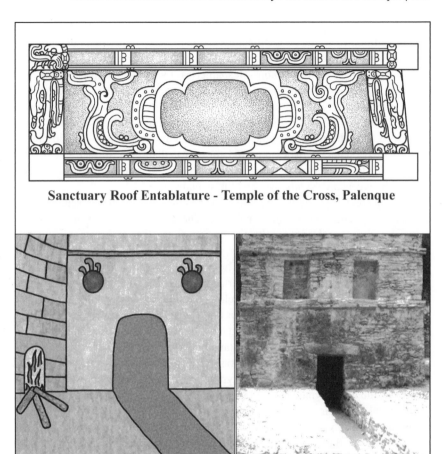

Sanctuary Roof Entablature - Temple of the Cross, Palenque

Aztec Sweatbath Florentine Codex
c. A.D. 1550

Sweatbath P7 Piedras Negras
c. A.D. 630-680

**Figure 12.5: Cave symbolism and animism of sweatbath architecture;
Santuary roof entablature (© Greene Robertson 1991: fig. 47);
Aztec sweatbath (after Sahagún 1961: fig. 180)**

of the Cross portray animistic beings that symbolize a cosmological cave. This symbolism is not only represented by the entrance/mouth, but is also embodied by the cartouche, a motif commonly seen throughout Mesoamerica (Fig. 12.5). Early representations of cave symbolism also portray the animistic nature of the cave as an entrance to the underworld, such as Middle Formative Monument 9 from Chalcatzingo (Grove 1984: 48). The outline created by the drain and benches of the functional sweatbaths at both Palenque and Piedras Negras represent the bottom half of this cartouche. Furthermore, cartouche representations depicted on the roof entablatures from the sanctuary of the symbolic sweatbaths at Palenque support the cosmological symbolism of caves (Greene Robertson 1991: 36).

In addition to animistic architecture and cartouche representations, the relationship between sweatbaths and caves is strengthened by the discovery of sweatbaths in various caves throughout Mesoamerica. One example in particular is a non-monumental sweatbath that was recently excavated in the mouth of a cave near Piedras Negras (Child 2002). This small structure was not only tightly sealed with a narrow entrance, but also contained burnt-calcified stones similar to those recovered from the eight monumental sweatbaths in the site core. In addition to the three basic characteristics required for a sweatbath, the artifact assemblage was similar to other sweatbaths at Piedras Negras, thus reconfirming the strict relation between cave symbolism and the sweatbath.

The second element that portrays cave symbolism is the presence of enshrined architecture on the interior façade. The earliest reflection of this architectural enshrinement occurs with the design of the firebox-hearth area within the sweat chambers at Piedras Negras, which are located on the back walls of the structures (Child & Child 1999). These fireboxes were elaborately built with vaults and stone lintels as symbolic structures enshrined within other buildings. When both enshrined and animistic architecture independently occur throughout Mesoamerica, they can symbolize other types of structures. However, the combination of these two architectural designs that typically symbolizes the sweatbath.

The visual comparison of floor plans between the sweatbaths of the Cross Group at Palenque and those at Piedras Negras demonstrates the similarity of these structures, regardless of their symbolic or functional nature (Fig. 12.6). However, the hieroglyphic texts from the *alfardas* of the Palenque temples (Fig. 12.3) reveal that their dedication was in A.D. 692 (9.12.19.14.12 5 Eb 5 K'ayab). Based on our excavations at Piedras Negras, ceramic dates from primary-sealed context indicate that four of the eight functional sweatbaths had been built by this time. The earliest, Structure R-13, was built around A.D. 450 (Child & Child 2000). This construction precedes the A.D. 490 *Lakam Ha'* event at Palenque and the founding event at Tortuguero twenty years later. Nonetheless, sweatbaths have yet to be associated with these early events in the Palenque region and are only relevant because they are mentioned in the hieroglyphic texts by rulers who use *Ahkal* "Turtle" as one of their names.

The earliest four sweatbaths of Piedras Negras were built upon open platforms without vestibules. Although the firebox-hearth area represented symbolic buildings and were enshrined within the vaulted sweat chamber, these small structures were no comparison to the larger and elaborate symbolic sweatbaths of Palenque. Thus, forty years later, Ruler 4, otherwise known as Itsam K'an Ahk III, changed the sweatbath landscape at Piedras Negras in a rage of architectural competition between neighboring polities. Between A.D. 729-757, Ruler 4 built vestibules around the sweat chambers of the first four sweatbaths. These vestibules not only had a symbolic function to enshrine the sweat chamber, but also were probably enclosed to obtain more privacy as places to rest and disrobe. Ruler 4 of Piedras

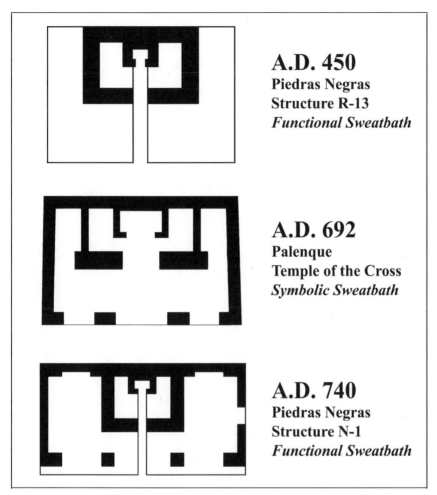

A.D. 450
Piedras Negras
Structure R-13
Functional Sweatbath

A.D. 692
Palenque
Temple of the Cross
Symbolic Sweatbath

A.D. 740
Piedras Negras
Structure N-1
Functional Sweatbath

**Figure 12.6: Plan views of symbolic and functional sweatbaths
from Piedras Negras and Palenque**

Negras built four new ones with vestibules. The architectural similarities between the symbolic sweatbaths at Palenque and the shift in functional sweatbath characteristics at Piedras Negras suggest the desire of Ruler 4 to compete with the grandeur and symbolism of the enshrined architecture at Palenque (Fig. 12.7). The fact that symbolic sweatbaths are similar to functional sweatbaths, in that they both have enshrined and animistic architecture, supports the cosmological relationship of cave symbolism and the sweatbath for the Classic Maya. Thus, the monumentality of the Maya sweatbath had reached its maximum form of cosmological expression of cave symbolism by the end of the Late Classic, through both enshrined and animistic architecture.

**Figure 12.7: Upper section: perspective of symbolic sweatbath–
Temple of the Sun, Palenque;
lower section: perspective of functional sweatbath–
Structure P7, Piedras Negras**

Ritual and the Sweatbath

The main ritual element that defines the ceremonial practices of the sweatbath is the cleansing process of purification. This process not only included the human element of sweating toxins through the pores, but also involved the setting up and the purification of the actual structure itself. Thus, the living entity of the sweatbath was set up at Palenque when the *och naah* "house entering" verb (Stuart 1998: 394) was used on the *alfardas* of the Cross Group structures to record their dedications in A.D. 692 (9.12.19.14.12 5 Eb 5 K'ayab). Although the dedicatory verb recorded on the *alfardas* refer to the entering of the gods, the so-called Death Head monument that was discovered in the Cross Group plaza contains the central element of fire for the same dedication date, which reads: **OCH-K'AK tu-pi-bi-NAAH-li**, *och k'ak' t-u-pib-naah-il*, or paraphrased as "fire entered into the sweatbath" (Fig. 12.3). David Stuart (1998: 418) makes the case that "by bringing the heat of fire into a building, the space is vivified and invested with its own soul." In addition to giving "the house a soul" as the Tzotzil Maya do today (Vogt 1969: 461), the element of fire is also used in many societies throughout the world to symbolically purify the structure for the process of sanctification. Furthermore, epigraphers have pointed out that the verb *och* not only signifies "to enter" in Maya languages, but also means "to become," referring to "changes in states of being" (Schele 1984: 301; Stuart 1998: 394). Thus, the change that occurred in the symbolic sweatbaths of Palenque on their dedication date not only provided these structures with souls, but also included the sanctification process of purifying these living entities.

As for the human element of purification, the cleansing process of the sweatbath functioned for two different types of ritual contexts, transportation rites and transformation rites (Child & Child n.d.). The former is a system of rites where the performers are transported to a supernatural realm, and then returned back to the same stage in life. Because of indigenous beliefs that an individual has to be spiritually clean before passing from the profane to the sacred realms, the sweatbath is used to purify the body and the soul for this purpose. Ethnographies reveal the importance of spiritually purifying oneself through ritual sweating before participating in any ceremonial activities, such as ritual dancing (Bucko 1998: 82). In addition, ethnohistorical records make known that the idea of ritual purification for participation in sacred events is of ancient origin (Lynd 1864: 168-171). This is evident from the Pre-Hispanic codices, such as the Codex Nuttal, which portrays the sweatbath as a purification device to cleanse the soul before playing the ball game (Nuttal 1975: 16). The association of monumental sweatbaths located in contiguous plaza space with ball courts and dance platforms at many of the archaeological sites throughout Mesoamerica reveal the significance of the sweatbath in ritual purification (Child 2002). In addition, the association of monumental sweatbaths built within sacred temple space also confirms the importance of ritually purifying oneself before participating in ceremonial activities.

The second ritual of purification consists of transformation rites, in which performers are transformed to a new stage in life, after which they do not return to their previous stage. Such rites can range from a different "phase" in life to the actual rebirth into a "new" life. These rituals are usually referred to as rites of passage, carried out at crucial moments of transition in an individual's life, such as puberty, adulthood, and marriage. Because of indigenous beliefs that an individual has to be spiritually clean before transforming to a new stage in life, the sweatbath is used to purify the body and the soul for this purpose. Communities today continue to use the sweatbath today to demonstrate that it is used to purify children during important rites of socialization (Eastman 1911: 84; Ichon 1977; Katz 1990: 180; Servain 1983). Ethnohistorical accounts reveal that the notion of ritual purification for personal rites of passage is a long-standing tradition (Sahagún 1970: 22-24). Furthermore, Pre-Hispanic codices confirm the ancient use of the sweatbath for rites of passage, such as puberty, adulthood, and marriage, especially those portrayed in the Mixtec codices from Oaxaca (Bellas 1997: 123-125).

In terms of the Classic Maya, there is evidence that indicates the use of the sweatbath in association with specific transformation rites. As mentioned earlier, the dedication date for the three symbolic sweatbaths of the Cross Group was in A.D. 692, when Kan Bahlam II was fifty-six years old. Nonetheless, all three of the sanctuary tablets located within the symbolic sweatbaths portray similar scenes of Kan Bahlam II before the dedication date as a six-year-old child and as a forty-nine-year-old adult. It has long been known that the A.D. 684 event (9.12.11.12.10 8 Oc 3 K'ayab) that portrays Kan Bahlam II as an adult is his accession to kingship. However, what is the significance of the A.D. 641 event (9.10.8.9.3 9 Akbal 6 Xul) that was so important to pair it with Kan Bahlam II's accession on three different monuments? It is most likely that these events are portrayals of transformation rites that required purification in the sweatbath to transform him to the "new stage" of puberty and the "new life" of kingship. The transformation of kingship was probably not considered a stage in life, since very few people ever experienced it. The new names that are given to Classic Maya rulers when they accede to the throne suggest that kings are reborn into a "new life" when they take upon themselves this responsibility. Thus, the sweatbath would be an appropriate device to aid in this sanctification process, which indicates that it was probably not a coincidence that these events were portrayed within symbolic sweatbaths.

Although the sanctuary tablets are located within the architectural context of a symbolic sweatbath, thus suggesting the use of a sweatbath for these events, the *pib-naah* glyph is only found on the Tablet of the Foliated Cross. However, further evidence indicates that the lexical data selected for these texts reveal that the A.D. 641 event was a rite of passage for puberty and would have required the purification element of the sweatbath. This event was recorded three different times, in the following ways (Fig. 12.8). First, the text above the figure on the

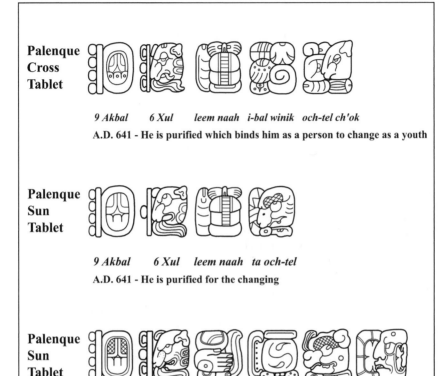

Palenque Cross Tablet

9 Akbal   6 Xul   leem naah i-bal winik och-tel ch'ok
A.D. 641 - He is purified which binds him as a person to change as a youth

Palenque Sun Tablet

9 Akbal   6 Xul   leem naah   ta och-tel
A.D. 641 - He is purified for the changing

Palenque Sun Tablet

9 Akbal   6 Xul   k'al-wan   u-jo-tal   och-te   k'inich
A.D. 641 - He is wrapped (accedes) as the fifth to change as the sun face

**Figure 12.8: Cross Tablet text (© Greene Robertson 1991: fig. 9);
Sun Tablet text (© Greene Robertson 1991: fig. 95)**

left of the Tablet of the Cross indicates that Kan Bahlam II was purified in the temple when he was six years old. The text reads: **le-ma-WITS-NAAH i-ba-la WINIK OCH-te-le ch'o-ko**, *leem wits naah i-bal winik och-tel ch'ok*, which roughly translates as "he is purified in the temple, which binds him as a person, to change as a youth." It is interesting to note that there are over twenty verbs that Maya scribes could have chosen to describe how Kan Bahlam II was introduced or entered the temple. However, the "introduction" verb chosen for this rite of passage deals specifically with purification. The verb expressing this rite of passage *leem*, not only signifies "to introduce" in Yucatec Maya, but also means "to alleviate the cold wind, pain, and sickness from the body" (Barrera Vásquez 1980: 445). If the verb *leem* signifies a purification context, then this would be congruent with ethnographic and ethnohistorical accounts that indicate that cold wind and infirmity were alleviated from the body through the ritual practice of the sweatbath. The second text is recorded on the inner part of the Tablet of the Sun, which reads: **le-ma-NAAH ta-OCH-te-le**, *leem naah / ta och-tel*, which roughly translates as, "he is purified in the temple, for the change." Although the youth glyph *ch'ok* doesn't directly follow, the preposition *ta* changes the structure of the meaning. In addition, this form uses the previously mentioned *och* verb, which not only signifies to enter, but also means to become, begin, or change. It is within this context that the *och* glyph best indicates the connotation of "change." This is also supported by the third text that is recorded on the outer portion of the Tablet of the Sun, which reads: **K'AL-wa-ni u-JO-TAL-la OCH-te K'INICH**, *k'al-wan u-jo-tal och-te k'inch*, which roughly translates as, "he is wrapped (accedes) as the fifth to change as the sun face." The verb used for a rulers accession, *k'al*, is also used to portray this puberty rite, thus reconfirming the context of transformation in this ritual. When the purification meaning behind the verbs *leem* and *k'al* are coupled with the "changing" verb *och*, it is most likely that the A.D. 641 event is a portrayal of Kan Bahlam II transforming to a new stage of puberty that required the sanctification element of the sweatbath.

Additional evidence that sheds more light on the transformation rite of the sweatbath is the event that directly follows, which is recorded twice on the Tablet of the Sun in A.D. 642 (9.10.10.0.0 13 Ajaw 18 K'ank'in). Although this event occurs when Kan Bahlam II was seven years old, it is significant because it happened at the next available period ending, thus suggesting the importance of period-ending celebrations for certain transformation rites. The lexical data in these texts indicate that this rite may have been the transformation between puberty

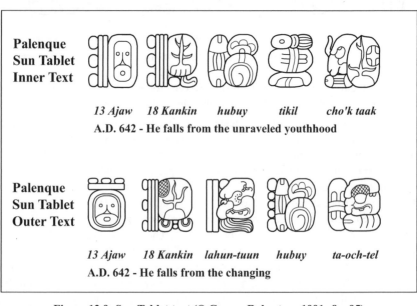

Palenque
Sun Tablet
Inner Text

13 Ajaw   18 Kankin   hubuy   tikil   cho'k taak
A.D. 642 - He falls from the unraveled youthhood

Palenque
Sun Tablet
Outer Text

13 Ajaw   18 Kankin   lahun-tuun   hubuy   ta-och-tel
A.D. 642 - He falls from the changing

Figure 12.9: Sun Tablet text (© Greene Robertson 1991: fig. 95)

and adulthood. The early age of Kan Bahlam II for this type of transformation would not be out of line with some modern ethnographic accounts, especially if he was considered heir to the throne. This event is recorded in the following two forms (Fig. 12.9). The first text appears on the inner part of the Tablet of the Sun, which reads: **hu-bu-yi ti-ki-li ch'o-ko TAAK**, *hubuy tikil ch'ok taak*, which roughly translates as, "he falls from the unraveled youthhood." The second text is recorded on the outer portion of the Tablet of the Sun, which reads: **hu-bu-yi ta-OCH-te-le**, *hubuy ta och-tel*, which roughly translates as, "he falls from the change." Although the *hubuy* verb is usually expressed as a warfare event in Maya hieroglyphic inscriptions, lexical data reveals that this verb has a different meaning in this context. The "falling" verb chosen for this rite of passage deals specifically with purification, which not only signifies "to fall" in some Cholan and Yucatecan languages (Josserand & Hopkins 1988), but also means "to alter or dissipate the harmony of the wind in the body" (Barrera Vásquez 1980: 238). Ethnographic and ethnohistorical data reveal that the main purpose of the sweatbath is to alter the harmony of the body by driving the cold wind out with the heat of steam. The other textual information from this event that supports a purification context for the use of the sweatbath is the meaning of the glyph *tikil*. Although the context of this glyph is in its adjectival form, meaning "unraveled or dissipated," lexical data for this glyph indicates a similar meaning to those previously mentioned, which is a word associated with change (Barrera Vásquez 1980: 792). Furthermore, this glyph is similar to those previously mentioned associated with purification, in that *tikil* means "to alter the sickness or pain by changing it back again" (Barrera Vásquez 1980: 793). The sweatbath is obviously the altering device that changes it back again by restoring one's corporal equilibrium.

The most likely scenario for the events portrayed on the tablets of the Cross Group sanctuaries are transformation rites of puberty, adulthood, and accession that all required the purification element of the sweatbath. The fact that these events are all portrayed within the context of symbolic sweatbaths strengthens this argument. In addition, it is not a coincidence that Classic Maya scribes chose the particular glyphs of *leem, och, k'al, hubuy,* and *tikil* to describe these transformation events, which can all be associated with the bodily concepts of sickness, purification, and change. These concepts are all crucial to indigenous beliefs of purifying oneself from a state of spiritual disequilibrium and restoring harmony with the gods before moving on to a new stage in life.

The Functional Sweatbath

An event that is recorded on the sanctuary tablets that occurs before the *och k'ak* dedication of the symbolic sweatbaths in A.D. 692 is a burning event (Fig. 12.4) that takes place in A.D. 690 (9.12.18.5.16 2 Cib 14 Mol). This event reads: **pu-lu-yi u-chi-ti-ni-il**, *pul-uy u-chitin-il*, translated by Houston as "the oven or sweatbath of the Triad is burning" (Houston 1996: 137). Houston points out that the alternative term for *pib-naah* was *chitin*, which also means "oven" in Yucatec Maya (Barrera Vásquez 1980: 651). Although Houston (1996: 145) argues that the heat generated in the Palenque sweatbaths was of a figurative sort, it is possible that this burning could have taken place in a nearby functional sweatbath, given that a different word *chitin* was used for this context. If the events portrayed on the sanctuary tablets were rites of passage that occurred at least fifty years before the dedication of these symbolical sweatbaths in A.D. 692, then where did these transformation rites take place? The most logical place would be near the source of the Otolum spring because the sanctuary texts reveal that these events occurred by a cave or spring, which is supported by the fact that the ancient Maya built sweatbaths around these cosmological elements. Therefore, it is likely that a functional sweatbath may have been built near the source of the Otolum spring. Although such a structure has yet to be encountered in this vicinity, there is architectural potential for such a structure (Fig. 12.2). The unexcavated mound, Structure 19AA, near the source of this spring could be a functional sweatbath due to its architectural layout and standing façade that still has niches similar to Sweatbath P7 at Piedras Negras. Only future investigations will determine the nature of this structure.

If this hypothesis cannot be confirmed, the significance of the Otolum spring does not diminish because two functional sweatbaths have been excavated along its course throughout the site. Based on current excavation data, the closest functional sweatbath to the ceremonial core during the reign of Kan Bahlam II is located in Group B between the Otolum and Murcielagos Cascades. This sweatbath, Structure B2, is in an ideal location because it is situated between two cascades and has constant access to flowing water (Fig. 12.2). These cascades make up the waterfall that is called the Queen's Bath, and the pools therein would have provided an area for cooling down and relaxing after an intense sweat.

Structure B2 has all three architectural indicators of a functional sweatbath. First, it has a low and narrow entrance that would have minimized heat loss. Within this entrance is the drainage area, a feature similar to other functional sweatbaths within the western Maya lowlands, whereby a narrow passageway divides the interior structure into two symmetrical parts and extends out to the exterior of the sweatbath (Fig. 12.10). This passageway leads to the second architectural indicator, which is the hearth area along the back wall; here, the hot rocks would have been placed to produce intense steam. The third architectural element is a low ceiling, which had the purpose of containing and maximizing the heat from the hot rocks, and is reflected by the low springline of the vault. In addition, the construction of this sweatbath is unique in that it is the only one in the Maya lowlands with three corbelled arches that intersect with the main vault of the sweat chamber. This was due to the fact that this building was not originally designed to be a sweatbath, but rather was later modified into one, as demonstrated by the stone sequence of its construction. Although this structure was modified into a sweatbath, ceramic evidence indicates that it was built during the Late Classic period (López Bravo 2000: 39).

Queen's Bath Architecture - Structure B2 (Sweatbath)

Figure 12.10: Structure B2 sweatbath photo and plan view (top); perspective illustration of Group B (bottom) (by Alonso Mendez)

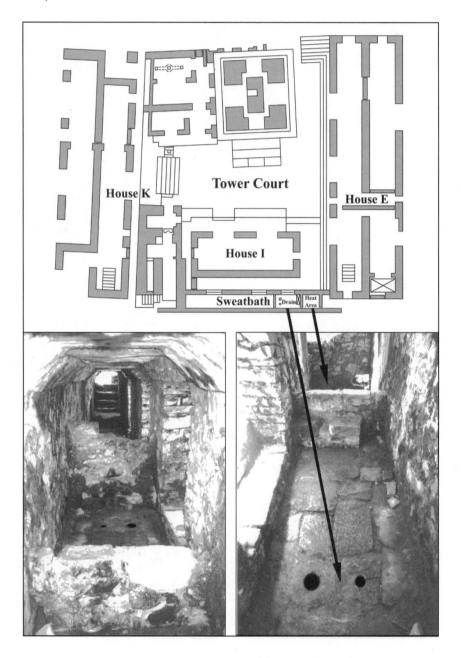

**Figure 12.11: Tower Court sweatbath within Palace complex
(plan after Green Robertson 1985: fig. 1)**

The second functional sweatbath at Palenque that was built along the Otolum is located in the southwest corner of the Palace, also known as the Tower Court (Fig. 12.11). It runs along the southern side of the court, between House H and House I. The elevation shows that it was constructed below House H as part of its frontal platform, and is situated on the same level as the court adjacent to House I. The location of this structure within the palace complex would have allowed members of the royal family the opportunity to use a sweatbath more frequently than just for ritual purposes. The prominence of sweatbaths as components of the royal palace in the western Maya lowlands, which is evident at the neighboring sites of Piedras Negras, Tonina, and Yaxchilan, suggests its importance at Palenque as well. The construction of this sweatbath, c. A.D. 764 (Greene Robertson 1985: 118), indicates that the royal family of K'uk' Bahlam II would have used it between A.D. 764-800. Although a sweatbath has yet to be confirmed within the Palace before A.D. 764, given the degree of hieroglyphic references to sweatbaths in earlier times, it is highly probable that an earlier version exists beneath this sweatbath in the Tower Court.

The Palace sweatbath has the architectural indicators of a functional sweatbath, but differs somewhat in its design compared to Structure B2 at the Queen's Bath. First, while it has a low and narrow entrance, it lacks a passageway that divides the interior structure into two symmetrical parts and extends out to the exterior. Second, the low ceiling makes it impossible for one to stand up straight because the springline of the vault was constructed low enough to contain and maximize the intense steam. And third, the "piles of loose stones" beneath the two circular holes in the floor of the central chamber indicates a hearth area, where water would have been poured over hot rocks to produce steam (Greene Robertson 1985: 80). These circular holes, which functioned as a drain for excess water, was a leading factor that led Alberto Ruz Lhuillier (1952: 51) to consider this structure a sweatbath. The dividing wall and bench, which sectioned off the room into chambers, was most likely constructed to protect the participants from the hot rocks that were placed on its opposite side. In addition, a small gap was left open in the dividing wall between the chambers that would have allowed excess water that was placed on the rocks to drain out.

Conclusion

Of all the archaeological indicators that make ancient Maya sites unique, the sweatbath is one that stands out at both Palenque and Piedras Negras. While both of these sites express the importance of the sweatbath through their monumentality, they vary in how this monumentality is expressed, which is crucial for understanding the ideological elements of this ancient practice. Piedras Negras differs from Palenque because its eight functional sweatbaths were constructed in association with ball courts, dance platforms, and temple complexes, while the two functional sweatbaths at Palenque are not located in these contexts. Although

Piedras Negras has long been considered the sweatbath "capital" of the Maya lowlands due to their monumental nature, Palenque is just as important because of the ceremonial features of its symbolic sweatbaths. Palenque's symbolic sweatbaths provide an abundance of architectural, iconographic, and epigraphic data to better understand the ideological elements of this ancient practice. Paradoxically, at Piedras Negras there are no symbolic sweatbaths or *pib-naah* glyphs. While both sites have information about the cosmological symbolism of caves and water, the spatial layout of functional sweatbaths at Piedras Negras indicates the importance of transportation rites, while hieroglyphic texts at Palenque reveal invaluable information about transformation rites.

Thus, if the practice of the sweatbath was so important at Palenque that it was expressed through the monumentality of symbolic versions in ceremonial space, then it is not unreasonable to assume that this site contains more than two functional sweatbaths. The pattern at Palenque, as opposed to Piedras Negras, suggests that more functional sweatbaths may be found in residential space, especially in those areas where springs supply the watercourses that move through the site core. Of the unexcavated structures that have been documented at Palenque thus far, twelve were built directly over or next to springs, and five of those displayed stone pools (French 2001: 15). The architectural potential of functional sweatbaths constructed near the source of springs awaits further excavation to determine the validity of this hypothesis.

References

Agrinier, Pierre
    1966   La casa de baños de vapor de San Antonio. *Boletin del Instituto Nacional de Antropologia* 25:29-32.

Alcina Franch, José, Andrés Ciudad Ruiz, and Josepha Iglesias Ponce de Leon
    1982   El "temazcal" en Mesoamerica: evolucion, forma, y funcion. *Revista Espanola de Antropologia Americana* 10:93-132.

Alva Ixtlilxóchitl, Fernando de
    1975   *Obras Historicas,* 2 vols. Universidad Nacional Autónoma de México, Instituto de Investigaciones Históricas, México, D.F.

Alvarado Tezozómoc, Fernando
    1975   *Crónica mexicayotl.* Universidad Nacional Autónoma de Mexico, Instituto de Investigaciones Históricas, Mexico, D.F.

Andrews, George F.
    1989   *Comalcalco, Tabasco, Mexico: Maya Art and Architecture.* Labyrinthos, Culver City, CA.

Andrews, E. Wyllys, IV, and E. Wyllys Andrews V
    1980   *Excavations at Dzibilchaltun, Yucatan, Mexico.* Publication 48. Middle American Research Institute, Tulane University, New Orleans, LA.

Arreola, José María
    1936   El temazcal o baño mexicano de vapor. *Ethnos* 1:28-33.

Barrera Vásquez, Alfredo
1980   *Diccionario maya.* Editorial Porrua, S.A., Mexico, D.F.

Bellas, Monica
1997   *The Body in the Mixtec Codices: Birth, Purification, Transformation and Death.* Unpublished Ph.D. dissertation, Department of Anthropology, University of California, Riverside.

Berdan, Frances F. and Patricia R. Anawalt
1992   *The Codex Mendoza,* 5 vols. University of California Press, Berkeley.

Bricker, Vicki R.
1973   *Ritual Humor in Highland Chiapas.* University of Texas Press, Austin.

Bucko, Raymond A.
1998   *The Lakota Ritual of the Sweatlodge: History and Contemporary Practice.* University of Nebraska Press, Lincoln.

Bunzel, Ruth
1967   *Chichicastenango: A Guatemalan Village.* University of Washington Press, Seattle.

Carrasco, Pedro
1946   El temazcal. In *México prehispánico,* edited by J. A. Viro, pp. 737-741.

Cheek, Charles D. and Mary L. Spink
1986   Excavaciones en el Grupo 3, Estructura 223 (Operación VII). In *Excavaciones en el Area Urbana de Copan, Tomo I,* edited by William T. Sanders, pp. 29-154. Instituto Hondureño de Antropología e Historia, Tegucigalpa, Honduras.

Child, Mark B.
2002   Ancient Rites of Passage and the Maya Sweatbath. In *Proceedings of the 34th Annual Chacmool Conference, "An Odyssey of Space,"* University of Calgary, Alberta, Canada.

Child, Mark B. and Jessica Child
1999   The Spatial and Temporal Distribution of the Ancient Maya Sweatbaths at Piedras Negras, Guatemala. Paper presented at the 98th Annual Meeting of the American Anthropological Association, Chicago.

2000   Los Baños de Vapor de Piedras Negras, Guatemala. In *XIII Simposio de Investigaciones Arqueológicas en Guatemala, Museo Nacional de Arqueología y Etnología, 1999,* edited by J. Laporte, H. Escobedo, A. Suasnávar, and B. Arroyo, pp. 1067-1090. Ministerio de Cultura y Deportes, Instituto de Antropología e Historia, Asociacion Tikal, Guatemala City.

2001   La Historia del Baño de Vapor P-7 en Piedras Negras, Guatemala. In *XIV Simposio de Investigaciones Arqueológicas en Guatemala, Museo Nacional de Arqueología y Etnología, 2000.* Ministerio de Cultura y Deportes, Instituto de Antropología e Historia, Asociacion Tikal, Guatemala City.

n.d.   Monumental Sweatbaths at Piedras Negras. In *The Land of the Turtle Lords: Urban Archaeology at the Classic Maya City of Piedras Negras, Guatemala,* edited by Stephen Houston and Hector Escobedo, University of Oklahoma Press, Norman. In press.

Chimalpahin Cuauhtlehuanitzin, Domingo
1965   Relaciones originales de Chalco Amaquemecan. Translated by Silvia Rendón, Fondo de Cultura Económica, Mexico, D.F.

258 | Mark B. Child

Códice Tudela
    1980   2 vols. Ediciones Cultura Hispánica de Instituto de Cooperación Iberoameri-
            cana, Madrid, Spain.

Códice Vaticano B. (3773)
    1972   Biblioteca Apostólica Vaticana. Akademische Drucund Verlagsanstalt, Graz.

Corona, Horacio
    1960   Deidades de la medicina y de los baños. *Boletin del Centro de Investigaciones
            Antropológicas de Mexico* 8:6-8.

Cosminsky, Shelia
    1972   *Decision Making and Medical Care in a Guatemalan Indian Community.* Ph.D.
            dissertation, Brandeis University, Waltham, MA. University Microfilms, Ann
            Arbor.

Cresson, Frank M.
    1938   Maya and Mexican Sweat Houses. *American Anthropologist* 40:88-104.

Cuevas Reyes, Francisco
    1997   *Malpasito, Tabasco.* Instituto Nacional de Antropología e Historia, Mexico,
            D.F.

Duran, Fray Diego de
    1964   *The Aztecs: The History of the Indies of New Spain,* translated by F. Horcasitas
            and D. Heyden, Orion Press, New York, NY.

    1967   *Historia de las Indias de Nueva España e Islas de Tierra Firma,* 2 vols.
            Editorial Porrúa, Mexico, D.F.

    1971   *Book of the Gods and Rites and the Ancient Calendar,* translated by F.
            Horcasitas and D. Heyden, Orion Press, New York, NY.

Eastman, Charles A.
    1911   *The Soul of the Indian.* Hougton Mifflin, Boston, MA.

Folan, William
    1996   Calakmul, Campeche. In *Estudios del México antiguo,* edited by B. Barba de
            Piña Chan, pp. 25-68. Instituto Nacional de Antropología e Historia, Mexico,
            D.F.

French, Kirk D.
    2001   The Precious Otolum of Palenque. *Pari Journal* II(2):12-16.

Furst, Jill L.
    1978   *Codex Vindobonensis Mexicanus I: A Commentary.* Publication 4, Institute
            for Mesoamerican Studies, State University of New York, Albany.

Gage, Thomas
    1969   *Thomas Gage's Travels in the New World.* Edited by J. Eric S. Thompson,
            University of Oklahoma Press, Norman.

Graham, Ian
    2002   *Alfred Maudslay and the Maya: A Biography.* British Museum Press, London.
            U.K.

Greene Robertson, Merle
    1985   *The Sculpture of Palenque: III. The Late Buildings of the Palace.* Princeton
            University Press, Princeton, New Jersey, NJ.

1991   *The Sculpture of Palenque: IV. The Cross Group, the North Group, the Olvidado, and Other Pieces.* Princeton University Press, Princeton, New Jersey, NJ.

Groark, Kevin P.
1997   To Warm the Blood, to Warm the Flesh: The Role of the Steambath in Highland Maya (Tzeltal-Tzotzil) Ethnomedicine. *Journal of Latin American Lore* 20(1):3-96.

Grove, David
1984   *Chalcatzingo: Excavations on the Olmec Frontier.* Thames & Hudson, New York, NY.

Hammond, Normand and Jeremy R. Bauer
2001   East Side Story: A Middle Preclassic Maya Sweathouse at Cuello, Belize. *Context,* Fall/Winter, 2000/2001, Vol. 15, No. 1, pp. 21-26. Boston University Center for Archaeological Studies, Boston, MA.

Houston, Stephen D.
1996   Symbolic Sweatbaths of the Maya: Architectural Meaning in the Cross Group at Palenque, Mexico. *Latin American Antiquity* 7(2):132-151.

Ichon, Alain
1977   A Late Postclassic Sweathouse in the Highlands of Guatemala. *American Antiquity* 42:203-209.

Jones, Chistopher
1996   *Tikal Report No. 16: Excavations in the East Plaza of Tikal, Vol. I.* The University Museum, University of Pennsylvania, Philadelphia.

Josserand, Kathryn and Nicholas A. Hopkins
1988   Final Performance Reports: National Endowment for the Humanities Grant, RT-20643-86, Chol (Mayan) Dictionary Database.

Katz, Ester
1990   El temazcal: entre religion y medicina. Paper presented at the III Coloquio de Historia de las Religiones en Mesoamerica y Areas Afines, November 28-30, Instituto de Investigaciones Antropologicas, Universidad Nacional Autonoma de Mexico, Mexico, D.F.

Kidder, Alfred and Edwin Shook
1959   A Unique Ancient Maya Sweathouse, Guatemala. In *Amerikanistische Miszellen,* pp. 70-74. Mitteilungen aus dem Museum fur Volkerkunde in Hamburg, No. 25. Kommissionsverlag Ludwig Appel, Hamburg.

Logan, Michael H.
1977   Anthropological Research on the Hot-Cold Theory of Disease: Some Methodological Suggestions. *Medical Anthropology* 1(4):87-112.

Lopatin, Ivan A.
1960   Origin of native steam bath. *American Anthropologist* 62(6):977-993.

Lopez Austin, Alfredo
1988   *The Human Body and Ideology: Concepts of the Ancient Nahuas.* 2 vols. Translated by T. and B. Ortiz de Montellano. University of Utah Press, Salt Lake City.

López Bravo, Roberto
2000   La veneracion de los ancestors en Palenque. *Arqueologia Mexicana,* Vol. VIII(45):38-43.

Lowe, Gareth W. and Pierre Agrinier
1960   Excavations at Chiapa de Corzo, Chiapas, Mexico. *Papers of the New World Archaeological Foundation* 8:1-105.

Lynd, James
1864   The Religion of the Dakotas. *Minnesota Historical Collections*, Vol. 2, Part 2, pp. 150-174.

Mason, J. Alden
1935   Mexican and Maya Sweat-Baths. *Museum Bulletin* 6(2):65, 67-69.

McKee, Brian R.
1990   Excavations at Structure 9. In *1990 Investigations at the Ceren Site, El Salvador: A Preliminary Report,* edited by P. Sheets and B. McKee, pp. 90-107. Department of Anthropology, University of Colorado, Boulder.

Moedana, N. Gabriel
1961   El temazcal, baño indígena tradicional. In *Tlatoani,* Sociedad de Alumnos de la Escuela Nacional de Antropología e Historia, Núm. 14-15, pp. 40-51, Mexico, D.F.

1977   El temazcal y su deidad protectora en la tradicion oral. *Boletin del Departmento de Investigacion de las Tradiciones Populares* 4:5-32.

Morley, Sylvanus G.
1935   *Guide to the Ruins of Quirigua.* Publication Supplement 16. Carnegie Institution, Washington, D.C.

Nuttall, Zelia (editor)
1975   *The Codex Nuttall: A Picture Manuscript from Ancient Mexico,* introduction by A. G. Miller. Dover Publications, New York.

Orellana, Sandra L.
1977   Aboriginal Medicine in Highland Guatemala. *Medical Anthropology,* 1(1):113-156.

1987   *Indian Medicine in Highland Guatemala: The Pre-Hispanic and Colonial Periods.* University of Chicago Press, Chicago, IL.

Pihó, Virve
1989   El uso del temazcal en la Altiplanicie Mexicana. In *Homenaje a Román Piña Chán,* coordinated by R. García Moll and A. García Cook, pp. 213-228. Colección Científica 187. Instituto Nacional de Antropología e Historia, México, D.F.

Riese, Berthold
1980   *Die Inschriften von Tortuguero, Tabasco.* Material der Hamburger Maya Inschriften Dokumentation 5. Universität Hamburg, Hamburg, Germany.

Rodríguez, Rouanet F.
1969   Practicas medicas tradicionales de los indígenas de Guatemala. *Guatemala Indígena* 4(2):51-86.

Ruppert, Karl
1935   *Caracol of Chichen Itza, Yucatan, Mexico.* Publication 454, Carnegie Institution, Washington, D.C.

1952   *Chichen Itza: Architectural Notes and Plans.* Publication 595. Carnegie
        Institution, Washington, D.C.

Ruz Lhuillier, Alberto
1952   Explorations en Palenque, 1951. *Anales del Instituto Nacional de Antropologia
        e Historia* 5:47-66.

Sahagún, Fray Bernardino de
1950-70 *Florentine Codex. General History of the Things of New Spain* (c. 1578-
        1579). Translated from Nahuatl into English, with notes and illustrations, by
        A. Anderson and C. Dibble. School of American Research, Monograph 14,
        Santa Fe, NM.

Satterthwaite, Linton
1936   An Unusual Type of Building in the Maya Old Empire. *Maya Research*
        3(1):62-73.

1952   *Piedras Negras Archaeology: Architecture; Pt. V. Sweathouses.* University
        Museum, University of Pennsylvania, Philadelphia.

Schele, Linda
1984   Some Suggested Readings of the Event and Office of Heir-Designation at
        Palenque. In *Phoneticism in Maya Hieroglyphic Writing,* edited by J. S.
        Justeson and L. Campbell, pp. 287-305. Institute for Mesoamerican Studies,
        State University of New York, Albany.

Schele, Linda and Peter Mathews
1998   *The Code of Kings.* Scribner's, New York, NY.

Seler, Edward
1963   *Códices Borgia,* 3 vols. Fondo de Cultura Económica, México, D.F.

Servain, Frédérique
1983   *Les bains de vapeur en Mesoamerica.* Master's thesis, University of Paris I:
        La Sorbonne, Paris, France.

1986   Tentative de classification des bains de vapeur en Mésoamérique. In *Traces,*
        9: 39-50.

Sheets, Payson D.
1992   *The Ceren Site: A Prehistoric Village Buried by Volcanic Ash in Central
        America.* Harcourt Brace Jovanovich, Fort Worth, TX.

Smith, A. Ledyard
1950   *Uaxactun, Guatemala: Excavations of 1931-37.* Publication 588. Carnegie
        Institution, Washington, D.C.

Stuart, David
1987   *Ten Phonetic Syllables.* Research Reports on Ancient Maya Writing, No. 14.
        Center for Maya Research, Washington, D.C.

1998   "The Fire Enters His House": Architecture and Ritual in Classic Maya Texts.
        In *Function and Meaning in Classic Maya Architecture,* edited by Stephen
        D. Houston, pp. 373-425. Dumbarton Oaks Research Library and Collection,
        Washington, D.C.

2000   Las nuevas inscripciones del Templo XIX, Palenque. *Arqueología Mexicana*
        VIII(45):28-33.

Stuart, David and Stephen D. Houston
1994   *Classic Maya Place Names*. Dumbarton Oaks Studies in Pre-Columbian Art and Archaeology, No. 33. Washington, D.C.

Taladoire, Eric
1975   Les bains de vapeur et les systemes d'eau dans leur rapport avec les terrain de jeux de balle, México. *Actas del XLI Congreso Internacional de Americanistas,* Vol. 1:262-269.

Tarn, Nathaniel and Martin Prechtel
1986   Constant Inconstancy: The Feminine Principle in Atiteco Mythology. In *Symbol and Meaning beyond the Closed Community: Essays in Mesoamerican ideas,* edited by Gary Gossen, 173-184. Studies on Culture and Society, Vol. 1. Institute for Mesoamerican Studies, State University of New York, Albany.

Tate, Carolyn E.
1992   *Yaxchilan: The Design of a Maya Ceremonial City.* University of Texas Press, Austin.

Taube, Karl A.
1988   *The Ancient Yucatec New Year Festival: The Liminal Period in Maya Ritual and Cosmology,* Unpublished Ph.D. dissertation, Department of Anthropology, Yale University, New Haven, CT.

1992   *The Major Gods of Ancient Yucatan.* Studies in Pre-Columbian Art and Archaeology, No. 32, Dumbarton Oaks Research Library and Collection, Washington, D.C.

Vogt, Evon Z.
1969   *Zinacantan: A Maya Community in the Highlands of Chiapas.* Belknap Press of Harvard University, Cambridge.

Wagley, Charles
1949   *The Social and Religious Life of a Guatemalan Village.* Memoir No. 71. American Anthropological Association, Menasha, WI.

Wauchope, Robert
1938   *Modern Maya Houses: A Study of their Archaeological Significance.* Publication 502, Carnegie Institution, Washington, D.C.

Part VI

CONTEMPORARY CONCERNS AND CONCLUSIONS

Chapter 13

Why Restore Architecture at Palenque?

C. Rudy Larios Villalta

Introduction

Although most previous restoration at Palenque did not result in unlimited reconstruction—instead derived from a desire to conserve—the more extreme European tendencies like full restoration or, conversely, mere conservation with no alterations whatsoever, so common in the nineteenth century, also influenced work at Palenque. Fortunately, the most visible tendency at the site is that of conservation, of conserving the monument exactly as it was found. As occurs in the rest of the Maya area, the work carried out was always the result of both archaeological investigation and the subsequent potential of utilizing the monuments as attractive tourist resources.

In other words, restoration has never been given the importance that has been accorded to archaeological investigation, to such a degree that literature about restoration, particularly regarding the reasons for doing it one way or another, is scarce or nonexistent. Nevertheless, these extraordinary monuments are precisely the reason for the existence of the archaeological investigation, and they represent the thoughts and actions of a remarkable culture, whose history is uniquely encapsulated in its architecture.

I am taking this opportunity to address the reasons that compel us to restore, and at the same time to describe and justify the methodology followed by the Proyecto Grupo de las Cruces. It is not a frequently debated topic, but for this very reason it is of vital importance to all who are in some way involved in the management of Pre-Hispanic Mesoamerican cultural remains.

The basic questions that arise when we consider the restoration of Pre-Hispanic architectural monuments are the following: What reasons do we have for restoring the ruins? How much do we restore? What will be the social function of the restored ruins? The answers to these can be quite diverse, and each project, each archaeologist, and each director of government institutions charged with the conservation of this cultural property have their own point of view and their own answers. Of course, we of the Proyecto Grupo de las Cruces are no exception. In this manner we will attempt to define some of the reasons that, we believe, can provide us with a model that is finally able to respond to the questions above with some degree of propriety.

International Norms

The restoration of monuments in Mesoamerica, with some notable exceptions, has never been guided by explicit, defined standards; rather each restorator or archaeologist has decided how to do it, without necessarily justifying why. Nevertheless, at the global level a series of guidelines has been proposed that only define whether to restore or not, but without explaining why. Some norms are so general that each restorator is able to liberally interpret and put them into practice according to their personal opinion or understanding, reaching such extremes that the monument in ruins may become a radically different structure from what it once was. The structure may be timidly left in ruins with nothing being done, leaving it in disorder and deformed, or more bravery and imagination than evidence can be used, leading to a misleading result.

On the other hand, we attempt to find a balance between these two extremes, as we lack the courage to try to reconstruct what time has destroyed. Instead we appreciate the monument as something unique, irreplaceable, and above all, a testament to the past that must continue into the future as a witness of that irreplaceable past. Moreover, such a vestige must, without exception, be integrated into modern society with a specific social function.

The concern and interest of many experts worldwide brought about the preparation of certain international documents, ratified by the Mesoamerican countries, which aim to standardize the restoration process, in order to obtain the best possible results. In this way, and in order to attain a better understanding, we think it opportune to briefly analyze a few fundamental concepts, beginning with two articles from the "Final Report of the Meeting on the Conservation and Use of Monuments and Places of Historical and Artistic Interest" (Normas de Quito, OEA, 1967). From this we will address only Numbers 3 and 4 of the "General Considerations," which state the following:

Norms of Quito:

General Considerations

3. Whatever the intrinsic value of an asset, or the circumstances that produce its historical or artistic significance, it will not constitute a monument as long as the State does not confer upon it an expressed declaration as such. The declaration of a National Monu-

ment implies its official documentation and registration. From that moment, the asset in question will be subjected to the regimen of exceptions designated by law.

4. Any cultural asset is implicitly destined to fulfill a social function. The state is responsible for bringing about said goal and to determine, in distinct cases, the degree to which said social function is compatible with the private property and interests of the parties involved.

In the previous articles we can distinguish two aspects of outstanding importance for the appreciation of monumental patrimony:

(1) The term Monument is not a designation of size but a category that the asset receives from the state, and it is based on its cultural significance.

(2) Any cultural asset must fulfill a social function.

In the first place, we understand that only the state can categorize and catalogue a place as a monument, and this will depend on its significance. If the cultural asset has already been designated as a monument, then it must be made to serve a social function, to fulfill the objectives specific to the future of the individuals in possession of the asset in question. In other words, the responsibility of the state is to conserve the monument, but at the same time, to define what is required to be done with it, and what purpose it will serve within current and future society.

Conservation tendencies, and the reasons behind them, have changed gradually, but perhaps we do not yet have a clear idea of the ultimate destiny of the monuments that we restore. In spite of the fact that many people see them only as potential hens that lay golden eggs, Pre-Hispanic monuments are becoming more relevant. Suffice it to say that the monument itself is valuable, not for the revenue it might create through tourism, but because it is the expression of a culture that no longer exists, but which nonetheless continually asserts its physical presence.

Modern societies are only depositories of cultural assets, consequently the most important social function of monuments, their primary current role, should not be tourism. Instead we should emphasize the quality that both identifies it with the past and that which joins it to the present; in other words, the nation as well as the neighboring communities must identify with it as a part of themselves, as inseparable from the present. When modern societies do not identify with the past, when they ignore their local history, such cultural assets cannot fulfill their social function.

We do not wish to suggest that tourism should be unimportant. Tourism, like any economic benefit derived from it, should ideally result from the intrinsic cultural value of the monument, but should not be the primary purpose of restoration. Consequently, the social function that the monuments should currently fulfill must be perfectly clear to the neighboring communities, so that they may become the caretakers of its future.

As caretakers for the future, the locals become conservators, not predators, of these cultural goods. This so-called predation has occurred in many cases in which both locals and outsiders see the sites merely as a source of profit, not as a connection with the past, and even less as something with which they themselves are integrated.

Social Function and Restoration

Exploration into archaeological monuments, which subsequently require restoration, cannot be removed from the process of understanding the past. Alone, however, it will not fulfill the primary objective, which is, among other things, to make the monument acquire a meaning to modern communities and to visitors. It is essential that the monument acquires, through archaeological investigation and restoration, both a comprehensible physical form, and an intelligible history of its ancient social function, in order to show us more completely and faithfully what it once was.

On another level, let us say that restoration is an operation of exceptional character; we cannot restore a monument that is in a good state of preservation, but when it is in a ruined state, then the problem and dilemma of the restorator is to determine to what extent restoration can be done. The restorator works to understand to what degree it is permissible and correct to intervene in the ruin, in order to transform it into something proper for exhibition and explanation to the visiting public. Regarding this point I choose to cite some comments of Hiroshi Daifuko:

> When an object is not well preserved, the problem is to determine the degree of treatment that should be applied. The minimum is to do only that which is necessary for its survival, but if the object remains unrecognizable it becomes apt to ask up to which point restoration should be undertaken (Daifuko 1969: 27).

As discussed before, the most important social objective is that groups of people appropriate the monument for its cultural value and significance in order to maintain it both as part of themselves and their future. Therefore restoration projects should work toward this end; that is to say, that through these projects, the monument or monuments restored may be understood in their entirety and for all that they are worth. This is especially true for those people who live from them, who invariably should be the neighboring communities, and who currently form part of the cultural value of the monuments.

When we carry out only what is necessary so that a structure does not collapse, and we leave the elements in the same state of decay in which they were encountered, we risk not fulfilling the social function, as the monument may remain unrecognizable. Moreover, when the treatment of the monument is more cosmetic than structural, in the long run, we risk a collapse of greater proportions, undermining the goal of conservation.

The more critical problem, as Daifuko would say, is to determine to what degree we are able to intervene so that the monument can be understood and fulfill its purpose, without rendering artificial its original characteristics or transforming it into something altogether different.

In order to explain our criteria and the purpose of our actions, especially regarding Temples XIX and XX at Palenque, it is necessary to refer to a document that, although old and perhaps obsolete in some aspects, is the product of many experts and contains many wise guidelines that are applicable to any act of restoration. Titled the "Venice Letter," we will not attempt to discuss this document in its entirety. Instead we will only analyze two essential articles that are very significant to the topic that concerns us. Within the letter we find the following two articles:

Venice Letter

Article 9. Restoration is an operation that must maintain an exceptional character. It has as its goal to conserve the historical and aesthetic value of the monument, and it is founded on a respect for ancient material and authentic documents. It stops at the point at which the hypothetical begins, moreover, any complementary work recognized as indispensable for technical or aesthetic reasons will depend on the architectural composition, and will carry the seal or mark of our current era. Restoration will always be preceded and accompanied by archaeological and historical study of the monument.

Article 15. All forethought will also be taken with the goal of facilitating the understanding of the monument that is revealed, without unnaturally rendering its meaning. All reconstructive work must, however, must be excluded a priori: Only the *anastilosis*, that is, the re-composition of the extant, but dismembered, parts, can be taken into account (Díaz-Berrio 1968).

While several interesting points unfold from these two articles of the Venice Letter, we only wish to emphasize three main aspects: the need to define a final point or limit of restoration; the integration of complementary elements; and *anastilosis*. These three actions in the restoration of monuments, put into practice with a modicum of sense, can make the difference between reality, fantasy, and the true social function that these cultural resources should fulfill.

Limits to the Restoration of Monuments

If we consider Article 9 of the Venice Letter valid, it becomes necessary to suspend restoration at the very moment when we begin to speculate about what will follow. In other words, when a hypothesis becomes the basis of an action, we enter into uncertain territory, and therefore we are ethically obliged not to continue.

Integration of Complimentary Elements

Article 9 authorizes the aggregation of complementary or absent elements, but advises that, "all complementary work recognized as indispensable for aesthetic or technical reasons will depend on the architectural composition, and will carry the seal or mark of our current era." Therefore this guideline authorizes the production of complementary elements. This has been the most controversial article in the document among innumerable restorators and archaeologists for almost half a century.

This type of reasoning is very simple, and when we approach an architectural element with some missing parts due to temporal deterioration, we can complement them only when they serve an aesthetic or structural function. Also, it is clear that the complementary architectural element must indeed exist in the first place, or else the work will lapse into reconstruction and mere hypothesis. We can also include the reconstruction of nonexistent parts along with what is sanctioned by the Venice Letter, as long as it is based only on other elements of the same structure, or in extreme cases, on those of other, similar structures. In other words, by analogy we can assume that the nonexistent part was the same as another, surviving, equivalent one. In any case, this type of work remains hypothetical, and without any real basis.

Article 15, with absolute clarity, also prohibits reconstruction. This refers not only to the replacement of absent elements, but also to the re-creation of some nonexistent part, whether by analogy or imagination. If a part of the structure does not exist, we do not have the right to invent it, as that would be a falsification of the truth. Thereby the monument, which is in reality a vestige of the past, becomes a false witness, as do the restorators involved.

Returning to the topic of the integration of complementary elements, we

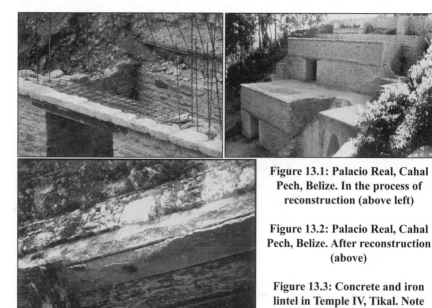

Figure 13.1: Palacio Real, Cahal Pech, Belize. In the process of reconstruction (above left)

Figure 13.2: Palacio Real, Cahal Pech, Belize. After reconstruction (above)

Figure 13.3: Concrete and iron lintel in Temple IV, Tikal. Note the iron destroying the lintel

should emphasize another controversial factor in the interpretation of this guideline, which is the mark, or seal, of the current era. Frequently, this part of the article is taken into account, but with a lack of consideration for the concept that any complement will depend on the architectural composition. Though commonly forgotten, this composition is in essence made up of four determining factors: shape, materials, color, and texture.

For example, we would mention that in many cases, the desire to leave the imprint of our era, along with the necessity of rendering the structure "stable and permanent," leads to the use of high ratios of Portland cement (Figs. 13.1 & 13.3), as well as steel supports, but fails to take into account the mechanics of Maya structures. In other cases, besides cement, restorators change other materials to mark the temporal difference, without taking into account that this will also change the structure's overall color and texture. Perhaps the most drastic mark of our time is the reconstruction of parts of the form or even entire walls, reset within 5-10 cm of the original parameters, altering a fundamental element of architectural composition (Figs. 13.4-13.9).

Figure 13.4: Calakmul, Campeche.
Reconstruction with the alteration of texture
(top left)
Figure 13.5: Yaxha, Guatemala. Complements altering material, texture, and color
(top right)
Figure 13.6: Tonina, Chiapas. Complements with reset parameters (lower left)
Figure 13.7: Palenque, Chiapas. Complements with reset parameters (lower right)

**Figure 13.8: Ek Balam, Yucatan. Partially empty spaces,
defining the integrated architectural features (left)
Figure 13.9: Dzibanche, Quitana Roo.
Complements with a continuous line of small cut stones (right)**

In other words, we do not have the right to change the architectural composition when what we are working on is not of our own design. Rather, the design is part of a distant time and culture, which we should work to accurately render. This position is based not only on the idea of respect for the monument and its creators, but also on what is dictated by the 'Burra Letter' or the 'Australian Letter,' which states:

> ARTICLE 19 Reconstruction is limited to the reproduction of fabric, the form of which is known physical and/or documentary evidence. It should be identifiable on close inspection as being new work. (Marquis-Kile and Walker 1992:71)

As an essential criterion for restorators, and for our work on Temples XIX and XX at Palenque, the imprint of our current time on architectural elements that are indispensable for structural or aesthetic reasons, must be both clearly identifiable upon close inspection, and harmoniously integrated with the original architectural design.

We also carried out work at Copan (1981-1996) with this in mind, using building material recovered from the original construction rubble, but outlining the reconstructed parts with a series of stainless steel braces. At El Pilar, Belize, we used aluminum nails to create a line of points that divide the reconstructed elements from the intact parts recovered in situ. At Palenque we are using the same method, but without metal, and instead we are employing small, machine-cut stone pieces. These have a completely rectangular shape, which clearly shows that they are not original components, but rather something made recently (Figs. 13.10 & 13.11).

With the application of this type of stone marker, we fulfill the objective of respecting the architectural composition, and, far from being interrupted, the structure continues without alterations in form, materials, proportions, color or texture. However, any close examination will reveal what our work has added, and it will also show that we only have done what is necessary for aesthetic or structural reasons, which will in turn help the visitor to clearly understand what they are observing.

**Figure 13.10: Temple XIX, Palenque, Chiapas.
Borders integrated in distant visual line**

**Figure 13.11: Temple XIX, Palenque, Chiapas.
Small rectangular stones define integrated architectural features**

Anastilosis or Reintegration

As we have seen, reconstruction is prohibited a priori, at least by the Venice Letter, in that any honest restorators must try to avoid inventing any element that

Figure 13.12: Structure 29, Copan, Honduras. Collapsed west façade

did not previously exist. However, these can be copied by analogy, but, according to these standards, only one approved and appropriate method of reconstruction exists: *anastilosis*, the re-composition or reintegration of existing, but dismembered or fallen, elements according to the definition within the written guidelines.

This term has been interpreted in different ways by different restorators, and in Europe it is used in a much broader manner than in our case. It is apparently taken to such a degree in Europe that entire monuments can be reconstructed, as long as the original architectural composition and construction materials remain the same.

In our work, this method does not simply consist of retrieving stones from rubble, in order to include them in restoration. First we must take into account that the specialist architects who composed the Venice Letter defined *anastilosis* as the re-composition of existing elements. In other words this includes original elements that have been dislocated, but which we can document as found in situ (Figs. 13.12-13.14).

Conclusion

In conclusion, the gains made by restoration, and the methods applied to Temples XIX and XX at Palenque, are the results of the social objectives we have chosen to pursue. If we wish to emphasize the past and make it so that the monuments endure and fulfill their commitment as faithful witnesses to humanity, restoration

Figure 13.13: Structure 29, Copan,
Honduras. Collapsed west façade (left)

Figure 13.14: Structure 29, Copan, Honduras. Reintegration of collapsed sculpture
(above)

must be truthful, avoid surpassing what is evident, and do only what is necessary so that the monument remains stable, but still comprehensible to the eye of the visitor. In other words, the monument becomes transformed into a didactic object from which we all learn, beginning with archaeologists and neighboring communities. Ultimately the nation in general can identify with the monument as part of the present, and exercise a commitment to conserve it forever.

On the contrary, if the aim is to create scenery for tourists, then there are no limits, and imagination can be the basis for reconstructing something inexistent, forgetting the monument's intrinsic cultural significance. The state of ruin in which monuments are generally encountered shows the antiquity and the passage of time, and we do not have the right to erase this imprint and thereby to transform the ruin into a new building, simply in order to make a site more attractive.

Temple XIX at Palenque is a very special example, as it shows not only the effects of time, but also a change in construction techniques. K'inich Ahkal Mo' Nahb III, its builder, who ruled Palenque between A.D. 721–c.740, tried to restore the prestige of the city. Palenque had suffered due to the capture and eventual death of the previous ruler, K'inich K'an Joy Chitam II, at the hands of the ruler of Tonina, a highland city south of Palenque. This incident may have subsequently left the city without a ruler for ten years (see, however, Marken & Straight, Chapter 14).

Ahkal Mo' Nahb III built Temples XIX and XXI in an attempt to demonstrate that Palenque was still powerful, and perhaps this feeling caused him to break the construction tradition of his ancestors, modifying and amplifying the distribution of interior space, and altering the binding mortar. As we understand it, the change in mortar took place prior to the reign of Ahkal Mo' Nahb III, when lime was no longer used in the binding agent, and instead a clay matrix, which was poor in lime, was employed (see Marken, Chapter 4). The result, in both of the structures, was a catastrophic collapse.

Under such conditions it does not make sense to reconstruct what was destroyed as a result of these documented events. If so, we would be responsible for erasing a characteristic that serves to help define a decadent and conflictive period of the city. The cultural significance then was the basis for defining the extent of the restoration, but also the social aims, which we defined earlier, play a determining part. The monument itself is a testament to that historic moment that, through the ruined remains, becomes the object of future research and preservation.

At Temple XX, where we are currently working, erosion and structural failures were so drastic that on the east and south sides, only the natural bedrock mound and some very small parts of the architecture remain. This seemed like a difficult mystery to explain, but excavations on the west façade and a small portion of the south façade during the 2002 season, demonstrated that the absence of architecture on the east and south sides of the substructure was the result of a total remodeling, in antiquity, of the entire structure. The west façade, and a small portion of the north side still retain a large sample from this remodeling, and they demonstrate that what is missing from the front and the south sides is nothing more than intentional destruction, as a preparation for the remodeling that was never finished.

Figure 13.15: Temple XIX, Palenque, Chiapas. Finalized restoration, March 2000 (photo by Graciela Sartori)

To date we have learned much about the architectural composition of this enormous monument, and we continue working to stabilize it. But we ask: What can we do about what no longer exists? To what point should we restore something that was not destroyed by time alone? The answer is simple. We will do what is necessary in order to stabilize what exists and leave clear evidence of both the remodeling and decay, as this is also part of the story. It also constitutes part of a cultural significance that we do not have the right to alter (Fig. 13.15).

References

Daifuko, Hiroshi
 1969 La importancia de los Bienes Culturales: La Conservación de Bienes Culturales, Museos y Monumentos - XI, UNESCO.

Díaz Berrio, Salvador
 1968 Comentarios a la Carta de Venecia Universidad de Guanajuato, México.

González C., Marcelino
 1977 Teoría y métodos de Restauración Arquitectónica de Monumentos Arqueológicos, Guatemala 1900–1975: Programa para la Conservación del Patrimonio Cultural de Centro América y el Caribe. UNESCO.

Larios Villalta, Rudy
 1986 Inédito Restauración y Arquitectura Residencial en Las Sepulturas, Copán. *Estudios Especiales del Área Urbana de Copán, Tomo VII*, edited by William T. Sanders. Instituto Hondureñode Antropología e Historia.

 2000 Criterios de Restauración Arquitectónica En El Área Maya: Versión digital, submitted to the Foundation for the Advancement of Mesoamerican Studies Inc.

Larios Villalta, Rudy and William L. Fash
 1985 Excavación y Restauración de un Palacio de la Nobleza Maya de Copán. *Yaxkin* VIII(1): 111-113.

Marquis-Kile, Peter and Meredith Walker
 1992 The Ilustrated Burra Charter. Published by the Australian ICOMOS Inc. with the Assistance of the Australian Heritage Commission.

Chapter 14

Conclusion:
Reconceptualizing the Palenque Polity

Damien B. Marken and
Kirk D. Straight

Archaeological and epigraphic investigations in the Maya area during the past few decades have altered the accepted views on the nature of Classic Maya centers and their development. Out is the old classification of Maya centers as empty "ceremonial centers" advocated by Eric Thompson (1956) and others, contradicted by extensive mapping and settlement research conducted at several sites, including Tikal (Carr & Hazard 1961; Puleston 1983), Dzibilchaltun (Andrews & Andrews 1980), Caracol (Chase & Chase 1987), and Copan (Webster & Freter 1990; Willey & Leventhal 1979). Following, and concurrent to, Gordon Willey's pioneering emphasis on regional settlement patterns (Willey et al. 1965), advances in epigraphy have brought Maya rulers and individuals to the threshold of history (e.g., Berlin 1958; Culbert 1991; Lounsbury 1974; Martin & Grube 2000; Proskouriakoff 1960, 1963, 1964; Schele & Freidel 1990; see Coe [1989] for a synopsis of the history of Maya hieroglyphic decipherment).

Although most Mayanists praise an equal merging of archaeological and epigraphic data, few are able to do so when describing a particular site and its surrounding polity (for an exception, see Fash 2001; Fash & Sharer 1991; Sharer 2004). Rarely do the archaeological and epigraphic records significantly overlap at any given site.[1] At Palenque for example, numerous retrospective inscriptions describe Early Classic individuals and events, such as the founding of *Lakam Ha'*, the Classic Maya toponym for Palenque's epicenter (Stuart & Houston 1994), in A.D. 497, but almost nothing is known about this period archaeologically.[2] The difficulty in coalescing archaeological and epigraphic data is compounded by the fact that epigraphic records in the Maya area only deal with Maya elites, to the exclusion of "commoners," and do not shed light on the more mundane aspects of ancient Maya society of interest to archaeologists. Furthermore, most purely archaeological

279

models (excepting macro-regional exchange models [e.g., Fash & Fash 2000]) of Classic Maya polities tend to be confined to local regions (e.g.,, Aoyama 1999; de Montmollin 1989; Webster 1988), while current epigraphic models concentrate on broad-based interpolity politics (although the inscriptions from certain areas, especially the Usumacinta subregion, hint at the existence of subregional political hierarchies). How then are we to synthesize the varying theories and models of ancient Maya polities expounded by both archaeologists and epigraphers?

The preceding chapters outline much of the research conducted at Palenque during the past five years. Diverse in their scope and focus, several chapters reflect upon social and political organization and structure during the Classic period at Palenque. While the debate as to the extent that Maya centers were urban remains unresolved (see Barnhart, Chapter 6), a general consensus as to the definition of what constitutes a Classic Maya polity is currently accepted (Culbert 1991; Sharer & Golden 2004). Maya polities (a group organized under a single ruling leader or family [Johnson & Earle 1987]) for the most part, consisted of the polity center, or site core, surrounding hinterlands, and subordinate secondary and tertiary centers. It is acknowledged that a high level of variability in spatial size and internal complexity existed between Maya polities, best viewed as a continuum of polity size and complexity. The lack of evidence for large-scale crop surplus storage (Tourtellot 1993: 223), makes it likely that each Maya polity was self-sufficient in subsistence goods, and that the "exchange of foodstuffs was limited to the local or intraregional level" (Demarest 1992: 142; see also Hammond 1991: 260; Hirth 1992: 20; Rice 1987: 77; Trigger 2003; Webster 1985; Wright 1999: 215). The reliance on human porters throughout Mesoamerica further highlight the probable limitations of Maya trade in perishable food products,[3] although additional bulk transport with canoes may have increased the potential "spheres of exchange" in some lowland areas, especially at those sites located near rivers, lakes, or the Caribbean coast.

When considering Palenque, a description of the entire polity is rendered more difficult by the paucity of demographic and settlement information for the local region, and/or sustaining area (i.e., the hinterlands), surrounding the Late Classic center. However, ongoing regional surveys by Rodrigo Liendo Stuardo (Chapter 5, 1999, 2002a, 2002b, 2003) now enable more complete local-level analyses. Contemporaneously, extensive research at the site of Palenque itself by Arnoldo González Cruz of the Instituto Nacíonal de Antropología y Historia (INAH) (1989-present), the Proyecto Grupo de las Cruces (PGC) (1997-present), and the Palenque Mapping Project (PMP) (1998-2000) has greatly increased the available data regarding the Palenque site core. These data enable a refined definition of the site core and the formulation of incipient generalizations concerning Late Classic settlement, elite residence, and political change within the core itself.

Following the discussions presented in this volume, the nature and extent of Palenque's external relationships with other Classic Maya sites can be considered in conjunction with its internal/local structure and organization. Using elements of the peer polity interaction model (Renfrew & Cherry 1986), location theory/central-place analysis (e.g., Chisholm 1968; Inomata & Aoyama 1996; Lösch 1954), and regional community analysis (Yaeger & Canuto 2000) these external relations are best viewed on three scales. The first scale of analysis is at the local level, which can serve as a preliminary assessment of the spatial extent of the Palenque polity. The second level examines Palenque's subregional area (the western Maya lowlands). Finally, the third level of analysis views Palenque within the overall Classic Maya regional political landscape, providing an indication of Palenque's "spheres of influence" in the Maya area. In order to achieve these goals, a cohesive merging of archaeological and epigraphic data is imperative.

Models of Classic Maya Polity Interaction

A myriad of models of Classic Maya interpolity political structure is currently available to researchers, none of which is by any means universally accepted. Variously derived from ethnographic (e.g., Vogt 1969) and ethnohistoric analogy (e.g., Marcus 1993), archaeology (e.g., Adams & Jones 1981; Sabloff 1986), and epigraphy (e.g., Marcus 1976; Martin & Grube 1995; Mathews 1991), as well as combinations of these lines of evidence, consensus among Mayanists is unknown.

Currently in vogue is the epigraphically based super-state model[4] where the sites of Calakmul and Tikal, and conflicts between them, dominated and directed the Classic Maya political landscape (Martin & Grube 1995). Within this model warfare is suggested to have served as the underlying mechanism for intersite interaction. David Webster has convincingly argued that one's view of Maya warfare is directly tied to the type of data set used for analysis. Acknowledging a shared elite culture which structured interactions among polities (including warfare), Webster (1993: 437) notes that "mature dynastic warfare" may involve territorial centers, but also intrapolity factions (Webster 1993: 431). We are left to wonder how Maya warfare was structured, who physically participated, where "battles" were fought, what weapons and tactics were used, and what the political and economic repercussions might have been. As an integration mechanism, warfare may be structured toward different goals in different societies, and may change over time. At present, while art and epigraphy provide insights into the distribution and frequency of "warfare events," the possible catalysts (e.g., population pressure, resource control, tribute, and domination) which shaped the nature of Maya warfare have not been thoroughly investigated in a systematic way. Even the "meanings" of specific warfare expressions are not sufficiently distinguished; they largely remain unknown interactions recorded in an ancient script still in the process of decipherment.[5]

The super-state model fails to explain the origins of the so-called "super-states"—why did Tikal and Calakmul grow larger and more "powerful" than other large and "wealthy" Classic sites?—overly relying on static assumptions of Classic period social structure, ignoring the archaeological and ethnohistoric evidence of dynamic states within the Maya area (Marcus 1993, 1998; Webster 1997). It is unlikely that a stable large-scale, territorially unified political hegemony ever existed in the Maya lowlands; instead the political size of individual polities could wax and wane quite quickly (within a generation or two) during the Late Classic period (Demarest 1992: 140). While Calakmul and Tikal were certainly the largest and most important Classic sites in the central lowlands, there is little archaeological evidence to support the super-state model, especially when considering the peripheral western lowland subregion. As Jeremy Sabloff states, "there are no clear data in the archaeological record which can be strongly linked with the inference that various sites *politically* controlled a number of other sites, particularly in regard to large sites controlling other large ones" (1986: 111; emphasis in the original).

That the Classic Maya were unable to maintain centralized regional states by no means diminishes their accomplishments; unstable and short-lived hegemonies were characteristic of other ancient complex societies:

> Regional Mesopotamian states were far from typical entities in the course of Mesopotamian political events. Rather, they were rare occurrences, unable to establish a legitimate and institutionalized method of governance over various city-states that guarded their local autonomies (Yoffee 1988: 63).

Thus the Classic Maya were not anomalous in world history. The apparently fleeting nature of Classic lowland Maya "political conquest," represents another case of how ancient polities in general had difficulty in consolidating political control over their peers. Robert Sharer (personal communication 2004) suggests that since new ruling lineages, such as that founded at Tikal in A.D. 379, still "counted back" to the original polity founder in subsequent king lists, Classic Maya warfare may have some parallels with Postclassic Mexica "conquests" that were motivated more by economic and ideological reasons than for political consolidation.

Beyond the theoretical limitations of the super-state model, several epigraphic particulars, such as crediting Caracol's "star-war" against Tikal on 9.6.8.4.2 (A.D. 562) to Calakmul, are often based on inferred elite interaction (Martin & Grube 2000: 90) without sufficient direct evidence.[6] When describing the Caracol-Naranjo wars (A.D. 626-631) Calakmul's primacy in these events is again assumed and evoked (Martin & Grube 2000: 92); such epigraphic analyses demand archaeological corroboration to inform about the nature of elite interaction which leads to alliance and territorial expansive states. The catch-all phrase "elite interaction" offers little in the way of explanation, while "focus on elites as the key explanatory concept may neglect bottom-up social processes and economic or other forces over which the powerful have little control" (Kowalewski et al. 1992: 261). The point here is that not all the epigraphic evidence leads to the same conclusions; connecting data across class lines is the necessary future for Maya studies. Unfortunately there is limited data regarding non-elite activities at Palenque, hampering the extent to which one can explain processes of social change. Instead the aim here is to define the Palenque polity in terms of development, organization, and influence within the Classic Maya political landscape and attempt to explain political and organizational changes within that polity.

In order to do so, a different theoretical framework is necessary to evaluate the extent of Classic Maya polities and gauge the intensity of their inter- and intrapolity interactions. Using multiple, distinct classes of evidence we intend to carry out analysis of the Palenque polity at multiple interaction scales: the local, the subregional, and regional (pan-Maya) levels. Within this framework, we place emphasis on the subregional and local level interactions. This framework analyses a short time span—the history of a particular site—in an attempt to define the extent and intensity of that site's economic, ideological, and political dynamics. This sort of polity definition is necessary before one can begin to place sites and polities within a larger regional political hierarchy. When identifiable, low-level (local) political organizations are deemed of particular importance; the applications of central-place theory (e.g., Inomata & Aoyama 1996: 292) and regional community theory (e.g., Pauketat 2000) have demonstrated that interaction between political authorities and local populations is key to understanding the relationship of a polity center and surrounding sites.

The peer polity interaction model, developed by Colin Renfrew (1986; see also Price 1977), examines interactions (in the broadest sense) between politically independent groups located in spatial proximity. Within this model, the extent of shared symbolic systems, such as spoken language, writing and numeric systems, political institutions, and religious beliefs, is greater than the "power span" of individual autonomous polities (Renfrew 1986: 2). While avoiding placing a priori emphasis upon relations of dominance and subordination between *societies*, the peer polity interaction model does not consider the polity in isolation, but rather as a part of a larger *regional* framework of loosely related, politically independent, interacting groups (Renfrew 1986: 1, 7).

The peer polity interaction model is particularly pertinent when considering the Late Classic Maya political landscape, especially that of Palenque, and may have been too quickly dismissed by some Mayanists. Furthermore, by reducing the scale of analysis of the peer polity interaction model to subregional and local levels, the nature of interaction between Classic Maya site cores and their neighbors can be better studied. These more frequent interactions likely had a greater role in the history and development of many Classic Maya polities. On the subregional level, Palenque seems to have played an important part in western Maya lowland Late Classic intersite relationships. More locally, Palenque is by far the largest site, and one of the fundamental facets of the peer polity model must be ignored at this level: in the model, peer polity analytical units are supposed to be of equal scale (Renfrew 1986). This divergence from Renfrew's perfected model is necessary to apply our approach to the archaeological record in the Maya area, and reflects our belief that a different methodological approach to describing Classic Maya polities is necessary before constructing theoretical models.[7] Instead of attempting to force data into a rigid theoretical hierarchy model, we emphasize scales of interaction and mechanisms of interaction; interactions between "major" and "minor" centers can be of substantive importance to polity development and organization at both site types.

Robert Fry (1990) compared the demographic growth at larger "regional capitals" (like Tikal) or "major central places" to smaller centers in the same subregion. He concluded that the dynamic occupation shifts seen archaeologically at major centers are not characteristic of smaller centers. While subsequent research has demonstrated that smaller centers, such as Dos Pilas (O'Mansky & Dunning 2004), also experienced dramatic fluctuations in occupation, Fry is correct in warning against generalizing trends from one type of center to another. He instead argues for investigation of the interactions between centers of different size, organization, and complexity. In regard to the applicability of generalizations about population growth, Fry states, "the heterogeneity of demographic trends should make us cautious in seeing pan-lowland patterns, and it reinforces the need for surveys and programs of regional scope" (Fry 1990: 296). Regional survey (Liendo, Chapter 5) suggests that demographic processes in the Palenque area were a major factor in shaping settlement at the site of Palenque. Nucleation within the Palenque site core is linked to possible migrations from the surrounding hinterlands, yet concurrent with the establishment of new settlements in these hinterlands during Balunte times.

A necessary complement to analyzing interaction at multiple spatial scales is to consider as well different kinds of interaction in an attempt to gauge their "intensity" and "frequency." In order to operationalize Palenque's inter- and intrapolity interactions, they have been divided into three broad interaction classes: economic, ideological/symbolic, and political. Other categories of Classic Maya interaction may be definable, but we deal with only these three because we feel they cover the most archaeologically visible forms of ancient interaction. Furthermore, each of these differing interaction types can be correlated to specific archaeological data sets. Space constraints limit evaluation in this chapter of all possible archaeological data sets; instead, we have selected the most abundant and, in our opinion, relevant data sets for analyzing Palenque's "spheres" of economic (ceramic exchange), ideological/symbolic (architecture and art styles), and political (epigraphic history) interaction.

Economic Interaction

While ceramics certainly do not equate directly with domination, politically or economically, exchanges in bulky utilitarian items do represent the physical remains of ancient contact. The frequency and intensity of production and movement of

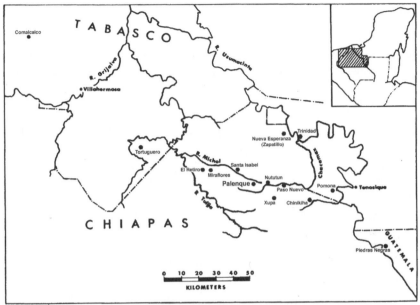

Figure 14.1: Map of the Palenque area (after Rands 1969)

goods in and around Palenque indicate possible economic and political structures once influencing interactions in the region. We recognize the limitations of using just one artifact class for analysis. However, the spatial distribution of ceramics related by design, form, and/or paste composition put Palenque's possible spheres of interaction in perspective.

Ceramic Exchange

Local, inter- and intraregional exchange studies have received various amounts of attention from Mayanists. Unfortunately the archaeological record limits reconstructing or modeling economic interactions on any level. While per-ishable goods are rightly assumed to have circulated within the Palenque core and to and from other areas, as archaeologists we rely on certain sturdy artifact classes to facilitate analysis of exchange patterns. Lithics and ceramics are most com-monly evaluated in terms of raw material procurement, manufacture, use, and ex-change. The "everyday" utilitarian, ritual, and "elite" forms of lithics and ceram-ics permit multifaceted analysis of exchange on differing social scales. However, only a single study of chipped stone artifacts from the Palenque area is readily available (Johnson 1976), and the Palenque artifact inventory is notably deficient in chert, flint, and obsidian artifacts. Fortunately, extensive work with the ceramic catalog at Palenque by Robert Rands and his colleagues (Bishop 1975, 1994; Bishop, Rands & Harbottle 1982; Bishop, Rands & Holley 1982; Rands 1967a, 1967b, 1973, 1974a, 1974b, 1977, 1987, 1988, 1994, Chapter 2, Chapter 3; Rands

& Bargielski Weimer 1992; Rands & Bishop 1980, 2003; Rands & Rands 1957, 1959; Rands et al. 1978) has brought us closer to understanding the production and exchange in pottery classes and traditions within the Palenque region. The detailed ceramic chronology for Palenque also facilitates dating cultural deposits at the site for ready comparison with other centers and regions. Detailed petrographic and compositional analysis of ceramics (Bishop 1975, 1994: 26-35; Bishop, Rands & Harbottle 1982; Rands & Bishop 1980) recovered from dozens of sites in the Palenque area permit an unusually detailed discussion of production and exchange trends within a large and environmentally diverse region.

The Palenque ceramics are difficult to work with; preservation in the high rainfall region is notably poor. The apparent low quality slips, heavy weathering, and complex regional exchange patterns (Bishop 1975; Rands 1974b, Chapter 2) have left archaeologists in a particularly intricate dilemma. Limitations notwithstanding, the extensive analysis of ceramics from the Palenque region offers a unique perspective on economic relationships and cultural contacts within and without the region. Following the ceramic chronology for Palenque (Rands 1974a, 1974b, 1987, Chapter 2) from earliest to latest times, some interesting affiliations, developments and patterns emerge.

The evidence for Preclassic occupation at Palenque comes entirely from ceramic data. No Preclassic architecture or monuments have been encountered at the site. Sealed Preclassic deposits or pure stratigraphic levels are likewise unknown. In general, the Palenque ceremonial center seems to lack the great time depth and architectural remodeling episodes characteristic of Copan or Tikal.[8] Very few early architectural phases have been located, and none appear to date earlier than the Cascada phase.

All Preclassic pottery from Palenque comes from redeposited contexts, typically plaza or structure fill. This fragmentary data set attests to some kind of occupation by the Middle Preclassic. Waxy red slips are a dominant horizon marker, though the fragmented nature of the redeposited sherds usually precludes more precise formal type designation or more precise temporal assignment. Modal similarities among Preclassic ceramics exist among Paso Nuevo, Chinikiha, and Palenque (Rands, Chapter 3) though strict type to type comparisons are unwarranted and not possible. Rands has noted the overall "non-Maya" character of the regional Preclassic ceramics, citing Greater Isthmian and Olmec area influences; the greater Peten traditions do not exert much influence on the Palenque area at this time.

Excavations at Paso Nuevo and Zapatillo (Rands, Chapter 3), as well as El Lacandón, have produced a fairly strong Middle Preclassic waxy ware assemblage. Thick walled carbonate temper dishes with flared everted rims, which Rands equates with Tierra Mojada resist, appear in levels alongside specular hematite waxy red slipped bowls, usually with some horizontal fluting (see Rands, Chapter 3: Figs. 3.9 & 3.10). This assemblage evidences relatively sophisticated production technology on this Middle Preclassic horizon. The consistency of form and double slipping or resist-finishing techniques suggest a shared technical knowledge in the local region or distribution from a single specialist potting community.

Aside from advanced technological skill, the consistent form of these vessels may legitimately be inferred to relate to broadly similar functions. It appears that on some level of local contact, Preclassic inhabitants within the Palenque region participated in exchange of wares or the technology to produce them in order to serve similar needs at multiple centers.

While not associated with monumental architecture or Long Count dates, the Picota phase (c. A.D. 250-400) appears to be temporally equivalent with the "Protoclassic" phenomenon known sporadically across the southern Maya lowlands (Brady et al. 1998; Pring 2000). Interestingly, the Picota phase is not well represented in epicentral construction deposits, rather appearing dominantly from surface collection and excavation approximately one kilometer west of the Palenque ceremonial center, adjacent to the Rio Picota. Orange gloss slips, dominant in the Protoclassic assemblages across the southern lowlands, are absent from this phase, which is dominated by matte red slips (when preservation permits detection) on distinctly local forms (Rands 1973, 1974b). On this temporal horizon, when a relatively small, pre-dynastic Palenque polity is best viewed as a small hamlet or chiefdom (Rands 1974b) recovered ceramics show a consistency of form and paste never encountered again at the site (Rands & Bishop 2003). It appears that locally manufactured pottery dominated at Palenque during Picota times.

In the subsequent Motiepa phase (c. A.D. 400-500), clearly imported ceramics make an initial appearance at Palenque (Rands, Chapter 2, Chapter 3). Peten gloss wares of the Aguila Orange and Balanza Black groups, recovered from deep mixed deposits in the epicenter, attest to some contact with areas to the south. This is the only time in Palenque history when appreciable amounts of Peten ceramics are imported into the site, possibly transported by way of the Usumacinta or San Pedro Rivers. Locally manufactured ceramics are present concurrent to the Peten gloss ware intrusion. Most commonly represented by deep serving dishes similar in form and matte red slip to Picota specimens, locally manufactured ceramics in Motiepa appear to grow out of the local Picota tradition. Preceding major epicentral architectural construction, Motiepa times evince continuation of the local pottery making tradition with modification along with some importation of distinctly foreign types (Rands, Chapter 3).

The subsequent Cascada phase (or subcomplex [see Rands, Chapter 2]) (c. A.D. 500-620) saw the cessation of Peten imports and further development, or "drift," in locally produced forms. Some hematite red slipped pottery at Palenque dating to the Cascada phase has strong correlates at the western site of Piedras Negras (Holley 1983, cited in Rands 1987); however, the majority of ceramics dating to the Cascada phase are overwhelmingly local in form. This dependence on local, or near-local, production continued into the Otolum phase (c. A.D. 620-700), when epicentral architecture construction boomed and Palenque took on more of the familiar form known today. Construction of the Palace and North Group began in this phase and the first monumental hieroglyphic inscriptions were erected.

While Otolum times saw Palenque growing into a more substantial settlement with the hallmarks of a Maya "city" (monumental architecture, sculpted monuments, aqueducts, and writing claiming a "king"), the ceramic assemblage is still distinctly local in form and design. For the first time, polychrome pottery represents a substantial percentage of the assemblage. Wide everted rim serving dishes are consistent in form and paste in Otolum times, though in a range of sizes; when sufficiently preserved, polychrome designs are evident on the vessel interiors. These dishes represent the most consistent local polychrome tradition at Palenque, though of limited duration (perhaps 70 years). Late Classic polychrome "palace-scene" vases are noticeably absent. Even during the Otolum phase at Palenque, when polychrome dishes abound, the absence of this near ubiquitous Classic Maya culture marker, the painted vase, reinforces the aberrant nature of the local ceramic assemblage in conforming to general tendencies known from the majority of lowland sites. Polychrome plates, dishes, and vases have much greater frequency at central Peten sites, and most Late Classic Maya polities produced or imported painted cylinders.

The site of Trinidad, less than 50 km northeast of Palenque on the lower Usumacinta River, was evidently influenced to a greater extent by central Peten ceramic trends. Roughly coeval in time with the Otolum phase at Palenque, Trinidad's Taxinchan complex (which Rands places on a Tepeu 1-2 horizon) is clearly within the Tepeu ceramic sphere (Rands 1969). Saxche and Palmar polychromes are present, although fine paste pottery with regionally distinctive forms and designs are also known at this time (Rands 1969: 9). The subsequent Naab ceramic complex at Trinidad witnessed localized monochrome wares with a more western Maya influence increase in frequency (Rands 1969: 11). This may well reflect the geographic position of Trinidad to water routes connecting to the northern Peten and shifting influence at the site from both Peten and western subregional trends. Rands notes that the distinct ceramic sequences at Palenque and Trinidad indicate, "that some sort of barrier existed between sites in the Trinidad zone and Palenque is evident, subject to certain important qualifications" (Rands 1969: 10). One is left with the impression that sites within 50 km of Palenque were influenced by contacts from outside the region as well as from sites in closer proximity. These influences or contacts seem to wax and wane over time, hinting at the complex subregional history of the area.

By Murcielagos times (c. A.D. 700-750), an influx of new paste classes appears in the Palenque assemblages (Rands 1974b; Rands & Bishop 1980). Well represented are pottery with paste compositions that correlate with both the near plains (10-15 km distance) and the Usumacinta floodplain (50 km distance). Most significantly, serving bowls and basins, manufactured almost exclusively in a heavily quartz sand tempered buff paste, have been sourced to the plains area north of Palenque (Rands 1987). The abundance and consistency of paste and form of these vessels indicate a regional specialization and incorporation of the plains region in either a complex redistribution or marketplace exchange network centered at Palenque.

Also during the Murcielagos phase, "tier-of-heads" *incensario* variants appear with frequency at Palenque and nearby sites (Bishop, Rands & Harbottle 1982: Fig. 2a). Compositional analysis indicates that most of these "tier-of-heads" *incensarios* from Palenque and elsewhere were produced at Palenque (Bishop, Rands & Harbottle 1982; Rands et al. 1978: 23). Other *incensario* variants from the following Balunte phase are of different origin (Rands et al. 1978: 25-26). Georgia West (2002) has postulated that these and other sorts of ritual items were exported from Palenque for utilitarian pottery forms. Although a valid interpretation of the data concerning Palenque *incensarios*, the few examples recovered outside of Palenque make it unlikely that the "*incensario* trade" alone could have supported the importation of utilitarian wares into the Palenque site core.

Fine paste ceramics, in a range of discernable specific paste classes, became increasingly popular at Palenque during the Murcielagos phase. These fine paste pieces probably represent importation from the Usumacinta floodplain and other as yet unidentified areas, possibly to the northeast. By late Murcielagos times, Yalcox Black and Chablekal Gray vases, beakers, and bowls augment the increasing diversity of fine paste ceramics in Palenque assemblages (Rands, Chapter 2). Yalcox Black group ceramics are reported for sites in the Tabasco region (Berlin 1956) and as far away as Mayapan (Smith 1971). Compositional analysis of Yalcox group ceramics indicate that they were produced at a number of locations, possibly even at Palenque itself (Rands & Bishop 1980). Chablekal group pots are known to have circulated widely in the Late Classic (from perhaps A.D. 730) down the Usumacinta corridor, though stylistic variables distinguish the recovered Palenque specimens from those of other sites such as Piedras Negras and Cancuen. Continuity from Murcielagos into Balunte phase (c. A.D. 750-820) is noted for fine paste imports, such as the previously mentioned Yalcox and Chablekal groups, as well as local fine paste expressions which slightly predate the introduction of these established types. "Ancestral" pieces appear first, followed by Fine Blacks,[9] with Fine Grays gaining in popularity throughout Balunte times. Murcielagos and Balunte equivalent ceramics have been recovered from various sites in the Palenque area survey zone (Rands 1967a, 1967b, 1987; Liendo Stuardo 1999, 2003, Chapter 5). An increase in frequency and strength of cultural contact among populations or communities living within the region are indicated on this temporal horizon.

Phase-defining large Balunte tripod serving dish/plates, which clearly marks the peak of occupation at Palenque, have been recovered throughout the Palenque area in a variety of pastes, indicating emulation and the dominance of Palenque form. This duplication of form in various paste classes suggests that Balunte times represent the culmination of cultural contact, diffusion of style, and exchange. Although ceramics do not clearly indicate political boundaries, by A.D. 780 the local region was apparently influenced to the greatest degree by the preferences in form at Palenque. The degree to which exchange networks overlap with political boundaries is an issue to be studied. However, the sustained contact between Palenque and ceramic production sites outside the immediate Palenque center is indicative of cultural contact and the movement of ideas and production technology in the region.

The final recognizable Palenque ceramic development is the ephemeral Huipale phase (post-A.D. 820). Known only from surface collections, this phase appears to postdate dynastic activity at the site. The extreme rarity of Fine Orange ceramics at Palenque indicates that the site did not continue to interact within exchange spheres past A.D. 830. The overall paucity of material assigned to this phase in conjunction with the cessation of monumental architecture and glyphic monument erections reinforces the abrupt decline and abandonment of Palenque.

The fifty years of research on the subject of production and exchange in ceramics in the Palenque region (e.g., Rands 1967, 1974b, 1977, 1987, 1988, Chapter 2, Chapter 3; Rands & Bishop 1980, 2003) have isolated much finer relations than we have discussed here. Our intent is not to recapitulate the extensive conclusions and questions formulated during this era of work, but rather to overview some of the major trends of exchange within and without the Palenque area to facilitate a more comprehensive discussion of the influence, interaction, and contact "spheres" which act to place Palenque in a local, subregional, and pan-Maya context.

While similarities in ceramics represent diffusion or culture contact, pottery or the technology to produce certain types or wares can be acquired through the mechanisms of trade, exchange, migration, and conquest (Arnold 1985: 1). Furthermore, ceramics may circulate independent of social or political spheres (Arnold 1985). While the spatial analysis of related ceramics can indicate frequency and intensity of contact between Palenque and other centers, the structure of these contacts must be pieced together from multiple lines of evidence. In combination with art and epigraphy, architectural analysis, and environmental data, these complementary data sets provide a framework within which to evaluate the direction and structures of information diffusion between Palenque and neighboring centers.

From Preclassic times on, Palenque ceramics are notably unaffected by central Peten trends on more than a general modal level. Forms appear to be more influenced by non-Maya traditions originating closer to Palenque itself. The exception to this long-standing independent trend at Palenque is the importation of Peten gloss wares during the Motiepa phase. This intrusive complex indicates that Palenque's greatest material contact with the Peten Maya "heartland" occurred in the Early Classic, never to be repeated in subsequent phases.

Ceramics tend to be predominantly local in design, style, and composition through Otolum times when the bulk of architectural growth occurred and hieroglyphic monuments make an initial appearance at the site epicenter. While a local polychrome dish-plate industry is sustained beyond the Otolum phase, local pottery exchange becomes more frequent in the archaeological record (Bishop 1994; Rands 1988; Rands & Bishop 2003). The decline in polychrome pottery manufacture and use is complemented by an influx of new paste classes into the Palenque center. Increases in the number of paste classes as well as distinct intrusive traditions probably indicative of micro-regional specialization clearly mark Palenque as a consumer of ceramics at this time. Murcielagos through Balunte phases see continued interaction among Palenque and nearby pottery producing areas, as well as importation of specific typologically consistent (Yalcox, Chablekal) fine paste specimens known to have wider distributions in Yucatan and down the Usumacinta River. It seems reasonable, on the basis of ceramic data, that the Palenque polity witnessed increased archaeologically visible interaction through time with neighboring centers within an approximately 50 km radius. What materials were produced and exported out of Palenque are unknown at present, yet the increased reliance or incorporation of local production does correlate directly with architectural growth, public works construction and (presumably) demographic growth at the center.

Ideological/Symbolic Interaction

Though under the heading of ideology, this section does not necessarily fit into a strict anthropological definition of the term (Geertz 1973). Instead focus here is placed on identifying the material remains of non-material sorts of interactions. In other words, how do we determine and define the results of different non-material types of interaction, such as emulation versus politically forced imitation? Similarities in monumental architecture and art styles between local and subregional communities may demonstrate difficult to define interactions in the absence of economic ties. Despite these acknowledged difficulties an effort is made to determine the nature and intensity of interactions that may produce similar, or differing, monumental architecture and art traditions at various sites.

Architecture

Palenque architecture can be characterized as part of the greater Classic Maya architectural tradition. However, as has long been noted (Roys 1934), Palenque monumental structures differ significantly from Classic Peten buildings in form and engineering (see Marken 2002; Marquina 1964). The wide galleries and lattice-type roofcombs of Palenque are distinctive of the Northwestern Maya architectural tradition (Andrews 1995). These "open" roofcombs are seen elsewhere in the western Maya subregion, specifically at Yaxchilan, Tonina, and Piedras Negras. Based on the currently known architecture, Palenque's architectural tradition appears fully developed in the early Late Classic (see Marken, Chapter 4). Whether the Palenque architectural tradition evolved locally or was imported directly is undetermined, as no earlier antecedents of this style are known, and much of the site remains unexcavated. However, Early Classic tombs (within razed or buried temples) with stepped vaults analogous to Temple V have been discovered within the Palenque site core, hinting that Palenque's architectural style was a local manifestation of a greater pan-Maya tradition.

During the reign of K'inich Kan Bahlam II (A.D. 684-702), Palencano temple structures underwent their most significant formal architectural addition. All the temple structures attributed to his reign contain an inner vaulted sanctuary in the rear primary axis room. Hieroglyphic evidence has shown that these sanctuaries functioned as symbolic ritual sweatbaths (Child, Chapter 12; Houston 1996). While the monumental, as well as more "private," symbolic sweatbaths seem to have continued in use following K'inich Kan Bahlam's reign (García Moll 1991: 241; Marken & González, Chapter 8), no other monumental inner sanctuaries were constructed at Palenque after A.D. 702.

At the westernmost Maya site of Comalcalco, Tabasco, the identification of similar "inner sanctuaries" has often been cited as indicative of Palenque's political dominance at that Late Classic site (Andrews 1975: 200; 1989: 79, 141; Houston 1996: 145). Other architectural and sculptural "parallels," such as similar sloping upper façades, are also seen as evidence of Palencano influence at Comalcalco (Andrews 1989: 34). Yet many architectural similarities between Palenque and Comalcalco are actually rather superficial, and alone fail to demonstrate any political integration between the two sites.

Overlooking differences in construction materials at the two sites (Andrews 1989: 28; Gallegos Gomora 1997: 214-216; Marken 2002), the plans of temple structures at Palenque and Comalcalco are substantially different. Both styles consist of two parallel vaulted galleries, but Palencano temples have three entryways connecting the two galleries, while Comalcalco temples have only one. Furthermore, temple façade pier arrangements do not match (compare Andrews 1989: Fig. 121, and Marken, Chapter 4: Fig. 4.2c). Palenque temple structures have lateral façade piers (see Marken, Chapter 4: Fig. 4.1); Comalcalco temples do not. In the absence of writing, central Andean archaeologists have used architectural forms and styles to identify political integration and control (Isbell 1991; Schreiber 1992). In several instances architectural similarities have been suggested as evidence of political control between different Mesoamerican sites, only to be invalidated by further analysis (e.g., Laporte 2003). If Palenque politically controlled Comalcalco in the Late Classic, it would be reasonable to expect Comalcalco temple structures to be exact (or near-exact) matches of Palenque temples.

We do not deny that some form of contact existed between the two sites and that Comalcalco architecture was heavily influenced by architectural styles from Palenque. In fact, the centers (and Tortuguero) have the same emblem glyph, which has led to speculation of familial ties between the dynastic lineages of both sites. The presence of nine sculpted stucco figures in the tomb underlying Comalcalco Temple IX and K'inich Janab Pakal I's tomb in the Temple of the

Inscriptions at Palenque has seemed to confirm interaction between the two centers. Yet these figures are of vastly different sculptural styles (Andrews 1989). Furthermore, Comalcalco rulers were buried in the site's Grand Acropolis, an accretion of monumental structures, while Palencano rulers were buried in their own monumental funerary pyramids.[10]

Unsubstantiated political integration and vague diffusion do not clarify the nature of interaction between the two sites. Exchange mechanisms may have existed in the form of perishable items, such as cacao from the Comalcalco area, but these are purely speculative. Consistent economic ties between the two sites seem unlikely; compositional differences between Fine Gray ceramics from each site indicate involvement in separate exchange systems (Bishop et al. 2004).

Mark Child (Chapter 12) has raised an intriguing line of inquiry into site interactions in his discussion of ancient Maya sweatbaths. The architectural similarities between Comalcalco and Palenque could possibly be the result of a sweatbath cult in the Maya area, and especially prevalent in the western lowlands. Within the western Maya subregion, the sites of Palenque and Piedras Negras seem to have been the dominant cult centers based on their extensive functional and symbolic monumental sweatbaths. The construction of symbolic sweatbaths at Palenque coincides with the principle occurrence of "tier-of-heads" *incensario* variants within the site core (Rands et al. 1978; see above). Local exchange of these ritual items (Bishop 1994), intimately associated with Palenque's monumental sweatbaths, may be an instance where economic and ideological interactions overlapped.

More locally, the smaller sites of Xupá and El Retiro, Chiapas apparently took part in this sweatbath cult. Symbolic sweatbaths identical to those of Palenque's Cross Group have been identified at both sites, as well as other small sites within the Palenque area (Blom 1923; Blom & La Farge 1926: Fig. 168; Liendo Stuardo 1999, 2002b). The monumental architecture of these sites is, unlike that of Comalcalco, identical in form to that of Palenque, likely indicating actual integration within the Palenque polity. At Xupá in particular, a limestone monument, now lost, was carved in Palenque style (Maler 1901: 17).

Our own studies (Marken, Chapter 4; Straight, Chapter 10) indicate that structure form could evolve with modification over time or change rapidly within the reign of a single ruler. While functionally analogous structures at geographically distant centers may indicate homologous social institutions, these need not be evidence for political integration, domination, or exploitation. Buildings were actively used by the ancient Maya to fulfill biological, social, and religious "necessity." Familiarity with concepts or institutions and the governmental, civic or ritual architectural expressions that structured them indicate fairly intense contact. Most interestingly, the ability to construct a "replica" building would require prolonged exposure to the original. Architecture may thus represent the diffusion of ideas among peer polities at a subroyal level, among architects and craftpersons. It is currently unknown how knowledge about constructed architectural forms circulated, perhaps architects and carvers were trained in a school system, sponsored by a dominant center. Alternatively, these knowledgeable persons may have moved from center to center seeking the greatest prestige and reward for their services.

Art

From global and historical perspectives Classic Maya art can be classified as belonging to a single, pan-Maya, art style, often specifically oriented toward legitimizing rulers' right to sovereignty (Miller 1996; Schele & Miller 1986). Classic Maya scribes also recorded their inscriptions in the same language (Houston & Lacadena 2003; Houston et al. 2000).[11] Furthermore, the Classic Maya elite shared similar religious beliefs; monuments of the Classic period throughout the Maya area often depict the same deities. For example, Triad expressions, though first identified in Palenque inscriptions (Berlin 1963), have been identified at several other Classic sites.

Despite these similarities, Proskouriakoff (1950) was able to identify stylistic differences in Classic Maya monumental sculptural art through time. Furthermore, subtle differences are apparent between the art styles of specific Classic Maya subregions. Most obvious are subregional differences in the mediums of monumental art at various Classic centers. During the Preclassic, substructures were adorned with large stucco masks at numerous sites throughout the Maya area, such as Calakmul, Nakbe, El Mirador (Hansen 1998), Cerros (Schele & Freidel 1990), and Uaxactun (Smith 1950). In the Early Classic, and more especially in the Late Classic, the diversity of mediums for monumental expression increased. This increase is evident in how the monumental art of many Maya sites can be equated with a particular art form: Caracol has its Ajaw altars, Yaxchilan its stone lintels, Tikal its twin-pyramid complexes and stela-altar pairings, while Copan and Tonina carved stelae in the round. Palenque rulers and sculptors chose wall panels to memorialize their ancestry and lives. These private (when compared to stelae) monuments located within temples on high pyramids were supplemented by public sculpture adorning these pyramids, similar to the stucco sculpture of Comalcalco (Andrews 1989). Like Comalcalco, but unlike the major sites of the Upper Usumacinta River (e.g., Yaxchilan, Piedras Negras, Bonampak), stelae are few at Palenque. Only three stelae are known from the site core: two are plain (Barnhart 2001; Blom & La Farge 1926), and one is carved in the round (Greene Robertson 1991). Furthermore, certain carving styles can be equated with the reigns of specific Palenque rulers. For example, the calligraphy-like incised glyphs of the Tablet of the 96 Glyphs, and the platform panels for Temples XIX and XXI coincide with the reigns of K'inich Ahkal Mo' Nahb III (r. A.D. 721-c.740) and his son K'inich K'uk' Bahlam II (r. A.D. 764-c.785). In contrast, certain compositional forms of K'inich Janab Pakal I's reign seem to have been maintained by his successors (Fig. 14.2).

While Palencano scribes reproduced Classic Maya language in their monumental inscriptions, they used a distinctly "western" Maya vocabulary. For example, *wa-ni* verbal endings are very common at Palenque, but are less frequently seen in Peten inscriptions. Palenque scribes are likewise anomalous in their practice of substituting the glyphic element *ta* for the locative *ti*. Palenque texts also demonstrate a narrative structure divergent from other Classic period sites (Josserand 1991). The Palenque pantheon also shows local manifestations.[12] As David Stuart (Chapter 11) has suggested, both a pan-Maya and a local Palencano version of the deity GI are described in the Temple XIX texts.

Palenque's divergence from other Classic Maya sites in subregional artistic style parallels the area's general ceramic isolation from central lowland Maya sites discussed above. However, some similarities in art styles are identifiable within the western Maya subregion and Palenque's local region. Monumental wall panels are most abundant at Palenque in the Maya world, but the captive panels of House C of the Palace are reminiscent of the numerous captive panels of Tonina (which postdate House C). The one known carved stela from Palenque

Figure 14.2: Accession scenes at Palenque:
a) Oval Palace Tablet; b) Tablet of the Slaves; c) Palace Tablet
(drawings courtesy of Merle Greene Robertson)

is carved in the round like the stelae from Tonina. Furthermore, the stucco human head on the "Frieze of the Dream Lords" at Tonina does not resemble the local elite depicted on the site's stelae. More locally, sculptural similarities, such as near identical dress (see Lizardi Ramos 1963: Figs. 1, 4) exist between Pomona and Palenque monumental art. Even more striking are the similarities in rendering the dress and "incense bags" of elites at Palenque and El Cayo, considered a secondary center of Piedras Negras.[13]

The question of ethnicity often comes into play when discussing art styles. Although the creators of the separate subregional Maya art styles were certainly all Maya, are the varying forms of monumental expression indicative of different "types" of Classic Maya, or instead the result of variable methods chosen by specific ruling lineages to help legitimize their authority? Issues such as this are beyond the scope of this chapter, but remain an interesting potential line of inquiry (see Canuto & Fash 2004).

Political Interaction

The best evidence we have in the Maya area for direct political contact between separate sites during the Classic period is the epigraphic record (Table 14.1). Notwithstanding this fact, Classic Maya inscriptions are full of poorly understood events and rarely elaborate on select few instances of interaction that are often separated by several years, even decades. Moreover, key elements of political integration, such as the giving and receiving of tribute, are generally omitted in Classic period hieroglyphic texts. Classic Maya inscriptions often focus on elite ancestry and ritual events. Unlike Linear A/B or cuneiform, Classic Mayan script was not used to record individual manufactory seals or numerated tribute schedules on durable media.

One of the strengths of epigraphic studies is how they document the "gifting" of elite women by rulers from one site to another. It is currently accepted that those receiving elite women in marriage were considered subordinate to the elites of the site of origin (Marcus 1993). However, in terms of interaction events, warfare may be the most abundant mechanism of intersite interaction mentioned in the epigraphic record.

At present, Classic Maya warfare is poorly understood. While some researchers feel that "the Maya seem to have generally deployed fairly small numbers of warriors with rather minimal organization" (Webster 1998: 329), others seem to envision the mobilization of large-scale "armies" (Martin & Grube 2000), similar in organization to Conquest period Aztec armies (Hassig 1988). However, smaller fighting bands or raiding parties seem the more common organization of most Classic Maya warfare.[14] As Hassig (1988, 1992) has pointed out in the case of Tenochtitlan, if a Mesoamerican polity were to ever deploy their entire military force in a single military venture, the polity center would be extremely vulnerable to attack from a third party. This is especially pertinent considering the few

Table 14.1: Palenque's Epigraphically Recorded Intersite Interactions

Year (A.D.)	Event	Interaction Site	Inscription Location	Palenque Ruler
603	capture of a lord by	Bonampak	Bonampak Lintel 4	Lady Yohl Ik'nal
610	attack against	Wa-Bird	Santa Elena panel	Aj Ne' Ohl Mat
611	attack by	Calakmul	T. Inscriptions/House C H.S.	Aj Ne' Ohl Mat
624	capture of a lord by	Piedras Negras	Piedras Negras Stela 26	K'inich Janab Pakal I
654	attack by	Calakmul	T. Inscriptions/House C H.S.	K'inich Janab Pakal I
659	capture of rulers from	Wa-Bird & Pomona	T. Inscriptions/House C H.S.	K'inich Janab Pakal I
663	capture of lords from	Wa-Bird & Pomona	House C façades	K'inich Janab Pakal I
687	capture of ruler from	Tonina	Tablet of the Warriors	K'inich Kan Bahlam II
690	visit by ruler of	Moral-Reforma	Moral-Reforma Stela 4	K'inich Kan Bahlam II
692	capture of a lord by	Tonina	Tonina M.27/M.145/M.p49	K'inich Kan Bahlam II
695	capture of lords from	Tonina	Tablet of the Warriors	K'inich Kan Bahlam II
711	"star-war" by	Tonina	Tonina M. 22	K'inich K'an Hoy Chitam II
714	visit by Palenque ruler	Piedras Negras	Piedras Negras Stela 8	K'inich K'an Hoy Chitam II
723	capture of a lord from	"La" (unknown)	Tablet of the Slaves	K'inich Ahkal Mo' Nahb III
725	capture of a lord from	Piedras Negras	Tablets of the Scribe & Orator	K'inich Ahkal Mo' Nahb III
725	attack against	"Kinal" (Piedras Negras)	Tablet of the Slaves	K'inich Ahkal Mo' Nahb III
729	attack against	"Ko-?" (unknown)	Tablet of the Slaves	K'inich Ahkal Mo' Nahb III
730	"star-war" against	"Chonal" (unknown)	Tablet of the Slaves	K'inich Ahkal Mo' Nahb III
c. 730	marriage of a Palenque woman	Copan	Copan Stela 8	K'inich Janab Pakal II?

known fortified western Classic Maya sites[15] and the generally lower populations of Classic Maya sites, particularly those of the western subregion (e.g., Barnhart, Chapter 6; Nelson 2004), compared to those of central Mexico (Sanders & Webster 1988). That the larger Classic Maya polities could on occasion mount and organize large, long-distance military ventures, as implied in some Classic period inscriptions, is a definite possibility that really has yet to be systematically explored across the Maya lowlands.[16]

As an interaction mechanism, warfare as presented in Classic inscriptions is rather vague and somewhat subjective. Monumental inscriptions and art describing and depicting warfare were propaganda monuments used to glorify and legitimize the authority of rulers. As investigators, we must remain wary of universally accepting the statements inscribed by past rulers as objective histories; many events (war included) are only recorded retrospectively within the context of royal legitimacy. Furthermore, "while violent conflict is an important part of all complex societies, we should remain cognizant that daily life continues even during some of the most extreme forms of conflict and that people often ignore the boundaries imposed by elites and combatants" (Stanton & Brown 2003: 7). Whether actual political integration occurs following warfare events recorded in the inscriptions is rarely clear. As David Webster (1993: 426) states, "currently the clearest part of the view [of Maya warfare] is provided by art and epigraphy; paradoxically, I believe that it is our preoccupation with these categories of evidence that distorts our conceptualizations of Maya warfare as a form of interaction." Other lines of evidence, namely sudden changes in archaeologically visible cultural patterns (Webster 1998: 315), are necessary to confirm the consequences of specific epigraphic warfare events. In the Maya area, these material effects of warfare are rarely investigated in conjunction with epigraphy to determine the validity of the epigraphic record. For example, we are generally unaware of where Maya battles were fought (Webster 1998: 331), yet often researchers equate an epigraphically recorded defeat with the sacking of a polity center (Braswell et al. 2004: 162; Martin & Grube 2000; Martin et al. 2002: II-17). In some cases where the sacking of a site is accepted as coinciding with an epigraphically recorded defeat, such as at hiatus-period Tikal, further analysis of the archaeology and epigraphy of the site reveal that the site was not sacked at that time (Guenter 2002: 100). In other cases, where the sacking and destruction of a site center is evident, the event is often not recorded epigraphically.

Even with a plethora of epigraphic and archaeological data at hand, reconstructing historic events remains problematic. Wooden Lintel 2 from Tikal Temple I clearly records a "sacking" or "defeat" phrase (*hubiiy u-tok u-pakal*) over the ruler of Calakmul in August A.D. 695. Combined with the stucco façade from structure 5D-57, portraying a supplicated Calakmul lord taken during this conflict (Martin & Grube 2000: 45, 76), these records have strongly suggested that Yichaak' K'ak' of Calakmul was captured and killed at this time. Indeed, the carved "captive bone" from Tikal Burial 116 (Ruler A) portraying a Calakmul captive associated with the name of a *new* Calakmul ruler in November of the same year, A.D. 695, further supports this idea. However, the 1997 recovery of a lavish royal tomb at Calakmul, most likely that of Yichaak K'ak' (see Martin & Grube [2000: 111] for a contextual case for this identification) has raised serious questions about capture and dispatchment resulting from belligerent interactions between centers. It appears that the ruler of Calakmul did die in late 695 A.D. and was interred with full reverence and care at Calakmul. If his death was a result of this conflict with Tikal (which seems most likely), where and how was he killed? And how was his body returned to Calakmul? Strong parallels with this situation surround the death of the Tikal ruler the same day as the "*entrada*" of Siyah K'ak' as well as the "capture" and return (?) of K'an Joy Chitam II at Palenque. Clearly the repercussions of Maya conflict are yet to be systematically and empirically explored.

However, it has proven difficult for many Mayanists to correlate the epigraphic histories of sites with the known archaeological record. For example, to date no rulers of Caracol have been identified in funerary chambers, although an abundance of epicentral tombs with securely dated texts have been excavated in the last twenty years. This is in stark contrast to centers where the funerary chambers of rulers, named on stone and stucco monuments (and ceramics), have been positively identified. It appears that some subregnal elites (including females) were buried in prominent positions in the major epicentral architectural compounds of Caracol. Unfortunately, the recorded interment dates, when compared to ruler death dates inscribed on stone monuments, preclude these unidentified tomb occupants from being kings of Caracol. There is no overlap between painted and carved texts. It should be pointed out that there are a few cases where the archaeological and epigraphic records do coincide well, such as at Early Classic Copan (see Sharer 2004).

More distressing, the difficult to date Tikal earthworks have been alternately assigned a "probable" date of construction more than once in order to make them fit the known epigraphic warfare events: either to correspond to the A.D. 378 event at Tikal, or just after the A.D. 562 "star-war" event (Chase & Chase 1987: 60). Based on the archaeological evidence for the El Mirador Basin, even a possible Preclassic date (c. A.D. 200) has been suggested (see Haviland 2003: 137-139; Webster et al. 2004 for reviews of this dating dilemma). As previously stated, precise epigraphic dating of events is difficult to correlate to less precisely dated archaeological features. Though not impossible, extreme prudence is warranted in such situations.

Despite the recognized limitations and pitfalls of the epigraphic record in detailing interaction mechanisms, hieroglyphic inscriptions do still provide an invaluable resource in analyzing interpolity interactions. As with other forms of interaction discussed, local and subregional level interactions are considered greater intensity mechanisms affecting site and polity formation and development than epigraphically recorded long-distance interactions. However, the point of this section is not to summarize every epigraphically recorded interaction between Palenque and other sites (see Table 14.1). Instead the goal is to highlight how analysis of the epigraphic record alone can place equal importance on long-distance interactions and potentially more intense local and subregional interactions.

Palenque-Calakmul Interactions

The oft-cited warfare events by Calakmul against the Palenque polity occurred on 9.8.17.14.14 10 Ix 7 Pop (A.D. 611) and on 9.11.1.16.3 6 Ak'bal 1 Yax (A.D. 654), during the reigns of Aj Ne' Ohl Mat (r. A.D. 605-612) and K'inich Janab Pakal I (r. A.D. 615-683), respectively, although until recently (Miller & Martin 2004), the A.D. 654 event was considered to have occurred on 9.8.5.13.8 6 Lamat 1 Sip (A.D. 599) during the reign of Lady Yohl Ik'nal (r. 583-604). These events are recorded retrospectively on two monuments from the reign of K'inich Janab Pakal I. With the accession of K'inich Janab Pakal I, a break in Palenque's dynastic patrilineal succession occurred. Previous researchers have demonstrated how K'inich Janab Pakal I and his successors used these retrospective texts, highlighting a past defeat of Palenque, in conjunction with local ideology, as propaganda to legitimize their lineage's right to rule (Schele & Freidel 1990; Schele & Miller 1986). The manipulation of history and ideology in hieroglyphic texts by specific Palenque rulers has been thoroughly analyzed and does not need to be further elaborated here (see Stuart, Chapter 11).

As of yet there is little archaeological confirmation of the Calakmul warfare events, including the "throwing down" of the principle deities of the Palenque rulers (Grube 1996: 3). However, subsequent rulers would have repaired and/or cleaned up any destruction of the Palenque site core. Unfortunately, almost nothing is known about the archaeology of the Palenque ceremonial center during the period of the earlier, A.D. 611, Calakmul event.[17] In contrast, the archaeological record during the reign of K'inich Janab Pakal I is well documented. Neither the Temple Olvidado (dedicated in A.D. 647) nor the early buildings of the Palace show any signs of destruction or willful damage. Furthermore, construction activity at Palenque continues unabated. The South Subterraneos of the Palace were "dedicated" on 9.11.1.12.8 9 Lamat 6 Xul (A.D. 654) (Martin et al. 2002: II-24) just before the Calakmul "attack," and shortly after, House E of the Palace, containing K'inich Janab Pakal I's accession monument, the Oval Palace Tablet, was dedicated on 9.11.2.1.11 9 Chuwen 9 Mak (A.D. 654). It thus seems odd that Calakmul warriors would "throw down" the Palenque gods, yet leave no evidence of their presence.

It is unlikely that K'inich Janab Pakal I "invented" these military defeats, though it is possible that he embellished their severity. As one of the two longest distance warfare events in the epigraphic record,[18] it is likely that the Palenque-Calakmul wars did not result in political integration, and that little subsequent interaction occurred between the two sites. Neither event is recorded at Calakmul (as nearly all the monuments from that site are eroded), nor any of the secondary sites cited as possible alternate protagonists. While the ceramics from this period (Cascada and Otolum phases) have some correlates at the subregional level (see above), they show no affiliation with central lowland wares; an important archaeologically visible line of evidence for conquest is the sudden intrusion of new pottery styles (see Bey 2003; Webster 1998: 315). Although difficult to fully prove or disprove, the continuity in Cascada and Otolum phase ceramics and the distance between Palenque and Calakmul seem to preclude frequent and sustained intersite contact. Despite the lack of evidence for sustained interaction between Palenque and Calakmul, the retrospective use of these isolated events was an integral part of K'inich Janab Pakal I's legitimization program.

The Tikal-Palenque alliance

Also recorded on the House C hieroglyphic staircase and the Temple of the Inscriptions West Panel is the "arrival" at Palenque of an individual carrying the name of the contemporaneous Tikal ruler, Nuun Ujol Chaak, on 9.11.6.16.17 13 Kaban 10 Ch'en (A.D. 659). Originally interpreted by Linda Schele (1994: 3-4; see also Anaya 2001) as evidence of a Tikal-Palenque alliance, the "arrival" event reading has been since revised (Zender 2002). Six days prior to the "arrival" event Palencanos captured several named individuals from Pomona and the Wa-Bird site (believed to be the site of Santa Elena, Tabasco) on 9.11.6.16.11 7 Chuen 4 Ch'en (Martin et al. 2002). The emblem glyph of the Wa-Bird site matches that of the individual "arriving" at Palenque (Stuart, personal communication 2003).

It has been suggested that this "arrival" is indicative of an alliance between Palenque, the Wa-Bird site, and Yaxchilan (Martin et al. 2002: II-25), but as Wa-Bird lords are depicted as captives on the western substructure of House C an alliance between Palenque and the Wa-Bird site seems unlikely. Marc Zender (2002) has instead proposed that Palenque warriors defeated Pomona and the Wa-Bird site, returning to the site core with captives from both sites. According to the epigraphic record of the subregion, Wa-Bird/Santa Elena was a highly contested site between Palenque to the west and Piedras Negras to the east. The A.D. 659 "arrival" event could then be interpreted as an attempt by Palenque to extend or maintain the bounds of its political authority at the subregional level (see Golden 2003). However, until archaeological work is undertaken at Wa-Bird/Santa Elena this scenario remains speculative.

Copan-Palenque Connections

The southeastern Maya site of Copan, Honduras, has also been proposed as a late Late Classic ally of Palenque based on parentage statements of Yax Pasaj Chan Yopaat, the sixteenth ruler of Copan (r. A.D. 763-c.810) (Martin & Grube 2000: 209). Stela 8 at Copan records that the mother of Yax Pasaj Chan Yoaat, Lady Chak Nik Ye' Xook, originally came from Palenque (Fash & Stuart 1991: 167). Kinship ties and the exchange of women to form alliance and reciprocity networks are well documented anthropologically at nearly all levels of social complexity. There is also evidence that intersite elite marriages were used to socially tie elite lineages from different polities together (Marcus 1993: 141-142), especially at the local and subregional levels.

At Copan, having a Palencano woman as the ruler's mother appears to have been emically important, as she is named in several inscriptions, while Yax Pasaj Chan Yoaat's father is rarely mentioned (Martin & Grube 2000: 209). Furthermore, Stela A (A.D. 730) of Copan marks Palenque, along with Copan, Tikal, and Calakmul, as one of the four major regional Maya capitals of the late Late Classic (see Marcus 1976).[19] It is thus rather clear that the late Copan rulers sought to use their kinship ties to Palenque to help legitimize their diminishing local authority (Fash 2001).

At Palenque however, Copan is never mentioned in the inscriptions and there is no archaeological evidence at either site to suggest frequent and sustained contact. The marriage of Lady Chak Nik Ye' Xook to a high ranking elite (it is unclear if he was ever a ruler) of Copan had little effect within the Palenque polity. Otherwise, the elite of Palenque would likely have mentioned this connection on one of several hieroglyphic monuments of the period. While these two sites, at the opposite peripheries of the Classic Maya, area share numerous similarities in eccentricity and Late Classic breakdown in centralized political authority, there is nothing to suggest that the single recorded kinship tie between the two sites resulted in any real form of political alliance or integration. This is not unexpected given the distance and unprotected[20] overland route between the two centers.

Local and Subregional Interactions

Space constraints prevent dealing with each and every epigraphically record-ed interaction event between Palenque and their local and subregional neighbors. We shall only briefly discuss the more frequently named interaction sites and refer the reader to the numerous epigraphic studies of the Palenque region (e.g., Bernal Romero 2002; Grube 1996; Guenter 2002; Martin 2003; Martin & Grube 2000; Mathews 1991, 2000; Schele 1991). Nor will we delve into the warfare events un-dertaken by the *sajal* (sublord) of K'inich Ahkal Mo' Nahb III, Chak Sutz', from A.D. 723-730 against the locations of "La" (location unknown, but also men-tioned at Bonampak), "Kinal" (Piedras Negras), "Ko-?" (location unknown), and "Ch'onal" (location unknown) (see Table 14.1).

The Wa-Bird/Santa Elena and Pomona warfare events shall not be reiterated, although a brief comment on the inscribed jade pendant discovered in Temple XII-sub at Palenque (Temple Oscuro) may elucidate postwarfare interactions (López Jiménez 2001). The Calendar Round date of the inscription of this carved jade pendant corresponds to 9.13.5.0.0 1 Ajaw 3 Pop (A.D. 697), incidentally after the death of the Pomona ruler named in the pendant inscription (Stanley Guenter, per-sonal communication 2003). It is possible that the Oscuro pendant was given to the Palenque elite as tribute or war booty, but tribute likely deemed of little value to the Pomona elite as the named ruler had already passed away.

Throughout its dynastic history, kinship ties connected Palenque to several lo-cal sites, such as the unidentified site of Ux Te' K'uh and the possible unidentified site of K'an Tok (see below). The Temple of the Sun sanctuary doorjamb panel in-scription names an individual from Ux Te' K'uh related to K'inich Kan Bahlam II of Palenque, possibly his maternal grandfather (Stuart, personal communication 2004). This individual is again mentioned on the Temple XIX west platform panel. According to the inscription from the Temple XXI platform panel, the mother of K'inich Ahkal Mo' Nahb III also came from Ux Te' K'uh (González Cruz & Ber-nal Romero 2003: 26). The central figure on the Temple XIX west bench panel, Sajal Bolon, carries the glyph *aj-ux-te'-k'uh* ("he from Ux Te' K'uh") in his name and is related to K'inich Ahkal Mo' Nahb III as well. The familial ties between the elites of Palenque and Ux Te' K'uh indicate that another polity using the Palenque emblem glyph, Tortuguero, Tabasco, was not an ally of the Palenque elites (see Martin & Grube [2000] and Guenter [2002] for a full discussion), at least during the reign of its most prominent ruler Bahlam Ajaw (r. A.D. 644-679). Excavations at Tortuguero have uncovered Palenque-style "tier-of-heads" *incensarios* (Arellano Hernández 1996), but the ceramics show fundamental differences (Bishop, personal communication 2002). Glyphic evidence, combined with the identified *incensarios* indicates that Tortuguero elites participated in the subregional sweat-bath cult (Child, Chapter 12).

According to the inscription from the K'an Tok Tablet from Temple XVI at Palenque, during the Classic period several individuals were "installed into the office of K'an Tok" by the rulers of Palenque (Bernal Romero 2002).[21] On 9.0.0.5.9 3 Muluk 17 Muwan (A.D. 445) the second Palenque ruler, nicknamed "Casper," "oversaw" the accession of his younger brother to the office of K'an Tok (Bernal 2002). Much later, another individual related to the Palenque royal lineage (Stuart, Chapter 11), named Janab Ajaw, was "installed" as K'an Tok by K'inich K'an Joy Chitam II (A.D. 718) (Stuart 2003: 2). On the Temple XIX south platform panel at Palenque, Janab Ajaw is depicted impersonating the deity Itzamnah at the accession of K'inich Ahkal Mo' Nahb III (r. A.D. 721-c.740) and handing him the rulership headband (Stuart, Chapter 11). Thus multiple Classic holders of the office of K'an Tok were members of the Palenque royal lineage, and the lack of interregional glyphic events recorded at Palenque after A.D. 730 demonstrate the overarching concern of the Palenque rulers with the internal interworkings of the polity. This shift is accompanied by post-A.D. 730 construction of "gallery-structures" (see Straight, Chapter 10) with elaborate platform thrones indicative of formal private meeting areas.

Tonina

One of Palenque's best-known "rivals" in the western lowland subregion was the site of Tonina to the south in the Ococingo Valley, Chiapas. Although located in the Chiapan highlands, Tonina has all the hallmarks of Classic Maya culture—stelae, hieroglyphic writing, Maya vaults, etc. A small site (estimated 660 inhabitants), Tonina was nevertheless the dominant Late Classic center of the Ocosingo Valley (Becquelin 1979). Like Palenque, Tonina was a peripheral Classic Maya site exhibiting local particularities in art and ceramic traditions. Aside from a few isolated architectural and sculptural similarities (Mateos González 1996), such as the aforementioned Temple of the Cross stela (at Palenque) and the Frieze of the Dream Lords (at Tonina), the only available evidence of interaction with Palenque comes from the epigraphic record of both sites (see Table 14.1).

The inscriptions from Palenque and Tonina record back and forth "capture" events between the two sites, including the "capture" of Ruler 2 of Tonina by K'inich Kan Bahlam II of Palenque in A.D. 687 (Mathews 2001). This event is soon followed by the erection of Palenque's only carved stela (A.D. 692), which is in the style of Tonina stelae. These events culminate in the "capture" of K'inich K'an Joy Chitam II (r. A.D. 702-711?), the Palenque ruler, and a "star-war" event, presumably against Palenque on 9.13.19.13.3 13 Ak'bal 16 Yax (A.D. 711). Yet there are several problems with this interpretation of K'inich K'an Joy Chitam II's capture. First, House AD of the Palace at Palenque was dedicated by K'inich K'an Joy Chitam II in A.D. 720 as recorded on the Palace Tablet (Schele 1986: 111). Second, the K'an Tok Tablet records K'inich K'an Joy Chitam II "overseeing" the accession of the aforementioned Janab Ajaw to the office of K'an Tok on 9.14.7.0.15 6 Men 13 K'ank'in (A.D. 718) (Bernal 2002; Stuart 2003: 2). Finally, K'inich K'an Joy Chitam II is mentioned on Piedras Negras Stela 8 (A.D. 714) participating in an event with the rulers from Piedras Negras and Santa Elena (Stuart 2003).

David Stuart has proposed that K'inich K'an Joy Chitam II continued to rule at Palenque following his defeat by Tonina, "perhaps even for several years under the watchful eye of Tonina's ruler" (2003: 3).[22] While we agree with Stuart's general interpretation that K'inich K'an Joy Chitam II continued to rule at Palenque after A.D. 711, there is little evidence of Tonina influence at Palenque following his "capture." Palencano style stucco sculpture at Tonina may be the only indication that Tonina exerted material influence on Palenque. As mentioned above, it is difficult to differentiate between shared ethnic traits and direct interaction, especially within a single subregional style.

A somewhat similar Late Classic epigraphic case has been extensively documented in the southeastern Maya lowlands. At the Classic Maya center of Copan, the decapitation of the thirteenth ruler, Waxklahun Ubab K'awil (18-Rabbit) at the hands of the somewhat distant and smaller polity of Quirigua was recorded epigraphically (Fash & Stuart 1991). Research from both Quirigua and Copan demonstrate that the former experienced a period of unprecedented construction in the ten years following the capture of "18-Rabbit," while at the latter little construction occurred and no monuments were erected during the same period (Sharer 1991, personal communication 2004). In contrast, the site of Palenque saw decades of architectural growth and new inscriptions following the "capture" of K'inich K'an Joy Chitam II by the smaller and distant site of Tonina. These examples indicate the variability in how violent conflict between sites may have affected archaeologically visible growth. We are however uncertain as to what archaeologically visible influence may have occurred during these times, such as how tribute or political control were affected and enforced.

Conclusion

Clearly in the Late Classic, Palenque was a major center of the western Maya lowlands, maintaining frequent, and at times sustained, interaction with surrounding sites at the local and subregional levels. At the local level these ties are most strongly manifested in economic and ideological interactions. At the subregional level, economic interactions nearly disappear, and ideological interactions seem to fade into a more loose-knit, indirect form of emulation and ideological sharing. While numerous political interactions occurred at the subregional level, and multiple interactions occurred between Palenque and specific subregional sites, these periods of interaction do not appear to have been very long-term—after a decade or so, neither site mentioned the other again. This contrasts with political interactions at the local level. Although few local sites are recorded in the inscriptions of Palenque, Ux Te' K'uh was frequently cited in later texts, and kinship ties between Ux Te' K'uh elites and the Palenque elite hint at sustained and long-term interaction.

One possible exception to the short-lived subregional interaction trend was the relationship between Palenque and the site of Piedras Negras, Guatemala. During the late Early Classic (Palenque's Cascada phase) ceramics from the two centers share some analogs, and the elite from both sites seem to have been heavily involved in the subregional sweathbath cult during the Late Classic. Architecturally, the Late Classic Temple of the Inscriptions at Palenque and Structure O-13 at Piedras Negras are nearly identical; both pyramid substructures have the same number of terraces and both superstructures have five doorways, and were constructed in front of large terraced hills (Héctor Escobedo, personal communication 2004). The two recorded warfare events between the two sites are significantly separated in time (A.D. 624 and A.D. 725), hinting at persistent intersite antagonism. Yet the mention of K'inich K'an Joy Chitam II on Piedras Negras Stela 8 shows that both friendly and antagonistic interactions occurred between the sites, and that intersite relations were ever shifting.[23]

One of the strengths of using multiple data sets to examine interactions at various geographic scales, especially when evaluating epigraphic data, is how it demonstrates and highlights the differing emic importance of events at one site versus another. For example, the Copan-Palenque connection was deemed of some importance by late Late Classic rulers at Copan, but not by their Palencano contemporaries. Conversely, the Calakmul-Palenque warfare events were used by K'inich Janab Pakal I as propaganda to legitimize the authority of his lineage, although due to the eroded nature of the hieroglyphic record at Calakmul we are unaware if the events were recorded at that site. From an etic perspective, as of yet the Calakmul-Palenque events have no material corroboration in the known archaeological record, and it is unclear at present what effect they may have had on the development of the settlement pattern and political organization of the Palenque polity. However, in Early Classic Motiepa times, prior to the Calakmul events, ceramic imports from the central lowlands may have inspired Palenque potters. These early influences were incorporated into, and adapted to local ceramic traditions. Altogether, the data from Palenque and its local areas does not support the super-state model in the western Maya lowlands, which ignores the varying importance of different sorts of interactions at multiple scales, as well as the variability between centers across the Classic Maya area.

In this chapter we have attempted to establish how combinations of interaction mechanisms may have contributed in establishing intrapolity integration and how interaction can manifest itself differently at different scales of analysis. During the late Late Classic occupation of Palenque, Tabasco plain ceramic pastes increase in frequency (Rands & Bishop 1980). At the same time, while emergent sites in this area show ties to Palenque-made pottery (Liendo, Chapter 5), Palenque's hinterland settlement increased and the elites of Ux Te' K'uh became more politically "intertwined" with the Palencano elite. If this site is eventually discovered, analysis of its ceramic and architectural assemblages could reveal whether economic and/or ideological interactions coincided with their strong Palencano political affiliation.

Throughout this chapter we have intentionally avoided the ongoing debate in Maya studies as to whether Classic Maya polities should be considered centralized or segmentary states (Fox et al. 1996). A priori, our approach favors neither model; "a simple dichotomy between two models sometimes blinds us to important details of political and economic organization" (Inomata & Aoyama 1996: 308). Instead a middle-ground between the two models as suggested by Marcello Canuto and William Fash (2004) may be a preferable line of investigation. Unfortunately research in the Palenque site core glaringly lacks archaeological investigation at the household level. This deficiency in data on core and hinterland demography and settlement precludes discussion at Palenque of bottom-up mechanisms of site community development and evolution. Partly for these reasons, we have emphasized interactions at the local and subregional levels in a conjunctive framework (Fash & Sharer 1991). The available data concerning Palenque's economic and ideological interactions do not demonstrate that the Palencano elite directly controlled ceramic exchange, nor that they were able to develop a large subregional state that imposed identical architectural and art styles on their subregional peers, although there is evidence for occasional, but unsustained hegemonic interaction. Conversely, Palenque's relative ceramic (and lithic [Johnson 1976]) isolation indicates that Palenque was never incorporated into any regional Maya super-state. The evidence from Palenque serves as an example of the very real diversity in material culture across the Classic Maya world.

Politically, Palenque was an important western Classic Maya site, but rarely became embroiled in interpolity politics outside its subregion. Epigraphically recorded long-distance "violent events," such as the ones between Calakmul and Palenque, and the appearance of the Palenque emblem glyph at sites such as Copan and Altar de los Reyes hint at larger political "spheres of interaction." Unfortunately, we do not yet have a full conception of essential details and contexts of long-distance interaction, such as the social/economic/ideological motives and/or consequences to different types of long-distance interaction, that could enable more interregional interpretations of ancient Maya history and culture. However, the impressive Late Classic architectural and sculptural traditions, as well as the abundance of imported greenstone in funerary contexts, support the notion that the Palenque rulers did not view themselves as anyone's subordinates. While similarities in ceramic and art styles are more apparent and pervasive at smaller spatial scales, variability between sites, even locally, indicate presently undetermined levels of autonomy within archaeologically reconstructable polities, possibly coinciding with ecological niches on a micro-regional scale.

Notes

[1] In contrast, the archaeological and epigraphic records at Copan, Honduras, do overlap through much of the site's occupation history (for a recent synopsis of the Early Classic at Copan, based on both archaeological and epigraphic data see Bell et al. [2004]).

[2] Roberto López Bravo of INAH is currently undertaking a test-pitting program throughout the Palenque site core. The Proyecto Crecimiento Urban de la Antigua Cuidad de Palenque (PCU) has identified several architectural groups with substantial Preclassic and Early Classic material (see López Bravo 2003, 2004).

[3] Hirth (1992) cites Drennan's (1984) estimate of 275 km as the maximum distance for a one-way human porter to travel with a full load. Others have questioned such a high estimate. See Malville (2001) for a review of travel costs, maximum distances, and average weight of human porter loads from cross-cultural examples.

[4] The label "super-state" is one originally applied by Martin and Grube (1995). In this chapter we have opted to continue to use this term in order to more succinctly discuss possible Classic hegemonies. While we have retained the unfortunate moniker "super-state model," derived from the title of Martin and Grube's (1995) *Archaeology* magazine article, it is noted that this is not a formal model of any kind. Furthermore, the article does not so much propose "super-states" as stress the current state of known epigraphic references concerning political relationships among Classic period Maya polities. In subsequent works, Martin and Grube (2000) have downplayed the term "super-states" in preference of the term "superpower" when making reference to Calakmul.

[5] While some glyphic expressions have been formally translated, others remain obscure. In particular, the "star-shell," or "star-war," glyphic compound has resisted decipherment, though it is certainly a verb. The *u-kahiiy* agency expression upon which so many "overlordship" relations rest has alternately been glossed as "he did it," "in the land of" (Schele & Freidel 1990), and "under the auspices of" (Martin & Grube 2000). The *hubiiy* "thrown down" verb, often in conjunction with the phrase *u-tok' u- pakal*, is generally considered to refer to the sacking of a center, although this phrase may alternately pertain to armed conflict and the "defeat" of an opposing force. The expressions, *chukaah* ("capture"), *u-baak'* ("his prisoner"), *u-chaan* ("his captor"), *yete* ("his captor," or "his owner"), and the *a-baak'* ("captive count") expression all relate to the taking and retaining of prisoners.

[6] The monument recording this particular "star-war" event is located at Caracol, and the glyph upon which Calakmul's involvement is based has never been legible. Martin and Grube (2000) argue that the name glyph for the contemporaneous Calakmul ruler could fit into the eroded glyphic cartouche naming the protagonist of the "star-war" event of Altar 21 at Caracol. However, Classic Maya scribes were well skilled in their craft, and could likely fit innumerable variable glyphic spellings into any cartouche. An example of this at Palenque is the name glyph K'inich Ahkal Mo' Nahb. This name, used by three separate Palencano rulers, is one of the most commonly recorded names at Palenque and demonstrates the cornucopia of variable spellings of ruler names available to Classic Maya scribes. For decades, the spelling of this name glyph was considered standardized until the

recent recovery of monuments from Temples XIX and XXI at Palenque revealed another two forms of the name (see Stuart, Chapter 11; see also Coe & Van Stone [2001: 81] for five glyphic spellings of K'inich Ahkal Mo' Nahb'). Likewise, the Caracol emblem glyph (which is an aberrant emblem glyph in that no "*ajaw*" postfix in conjunction with a top-onym is ever present) shows extreme variation in glyphic rendering. Furthermore, there is precedent at Caracol (Altar 23) for using the *u-kahiiy* compound to link the actions of one Caracol ruler to another Caracol ruler.

Since C. C. Coggins' (1975) work at Tikal, researchers have noted archaeological evidence of obtrusive influence from the region east or southeast of Tikal based on tomb occupants (Coggins 1975: 333, 379, 386), mortuary practices (Chase & Chase 1987: 15, 43), architectural "grammar" (Becker 2003: 269, 274-275), settlement patterns (Haviland 2003: 141), ceramics (Culbert 2003: 81; also compare Culbert [1993: Figs. 39-42] with Chase & Chase [1987: 16-17, Fig. 11], especially Arlen Chase's observation that the "ajaw" vessels correlate with the Uaxactun type) and stone monument styles and dates (Chase & Chase 1987: 61).

[7] Nearly all theoretical models thus far applied to the Classic Maya have proved inadequate in describing the variation seen in the archaeological record (Sharer & Golden 2004). Despite the usefulness and applicability of its assumptions in analyzing Maya polities, the peer polity model as a developmental explanation is likewise deficient is some respects. While further work is necessary to substantiate some claims, it currently appears unlikely that the site of El Mirador, Guatemala had any "peers" in the Maya area during the Preclassic period, although William Folan has forwarded Preclassic Calakmul as a definite peer (and rival) of El Mirador (Pennsylvania State University Mesoamerican Urbanism Conference held September 17-24, 2004, William Sanders presiding). Certainly during the Late Classic some Maya centers were clearly larger, had earlier developmental sequences, and housed more influential elites, than others. However, the number of large and materially "wealthy" sites increases with every new major archaeological project in the lowlands.

[8] This has been demonstrated in the Palenque ceremonial center by extensive excavations by both INAH and foreign archaeological projects (see Marken, Chapter 4). While recent test pit excavations elsewhere in the site core by the PCU have discovered earlier archaeological deposits to the west of the ceremonial center, these deposits lack significant stratigraphic depth as well (López Bravo 2003, 2004).

[9] While Yalcox Fine Blacks are known sporadically from the Cascada phase on, their greatest frequency is just prior to, and concurrent with, the influence of Chablekal Fine Gray wares.

[10] While the only securely identified ruler's tomb at Palenque is that of K'inich Janab Pakal I, the similarities in burial goods, and funerary architecture between Pakal the Great's tomb and those of Temples XVIIIa-sub and XX-sub suggest that both the latter were also the burials of Palencano rulers (Marken 2003).

[11] The recently recovered Late Preclassic mural painting at San Bartolo, Guatemala, contains a hieroglyphic phrase ending with a probable early version of the *ajaw* glyph (Taube, et al. 2004), suggesting the antiquity of glyphic Mayan.

[12] We have used the term "pantheon" for convenience; however, we acknowledge that the distinctions among "gods," "deity aspects," "supernaturals," and other representations are not always clear.

[13] Compare Altar 4 at El Cayo (A.D. 731) to the Lápida de los Ayudantes (A.D. 734) from Palenque Temple XIX. Interestingly, the carver's signature on El Cayo Altar 4 indicates that he was a Piedras Negras lord (Martin & Grube 2000: 150). Other Piedras Negras sculptors were responsible for producing monuments at both Piedras Negras and El Cayo (Martin & Grube 2000: 153).

[14] The Classic Maya hieroglyphic/iconographic record is fully consistent with raiding and limited warfare. For instance, no u-baak' ("count of captives") title records the taking of more than twenty captives, though this is open for further interpretation. Most securely deciphered glyphic compounds relate specifically to the taking and "owning" of captives (see above). By analogy, the Postclassic Mexica maintained a state of perpetual war with their traditional enemies, the Tlaxcalans, supplying a constant influx of sacrificial victims, as well as a ready training ground for young warriors. As Leon-Portilla (1962: xli) explains, "regardless of the ostensible purpose of a military campaign—to conquer new territory, punish a rebelious vassal state, or repel an aggressor—the Aztec warriors never forgot that their first duty was to take captives to be sacrificed."

[15] This conception of unfortified western Maya sites should change in the near future. Stanley Guenter (personal communication 2004) has informed us that there are several fortified sites near Boca del Cerro, Tabasco, and Edwin Roman (personal communication 2004) and Charles Golden (Golden et al. 2004) have also encountered walls near the site of Tecolote, Guatemala, while doing reconnaissance in the Sierra Lacandon. However, as of yet no archaeological work has been undertaken to determine neither the chronological placement of these features, nor to confirm their possible functions. Even the oft-cited Tikal "defensive earthworks" (Puleston & Callendar 1967) are in no way securely dated, nor their exact configuration and function known (Webster et al. 2004.) It appears that considerable variation exists in size, construction, and probable function of "walls," or "perimeters" around sites.

[16] Evidence for possible siege-like warfare is available from the Terminal Classic Petexbatun area (Demarest 2004), demonstrating that at times, and at least in certain subregions, conflictive groups could be mobilized to attack or defend sites.

[17] The known archaeological deposits from Palenque corresponding to the Cascada phase (the A.D. 611 event) are few, although they include the Temple XVIIIa-sub and Temple XX-sub tombs, one subfloor tomb from behind Temple XV, and excavations behind the North Group (Temple VIII) (Marken, Chapter 4; Rands, personal communication 2003, 2004). Mixed Cascada deposits also underlie the Temple of the Count (Rands 1974a, 1974b). It is possible that the early excavations in the Palace at Palenque may have missed or not recognized the sorts of termination deposits that could confirm these epigraphic warfare events. That termination deposits similar to those identified elsewhere in the Maya area (e.g., Pagliaro, Garber & Stanton 2003; Sharer 2004) are present at Palenque is clear from the Temple XIX excavations, supervised by the authors as part of the PGC, as well as from the INAH-sponsored Temple XXI excavations (González Cruz 2003). Whether these termination deposits were "desecratory" or "reverential" (Pagliaro, Garber & Stanton 2003) is difficult to determine, although we tend to view the Temple XIX deposits as reverential (see Straight, Chapter 10).

[18] The other is the attack on Dos Pilas by Calakmul in A.D. 650 (Houston 1993).

[19] Altar 3 from the site of Altar de los Reyes in southeastern Campeche records thirteen different emblem glyphs, including that of Palenque (Sprajc 2003), indicating the emic

importance of the Palenque polity within the Classic Maya political landscape, along with several other contemporaneous Classic Maya centers.

[20] While the exaction of tribute from "conquered" centers is expected and assumed, to our knowledge no clear model of how this system worked has been proposed. We stress the fact that a raiding or war party contact is quite a different situation than sustained movement of precious goods, which requires a secure land route.

[21] Guillermo Bernal Romero (2002) and Arnoldo González Cruz (González Cruz & Bernal Romero 2000) consider K'an Tok to be a nearby Classic Maya site, possibly Jonuta, Tabasco. Berthold Riese (2001) has raised some objections to the identification of Jonuta as K'an Tok. Furthermore, neither David Stuart (personal communication 2004) nor Stanley Guenter (personal communication 2004) believe that the K'an Tok glyph is a toponym. Instead they feel that K'an Tok was some sort of "priestly" office closely tied to the Palenque ruling elite. The carving of the K'an Tok Tablet would then coincide with the increasing presence of subregnal elites in the Palenque epigraphic record during the late Late Classic. However, if future epigraphic analysis does confirm that K'an Tok is indeed a location, it would only further support our general impression that the Palencano rulers were most directly concerned with their local "political" connections. For example, if K'an Tok is another site, multiple Classic rulers of K'an Tok were members of Palenque's ruling lineage, indicating that a high degree of political integration existed between the two sites. The size of Palenque and its superordinate status in the inscriptions would then indicate that the Palenque elite had some sort of political control over K'an Tok. However, Janab Ajaw's position on the Temple XIX south platform would demonstrate the potentially reciprocal relationship between primary and secondary Classic Maya sites.

[22] Personally, we question the accepted placement of the Calendar Round date 13 Ak'bal 16 Yax in the Long Count at 9.13.19.13.3. If the Calendar Round date is moved forward one cycle (52 years), the "capture" event would occur on 9.16.12.8.3 13 Ak'bal 16 Yax (A.D. 763), less than a year before the accession of K'inich K'uk' Bahlam II on 9.16.13.0.7 9 Manik' 15 Wo (A.D. 764). However, as there is no currently known ruler named K'inich K'an Joy Chitam during this period, this possibility remains speculation.

[23] Early Spanish contact period accounts make it clear that human messengers or "ambassadors" throughout the Basin of Mexico and beyond were traditionally allowed safe passage in order to keep lines of communication open among centers, even traditional enemies (Leon-Portilla 1962: 46). A lowland Maya example of developing relations following "warfare" can be found in the monuments of Caracol. While Altar 23 (A.D. 800) depicts a bound captive from Ucanal, two altars (12 and 13) erected twenty years later (A.D. 820) portray the ruler of Ucanal and the king of Caracol engaged in what appear to be joint activities (Martin & Grube 2000: 98).

References

Adams, Richard E. W. and Richard C. Jones
    1981   Spatial Patterns and Regional Grown among Classic Maya Cities. *American Antiquity* 46(2):301-322.
Andrews, E. Wyllys IV and E. Wyllys Andrews V
    1980   *Excavations at Dzibilchaltun, Yucatan, Mexico.* Middle American Research Institute Publication 48, New Orleans, LA.

Andrews, George F.
1975   *Maya Cities: Placemaking and Urbanization.* University of Oklahoma Press, Norman.
1989   *Comalaclco, Tabasco, Mexico: Maya Art and Architecture.* 2nd edition. Labyrinthos, Culver City, CA.
1995   Arquitectura maya. *Arqueología Mexicana* 2(11):4-12.

Aoyama, Kazuo
1999   *Ancient Maya State, Urbanism, Exchange, and Craft Specialization.* University of Pittsburgh Memoirs in Latin American Archaeology No. 12, Pittsburgh, PA.

Anaya Hernández, Armando
2001   *Site Interaction and Political Geography of the Upper Usumacinta Region during the Late Classic: A GIS Approach.* BAR International Series 994. Hadrian Books Ltd., Oxford, U.K.

Arellano Hernández, Alfonso
1996   Algunas Notas Sobre Tortuguero, Tabasco. In *Eighth Palenque Round Table–1993,* edited by Merle Greene Robertson, Martin Macri, and Jan McHargue, pp. 135-142. Pre-Columbian Art Research Institute, San Francisco, CA.

Arnold, Dean E.
1985   *Ceramic Theory and Cultural Process.* Cambridge University Press, Cambridge, U.K.

Barnhart, Edwin L.
2001   *The Palenque Mapping Project: Settlement and Urbanism at an Ancient Maya City.* Unpublished Ph.D. dissertation, University of Texas, Austin.

Becker, Marshall J.
2003   Plaza Plans at Tikal: A Research Strategy for Inferring Social Organization and Processes of Culture Change at Lowland Maya Sites. In *Tikal: Dynasties, Foreigners, & Affairs of State,* edited by Jeremy A. Sabloff, pp. 253-280. School of American Research Press, Santa Fe, NM.

Becquelin, Pierre
1979   Tonina, a City-State of the Western Maya Periphery. Paper presented at the XLIII International Congress of Americanists, Vancouver, Canada.

Bell, Ellen E., Marcello A. Canuto, and Robert J. Sharer, eds.
2004   *Understanding Early Classic Copan.* University Museum, University of Pennsylvania, Philadelphia.

Berlin, Heinrich
1956   Late Pottery Horizons of Tabasco, Mexico. *Contributions to American Anthropology and History* 11(59):95-153. Publication 606. Carnegie Institution of Washington, Washington, D.C.
1958   El glifo emblema en las inscripciones mayas. *Journal de la Société de Américanistes* 47:111-19
1963   The Palenque Triad. *Journal de la Société des Américanistes* 52:91-99.

Bernal Romero, Guillermo
    2002   Análisis epigráfico del Tablero de K'an Tok, Palenque, Chiapas. In *La Organización Social Entre los Mayas. Memoria de la Tercera Mesa Redonda de Palenque, Vol. I*, edited by V. Tiesler Blos, R. Cobos, and M. Greene Robertson, pp. 307-327. Conaculta-INAH, Mexico, D.F.

Bey, George J., III
    2003   The Role of Ceramics in the Study of Conflict in Maya Archaeology. In *Ancient Mesoamerican Warfare*, edited by M. Kathryn Brown and Travis W. Stanton, pp. 19-30. AltaMira Press, Walnut Creek, CA.

Bishop, Ronald L.
    1975   *Western Lowland Maya Ceramic Trade: An Archaeological Application of Nuclear Chemical Geological Data Analysis*. Unpublished Ph.D. dissertation, Southern Illinois University, Carbondale.

    1994   Pre-Columbian Pottery: Research in the Maya Region. In *Archaeometry of Pre-Columbian Sites*, edited by David A. Scott and Pieter Meyers, pp. 15-66. The Getty Conservation Institute, Los Angeles, CA.

Bishop, Ronald L., Robert L. Rands, and Garman Harbottle
    1982   A Ceramic Compositional Interpretation of Incense-Burner Trade in the Palenque Area, Mexico. In *Nuclear and Chemical Dating Techniques*, edited by L. A. Currie, pp. 411-440. ACS Symposium Series 176. American Chemical Society, Washington, D.C.

Bishop, Ronald L., Robert L. Rands, and George R. Holley
    1982   Ceramic Compositional Analysis in Archaeological Perspective. *Advances in Archaeological Methods and Theory, Vol. 5*, edited by Michael B. Schiffer, pp. 275-330. Academic Press, New York.

Bishop, Ronald L., Erin L. Sears, and M. James Blackman
    2004   A Través del Rio del Cambio. Paper presented at the Congreso Internacional de Mayistas. Villahermosa, Tabasco, Mexico. July 11-17, 2004.

Blom, Franz
    1923   *Las Ruinas de Palenque, Xupá y Finca Encanto*. INAH, Mexico, D.F.

Blom, Franz and Oliver La Farge
    1926   *Tribes and Temples: A Record of the Expedition to Middle America Conducted by the Tulane University of Louisiana in 1925, Vols. I & II*. Tulane University of Louisiana, New Orleans, LA.

Brady, James E., Joseph W. Ball, Ronald L. Bishop, Duncan C. Pring, Norman Hammond, and Rupert A. Housley
    1998   The Lowland Maya "Protoclassic": A Reconsideration of Its Nature and Significance. *Ancient Mesoamerica* 9(1):17-38.

Braswell, Geoffrey E., Joel D. Gunn, María del Rosario Domínguez Carrasco, William J. Folan, Laraine A. Fletcher, Abel Morales López, and Michael D. Glascock
    2004   Defining the Terminal Classic at Calakmul, Campeche. In *The Terminal Classic in the Maya Lowlands*, edited by Arthur A. Demarest, Prudence M. Rice, and Don S. Rice, pp. 162-194. University Press of Colorado, Boulder.

Canuto, Marcello A., and William L. Fash
    2004   The Blind Spot: Where the Elite and Non-Elite Meet. In *Continuities and Changes in Maya Archaeology: Perspectives at the Millennium*, edited by Charles W. Golden and Greg Borgstede, pp. 51-75. Routledge Press, New York.

Carr, R. F. and J. E. Hazard
    1961   *Map of the Ruins of Tikal, El Peten, Guatemala*. Tikal Report No. 11. University Museum Monograph 21, University of Pennsylvania, Philadelphia.

Chase, Arlen F. and Diane Z. Chase
    1987   *Investigations at the Classic Maya Center of Caracol, Belize: 1985-1987*. Pre-Columbian Art Research Institute Monograph 3, San Francisco, CA.

Chisholm, Michael
    1968   *Rural Settlement and Land Use*. Hutchinson & Co. Ltd., London, U.K.

Coe, Michael D.
    1989   *Breaking the Maya Code*. Thames & Hudson, New York, NY.

Coe, Michael D. and Mark Van Stone
    2001   *Reading the Maya Glyphs*. Thames & Hudson, London, U.K.

Coggins, Clemency C.
    1975   *Painting and Drawing Styles at Tikal: An Historical and Iconographic Reconstruction*. Unpublished Ph.D. dissertation, Harvard University, Cambridge, MA.

Culbert, T. Patrick
    2003   The Ceramics of Tikal. In *Tikal: Dynasties, Foreigners, & Affairs of State*, edited by Jeremy A. Sabloff, pp. 47-82. School of American Research Press, Santa Fe, NM.

Culbert, T. Patrick, ed.
    1991   *Classic Maya Political History: Hieroglyphic and Archaeological Evidence*. Cambridge University Press, Cambridge, U.K.

    1993   *The Ceramics of Central Tikal*. Tikal Reports No. 25A. University Museum Publications, University of Pennsylvania, Philadelphia.

de Montmollin, Olivier
    1989   *The Archaeology of Political Structure: Settlement Analysis in a Classic Maya Polity*. Cambridge University Press, Cambridge, U.K.

Demarest, Arthur A.
    1992   Ideology in Ancient Maya Cultural Evolution: The Dynamics of Galactic Polities. In *Ideology and Pre-Columbian Civilizations*, edited by Arthur A. Demarest and Geoffrey W. Conrad, pp. 135-157. School of American Research Press, Santa Fe, NM.

    2004   After the Maelstrom: Collapse of the Classic Maya Kingdoms and the Terminal Classic in Western Petén. In *The Terminal Classic in the Maya Lowlands*, edited by Arthur A. Demarest, Prudence M. Rice, and Don S. Rice, pp. 102-124. University Press of Colorado, Boulder.

Drennan, Robert D.
    1984   Long-Distance Transport Costs in Pre-Hispanic Mesoamerica. *American Anthropologist* 86:105-112.

Fash, William L.
2001   Scribes, Warriors and Kings: The City of Copan and the Ancient Maya. Revised Edition. Thames & Hudson, London.

Fash, William L. and Barbara W. Fash
2000   Teotihuacan and the Maya: A Classic Heritage. In Mesoamerica's Classic Heritage: From Teotihuacan to the Aztecs, edited by D. Carrasco, L. Jones, and S. Sessions, pp. 433-463. University of Colorado Press, Niwot.

Fash, William L. and Robert J. Sharer
1991   Sociopolitical Developments and Methodological Issues at Copan, Honduras: A Conjunctive Approach. Latin American Antiquity 2(2):166-187.

Fash, William L. and David Stuart
1991   Dynastic History and Cultural Evolution at Copan, Honduras. In Classic Maya Political History, edited by T. Patrick Culbert, pp. 147-179. Cambridge University Press, Cambridge, U.K.

Fox, John W., Garrett W. Cook, Arlen F. Chase, and Diane Z. Chase
1996   Questions of Political and Economic Integration: Segmentary versus Centralized States among the Ancient Maya. Current Anthropology 37(5): 795-801.

Fry, Robert E.
1990   Disjunctive Growth in the Maya Lowlands. In Precolumbian Population History in the Maya Lowlands, edited by T. Patrick Culbert and Don S. Rice, pp. 285-300. University of New Mexico Press, Albuquerque.

Gallegos Gomora, M. Judith
1997   Forma, Materiales y Decoracion: La Arquitectura de Comalcalco. In Los Investigadores de la Cultura Maya 5(1), 212-226. Universidad Autonoma de Campeche, Mexico.

García Moll, Roberto, ed.
1991   Palenque 1926-1945. Antologias. Serie Arqueologia. INAH, Mexico, D.F.

Geertz, Clifford
1973   The Interpretation of Cultures. Basic Books, New York.

González Cruz, Arnoldo
2003   Los Templos XXI y XXII. Dos Monumentos Arqueológicos Explorados en Palenque, Chiapas. Lakamha' 2(9):4-9.

González Cruz, Arnoldo and Guillermo Bernal Romero
2000   Grupo XVI de Palenque: Conjunto arquitectónico de la nobleza provincial. Arqueología Mexicana VIII(45):20-25.

2003   The Throne of Ahkal Mo' Nahb' III: A Unique Finding at Palenque. INAH/ Nestlé, Mexico, D.F.

Golden, Charles W.
2003   The Politics of Warfare in the Usumacinta Basin: La Pasadita and the Realm of Bird Jaguar. In Ancient Mesoamerican Warfare, edited by M. Kathryn Brown and Travis W. Stanton, pp. 31-48. AltaMira Press, Walnut Creek, CA.

Golden, Charles W., Luis A. Romero, Rene Muñoz, Andrew Scherer, and James L. Fitzsimmons
    2004   Reconocimiento y patrones de asentamiento en la Sierra Lacandon. Paper presented at the XVIII Simpsio de Investigaciones Arqueologicas en Guatemala. Guatemala City, July 19-23, 2004.

Greene Robertson, Merle
    1991   *The Sculpture of Palenque, Vol. IV: The Cross Group, the North Group, the Olvidado, and Other Pieces.* Princeton University Press, Princeton, NJ.

Grube, Nikolai
    1996   Palenque in the Maya World. In *Eighth Palenque Round Table–1993*, edited by Merle Greene Robertson, Martin Macri, and Jan McHargue, pp. 1-14. Pre-Columbian Art Research Institute, San Francisco, CA.

Guenter, Stanley P.
    2002   *Under a Falling Star: The Hiatus at Tikal.* Unpublished M.A. thesis, La Trobe University, Melbourne, Australia.

Hammond, Norman
    1991   Inside the Black Box: Defining Maya Polity. In *Classic Maya Political History: Hieroglyphic and Archaeological Evidence*, edited by T. Patrick Culbert, pp. 253-284. Cambridge University Press, Cambridge, U.K.

Hansen, Richard D.
    1998   Continuity and Disjunction: The Pre-Classic Antecedents of Classic Maya Architecture. In *Function and Meaning in Classic Maya Architecture. A Symposium at Dumbarton Oaks, 7th and 8th October 1994*, edited by Stephen D. Houston, pp. 49-122. Dumbarton Oaks Research Library and Collection, Washington, D.C.

Hassig, Ross
    1988   *Aztec Warfare: Imperial Expansion and Political Control.* University of Oklahoma Press, Norman.

    1992   *War and Society in Ancient Mesoamerica.* University of California Press, Berkeley, CA.

Haviland, William A.
    2003   Settlement, Society, and Demography at Tikal. In *Tikal: Dynasties, Foreigners, & Affairs of State*, edited by Jeremy A. Sabloff, pp. 111-142. School of American Research Press, Santa Fe, NM.

Hirth, Kenneth
    1992   Interregional Exchange as Elite Behavior: An Evolutionary Perspective. In *Mesoamerican Elites*, edited by Dianne Z. Chase and Arlen F. Chase, pp. 18-29. University of Oklahoma Press, Norman.

Houston, Stephen D.
    1993   *Hieroglyphs and History at Dos Pilas.* University of Texas Press, Austin.

    1996   Symbolic Sweatbaths of the Maya: Architectural Meaning in the Cross Group at Palenque, Mexico. *Latin American Antiquity* 7(2):132-151.

Houston, Stephen D. and Alfonso Lacadena García-Gallo
2003   Maya Epigraphy at the Millennium: Personal Notes. In *Continuities and Changes in Maya Archaeology: Perspectives at the Millennium*, edited by Charles W. Golden and Greg Borgstede, pp. 113-121. Routledge Press, New York.

Houston, Stephen D., John Robertson, and David Stuart
2000   The Language of Classic Maya Inscriptions. *Current Anthropology* 41(3):321-356.

Inomata, Takeshi and Kazuo Aoyama
1996   Central-Place Analyses in the La Entrada Region, Honduras: Implications for Understanding the Classic Maya Political and Economic Systems. *Latin American Antiquity* 7(4):291-312.

Isbell, William H.
1991   Huari Administration and the Orthogonal Cellular Architecture Horizon. In *Huari Administrative Structure: Prehistoric Monumental Architecture and State Government*, edited by William H. Isbell and Gordon F. McEwan, pp. 293-316. Dumbarton Oaks Research Library and Collection, Washington, D.C.

Johnson, Allen W. and Timothy Earle
1987   *The Evolution of Human Societies: From Foraging Group to Agrarian State*. Stanford University Press, Stanford, CA.

Johnson, Jay K.
1976   *Chipped Stone Artifacts from the Western Maya Periphery*. Unpublished Ph.D. dissertation, Southern Illinois University, Carbondale.

Josserand, J. Kathryn
1991   The Narrative Structure of Hieroglyphic Texts at Palenque. In *Sixth Palenque Round Table–1986*, edited by M. Greene Robertson and V. M. Fields, pp. 12-31. University of Oklahoma Press, Norman.

Kowalewski, Stephen A., Gary M. Feinman and Laura Finsten
1992   "The Elite" and Assessment of Social Stratification in Mesoamerican Archaeology. In *Mesoamerican Elites: An Archaeological Assessment*, edited by Diane Z. Chase and Arlen F. Chase, pp. 259-277. University of Oklahoma Press, Norman.

Laporte, Juan Pedro
2003   Architectural Aspects of Interaction between Tikal and Teotihuacan during the Early Classic Period. In *The Maya and Teotihuacan*, edited by Geoffrey E. Braswell, pp. 199-216. University of Texas Press, Austin.

Leon-Portilla, Miguel
1962   *The Broken Spears: The Aztec Account of the Conquest of Mexico*. Beacon Press, Boston, MA.

Liendo Stuardo, Rodrigo
1999   *The Organization of Agricultural Production at a Classic Maya Center: Settlement Patterns in the Palenque Region, Chiapas, Mexico*. Unpublished Ph.D. dissertation, University of Pittsburgh, Pittsburgh, PA.

2002a   Organización Social y Producción Agrícola en Palenque. In *La Organización Social Entre los Mayas. Memoria de la Tercera Mesa Redonda de Palenque ,Vol. I*, edited by V. Tiesler Blos, R. Cobos and M. Greene Robertson, pp. 307-327. Conaculta-INAH, Mexico, D.F.

2002b   *The Organization of Argicultural Production at a Classic Maya Center: Settlement Patterns in the Palenque Region, Chiapas, Mexico.* University of Pittsburgh Press, Pittsburgh, PA.

2003   Centro y Periferia: Dinamica de Asentamientos en el Reino de "Baak." Paper presented at the XVII Simposio de Investigationes Arquelogicas en Guatemala, Guatemala City.

Lizardi Ramos, César
1963   Inscripciones de Pomona, Tabasco, México. *Estudios de Cultura Maya* 3:187-202.

López Bravo, Roberto
2003   Del Motiepa al Picota: la primera temporada del Crecimiento Urbano de la antigua ciudad de Palenque (PCU). *Lakamha'* 2(9):10-15.

2004   *Informe Técnico Parcial de la 1ª Temporada de Campo del Proyecto Crecimiento Urbano de la Antigua Ciudad de·Palenque.* Conaculta-INAH. Unpublished field report.

López Jiménez, Fanny
2001   El Descubrimiento de la Tumba I del Templo de la Calavera y su Contexto Arquitectónico en Palenque, Chiapas. *Pueblos y Fronteras* 1:115-129. Universidad Nacional Autónoma de Mexico, Mexico, D.F.

Lösch, August
1954   *The Economics of Location.* 2nd edition. Translated by Wolfgang F. Stolper. Yale University Press, New Haven, CT.

Lounsbury, Floyd G.
1974   The Inscription of the Sarcophagus Lid at Palenque. In *Primera Mesa Redonda de Palenque, Part II*, edited by Merle Greene Robertson, pp. 5-19. Robert Lewis Stevenson School, Pebble Beach, CA.

Maler, Teobert
1901   *Researches in the Central Portion of the Usumacinta Valley, Vol. I.* Memoirs of the Peabody Museum of Archaeology and Ethnology, Harvard University, Vol. 2, Cambridge, MA.

Malville, Nancy
2001   Long-Distance Transport of Bulk Goods in the Pre-Hispanic Southwest. *Journal of Anthropological Archaeology* 20:230-243.

Marcus, Joyce
1976   *Emblem and State in the Classic Maya Lowlands.* Dumbarton Oaks Research Library and Collection, Washington, D.C.

1993   Ancient Maya Political Organization. In *Lowland Maya Civilization in the 8th Century A.D.*, edited by Jeremy A. Sabloff and John S. Henderson, pp. 11-184. Dumbarton Oaks Research Library & Collection, Washington, D.C.

1998 The Peaks and Valleys of Ancient States: An Extension of the Dynamic Model. In *Archaic States*, edited by Gary M. Feinman and Joyce Marcus, pp. 59-94. School of American Research Press, Santa Fe, NM.

Marken, Damien B.

2002 *L'Architecture de Palenque: Les Temples.* Unpublished M.A. thesis. Université de Paris I: La Sorbonne, Paris, France.

2003 Elite Political Structure at Late Classic Palenque, Chiapas, Mexico. Paper presented at the 5th World Archaeology Congress. Washington, D.C., June 23rd, 2003.

Martin, Simon

2003 Moral-Reforma y la Contienda por el Oriente de Tabasco. *Arqueología Mexicana* XI(61):44-47.

Martin, Simon and Nikolai Grube

1995 Maya Superstates. *Archaeology* 48(6):41-46.

2000 *Chronicles of the Maya Kings and Queens: Deciphering the Dynasties of the Ancient Maya.* Thames & Hudson, London, U.K.

Martin, Simon, Marc Zender, and Nikolai Grube

2002 Palenque and Its Neighbors. *Notebook for the XXVIth Maya Hieroglyphic Forum at Texas*, Austin.

Marquina, Ignacio

1964 *Arquitectura Prehispanica.* INAH; Mexico, D.F.

Mateos González, Frida

1996 Toniná, un Recorrido por sus Relieves. In *Eighth Palenque Round Table– 1993*, edited by Merle Greene Robertson, Martin Macri, and Jan McHargue, pp. 143-152. Pre-Columbian Art Research Institute, San Francisco, CA.

Mathews, Peter

1991 Classic Maya Emblem Glyphs. In *Classic Maya Political History: Hieroglyphic and Archaeological Evidence*, edited by T. Patrick Culbert, pp. 19-29. Cambridge University Press, Cambridge, U.K.

2000 Guerra en las tierras bajas occidentales mayas. In *La Guerra Entre los Antiguos Mayas. Memoria de la Primera Mesa Redonda de Palenque*, edited by Silvia Trejo, pp. 125-156. INAH, Mexico, D.F.

2001 The Dates of Tonina and a Dark House in Its History. *PARI Journal* II(1):1-6.

Miller, Mary E.

1996 *The Art of Mesoamerica.* Revised edition. Thames & Hudson, London.

Miller, Mary E. and Simon Martin

2004 *Courtly Art of the Ancient Maya.* Fine Arts Museum of San Francisco, CA.

Nelson, Zachary

2004 De la Cartografía al Cálculo de Población de Piedras Negras, Guatemala. In *XVII Simposio de Investigaciones Arqueologicas en Guatemala, 2003*, edited by J. P. Laporte, B. Arroyo, H. Escobedo, and H. E. Mejía, pp. 7-16. Ministerio de Cultura y Deportes, Instituto de Antropología e Historia, Asociación de Tikal, Guatemala City.

O'Mansky, Matt and Nicholas P. Dunning
    2004   Settlement and Late Classic Political Disintegration in the Petexbatun Region, Guatemala. In *The Terminal Classic in the Maya Lowlands*, edited by Arthur A. Demarest, Prudence M. Rice, and Don S. Rice, pp. 83-101. University Press of Colorado, Boulder.

Pagliaro, Jonathan B., James F. Garber, and Travis W. Stanton
    2003   Evaluating the Archaeological Signatures of Maya Ritual and Conflict. In *Ancient Mesoamerican Warfare*, edited by M. Kathryn Brown and Travis W. Stanton, pp. 75-90. AltaMira Press, Walnut Creek, CA.

Pauketat, Timothy R.
    2000   Politicization and Community in the Pre-Columbian Mississippi Valley. In *The Archaeology of Communities: A New World Perspective*, edited by Marcello A. Canuto and Jason Yaeger, pp. 16-43. Routledge Press, New York, NY.

Price, Barbara
    1977   Cluster Interaction Shifts in Production and Organization. *Current Anthropology* 18(2):209-233.

Pring, Duncan C.
    2000   *The Protoclassic in the Maya Lowlands*. BAR International Series 908. Hadrian Books Ltd., Oxford, U.K.

Proskouriakoff, Tatiana
    1950   *A Study of Classic Maya Sculpture*. Carnegie Institute of Washington Publication 593, Washington, D.C.

    1960   Historical Implications of a Pattern of Dates at Piedras Negras. *American Antiquity* 25(4):454-475.

    1963   Historical Data in the Inscriptions of Yaxchilan, Part 1. *Estudios de Cultura Maya* 3:149-167.

    1964   Historical Data in the Inscriptions of Yaxchilan, Part 2. *Estudios de Cultura Maya* 4:177-201.

Puleston, Dennis E.
    1983   *The Settlement Survey of Tikal*. Tikal Report 13. University Museum Monograph 48, University of Pennsylvania, Philadelphia.

Puleston, Dennis E. and Donald W. Callendar Jr.
    1967   Defensive Earthworks at Tikal. *Expedition* 9(30):40-48.

Rands, Robert L.
    1967a   Céramica de la región de Palenque, Chiapas. *Estudios de la Cultura Maya. Vol. VI*, edited by Alberto Ruz Lhuillier, pp. 111-148. Universidad Nacional Autónoma de Mexico, Mexico, D.F.

    1967b   Ceramic Technology and Trade in the Palenque Region, Mexico. In *American Historical Anthropology: Essays in Honor of Leslie Spier*, edited by C. L. Riley and W. W. Taylor, pp. 137-151. University of Southern Illinois Press. Carbondale, IL.

    1969   Maya Ecology and Trade: 1967-1968. A progress report of work carried out under the auspices of the National Science Foundation Grant of 1455X. University Museum, Southern Illinois University, Carbondale.

1973   The Classic Maya Collapse: Usumacinta Zone and the Northwestern Periphery. In *The Classic Maya Collapse*, edited by T. Patrick Culbert, pp. 165-206. University of New Mexico Press, Albuquerque.

1974a   A Chronological Framework for Palenque. In *The Art, Iconography and Dynastic History of Palenque, Part I. Primera Mesa Redonda de Palenque*. Vol. I, edited by Merle Greene Robertson, pp. 35-40. Robert Lewis Stevenson School, Pebble Beach, CA.

1974b   The Ceramic Sequence at Palenque, Chiapas. In *Mesoamerican Archaeology: New Approaches*, edited by Norman Hammond, pp. 51-76. University of Texas Press, Austin.

1977   The Rise of Classic Maya Civilization in the Northwestern Zone: Isolation and Intergration. In *The Origins of Maya Civilization*, edited by Robert E. Adams, pp. 159-180. School of American Research Advanced Seminar Series, University of New Mexico Press, Albuquerque.

1987   Ceramic Patterns and Traditions in the Palenque Area. In *Maya Ceramics. Papers from the 1985 Maya Ceramic Conference*, edited by Prudence M. Rice and Robert J. Sharer, pp. 203-238. BAR International Series 345(i). Hadrian Books Ltd., Oxford, U.K.

1988   Least-Cost and Function-Optimizing Interpretations of Ceramic Production: An Archaeological Perspective. In *Ceramic Ecology Revisited, 1987: The Technology and Socioeconomics of Pottery*, edited by Charles C. Kolb, pp. 165-198. BAR International Series 436(ii), Hadrian Books Ltd., Oxford, U.K.

Rands, Robert L. and Monica Bargielski Weimer
1992   Integrative Approaches in the Compositional Characterization of Ceramic Pastes. In *Chemical Characterization of Ceramic Pastes in Archaeology*, edited by Hector Neff, pp. 31-57. Monographs in World Archaeology No.7. Prehistory Press, Madison, WI.

Rands, Robert L. and Ronald L. Bishop
1980   Resource Procurement Zones and Patterns of Ceramic Exchange in the Palenque Region, Mexico. In *Models and Methods in Regional Exchange*, edited by Robert E. Fry, pp. 19-46. SAA Papers No. 1. Society for American Archaeology, Washington, D.C.

2003   The Dish-Plate Tradition at Palenque: Continuity and Change. In *Patterns & Process: A Festschrift in Honor of Dr. Edward V. Sayre*, edited by Lambertus van Zelst, pp. 109-132. Smithsonian Center for Materials Research & Education, Suitland, MD.

Rands, Robert L., Ronald L. Bishop, and Garman Harbottle
1978   Thematic and Compositional Variation in Palenque Region Incensarios. In *Tercera Mesa Redonda de Palenque. Vol. IV*, edited by Merle Greene Robertson and Donnan Call Jeffers, pp. 19-30. Pre-Columbian Art Research Institute, San Francisco, CA.

Rands, Robert L. and Barbara C. Rands
1957   The Ceramic Position of Palenque, Chiapas. *American Antiquity* 23(2):140-150.

1959   The Incensario Complex of Palenque, Chiapas. *American Antiquity* 25(2):225-236.

Renfrew, Colin
1986   Introduction: Peer Polity Interaction and Socio-Political Change. In *Peer Polity Interaction and Socio-Political Change*, edited by Colin Renfrew and John F. Cherry, pp. 1-18. Cambridge University Press, Cambridge, U.K.

Renfrew, Colin and John F. Cherry, eds.
1986   *Peer Polity Interaction and Socio-Political Change*. Cambridge University Press, Cambridge, U.K.

Rice, Prudence M.
1987   Economic Exchange in the Lowland Maya Late Classic Period. In *Specialization, Exchange and Complex Societies*, edited by Elizabeth M. Brumfeil and Timothy K. Earle, pp. 76-85. Cambridge University Press, Cambridge, U.K.

Riese, Berthold
2001   Los "Relieves de Jonuta." *Arqueología Mexicana* VIII(48):8.

Roys, Lawrence
1934   The Engineering Knowledge of the Maya. In *Contributions to American Archaeology Vol. II*. No. 6, pp. 27-105. Carnegie Institution of Washington, Washington, D.C.

Sabloff, Jeremy A.
1986   Interaction among Classic Maya Polities: A Preliminary Examination. In *Peer Polity Interaction and Socio-Political Change*, edited by Colin Renfrew and John F. Cherry, pp. 109-116. Cambridge University Press, Cambridge, U.K.

Sanders, William T. and David Webster
1988   The Mesoamerican Urban Tradition. *American Anthropologist* 90(3):521-546.

Schele, Linda
1991   An Epigraphic History of the Western Maya Region. In *Classic Maya Political History: Hieroglyphic and Archaeological Evidence*, edited by T. Patrick Culbert, pp. 72-101. University of Cambridge Press, Cambridge, U.K.

1994   Some Thoughts on the Inscriptions of House C. In *7th Palenque Round Table–1989*, edited by M. Greene Robertson and V. M. Fields, pp. 1-10. Pre-Columbian Art Research Institute, San Francisco, CA.

Schele, Linda and David A. Freidel
1990   *A Forest of Kings: The Untold Story of the Ancient Maya*. William Morrow and Company, Inc., New York.

Schele, Linda and Peter Mathews
1991   Royal Visits and Other Intersite Relationships among the Classic Maya. In *Classic Maya Political History: Hieroglyphic and Archaeological Evidence*, edited by T. Patrick Culbert, pp. 226-252. University of Cambridge Press, Cambridge, U.K.

Schele, Linda and Mary Miller
1986   *The Blood of Kings*. George Braziller, Inc., New York, NY.

Schreiber, Katharina J.
1992   *Wari Imperialism in Middle Horizon Peru.* Museum of Anthropology of Michigan Anthropological Paper No. 87, Ann Arbor.

Sharer, Robert J.
1991   Diversity and Continuity in Maya Civilization: Quirigua as a Case Study. In *Classic Maya Political History: Hieroglyphic and Archaeological Evidence*, edited by T. Patrick Culbert, pp. 180-198. University of Cambridge Press, Cambridge, U.K.

2004   External Interaction at Early Classic Copan. In *Understanding Early Classic Copan*, edited by Ellen E. Bell, Marcello A. Canuto, and Robert J. Sharer, pp. 297-318. University Museum, University of Pennsylvania, Philadelphia.

Sharer, Robert J. and Charles W. Golden
2004   Kingship and Polity: Conceptualizing the Maya Body Politic. In *Continuities and Changes in Maya Archaeology: Perspectives at the Millennium*, edited by Charles W. Golden and Greg Borgstede, pp. 23-50. Routledge Press, New York.

Smith, A. Ledyard
1950   *Uaxactun, Guatemala: Excavations of 1931-37.* Publication 588, Carnegie Institution of Washington, Washington, D.C.

Smith, Robert E.
1971   *The Pottery of Mayapan.* Papers of the Peabody Museum of Archaeology and Ethnology, Harvard University, Vol. 66, Cambridge, MA.

Sprajc, Ivan
2003   *Archaeological Reconnaissance in Southeastern Campeche, México: 2002 Field Season Report.* FAMSI report. www.famsi.org/reports/01014/index. html

Stanton, Travis W. and M. Kathryn Brown
2003   Studying Warfare in Ancient Mesoamerica. In *Ancient Mesoamerican Warfare*, edited by M. Kathryn Brown and Travis W. Stanton, pp. 1-16. AltaMira Press, Walnut Creek, CA.

Stuart, David S.
2003   Longer Live the King: The Questionable Demise of K'inich K'an Joy Chitam of Palenque. *PARI Journal* IV(1):1-4.

Stuart, David S. and Stephen D. Houston
1994   *Classic Maya Place-Names.* Dumbarton Oaks Research Library & Collection, Washington, D.C.

Taube, Karl A., William Saturno, and David Stuart
2004   El Muro Oeste de las Pinturas de Sub-Estructura 1 de San Bartolo en Guatemala. Paper presented at the XVIII Simposio de Investigaciones Arqueológicas en Guatemala. Guatemala City, July 23, 2004.

Thompson, J. Eric S.
1956   *The Rise and Fall of Maya Civilization.* 3rd edition. University of Oklahoma Press, Norman.

Tourtellot, Gair
1993   A View of Ancient Maya Settlement Patterns in the 8th Century. In *Lowland Maya Civilization in the 8th Century A.D.*, edited by Jeremy A. Sabloff and John S. Henderson, pp. 219-241. Dumbarton Oaks Research Library & Collection, Washington, D.C.

Trigger, Bruce G.
2003   *Understanding Early Civilization: A Comparative Study.* Cambridge University Press, Cambridge, U.K.

Vogt, Evon Z.
1969   *Zinacantan: A Maya Community in the Highlands of Chiapas.* Harvard University Press, Cambridge, MA.

Webster, David
1985   Surplus, Labor, and Stress in Late Classic Maya Society. *Journal of Anthropological Research* 41(4):375-399.

1988   Copan as a Classic Maya Center. In *The Southeast Maya Zone*, edited by Elizabeth H. Boone and Gordon R. Willey, pp. 5-30. Dumbarton Oaks Research Library and Collection, Washington, D.C.

1993   The Study of Maya Warfare: What It Tells Us about the Maya and What It Tells Us about Maya Archaeology. In *Lowland Maya Civilization in the 8th Century A.D.*, edited by Jeremy A. Sabloff and John S. Henderson, pp. 415-444. Dumbarton Oaks Research Library & Collection, Washington, D.C.

1997   City-States of the Maya. In *The Archaeology of City-States*, edited by Deborah L. Nichols and Thomas H. Charlton, pp. 135- 154. Smithsonian Institution Press, Washington, D.C.

1998   Warfare and Status Rivalry: Lowland Maya and Polynesian Comparisons. In *Archaic States*, edited by Gary M. Feinman and Joyce Marcus, pp. 311-351. School of American Research Press, Santa Fe, NM.

Webster, David and Ann Corinne Freter
1990   Settlement History and the Classic Collapse at Copan: A Redefined Chronological Perspective. *Latin American Antiquity* 1(1):66-85.

Webster, David, Jay Silverstein, Timothy Murtha, Horacio Martinez, and Kirk Straight
2004   *The Tikal Earthworks Revisted.* Occasional Paper in Anthropology No. 28, Pennsylvania State University, University Park.

West, Georgia
2002   Ceramic Exchange in the Late Classic and Postclassic Maya Lowlands: A Diachronic Approach. In *Ancient Maya Political Economies*, edited by Marilyn A. Masson and David A. Freidel, pp. 140-196. AltaMira Press, Walnut Creek, CA.

Willey, Gordon R., William R. Bullard Jr., John B. Glass, and James C. Gifford
1965   *Prehistoric Settlement in the Belize Valley.* Papers of the Peabody Museum of Archaeology and Ethnology, Harvard University, Vol. 54, Cambridge, MA.

Willey, Gordon R. and Richard M. Leventhal
1979   Prehistoric Settlement at Copan. In *Maya Archaeology and Ethnohistory*, edited by Norman Hammond and Gordon R. Willey, pp. 75-102. University of Texas Press, Austin.

Wright, Lori E.
  1999   The Elements of Maya Diets: Alkaline Earth Baselines and Paleodietary
          Reconstruction in the Pasión Region. In *Reconstructing Ancient Maya Diet*,
          edited by Christine D. White, pp. 197-219. University of Utah Press, Salt
          Lake City.

Yaeger, Jason and Marcello A. Canuto
  2000   Introducing an Archaeology of Communities. In *The Archaeology of
          Communities: A New World Perspective*, edited by Marcello A. Canuto and
          Jason Yaeger, pp. 1-15. Routledge Press, New York.

Yoffee, Norman
  1988   The Collapse of Ancient Mesopotamian States and Civilization. In *The
          Collapse of Ancient States and Civilizations*, edited by Norman Yoffee &
          George L. Cowgill, pp. 44-68. University of Arizona Press, Tucson.

Zender, Marc
  2002   Retreading the House C Stairs: Warfare and Political Expansion in Reign of
          K'inich Janaab' Pakal. Paper presented at the 67th Annual Meeting of the
          Society for American Archaeology. Denver, CO. March 2002.

Index

About the Contributors

Joshua Balcells González received his Licenciatura in archaeology from the Universidad Autónoma de Yucatán in 2002. He is currently working on his Maestria at the same institution. Besides conducting archaeological work at Palenque as a member of the Proyecto Grupo de las Cruces (PGC) from 1998-2002, he has also worked at the Maya site of Dzibilchaltun, Yucatán.

Edwin L. Barnhart, director of the Maya Exploration Center, has over a decade of experience in Mesoamerica as an archaeologist, an explorer, and an instructor. He has published over a dozen papers and given presentations at five international conferences. He has worked as an archaeologist at Copan, Honduras, and between 1994 and 1997 he discovered and mapped the site of Ma'ax Na in Northwestern Belize. During 1998-2000 he directed the Palenque Mapping Project (PMP). In 2001, he received his Ph.D. in anthropology from the University of Texas, Austin, with his dissertation entitled *The Palenque Mapping Project: Settlement Patterns and Urbanism in an Ancient Maya City*. He is currently a Fellow of the Explorer's Club and teaches National Science Foundation classes for college professors on Maya astronomy and sacred geometry.

Mark B. Child specializes in the study of Mesoamerican religion. His research interests include the detection and reconstruction of the essential beliefs and practices of ancient religious movements by utilizing a comparative approach that integrates architectural, epigraphic, and iconographic analyses to a framework of ethnohistoric and ethnographic data. Child served as Field Director of the Piedras Negras Archaeological Project in Guatemala from 1997-2000, where he carried out his doctoral dissertation research for Yale University. His research on the ancient Maya sweatbath was supported by the National Science Foundation, the Fulbright-Hays Program, and the Albers Foundation. Child has also carried out archaeological field research in Mexico, Honduras, and Belize.

Kirk D. French received his M.A. in anthropology from the University of Cincinnati in 2002. He has published and presented several papers on water management at Palenque. From 1998-2000 he surveyed the Palenque ruins as a member of the PMP. He has also conducted archaeological work at the site of Blackman Eddy, Belize as well as extensive CRM fieldwork in Texas. He is currently a Ph.D. candidate in anthropology at Pennsylvania State University in State College, PA.

Arnoldo González Cruz is the archaeologist in charge of the Archaeological Ruins of Palenque, Chiapas, for the Instituto Nacional de Antropología e Historia of Mexico, a position he has held since 1989. As the national site archaeologist, he has directed the Proyecto Arqueológico de Palenque and the Proyecto Especial Palenque. He has published several articles and papers on his extensive excavations and discoveries at Palenque. In 1993, during his excavation of the substructure of Temple XIII, he discovered a female royal tomb, now affectionately known as the "Red Queen." More recently, while working on Temple XXI, he discovered a beautiful limestone tablet that was included in the exhibition "Courtly Art of the Ancient Maya" at the National Gallery of Art in Washington, D.C. and the Fine Art Museum of San Francisco at the Legion of Honor in San Francisco, CA.

Merle Greene Robertson is the director of the Pre-Columbian Art Research Institute, as well as the Proyecto Grupo de las Cruces in Palenque. She is the author of the four-volume set *The Sculpture of Palenque*, published by the University of Princeton Press. She holds an honorary Ph.D. from the University of Tulane, New Orleans. In 1973, she organized the first Palenque Mesa Redonda conference, a conference she organized for the following 20 years. She has spent 45 years recording Maya sculpture by means of over 4,000 rubbings, which are currently at the Tulane University Library. During her career, she has worked at 100 sites, the most important being Palenque, Chichen Itza, Seibal, and Tikal. She has received the "Order of the Aztec Eagle" award from the Mexican government, and last year was named to the "Order of Pop" by the Popol Vuh museum in Guatemala City.

C. Rudy Larios Villalta, as both an architect and an archaeologist, has worked at several Maya sites, namely Palenque, Copan, Honduras, and Tikal and Cancuen, Guatemala. From 1970 to 1980, he was the director of the Tikal National Park in Guatemala. He has been the director of Architectural Restoration for the PGC (1999-2003), the Proyecto Arqueológico Copan Segunda Fase (1981-1996), and the Proyecto Arqueológico Cancuén (2000-2004). During 1988-1996, he was also codirector of the Proyecto Aqueológico Acrópolis de Copan.

Rodrigo Liendo Stuardo is a researcher at the Instituto de Investigaciones Antropológicas, Universidad Autonoma de México. He received his Ph.D. in Latin American Archaeology from the University of Pittsburgh in 1999. He has conducted extensive fieldwork in Yucatán, Chiapas, and Central Mexico. His main research focus is the economic and political development of Pre-Hispanic Maya society, and is currently involved in a multi-year project centered on the development of the Palenque regional polity.

Damien B. Marken began working as an archaeologist at Palenque in 1997. As a member of the PGC from 1997 to 2002, he participated in excavations of the Temple of the Cross, Temple XIX, and Temple XX at Palenque. In 2002, he received his M.A. in archaeology from the Université de Paris I: La Sorbonne, France, with the thesis *L'Architecture de Palenque: Les Temples*. His research foci include ancient Maya architecture and social organization. He is currently part of the mapping team for the Proyecto Arqueológico El Perú-Waka' in Guatemala and is a Ph.D. candidate in anthropology at Southern Methodist University.

Peter Mathews, an accomplished archaeologist and epigrapher, is professor of archaeology at La Trobe University in Melbourne, Australia. He received his Ph.D. in anthropology from Yale University in 1988. An expert on Maya hieroglyphs, he is co-author with the late Linda Schele of the books *The Code of Kings* and *The Bodega of Palenque*, and has published numerous articles on Classic Maya history. Throughout his thirty-year career in Maya archaeology, he has worked at numerous sites in Mexico and Guatemala, including Palenque, Tonina, Yaxchilan, El Cayo, and Dos Pilas.

Robert L. Rands has over fifty years of experience working with the ceramics of Palenque. His field experience includes excavation and survey at the sites of Palenque, Comalcalco, Tabasco, and numerous sites in the Palenque region, among others. He has been the recipient of numerous research grants from several institutions, including National Science Foundation, the Foundation for the Advancement of Mesoamerican Studies Inc., the Institute of Andean Research, and the University Museum, University of Pennsylvania. He has been professor of anthropology at the University of Mississippi, and the University of North Carolina, and is currently professor emeritus at Southern Illinois University at Carbondale. His research interests include ceramic analysis (the synthesis of paste compositional analysis, production technology, vessel shape, and stylistic data) and exchange patterns.

Kirk D. Straight received his M.A. in anthropology from California State University at Hayward, and is currently a Ph.D. candidate in anthropology at Pennsylvania State University. Prior to joining the PGC in 1998, he worked numerous years at the site of Caracol, Belize. At Palenque, he and Christopher Powell were the archaeologists in charge of the excavation of Temple XIX. During his tenure with the PGC, he was also the ceramic illustrator for Robert Rands. Currently a member of the Pennsylvania State University Tikal Earthworks Project, his primary research focus is ceramic exchange and its relation to Classic Maya economic and social structure.

David Stuart, the Linda Schele Professor of Mesoamerican Art & Writing at the University of Texas at Austin, is one of the premier scholars of Classic Maya history. At the age of fifteen he presented his first professional paper on Maya epigraphy at the third Palenque Mesa Redonda. He received his Ph.D. in anthropology from the University of Vanderbilt in 1995. As well as publishing numerous articles and papers on ancient Maya writing, art, and history, he is the author of the monographs *Classic Maya Place Names*, with Stephen Houston, and *Ten Phonetic Symbols*. As part of Harvard University's Maya Hieroglyphic Corpus project, he has worked all over the Maya lowlands, most notably at Copan, Honduras, Dos Pilas, Guatemala, and Palenque, Mexico.